The Best American Sports Writing 2011

GUEST EDITORS OF
THE BEST AMERICAN SPORTS WRITING

1991   DAVID HALBERSTAM
1992   THOMAS MCGUANE
1993   FRANK DEFORD
1994   TOM BOSWELL
1995   DAN JENKINS
1996   JOHN FEINSTEIN
1997   GEORGE PLIMPTON
1998   BILL LITTLEFIELD
1999   RICHARD FORD
2000   DICK SCHAAP
2001   BUD COLLINS
2002   RICK REILLY
2003   BUZZ BISSINGER
2004   RICHARD BEN CRAMER
2005   MIKE LUPICA
2006   MICHAEL LEWIS
2007   DAVID MARANISS
2008   WILLIAM NACK
2009   LEIGH MONTVILLE
2010   PETER GAMMONS
2011   JANE LEAVY

The Best AMERICAN SPORTS WRITING™ 2011

Edited and with an Introduction
by Jane Leavy

Glenn Stout, *Series Editor*

A Mariner Original
HOUGHTON MIFFLIN HARCOURT
BOSTON • NEW YORK   2011

www.hmhbooks.com

ISSN 1056-8034
ISBN 978-0-547-33696-1

Printed in the United States of America

DOC 10 9 8 7 6 5 4 3 2 1

Contents

Foreword

IT'S YOUR BOOK, and by "you" I mean the readers who view these pages and the writers who labor to produce them.

Every once in a while I have to correct the misconception that this book is "mine" or that I have undue influence over its contents. Over the more than two decades that I have sat in this chair, I have developed a metaphor that I think best explains the process.

My grandfather Earl was a trainer of horses, and I've always viewed my role as something akin to his. Over the course of each year I spend most of my time either in the barn or standing along the rail in the dewy mornings, using what I have learned from a lifetime of writing and reading to take care of the horse and help it prepare for the only race it will ever run.

This book, of course, is the horse. During that year, as I take story suggestions from readers, writers, and editors and add my own accumulated knowledge and insight to the process, it is my privilege to watch the horse grow and develop until it is finally ready to run.

But the horse is not mine. It belongs to the publisher, who nevertheless entrusts me to make sure that when race day comes, the horse is ready to run. Our guest editor each year is the jockey who shows up a couple weeks before the race and gets the mount. The publisher trusts that the jockey has been around the track before, respects the traditions of the process, knows what he or she is doing in the saddle, and can get the horse not only to the gate but, when the bell sounds, around the track safely without falling off. At that point all I can do is tell the jockey what I know about the horse in the form of about 75 stories I have selected for his or her consideration, turn over the reins, and send horse and jockey off together. At that instant it is out of my hands. The jockey is free either to make use of my suggestions or, as in this year's edition, to add some of his or her own. Yet as soon as this book breaks from the gate each year and the first page is opened and read, the book becomes the property of those who are the reason for its existence and the only figures in this metaphor who really matter—the writers and their readers.

I liken the readers to the fans in the grandstand, all of whom have a stake in the race and the full right either to cheer or to jeer our cumulative effort. I view the writers as my fellow workers in the barn—the other trainers, grooms, riders, apprentice jocks, and blacksmiths who have helped out over the course of the year as I've tried to nurture the colt through to adulthood and all of whom appreciate the work that entails. On the day of the race—when the book appears—they all gather at the rail to watch the big horse run, hoping to applaud at the end and praying that it takes no false steps on the journey.

By the time that happens and you read this, however, I'm back in the barn. My work is done and I am already looking over the new year's prospects, always hoping that no matter how well the last horse ran, next year's candidate will be even better.

Every season I read every issue of hundreds of sports and general interest magazines in search of writing that might merit inclusion in *The Best American Sports Writing.* I also contact the editors of hundreds of newspapers and magazines and request their submissions, and I send email notices to hundred of readers and writers whose addresses I have culled over the years. I survey writing on the Internet and make regular stops at online sources like sportsdesk.org, gangrey.com, longform.org, sportsjournalist.com, ladyjournos.tumblr.com, and other websites where notable sports writing is valued and discussed. Yet not even these efforts are enough to ensure that I see all of the best writing, so I still encourage everyone reading this—readers and writers—to send me stories they would like to see reprinted in this volume. Writers should not feel shy about sending me either their own work or the work of others for consideration for *The Best American Sports Writing 2012.* All submissions, however, must be made according to the following criteria. Each story

- must be column-length or longer.
- must have been published in 2011.
- must not be a reprint or book excerpt.
- must be published in the United States or Canada.
- must be received by February 1, 2012.

All submissions must include the name of the author, the date of publication, and the publication name and address. Photocopies, tear sheets, or clean copies are fine. Readable reductions to 8½-by-11 are preferred. Submissions from online publications must be made in hard copy, and newspaper stories should be submitted in hard copy as published. Since newsprint generally suffers in transit, newspaper stories are best copied and made legible. If the story also appeared online, providing the URL is often helpful.

While there is no limit to the number of submissions either an individual or a publication may make, please use common sense. Due to the volume of material I receive, no submissions can be returned or acknowledged, and it is inappropriate for me to comment on or critique any submission. Publications that want to be absolutely certain their contributions are considered are advised to provide a complimentary subscription to the address listed below. Those that already do so should make sure to extend the subscription.

No electronic submissions will be accepted, although stories that only appeared online are eligible. Please send all submissions by U.S. mail—weather conditions in midwinter here at *BASW* headquarters often prevent me from receiving UPS or FedEx submissions. The February 1 deadline has been in place for more than two decades and is not arbitrary.

Please submit either an original or clear paper copy of each story, including publication name, author, and date the story appeared, to:

Glenn Stout
PO Box 549
Alburgh, VT 05440

Anyone with questions or comments may contact me at basweditor @yahoo.com. Copies of previous editions of this book can be ordered through most bookstores or online book dealers. An index of stories that have appeared in this series through 2011 can be found at my website, glennstout.net, as can full instructions on how to submit a story. For updated information, readers and writers are also encouraged to join *The Best American Sports Writing* group on Facebook.

Thanks again go out to all at Houghton Mifflin Harcourt who support this book, and to my family, Siobhan and Saorla, who continue to share our home with its accumulated contents. As always, however, my greatest thanks go to those writers who earned their way into the pages of this edition on the strength of their talent alone—the ability to write words that matter—and not according to any other criteria.

GLENN STOUT
Alburgh, Vermont

Introduction: In Extremis

ONE FROSTBITING AFTERNOON in February 1980 I stood beside the luge track on Mount Van Hoevenberg in Lake Placid, contemplating a slip 'n' slide ride down the icy, twisting Olympic chute, the first such facility built in the United States.

I was tempted. After all, I was a proud charter member of the newly formed U.S. Luge Writers Association and a sportswriter on deadline trying to get 16 inches out of *whoosh*. I was also slightly tipsy, thanks to several construction drums full of premixed White Russians (one half-gallon vodka to one half-gallon Kahlúa plus eight quarts of milk) hauled to the speed skating oval that morning by a Connecticut milkman in honor of Eric Heiden.

John Powers, my colleague from the *Boston Globe*, gallantly offered to escort me, which would have made us the first and last mixed-doubles luge team in history.

We were stationed at Curve 12, known as "Omega." A couple of bottles of French champagne were buried in the snow at our feet, imported by an Emerson College student who used the money he saved on a discounted ticket ($2 for a $22 ticket) to procure the bubbly. An ambulance was parked opposite us on the other side of Omega.

The pop of the cork punctuated a defining moment of realization. I am not a "because it's there" person, except maybe when it comes to good champagne. My idea of risk is leaving home without a fully charged cell phone. I opted to hold on to the extremities I could no longer feel. Besides, I had already taken my life in my hands for the *Washington Post* by hitching a ride into town from the

Albany airport with two KGB agents masquerading as reporters from *Soviet Life* magazine. When the big galoot behind the wheel briefly considered pausing at a four-way stop sign at the crest of a hill a block from our quarters, I leaped from the car and slid down the street on my luggage.

Thirty years later, Powers was in Vancouver, covering his 17th Olympic Games for the *Globe,* when Nodar Kumaritashvili, a 21-year-old slider from the Republic of Georgia, heaved himself down the lethal track called the "Elevator Shaft." The ice was as treacherous as it was manicured—hosed between runs with a fine mist of water, scraped and polished and buffed to a diabolical sheen and chilled by ammonia-filled pipes that sucked heat from the concrete walls. Kumaritashvili was wearing gloves with small spikes on the fingertips for extra traction when he began his descent, the last anyone would make from the men's starting house 1,374 meters from the finish line.

Curve 16, the last, was called "Thunderbird," in homage to the indigenous people who consider Mount Whistler a "wild spirit place" and also to signify the thunder of sleds crossing the finish line. Just past a blue banner emblazoned with the Olympic rings and the motto "Des plus brillants exploits" ("Ever more brilliant exploits"), Kumaritashvili slammed into the lip of a curve that sneered at sanity. He ricocheted from one iced concrete wall to another like a crash dummy and was thrown out of the track and into a steel pole.

He was traveling 90 miles per hour—20 miles per hour faster than the gold-winning time at Lake Placid. And it was only practice.

"Even at Olympus, speed kills," Powers wrote in the *Globe.*

One decade into the new millennium the world of sports is in extremis. Everything is more extreme—hits and hip checks, endeavor and entitlement, compensation and consequence. Forget "faster, higher, stronger." Try "deeper, steeper, crazier."

When I signed on for this gig, I expected a full complement of gnarly surfer dude stories and ultra-tortured ultra-marathon confessionals. I didn't expect the death wish that suffuses the language and the actions of so many competitions and competitors; among the stories submitted for consideration this year were tales about

high-altitude skiers who take their lives in their hands to ski in the
"death zone"; an annual Vermont "Death Race" organized by tri-
athletes whose stated ambition is "to break you"; and a breathtak-
ingly reckless pickup skateboarder named Danny Way.

The need to declare oneself a world champion of *something*, to
create worlds to conquer, even if it means maybe getting killed in
the process, has spawned proto-playing fields unheard of when my
hero, Red Smith, filed his first piece for the *St. Louis Star* in 1927
—an account of the first night football game at Washington University written from the point of view of a glowworm outshone by
the newly installed stadium lights. As Red saw it, his job was to help
readers "recapture the fun they had at yesterday's game or find a
substitute for the fun they didn't have because they had to go to
work instead."

He also said that his job was to provide "momentary pleasure,
like a good whore."

By the time I joined the *Washington Post* sports staff in 1979, Red's
Runyonesque notion of sports writing was obsolete. "Juggling,"
Robert Lipsyte, then Red's colleague at the *New York Times,* called
it. (Juggling may be the only subject not covered by this year's submissions, which included pinball, bridge, birding, and competitive
computer programming.)

Led by a new generation of edgy sportswriters like Lipsyte, we
found new purpose in the great issues of the day—race, equal opportunity, drugs, and labor disputes. We became personality journalists, medical writers, and business reporters. Red quit juggling
and won a Pulitzer Prize in 1976 for columns devoted to grown-up
subjects, including off-track betting, baseball free agency, and
Olympic hypocrisy.

The toy department, as he called it, was all grown up.

Today fun is all but gone from the sports page. No one needs us
around for a good time with virtual fields of play beckoning at
home at the touch of a joystick. Pretty soon no one will feel the
need to go to a game because now you can be *in* a computer-
generated game with graphics so graphic, violence so violent, sty-
lin' so stylish, that NFL players have taken to imitating their virtual
clones.

Nobody needs us to report *any* score. With YouTube highlights,
streaming video, and 24/7 saturation bombing of Fanboy sensibili-

ties on a proliferating array of dedicated cable channels—MLB, UFC, WWE, Archery TV, Board Riders TV, Fourth and Long, Cricket Ticket, NASCAR HotPass, Golf Bug, Futbol Mundial, not to mention the networks created by teams and for teams, like YES— there's precious little sports left in *sports* writing.

And precious little news. Team-sponsored websites routinely give access—and scoops—to their own "reporters"—who are quite literally the new "house men," as hacks of old were called. End zone Twitter feeds by athlete auteurs preempt the fastest press box scribes.

Sports journalism is in the midst of an identity crisis so profound that we no longer know whether we're made up of one word or two. "Sportswriting Is One Word," Frank Deford declared in his 2010 Red Smith Lecture in Journalism at Notre Dame. A master of the long form in his glory days at *Sports Illustrated,* Frank saluted our business as the only journalistic endeavor to merit its own signifier, while mourning the passage of in-depth "takeouts." "Sports stories—two words—are disappearing," he said.

Glenn Stout, the indomitable editor of the *Best American Sports Writing* series, published by Houghton Mifflin since 1991, prefers two words—sports writing—as does spell-check. "The intention is to celebrate good writing that happens to be about sports," he explains, "rather than 'sportswriting,' a definition which tends to mean sports reporting, usually confined to news stories that appear in newspapers and . . . far more narrow in scope."

Red Smith used two words—sports writer—in a 1937 letter to a young man seeking advice on a career in journalism. Decades later he took the opposite approach. In the introduction to an anthology of columns called *Strawberries in the Wintertime,* he noted that the title "captures, I think, some of the flavor of the sportswriter's existence."

Like losing coaches at halftime, we have adjusted. Sports writing may be as popular as ever, Deford says, but it's as likely to be measured now in characters as in column inches. Newspaper columnists and beat writers have reinvented themselves as prolific bloggers and tweeters, attracting cultlike followers with their digital haiku —not quite what E. B. White meant by the "clear crystal stream of the declarative sentence." (Red considered it part of his job to read *Elements of Style* every year.)

But long-form sports stories are flourishing in new soil—popping up on new websites where space is infinite and nobody says, "Cut from the bottom." I'm happy that so many of those sources are represented in this collection.

It's anybody's guess how many published words are devoted to sports every year. Two things are for sure: fewer and fewer of them appear in traditional outlets, and Glenn Stout has read more of them than anyone else. He read 10,000 or so stories and sent 71 for my consideration. I lobbied for a couple of others that somehow eluded his in-box—Powers's column about death in Vancouver and two stories from the ABC News series about the sexual molestation of female swimmers by their coaches—because they exemplify the risks and risk-taking behavior that is the subject of so much of today's best sports writing (and sportswriting).

Lunatic endeavor has become ubiquitous, both on and off the field. To wit: an American BASE jumper—BASE stands for "buildings, antennas, spans, and earth"—who makes his leaps in a hand-tailored Italian neoprene suit like "Rocky the Flying Squirrel"; an Austrian free-diver whose ambition is to prove he can descend 20,000 leagues beneath the sea, give or take, without his head exploding; surfers who charge manfully into the waters of a Norwegian fjord in winter in order to be able to say they surfed above the Arctic Circle; English schoolmates who took the treacherous route to the summit "because it was there" and lost their lives on Mont Blanc.

The roster of all-star risk-takers also includes "sexting" quarterbacks, concussed quarterbacks, and the team doctors who send them back into the huddle; bong-sucking swimmers and blood-doping bikers; monied homeys like Marvin Harrison, the wide receiver on the other end of so many Peyton Manning heaves, who can't *not* go home again; and his extreme opposite, Darryl Dawkins, the first man to go straight from high school to the NBA, "the Man from Lovetron" who took a risk and applied for a job as a college coach.

General managers who pay a gazillion dollars for a .230 shortstop are risk-takers. Owners who shut down the most profitable game in the history of humankind are risk-takers. And truth tellers like Cincinnati Reds manager Dusty Baker are as rare as candor is risky. His admission of the impotence and incontinence caused by prostate cancer surgery—telling Howard Bryant what it's like to wear diapers in a major league clubhouse—was as daring as any daredevil flight of fancy.

Their risk is our salvation.

Red, who called himself "just a boy reporter" until the day he died, counseled every young writer who'd listen—and who didn't?—"You gotta get the smell of the cabbage cooking in the halls." Some took his advice more literally than others. In 1988 my pal Powers took the trip I declined eight years earlier, rocketing down Mount Van Hoevenberg in a pair of jeans. He likened the journey to "falling off the edge of the 14th-century earth."

Last year one author, in pursuit of a story, "unintentionally pitch-forked a load of manure" into his mouth. Jake Bogoch, who grew up playing hockey in western Canada—where, as he writes, "you play until your trajectory stalls or your father allows you to quit"—enrolled in kiddie goon camp and ended up with blood in his urine and "a deep bruise that was larger than a slice of processed cheese."

This is not what Red meant by legwork. But the 29 stories in this collection prove that there are still places only words can take us. The authors in this anthology followed Red's lead down sometimes dark and unlikely corridors, chasing stories about sexual reassign-ment surgery, intersex athletes, sexual assault, drug addiction, and neurological disorders, including Asperger's syndrome, a high-functioning form of autism.

Techno-gimmicky wizardry can fast-forward, slo-mo, rewind, and record experience. But the right word, still as hard to find as the hole in a slugger's swing, and a perfectly turned phrase as exqui-site as any triple lutz can summon a feeling, a place, a moment in time, with irrefutable specificity.

Words can slow the synapses and let us savor those moments, as in "Eight Seconds," Michael Farber's piece about the time it took to score the gold medal–winning goal in hockey in Vancouver. The story is as exceptional as it is an exception. "Consider a moment," he begins. "Now take that moment—maybe the most significant in sports in 2010—and break it down frame by frame into 100 or so smaller moments."

That's what words can do.

Words have the power to change the status quo—as Megan

Chuchmach and Avni Patel did by exposing 36 swimming coaches and compelling USA Swimming to change the rules governing the men who coach young women.

Words let us feel what a luger feels after a crash, when ice turns to fire. Words let us hear what people say and let us decide what their words say about them. Red told me years ago, "I crow with pleasure at this kind of usage: 'I know the man that that's the house of's daughter.'" He would have delighted at this from a member of the U.S. National Homeless Soccer Team profiled by Wells Tower, one Jason Moore, who introduces himself at the New York City shelter he calls home as Reverend Pimpin': "Being a reverend, you kind of learn to be pimpalicious."

Courtly as he was, Red would have recoiled at Ben Roethlisberger's crude barroom command cited by Sally Jenkins: "All my bitches, take some shots!" But he would have recognized the ugly truth of entitlement in the language of a quarterback accustomed to barking orders at the line of scrimmage and having them obeyed.

Words give us access to unknown territory—a crash site revisited 40 years later, the habitat of America's dwindling population of wild mustangs, the workshop of a master carver of Native American lacrosse sticks. And words fill the interior places in the heart and soul. Here is the ineffable John McPhee describing a last visit to the hospital to see his dying father. "I looked out the window for a time, at Baltimore, spilling over its beltway. I looked back at him. Spontaneously, I began to talk. In my unplanned, unprepared way, I wanted to fill the air around us with words, and keep on filling it, to no apparent purpose but, I suppose, a form of self-protection."

Sometimes words just plain take your breath away.

These 29 stories represent a panoply of excellence, reporting, and tone. They are by turns melodic, comedic, elegiac, and always idiosyncratic. I resolved to have as many voices heard as possible, eliminating some otherwise worthy picks because I had already chosen another piece by the author. Glenn dutifully removed the author's name and publication from the weighty batches that thudded at my front door. But some of the voices were so distinct, I recognized them anyway.

Voices of conscience: Sally Jenkins of the *Washington Post*, my pick for the best sports columnist writing today, and Selena Roberts of *Sports Illustrated*. It's no coincidence, I think, that two of the strongest voices in these pages belong to women writing about issues affecting women that wouldn't have made the agate page in Red's day.

Voices of whimsy: P. J. O'Rourke's lessons on child-rearing as gleaned from a 1961 field dog manual; Yoni Brenner's hilarious send-up of the verbal grandiosity of Any Given Sunday in the NFL. The last of his "Trick Plays" gives a whole new meaning to a Hail Mary pass: "In the waning seconds of the first half of the NFC championship game, the pious visiting quarterback leads a masterly 80-yard drive, culminating in a 15-yard touchdown strike. As his teammates celebrate, the quarterback drops to one knee to thank Jesus. Just then, the Rapture comes, and the quarterback is instantly beamed up to Heaven, leaving only his cleats behind."

Voices of grace: Mark Pearson writes of his cauliflower ear, a legacy of his college wrestling days and the love of the sport he inherited from his father. The burdens bequeathed by fathers (present, omnipresent, jailed, dead, remembered) are the subtext of this and so many other stories. Pearson's father taught him to wrestle with pain and left him glad to be the father of daughters. "As much joy and pride as there is between a father and a son, I don't know that I could endure much more of the unspoken pain that marks the lives of fathers and sons."

Voices that expose just how far otherwise rational people will go to win: Bill Shaikin introduces us to Vladimir Shpunt, an émigré Russian physicist hired by baseball's former power couple, Frank and Jamie McCourt, to help the Dodgers win by sending positive energy over great distances. From his living room in Boston. Via cable TV. No word who got custody of him in the divorce.

Voices that speak to the enduring importance of having a voice: Bill Plaschke's autobiographical ode to an old-fashioned notebook that gave a stuttering young boy a voice he didn't know he had speaks volumes about the enduring import of words.

Together, and in unexpected harmony, these 29 voices are sports writing's Greek chorus, by turns singing the praises of risk-takers and bearing witness to risk's pathological excess. On principle, I declined to include any of the multitudinous entries, no matter how well executed, detailing the sexploitation of others by risk-takers named Brett and Tiger. I also eliminated stories about women — racecar driver Danica Patrick and a whole roster of scantily clad femme fatale football players — who allow the sexploitation of themselves.

The need to risk self and sanity was the subject of many of this year's best submissions. Craig Vetter's admirably restrained profile of BASE jumper Dean Potter in *Playboy* reveals a man unable to accept the limits of humanity. Potter isn't satisfied with having flown four miles at 120 miles per hour with a parachute strapped to his back. No, he aims to fly without his hand-tailored Italian wingsuit or a parachute and walk away — like my pal Powers — in a pair of jeans.

Vetter sets the only appropriate tone for such a story — deadpan.

Bret Anthony Johnston sees art and aspiration — Pablo Picasso and Mike Tyson — in the daredevil skateboarder Danny Way, broken in so many places and in so many ways, "pushing not merely the limits of skateboarding but the boundaries of the human spirit, the soul."

The cultivation of confected risk in extremely extreme sports — and the astonishing number of stories devoted to those pursuits — may say something about how far we've come as a species, with leisure time to kill, disposable income to spend, and complacency to defy. It says as much about how far we have to go.

As I whittled and fiddled, and read and reread, the earth opened up and swallowed Japan. Neptune reared his gnarly head and let loose an epic wave that was definitely not surfable. Those running for their lives did not have to pay an entry fee for this "Death Race."

I wondered how those images registered, if they registered, with the corporately funded, apparel-endorsing, move-busting, family-busting, serotonin-depleted thrill-seekers who push the extremes of extreme. Do these explorers of human possibility know there was a guy named Magellan who navigated uncharted waters without GPS?

I wanted to tell Danny Way to read Mark Kram's series for the *Philadelphia Daily News* about a young boxer killed in the ring who became an organ donor and saved five lives. I wanted to tell Austrian aqua man Herbert Nitsch to read Chris Ballard's ode to a dying coxswain, Jill Costello, who steered her last race less than a month before her death from lung cancer. I wanted to tell Dean Potter to read Wright Thompson's homage to the soccer-playing Chilean miners whose old teammates joined the dusty vigil aboveground because, as one said, "we are not friends just of games. We are friends of the heart."

In its own decidedly nonlethal way, writing is also a kind of risk: these guys take their lives in their hands, and we take their lives in ours when we choose what to reveal about them — and sometimes about ourselves. Nancy Hass's elegy to Mike Penner, a longtime writer for the *Los Angeles Times*, should be required reading for all the leapers, sliders, skaters, and divers who leap, slide, skate, and dive in the name of human fulfillment. Penner risked everything to become the woman he knew himself to be, revealing to his readers that the Old Mike was now the New Christine. In her debut at a press conference introducing David Beckham to L.A., Christine wore "a golden-hued top from Ross and a multi-colored paisley skirt from Ames and a pair of open-toed heels from Aerosoles." In the end, she was unable to live in her new skin. The life and death of Mike Penner/Christine Daniels bears witness to just how far human beings will go to become fully themselves and the limits that fate places on the enterprise.

Mike/Christine's last byline was a suicide note. Hass writes: "For two decades, Mike Penner had crafted subtle sentences that teased the ironies out of the self-important world of sports: Christine Daniels, the woman he became for 18 months, added self-revelation and raw emotion to the mix. But in the end, there were only terse instructions."

That was a risk worth dying for.

JANE LEAVY

The Best American
Sports Writing
2011

Risks, Danger Always in Play

FROM THE BOSTON GLOBE

RUBEN "SPEEDY" GONZALEZ was always the last kid picked in physical education class, but he wanted to be in the Olympics. So he settled on luge by default.

"I needed a sport with lots of broken bones because I knew there would be quitters—and I never quit," he told Reuters last week. "I'll be the last man standing."

Or at least sitting. Gonzalez, who lives in Texas and competes for Argentina, is 47 now and yesterday he was bidding to become the first man to compete in four Winter Games across four decades. The secret to his survival is that he doesn't mind busting up a hand, a foot, an elbow, a rib when he slams into iced concrete and that he's invariably the slowest man on the track.

After the first two of four runs, Gonzalez is sitting a distant last among 38 competitors, more than eight seconds behind German leader Felix Koch and more than two seconds out of 37th place in a sport that is measured to the thousandth.

Until Friday, Gonzalez, a former photocopier salesman, was one of those charming quadrennial oddities, like Eddie The Eagle and Eric The Eel, who capture the public's imagination because they're Everyman, our Plimptonian ambassador to Olympus. But once Georgian luger Nodar Kumaritashvili died after a terrifying crash during a practice run on the Whistler speedway, watching Gonzalez slip-slide his way down the world's fastest run lost its amusing allure.

Luge always has attracted more Olympic "tourists" than the rest of the winter sports because anyone can do it. Just lie on your back and let gravity handle the rest. But once the amateur's amateur finds himself hurtling along at 90 miles an hour and ping-ponging from wall to wall before flipping over and ending up in a plaster cast, he learns a painful lesson. These Games can kill you.

There are 15 sports on the winter program and half of them can be fatal if you don't know what you're doing or simply have bad luck. All of the sliding sports—bobsled, luge, skeleton—are an orthopedic surgeon's dream. Ski jumping is flying without wings. Freestyle aerials are an upside-down lottery. The downhill is heartstopping, even for gold medalists. And the snowboard halfpipe is the plaything of the devil as Kevin Pearce, who suffered a severe head injury in the Olympic trials, can testify.

Even short-track speed skating can put you in the hospital for weeks. Allison Baver, who'll be competing here, shattered her right tibia last season after colliding with teammate Katherine Reutter in a World Cup race. At the trials, J. R. Celski ripped open his left thigh with his right skate blade after hitting the wall, nearly severing his femoral artery.

The Winter Games are dangerous enough for elite athletes who have been competing for years. They're no place for adventure seekers like the Latin American skier who'd never even been on a bunny slope but wanted to compete in the 1992 Games in Albertville. To prepare himself, he promised, he'd take a week of lessons in Val d'Isère.

By establishing qualifying standards before the 1994 Games, the International Olympic Committee tried to put a stop to absolute amateurs who'd convinced their countries to give them a parade uniform and a starting number. Even so, a sobering number of qualifiers probably have no business in the Games.

Kumaritashvili was no neophyte. He'd spent two years on the World Cup circuit, competed in five races this season, four of them on Olympic tracks, and ranked 44th in the overall standings. But he clearly was in over his head here.

The Whistler track is known as the "Elevator Shaft" because it plunges downward like the express elevator in a Manhattan skyscraper. It's fast and technical and even the best sliders in the world, like two-time champion Armin Zoeggeler of Italy, flipped during training runs last week. At high speed, even modest crashes are scary.

"When you hit that ice, it turns into fire," testified U.S. doubles slider Christian Niccum, a two-time Olympian who rolled over in training here. "I wanted to rip my suit off and yell, 'I'm on fire! I'm on fire!' It's hard when you're burning and the only thing to cool you down is ice."

Kumaritashvili had struggled all week to stay on his sled during training and already had crashed once. His final run, though, was proceeding reasonably well until he came late out of Curve 15, which sent him late into the finish curve and up toward the top of the wall, where the G-forces made him lose control.

"Once this happened," said Svein Romstad, secretary general of the International Luge Federation, "he was literally at the mercy of the sled."

Kumaritashvili came rocketing down, slammed into the opposite wall, and was catapulted out of the track and into a steel pole. It was terrible luck, but it was also an example of what can happen when physics and inexperience meet.

It was the first fatality on an artificial track in 35 years and it prompted the federation to make significant changes before yesterday's men's event. The starting line was moved down to where the women begin, the outer wall was raised at the point where Kumaritashvili went over, and the ice profile was changed. So the competition will be safer, but it can never be safe.

The Olympic motto, devised by founder Pierre de Coubertin himself, is "Faster, Higher, Stronger," and the Whistler track was designed to be the fastest on the planet. The Germans, who have dominated the sport for decades, love it. U.S. slider Erin Hamlin, the women's world champion, has proclaimed it fun.

But one thing that the true amateurs learn immediately is that there is no steering wheel or brakes on a luge sled and no safety nets. Even at Olympus, speed kills.

CHRIS JONES

Breathless

FROM ESPN THE MAGAZINE

EVEN BEFORE HE WAS A FREE-DIVER, Herbert Nitsch dreamed
he could stay underwater. He wouldn't need a fish's gills or tanks
filled with oxygen. In his dreams, he could live underwater as he
did on land—could live a better life, maybe even a perfect one.
Hidden below the ocean's surface, he could move effortlessly in
three dimensions and know the freedom of birds without having to
fly. All he had to do was trade liquid for air.

Today, sitting on a sailboat just off the Greek island of Crete,
feet dangling in the blue water, Nitsch is as close to that dream as
he has ever been. (When he is near water, he must touch it, if only
with his toes.) He is 40 years old, long and lean, having shaped
his body into a near-perfect submersible, efficient and technically
sound. He has conducted experiments on it, unraveled its myster-
ies. Through trial and error, says the Austrian, he has glimpsed its
truest potential and believes he has not yet reached it. Already, he
has set 31 free-diving records, including the most reason-defying,
for "no limit" diving, in which a person uses any means available
to dive as deeply as he can on a single breath. In 2007, Nitsch
strapped himself to a sled weighted with 180 pounds of lead, filled
his lungs with air, and disappeared into blackness off the Greek isle
of Spetses, dropping 702 feet—almost as deep as Rockefeller Center is tall—before returning to the surface alive. He believes that
within a year or two, he will dive 1,000 feet—that is, from the top
of the Chrysler Building to the sidewalk, then back to the tip of its
antenna.

Dreams are not enough at that depth. There are limits to the power of belief. Nitsch is a man of evidence, of science and measurements, of math. (In his spare time, he is a commercial pilot for an Austrian airline.) And through his trials, he has come to see one body part as crucial to his arithmetic: the spleen. His spleen is no different from your spleen: a mottled purple and gray organ about the size of your fist, on the left side of your abdomen between your heart and diaphragm. Its function is somewhat mysterious but includes the filtering of blood and the recycling of iron. Inside, small pockets called sinusoids collect oxygen-rich blood while it awaits processing. For every 33 feet a person descends underwater, organs are burdened by an extra 14.7 pounds of pressure per square inch. (When Nitsch reached the bottom of his record dive, the equivalent of an NFL lineman was sitting on each of his eyeballs.) Right around the time a diving Nitsch needs air, his spleen is squeezed by that pressure, forcing the oxygen-rich blood into his arteries like water from a sponge. Most of us associate liquid with drowning. But in his spleen, Nitsch sees a breath we never knew we had.

If the idea sounds crazy—our spleen as a third lung—know that Nitsch is, in fact, alarmingly rational. He is quick to point out that one of the ocean's greatest swimmers, the seal, can remain submerged for more than an hour in part because of the enormous capacity of its giant, enviable spleen. Nitsch believes blood squeezed from his own spleen can sustain him through the most difficult parts of his dives. In that fist-size organ, he sees remarkable adaptability and a reason to believe humans, like seals, are purpose-built to dive. "I don't think we know what we're capable of," he says in accented English. "In free-diving, we're still in the pioneering stage. The Wright brothers were once where we are. Now look how well we fly."

When asked what's too deep, what's an impossible depth to dream of reaching, Nitsch shrugs. "Something like 1,000."

Meters, he means. More than 3,000 feet.

Yesterday, Nitsch went spearfishing with some Greek friends. The Greeks, sponge collectors and fishermen, are legendary for their underwater lives. Yet they watched dumbfounded when Nitsch—tall and thin with a shaved head, black wetsuit, and long fins, a torpedo come to life—easily dropped 150 feet for minutes at a time. Nitsch has spent so much time underwater he has learned the body language of fish, acting timid or jumpy to attract their curiosity.

He has always been at home there. His father was an ardent sailor, and they spent a lot of time together touring the world's oceans. Nitsch became a snorkeler, then a scuba diver. He became an accidental free-diver when, in 1998, on a diving trip to the Red Sea, the airline lost his gear. Rather than squander a vacation on dry land, he decided to hold his breath and go for it. By week's end, he had hit 106 feet. He had no idea he'd missed the standing Austrian free-diving record by just over six feet, but he was sure about what he wanted to do with the rest of his life.

Even without the advantage of a lead-packed sled, he has already dropped a record 407 feet in the free-diving discipline known as constant weight, a giant fin attached to his feet. And though he no longer holds the record for simple breath-holding, he did once, staying underwater for 9:04 in 2006. He felt not the slightest urge to inhale until well past six minutes.

The Greeks posed for pictures after their time together. They asked why he does what he does. His answer: diving gives him pure joy, an otherwise unknowable freedom. And so down he must go. For them, watching him in the water, so effortless, he becomes something otherworldly. And yet he is built like the rest of us. Only his dreams are different.

"My body is just like everybody else's," Nitsch says. "My lungs may be slightly bigger, but everything else is the same. So yes, sometimes I ask myself, Why can I do these things when others can't? The truth is, it's no longer physical."

Nothing burns oxygen like panic. A few years ago, Nitsch went exploring with a friend deep inside a cave outside Vienna. Each carried a small emergency oxygen tank because some parts of the expedition led underwater, requiring them to hold their breath and swim. The cave's water was turgid, the light low, and in the darkness Nitsch's friend panicked. He quickly ran through his own tank and most of Nitsch's. Beneath the earth's surface, with only a few sips of air remaining, Nitsch wasn't sure they would make it out. But after they completed that terrifying exercise in stamina and will—"We just had to make it," Nitsch says matter-of-factly— he was overcome with relief. Not because he survived, but because he had learned what he needed to do to live without air.

"You must be absolutely calm," he says. The cave taught him the value of an economy of movement, of strapping a governor to emotion. It taught him he needed to dive as deeply inside himself as he dreamed of diving into the sea. He needed a new serenity.

Since the scare in the cave, he has become very good at slowing the processes of his body. Before his deepest dives, Nitsch enters a meditative state, a kind of trance. "I've trained myself to leave the situation," he says. At the surface, he inhales and exhales giant breaths several times over, approaching hyperventilation to rid his body of the carbon dioxide that triggers the body's inhalation reflex. Meanwhile, his brain begins to narrow focus. Sometimes, his tunnel vision is so intense, Nitsch experiences an out-of-body sensation. "Hydrodynamics and aerodynamics are not that different," he says, and that morning off Spetses he felt himself floating in the sky rather than the water. His brain carried him above the scene, high enough to see himself, breathing in, breathing out, along with everyone watching him, their boats floating in the water. He felt as though he were watching someone else about to attempt the impossible, and he went slack.

Nitsch conserves oxygen in many ways. He fasts for a day before a big dive; digestion burns oxygen. (Those gases also cause a particular danger: on steep ascents, a trapped fart can blow teeth out a diver's nose.) Rather than wear a mask, which would need to be equalized—the air inside it would painfully compress without more precious air exhaled into it—Nitsch built himself a pair of glasses. Made of fiberglass, with small, thick lenses, they allow him to check his depth gauge and spot the guide rope he follows into darkness, to see as clearly as with a mask, but with the sea flowing freely over his eyes.

Most important, Nitsch has perfected something called bloodshifting, an elaborate predive preparation commonly practiced by expert free-divers to trick the body into thinking it's drowning. When the brain believes the body is going to die, Nitsch has found in caves and other dark places, it becomes coldly efficient. Nitsch promotes bloodshifting by making preliminary dives with empty lungs, up and down and back again, before his real effort. In response, the human body—his body, your body—takes blood from its extremities and packs it into its core. The same reflex occurs naturally when you are cold, which is why when temperatures dip, fingertips are the first part of you to go numb. In either instance, starving your arms and legs of blood saves oxygen. In Nitsch's case, it also prepares his body for the pressure it is about to bear. Blood is pushed into the labyrinth of vessels in his lungs, and just as it's harder to crush a full can than an empty one, that blood protects his lungs from being ruptured by the weight of deep water. He can feel it happening, can imagine transforming into an aquanaut. Sitting at the surface, waiting for the word "go," Nitsch knows his body is doing everything it can to make his dreams come true. He is at peace then, just another stone waiting to sink.

Herbert Nitsch is lying to himself. There are some limits he cannot transcend. Because he can go so deep for so long, he risks decompression sickness each time he ascends, nitrogen bubbling out of his blood and into his brain and joints—the bends. That same nitrogen inevitably causes nitrogen narcosis on the way down too, starting at around 100 feet. There's nothing Nitsch can do to duck it. As alcohol affects people differently, divers respond to "getting narced" in their own way. Some feel happy, some tense. Some feel liberated, some trapped. For Nitsch, narcosis "is just a bitch," making him feel out of control on every dive, as though everything is about to slip from his grasp, a terrible feeling when you're riding nearly 200 pounds of lead to the bottom of the sea.

Still, the greatest threat to a submerged Nitsch has nothing to do with nitrogen. It has nothing to do with his brain or his heart or his lungs. It has to do with the ears and the reality that we are limited in the depths we can reach by their delicate architecture. What keeps Nitsch from reaching 1,000 feet is a mere fraction of an inch thick: the translucent tympanic membranes in the auditory canals otherwise known as eardrums.

It doesn't take much pressure to burst an eardrum. If you go swimming and don't equalize your ears by plugging your nose and pushing air into your Eustachian tubes, the weight of the water knocking on your door can snap that thin membrane at a dozen feet, give or take. It has never happened to Nitsch, but he knows it's an extraordinarily painful sensation. In cold water—and deep water is always cold water—it can also be deadly. When cold water rushes in, your ears' mechanics cramp and seize, affecting your sense of spatial awareness, including the sense of up and down. You don't know which way points toward permanent blackness and which way points toward light. Eventually, your body will warm the water trapped inside your head, and your ears will relax, opening up the world to you once more. By then, though, your lungs will have opened up too, and the water in your ears will be low on your list of concerns.

The only way to counter this danger is to pressurize the inside of your ears. But Nitsch's lungs—your lungs—only hold a finite amount of air. And when that air is compressed the deeper he travels, there is less and less to push into his Eustachian tubes. Eventually, he runs out. He always runs out. And always at the moment his eardrums inform him they're about to break.

He has searched for every known fix. In addition to conserving air, Nitsch takes in as much as he can. For his final breath, he practices what free-divers call packing: taking a normal breath, then 30 or so small swallows of air to fill every nook and cranny of his respiratory system with oxygen. Once below water, he stops his weighted sled at around the 75-foot mark and expels that stored air, through a tube, into a plastic Coke bottle. (These are the homespun instruments of a pioneering profession.) As he continues to descend, he takes sips from the bottle whenever his ears cry out. At depth, it is easier to sip air from a bottle than to squeeze it from crushed lungs.

It's also one more mind trick Nitsch is playing, fooling his brain into thinking he's actually breathing, even if the air he's taking in has already been stripped of oxygen. It's the same as a thirsty man spitting back a glass of water without swallowing it; he would feel as if he were drinking, but his body would be drying out all the same. The charade can't go on forever, maybe not even as far as 1,000 feet. The air in the Coke bottle may protect his eardrums, but packing expands the esophagus, restricting blood flow to the brain. To prevent a blackout, Nitsch's body amps up his heart rate, which burns a lot of oxygen. What air gives him, it also takes away.

Nitsch and other free-divers, then, are trying to determine if it's more effective to dive with nearly empty lungs, to sacrifice oxygen for the body's reaction to the absence of it: the slow, gradual shutting down, the gentle drift to death's door. He has begun to wonder if air is the enemy.

Liquid is life—Nitsch finds himself thinking that over and over again. Maybe we drown only because we haven't learned enough about what we're capable of. Maybe we drown only because our brain associates air with breathing and liquid with drowning. Aren't we made mostly of water? Weren't we born in the oceans?

And so he has experimented with a technique used by a vanguard of free-divers called wet equalization. Before a dive he fills his head with water, snorting scary amounts through his nose, driving it deep into his sinuses and Eustachian tubes. (The epiglottis, the flap of tissue at the back of our tongues, keeps the water out of his lungs.) On either side of his eardrums, water sits in a kind of static harmony. It is both inside and outside the door, a perfect balance. With it, Nitsch is able to dive as deeply as he wants. So long as there is water inside his head, he can dive forever.

Problem is, filling his head with water makes Nitsch feel as though he is dying. "It is very unpleasant," he says with typical understatement. The feeling is all that stands in his way, all that separates him from the only thing he's ever wanted. He's so close. But it's hard to evolve so quickly. Even Nitsch can't suddenly ignore the feeling he's drowning, that he is about to die.

You would feel the same way, as the water trickles out of your sinuses and down the back of your throat. You would feel it collecting in your stomach and running like a river into your intestines, first small, then large. Some might even slip past your epiglottis and rattle around in your lungs. You would taste the salt, choke on the bubbles, feel the weight dragging you down. You would feel the water making its inevitable way down every corridor of your body, into every chamber as you sink not like a stone, but like a foundering ship, picking up speed the deeper you went. You would feel your one-way valves and muscles struggling to fight the incoming tide. You would feel blood rushing into your pounding heart and convulsing lungs.

Nitsch might be wrong, but he thinks he knows what comes next. He's done the math, taken the measurements. He knows that, eventually, his body, your body, will stop fighting. Eventually, it will give in. Your brain will accept its fate and shut you down piece-by-inessential-piece, segment-by-unnecessary-segment. It will decide there is nowhere to go but down, that life on the surface is over and a new one awaits below. You will begin to adapt, feel yourself transform. Only then will you find a new serenity, euphoria even, your body no longer itself but something else, some new, mysterious vessel you never imagined you were capable of being. You will become a submersible, a torpedo, a seal with a giant, enviable spleen. And you will feel one with the water, as though you could dive forever, thousands and thousands of feet, where black becomes blue again, and where every one of your dreams comes true.

PAUL SOLOTAROFF

The Surfing Savant

FROM ROLLING STONE

PUT HIM IN THE WATER and Clay Marzo is magic, a kid with so much grace and daring that you laugh in disbelief to watch him surf. Every day he's out there in the South Pacific, shredding huge swells till he's faint with hunger and near the verge of dehydration. He doesn't really ride waves as much as *fly* them, soaring above the sea foam upside down and spinning the nose of his board in whip-lash twists. Just two years out of high school, Marzo is remaking a sport held hostage by rules and hack judges, turning it into a cross between aquatic parkour and X Games stunt work. Call it what you want, it's a sight to behold. *Sorry, but humans can't do that,* you keep thinking. Then he goes and does it all morning long.

But if you sit and list the things that Marzo has trouble doing, they quickly outrun the things he finds easy. He's unable, for in-stance, to eat a simple meal without much of it ending up on his shirt or the floor. Out of water, he has trouble interacting with other people, either staring in bafflement at their grins and jokes or avoiding casual contact altogether. He blurts things out, chants rap songs to himself, and pulls out clumps of his hair when anx-ious. When he speaks, which isn't often, he seems younger than his 20 years, mumbling like a bashful eighth-grader. For years, the rap on Marzo has been that, for all his talents, he's a pothead who chokes in competitions. And then there are the even-nastier names he's had to deal with, slurs that burned in deep: retard, moron, slacker, zombie. In middle school, Marzo was treated so badly that his mother, Jill, had to pull him out and teach him at home, where he wouldn't be punched for staring at wannabe thugs. His agoniz-

ing shyness has fractured his family and sparked ugly set-tos with
his father, Gino, an old-school hard-hat striver who accused him of
flaking off and screwing up his shot at stardom. That charge hurts
Clay more than the others combined: when your own father mis-
conceives you so badly, how can you hope that strangers will understand?

Now, pushing back from lunch at a Maui fish stand, bits of ahi
po'boy dotting his face and lap, Marzo wears the grin of a birthday
boy who gets to eat as much cake as he wants. To see him like this,
hands clasped across belly, is to encounter a kid whose first and
last directive is pure, physical joy. But the facts are more complex
and less happy. Marzo has Asperger's syndrome, a form of high-
functioning autism that causes no end of social confusion and anguish, and that commonly burdens those afflicted with a single,
smothering obsession: bird songs or train routes or the history of
naval warfare. "Though Asperger's teens are typically bright and
verbal, they can't connect with kids their age or with people they
don't know well," says Dr. Michael Linden, an autism specialist who
diagnosed Marzo at the age of 18, after a dozen years of botched
assessments. "Feelings are a foreign language to them, and they're
unable to pick up social cues. A lot of them retreat from relationships and get stuck in a special activity or interest that they devote
themselves to intensely."

Like a lot of adult Aspies, as some with the diagnosis have taken
to calling themselves, Marzo is a baffling mix of powers and defi-
cits. He has no interest in the written word (and has read few of the
dozens of stories about him in sports magazines, which regularly
anoint him one of surfing's saviors) but is brilliant, even clairvoy-
ant, in the water. Looking at the horizon, Marzo can read waves
that others can't and intuit where they'll break before they crest.
Traveling fills him with such dread that he's sick with nausea days
before boarding a plane, but he gets up each day and surfs lethal
points on Maui's western shore. The kinds of waves he lives on
don't crash near sandy beaches; instead, he climbs down lava cliffs
to reach breaks rife with boulders and a seafloor of spear-tipped
coral reefs that can turn a surfer's chest to chum. His body is a trav-
elogue of scars and welts, but it bores him to talk about the dangers
he courts—the boards he routinely snaps taking hellish falls; the
waves that hold him down till his lungs scream, half a minute or

more during really heavy sets. Only once, he says, has he been afraid of the surf. "There were tiger sharks behind me," he says, wiping a quarter-size splotch of mayo off his cheek. "They were pretty big, so I bailed quick."

After lunch, Marzo pays a visit to Adam Klevin, a muscular, bald-shaved man who's seen more of Clay in water than anyone besides his mother. For the past five years, Klevin has risen at dawn to film every wave that Marzo catches and compile the highlights. Today, on one of the flatscreens in the unkempt room that Klevin uses as an editing suite, Marzo is up and riding a 12-foot swell. Dancing on the wave front with cha-cha turns that brace him for a bigger move, he whips the back of the board into a savage 360 that surfers call a throw-tail reverse. It's a common trick, but there are few people on the planet who can successfully nail it in Maui after a recent storm has raised waves the size of houses. Marzo is barely upright as he exits the spin, his mouth a perfect *O* of exaltation. He bangs a hard left into the next section of wave and throws a front-side snap that lifts him clean out of the water, arms and knees in vehement op-position. He can't possibly make it—his rear end's gone, and God knows what he's looking at over his shoulder as he grabs the rail of the board for dear life. The wave collapses on the jagged floor, blowing up a squall of white-capped spray in which the boy and board go missing. For a moment there's nothing, just the chaos of foam. Then the chop parts, and here he somehow comes, half off the board but still in charge. This isn't surfing, this is sorcery, a kid so alive and electrically good that he makes this look like the world's one true religion.

But when I turn to say as much, Marzo is somewhere else, head down and eyes fixed on some inner shore. He has everything he needs to be his sport's Shaun White—the face, the body, the game-changing skill—and a chance to be a beacon for the 1.5 million kids in this country with autism-related disorders. But Marzo has neither the drive nor the nervous system to handle being famous. No, if it's all the same, he'd rather be alone, paddling back out, through the churn and boulders, to where the big waves break. It's the one place on Earth he feels safe.

For an island synonymous with God-sent waves and the goofy-foot cool of surf kitsch, Maui has produced shockingly few riders driven enough to compete with the sport's name-brand stars. "There's a small-town vibe here that's held guys back when they surfed the bigger stages," says Erik Aeder, a surf photographer and Maui native who has shot every local kid who showed much promise. "Plus, the trade winds make the waves choppy, which made it hard to learn the elegant moves that used to win tournaments."

But in the late eighties, a new breed of riders stood the game on end. Inspired by the halfpipe pyrotechnics of skate- and snowboarders, surfers like Kelly Slater and Christian Fletcher started to approach waves differently, shooting over the top of the lip, using the wave's speed to do airs and inverts and sudden, violent turns. "Those guys made their style a global phenomenon through videos and photo spreads," says Matt Warshaw, author of the forthcoming *The History of Surfing* and former editor of *Surfer* magazine. "Kids everywhere went to school on their hi-fi moves, and that next generation went bigger and faster, trying for stunt-show things in junior contests."

Among that contingent was a brood from Maui of exceptionally gifted boys. Raised within an hour's drive of each other, they came up together through the Pee-Wee ranks and traveled as extended family, becoming stars before they were in their teens. Dusty Payne was the first to join the pro-surfer tour after winning an international juniors competition in 2008. Kai Barger and Granger Larsen are right behind him, and all three, according to an industry insider, "should be solid fixtures" on the top-money list for years to come.

But the best of that bunch, from boyhood on, was Marzo. With his bottomless hunger for huge maneuvers and unsinkable sense of balance and intuition, he looked, to all who saw him, like the future of the sport while he was still in grade school. He was fiercely competitive in tournaments, racked up wins in every age division, and seemed an inevitable heir to Slater, the great soul surfer with nine world titles. "When he showed up for the national championships and put down perfect 10s at age 15, the media declared him the next great icon," says Warshaw. "Other kids could do some of the things he did, but not with his power and naturalness and skill at getting out of tight spots."

Though tournaments aren't as crucial to surfing fans as they are in other sports—there's a widespread sense that the rules are too archaic, favoring cautious riders over hellions—the hope was that Marzo and his class of big-air starlings would push the game up the board-sport totem and land it in the mainstream. (Surfing, eclipsed by X Games theatrics, remains virtually invisible on TV.)

Marzo seemed made to order for the thresher of pro surfing, which has cut down many kids with outsize talent. It begins with the yearlong World Qualifying Series, a continent-hopping gauntlet of contests against hundreds of amateur riders, all of them vying for 16 slots on the World Tour. Once Marzo turned pro and moved on to the big leagues, he would compete against the world's top 44 surfers in a globe-spanning season that lasts 10 months.

But it's one thing to rule the scholastic circuit, where no one's really watching but the families of other surfers, and a kid with Marzo's gifts could crush opponents by going bigger, faster, and braver. It's another to dominate the junior tour, where Marzo encountered battle-tested surfers with three or four years on him, most of them versed in the mind games and sly mechanics of contest strategy. The fake-outs on the waves, the jockeying for position—it was a language his Aspie brain couldn't process, blind as it is to tacit cues. Add in the crowds of fans, the announcers blaring scores over the PA system, and the cameramen in the water shooting action footage, and Marzo was sabotaged by his own senses. Nor did he fully grasp the rudiments of tournament rules, which give riders a half-hour to produce two scoring runs. Often, Marzo would land a hellfire move on an early wave, then bob like a buoy as time ran out, waiting for the perfect swell. "He had a couple of years there of brilliance, but then something happened," says Warshaw. "We figured maybe it was the pressure or the travel or—well, no one really knew at the time."

Including Clay. Almost from birth, he's had a sizable gift for confounding expectations. Born in San Diego, he moved at nine months to the small town of Lahaina, steps from the sea in Maui; his mom and dad, both avid surfers, wanted to be closer to the waves. "Clay was wading before he could walk, and he walked at seven and a half months," recalls Jill. "At three months, he swam with his head under water, and by one he was on the front of his dad's surfboard, riding waves all the way in." Both parents were fine, if workaday, athletes—Jill, a massage therapist, loved volleyball as a kid; Gino, a carpenter, played baseball in college—and they organized their lives around the care and feeding of not one but two surf prodigies. Clay's half-brother, Cheyne, who is seven years older, was signed by sponsors at the age of 13. "Clay adored Cheyne and wanted to be like him, right up to the stickers on his board," says Jill. "And it went both ways: Cheyne bragged him up to sponsors, saying, 'Wait'll you get a load of my younger brother.'"

Clay entered his first contest at the age of five, and took home a trophy for finishing fourth. By seven, he'd joined the kiddie corps of local prodigies, sharing sleepovers, picnics, and family trips with Payne, Barger, and Larsen. "We were doing bigger, wilder stuff because we always had waves to play with," Clay recalls. "It's the Maui style: trying to top each other and look like we weren't even trying." There'd be half a dozen boys in the back of Jill's van, burping and farting the 15 miles to surf the North Shore breaks. "That was a magical time for Clay, the best years of his life," says Jill. "They were wonderful with him, really treated him like a brother, though even then they could see that he was different."

Clay's mother and father were divided over his odd behavior. Jill had long been flustered by the passel of tics that presented when Clay was four. "He made these weird faces and couldn't stop doing it," she says. "He was humming and flapping and pulling his hair, and was always just very intense and nervous when he wasn't in water." He staged shrieking tantrums if anyone touched the baseball cards or seashells he collected, and soothed himself by reciting lines from movies he'd learned by heart. He was uneasy wearing anything but the softest fabrics, was easily spooked by sudden noises, and for years allowed no one but Jill to hug him, pulling away from others. But his father refused to concede there was anything wrong. "He never really shared much or let you in, but I figured that was who Clay was," Gino says. "He was always a great athlete, and loved running around to the contests together, the two of us hanging out and having fun. If he had anything, I thought he'd outgrow it. Learn to finally look you in the eye."

In grade school, Clay was diagnosed with attention deficit disorder and consigned to special ed. Jill tried him on Ritalin, but the drug exacerbated his moods and fits, made him a "kicking, screaming monster." Gino, meanwhile, derided the label. "He didn't need drugs," he says. "He needed to mind his teacher and stop drawing waves in his pad." By then, Clay's obsession with all things surfing completely filled the screen. No matter the assignment, each paper he wrote had to do with surfing. At night, he'd watch the tapes that Jill shot of his rides and study himself frame by frame. Then he'd go to bed and surf in his dreams: she would find him moving around but fast asleep, yelling, "Get off of my wave!" "You didn't want to wake him from one of those dreams," she recalls. "He could be violent in that state."

While Clay's schoolwork suffered, his surfing flourished. As a 10-year-old, he would fly long hours to competitions in California, where he would routinely whip the country's best 13-and-unders. If you're raised in Hawaii and can surf rings around older kids, you'll pop up pretty early on the radar of companies that make board-shorts and energy drinks. "I saw Clay for the first time when he was 10, and offered him a contract on the spot," says John Oda, the surf-team manager for Spy Optic eye-wear, which designs sunglasses for action sports. "He had so much speed and took such big risks that I knew, even then, that he'd be a star." By middle school, Clay had a deal with Quiksilver, and he was winning so many trophies that his parents had to cram them in the garage. Gino chauffeured him to meets and fussed over his gear and sponsor decals, making sure they were splashed on his boards. (Clay didn't like the stickers, which only served to draw unwanted attention to him.)

At 14—the year before his biggest triumph, the men's open title at the national finals—Clay sent a three-minute tape of himself surfing to Strider Wasilewski at Quiksilver. Wasilewski, who was then the team manager for Slater and several of the world's top pros, screened the loop in something like drop-jawed awe. "I'd never seen anyone near that young be so tuned in to the wave," he recalls. "His mechanics, his flow were comparable to Slater's, but Slater in his 20s, not teens. I thought, 'Holy shit, the world *has* to see this. We've got to book him onto the *Young Guns II* trip.'"

The *Young Guns* series of DVDs was a breakout marketing tool, showing off Quiksilver's future stars in exotic surf locales. Clay boarded an enormous yacht in Indonesia, where Slater and a film crew were shooting a handpicked group of the sport's best up-and-comers. Pitted against phenoms like Ry Craike and Julian Wilson, Clay astonished the pros with his flying-fish maneuvers, surfing the barrels with such command that he'd slow himself down to prolong his ride. For Slater, arguably the best surfer who has ever lived, it was a kind of a Clapton-meets-Hendrix moment, the jolt of new-found genius. "I didn't know anything about him, but he blew my mind," Slater recalled later. "I don't get intimidated by 15-year-olds often, but he was charging every wave, throwing the biggest, craziest reverses. He knows things about surfing that I don't."

The video that emerged moved a million units as a promo in surfing mags, and introduced Clay to a global public of preteen surfers. Soon, he appeared in a slew of new titles, signed six-figure deals with Quiksilver and others, and was trailed by groupies at media events, a sex symbol before his first girlfriend. "I'd be with him on a beach, just hanging out surfing, and suddenly all these kids would chase him down," says Klevin. "That really freaked him out and made it less fun, being in the bull's-eye of all these strangers." Whisked to late-night parties by sponsors' reps and roused for morning meet-and-greets and in-store signings, he began hiding out in foreign hotel rooms to avoid the stares and pleas of fans downstairs. "As a kid, he'd dreamt of going on trips with his heroes like Kelly," says Gino. "But suddenly, he was with them every week, in Tahiti one day, Australia the next, and he got sick of it pretty fast."

To earn his keep from the sponsors who pay him, a top rider lives out of a duffel bag, constantly jetting to end-of-the-world beaches for four-day "surf adventures." There he is shot, like the product he is, for photo spreads, online clips, and DVDs, all the while supplying punchy quotes about the "bombing reefs in Malaysia." He's also expected to pile up points on the tour circuit, flying to contests in Europe or Asia on weeks when he's not doing junkets. Finally, there are trade shows and promo tours and media events to do, a teeth-grind gamut of jostling cameras and sensory overload. It all so unstrung Clay that he eventually shut down, hiding behind headphones with the volume cranked, a mute, sullen kid who kept apart. His surfing cratered on the junior tour, he staged sudden ailments to get out of trips, and wouldn't leave his hotel bed when it was time to surf a heat. "All the guys were talking about this crazy kid, saying he's Pigpen in *Peanuts*," recalls Jamie Tierney, a senior Quiksilver producer who befriended Clay. "He'd lose his wallet and cell phone, and he'd lay down on the floor after he got done eating, rapping to himself over his iPod. It wasn't, let's just say, the greatest entrance."

One of his sponsors dumped him for odd behavior, and Clay

came within a lash of losing Quiksilver, by far his biggest backer. Interviewed once during a promo for his sponsor's line of goods, he was asked how the board-shorts felt. "They should be a little longer, maybe with better material too. And I don't like the color," he said. "Why—do you want me to like them?"

Several days after the monster storm that raised 50-footers off the coast, I arrange to meet Marzo at a forbidding break on the far west shore of Maui. A rock beach hidden from highway views by a copse of Cook pines and palms, it's reachable only by a bone-jarring track down the side slope of a cliff. At the bottom, several hard-boys in the beds of pickups have their feet up, smoking a fat-tie. The surf is mush, dreary three-footers that crumble like stale saltines, and the place has the last-dregs air of a keg party gone too long. Marzo and his girlfriend, Alicia Yamada, are slouched in the cab of her truck, hoping for an offshore breeze to kick up bigger waves. "Surf's beady," he yawns through the rolled-down window. "Barely worth getting out of bed."

"No biggie," says Yamada, nut-brown and pretty, with hair almost down to her waist. "You've surfed worse than this, so what the hell. Go out there and rip it up."

They're a curious pair. She: short, dark, and dazzling. He: tall, impassive, and half-present. Though Yamada won't discuss it, I've heard from others that Marzo can be a difficult mate. He grabs food from her without thinking to ask, gets jealous when she talks to friends, and used to say vicious things if he didn't get his way. "She's a tough cookie and doesn't take shit, but I worry 'cause they're together noon and night," says Jill. "Clay's real possessive, and they're both so young. The good news is they're in couples counseling now."

They met four years ago, when he surfed with her brothers and was shy to the point of anguish around her. But they were thrown together enough that a friendship developed, and by 16 and 18 (she's two years older) a fumbling romance began. This caused a lot of grousing in the Marzo household: Gino, suspicious of Alicia's motives, resented her frequent visits to Clay, particularly when she slept in his room. "Here's my son, with no experience in life but earning lots of money from sponsors, and she comes around with no job or cash, making herself right at home," he says. "Next thing

I know, he stops going on trips or wanting to compete. They won't keep paying you if you won't leave Maui, no matter *how* great you surf." There were constant battles at the dinner table, where he hectored Clay to be like his old Maui buddies, who traveled full-time to earn points and exposure on the junior circuit. Jill pushed back on Clay's behalf, saying he couldn't handle the punitive schedule of the typical top-shelf surfer. The fights so upset Clay that he'd flee upstairs or hide in the yard with his dogs. After a while, he stopped coming home altogether, staying with Alicia for days or weeks in the condo Jill had bought him with his earnings. Sides were drawn, and the siblings dragged in. Cheyne, the oldest, turned on Clay and accused him of hyping his ailment. Their younger sister, Gina, who's now 12, aligned with Jill and eventually stopped speaking to Gino. Last summer the couple split, after 21 years of marriage. Clay has no contact with Cheyne, whom he still reveres, and barely speaks to his father.

It takes more cajoling, but Marzo gets out of the truck; per usual, he's wearing just his trunks. Staring past the jetty to where the small sets form, his emerald eyes gain light and lose it, tracking currents the way a cat tracks birds. He's perfectly built for surfing: tall and broad-shouldered, with long, muscular arms to paddle hard, and short, rubbery legs that hold their line in the heaviest conditions. He's also strong in slop, carving whiplash turns in the flume of blah three-footers, but bored and saddened by the sight of them. Come summer, when the offshore winds die down and the surf here becomes a rumor, Marzo slides into a deep funk, moping on the couch with his laptop out, eyeing the conditions in Peru. "I'm eggy," he says now, Clay-speak for "vexed." "I checked the swell charts. It was s'posed to *go off.*"

There's a small group gathered on this rutted slope that over-looks the ocean: Tierney, who's visiting from California and who, two years ago, made *Just Add Water,* a wise and affectionate docu-mentary about Marzo and his condition; Klevin, on hand to film Clay's rides; and Yamada and her father, a surf-battered man who claims to have ridden 40-footers. They gently coax Marzo to ride for an hour, but he stalls them, eyeing the tide. The prospect of be-ing watched by even five admirers is enough to make him want to get back in the truck and go hide out in his room. His panic ratch-ets tenfold at tournaments, where he's still so pained by the crowd noise and cameras that he recently blew his chance to win the World Junior title by showing up late to his own heat. Nor is fear the only thing holding him back. In contests, he's incapable of playing it safe, going for broke on each wave. Time and again he has coughed up leads by failing to land an inverted blowtail when a modest, two-turn ride would seal the win. "Strategy's a huge part of contest surfing, which is how the hack guys earn their living, doing the same move over and over," says Tierney. "Clay can't do that, or says he can't. Me, I think he could if it really mattered."

Tierney, the son of two psychologists, seems to have a feel for handling Marzo. "C'mon, dude," he tweaks him. "I came all the way from SoCal. Show me how you surf this right-hand trash."

A half-smile tugs the corner of Marzo's mouth. "Even you could do it today," he murmurs.

"Well, let's go, then," says Tierney. "I brought my board along. Meet you where the dry rock sticks out."

Marzo hefts his six-foot Super and starts down the path to the shore, bumbling over roots, barefoot. To the consternation of his parents and backers, Marzo often responds to anxiety by getting stoned. It seems to brace his moods, which can reel on a dime, and allays the jitters that overtake him when he heads out into the world. As a maintenance drug, though, pot has its limitations. Marzo has ducked so many trips and promo junkets that he almost lost his meal ticket in 2008. "All the suits were on me hard to get rid of him, saying, 'He's a stuck-up, pot-smoking slacker,'" recalls Quiksilver's Wasilewski. "But I knew he was special, a once-in-a-lifetime talent who needed understanding and hope."

To save Marzo's career, Wasilewski pushed his parents to have him examined for autism. Jill, who had already put him through years of tests for everything from learning disabilities to depression, was loath to subject him to more doctors. After months of prodding, though, she accompanied Clay to California for a week of tests by autism specialists. In waiting rooms full of three-year-old boys who flapped their arms and wailed, she knew the truth before the findings came. "I went online to look Asperger's up and cried and cried, saying, 'That's Clay,'" she says. "The years we let pass, the push to do the contests—it all just hit me really hard. I thought from now on, it's only about him being happy. Whatever he wants to do, that's what we'll do."

"Clay drew comfort from the diagnosis," says Mitch Varnes, his manager. "It turned off the heat to finally know the facts and also took the heat off from his sponsors. They said, 'Forget doing promos and the junior tour—just go surf and have fun.' He still wound up in tons of films and mags, but on his terms, not theirs."

Marzo cut his trips down to six or ten a year, and began seeing a behaviorist who taught him cues for managing the fans and press. The treatments salved his panic. Though sparingly seen in contests, he won his sport's Oscar for Best Male Performance at the 2008 Surfer Poll Awards and became a bigger rock star in near-absentia than most of the tour's top guns. Marzo can go on earning a substantial living even if he never wins a championship or the handful of tourneys he enters when the mood occurs. The public adores him, especially kids, who seek him out in the trade publications and online sites where surfers gain exposure. "If he wants to surf contests, great," says Wasilewski. "If not, we'll film him wherever he roams, do Webisodes fans kill to see, which justifies what we pay him. He'll be with us as long as he wants. He's a part of our family."

But even with the fact of his diagnosis, the surf world expects things of Marzo. Tierney thinks he should "bite the bullet" and do the Qualifying Series, which can now be completed in a "doable" six months instead of a hellish year. "It would be a tough haul, but he'd get to join the World Tour and surf against his idols in great waves," Tierney insists. "He's one of the five best on the planet in terms of talent, and with focus and a couple of years' experience he could be one of the best who ever did it." Marzo's manager is pinning hopes on a prospective new pro tour for big-air, balls-out riders. "Just 16 guys, the best progressive surfers, and an hour, not a half-hour, for heats. No one knows if it'll go yet—there's no sponsor attached—but it would be perfect for Clay," says Varnes. Even Marzo is prone to grand ambitions, though they change each time you ask him. "The new tour would be cool—I could deal," he says. But the next day he's talking about the free-surf option, in which the great alternative riders—Dane Reynolds, Bruce Irons—command big money to travel the globe for films and photo shoots.

Still, as I stand on the rise overlooking the beach in Maui, it's hard to imagine how a kid like Marzo could manage any of those options. I think back on our first—and last—sit-down chat, in which he all but fled the room, screaming. It began well enough, with Marzo talking about his childhood and name-checking his heroes, Bruce Irons and Kalani Robb. "Those guys invented the moves," he says. "We were just trying to take them farther." Then, out of the blue, he announces that surfing is the thing that "saved" him. "It's the best drug ever," he says, "and I'm lucky to have it."

I gently ask what it saved him from. He stares out the window and starts to yank his forelock. "I just . . . see things different, from the back of my brain," he says. "Other people see 'em from the front, I guess. It's not good or bad, just how I am. Sort of makes it harder, though, you know?"

"How so?"

His free hand paws the side of his trunks, damp in the air-chilled room. "Well, I need people's help to get stuff done. Telling me where to go and what to say, and sometimes I don't like that, or I'm tired and don't want . . ."

The sentence just hangs there, whirring in space. I hold off, giving him room to work through the tangle of half-formed thoughts. Instead, he tugs his hair so hard that a clump comes off in his fingers. Panicked, I ask about the feeling he gets when he does something splendid on a wave. "I can't describe it," he says, slouching so low that he burrows into his chest. "Just pleasure, I guess. Where you want it over and over, and do anything to get it . . . Are we almost done?"

"Just one more," I say, looking at a poster-size photo on the wall. In it, Marzo is stock-still on his board, raising his arms in benediction as a 20-foot wave hulks above him. In the undepicted instant after the photo was taken, he paddled coolly around the edge of the wave before it smashed him to bits on the rocks. "What do you think when you see that picture?" I ask.

He mashes his lower lip, but releases the hair he's wrapped around a clenched index finger. "I was stoked," he says. "That wave was *bombing,* and there was another, even bigger, right behind it."

What he doesn't add is that he had just returned from a nightmare trip and felt blessed to be home again. Marzo is a creature of waves, but of *these* waves, the rocky, shark-toothed waters of Maui that he knows by heart. Look at him now, out beyond the reef, doing tricks to raise his flagging spirits. In surf no bigger than a picket fence, he's positioned himself above the swell, skimming like a coin from crest to crest. Just as each dies, he spies a new section to carve his name upon, hurling his board up the short-sleeve face to ride the foam again. He's forgotten the guys watching from their pickup trucks, and the small crowd up here with our mouths agape, and the father he can't please, and the brother who cut him dead—all of that's gone now, carried away by the hunchbacked westerly waves. He'll surf until lunchtime, then come back after a nap, and if not for the tiger sharks that hunt these waters once the sun goes down, he might never get out of the bliss machine, which makes no claims, only grants them.

JAKE BOGOCH

School of Fight: Learning to Brawl with the Hockey Goons of Tomorrow

FROM DEADSPIN.COM

TOM BLOOMBERG DECIDED to teach me how to punch another kid unconscious on a hot summer day in rural Manitoba. He called this unsolicited lesson "the moves." I was 15. Tom, an oak trunk of a man who lived two doors down from my family's cottage, knew that I was entering a tough age for hockey players and decided I was ready.

Tom had done well in hockey. He'd earned himself a tryout for the St. Louis Blues. Now he sold real estate. We stood above Falcon Lake on his dock, sticky with freshly lacquered stain, and Tom began the lesson with a story about a fight he'd won. The morning after the brawl, he'd woken up with a throbbing hand and driven to a hospital. Tom attributed the pain to a broken bone in his hand; the X-ray found that in fact the pain originated in his knuckle, into which his opponent's tooth had interred itself.

Tom segued into hockey fighting's rules of engagement: 1. Never fight with your visor on. 2. Don't antagonize only to back down. 3. Star players have immunity. 4. Enforcers only battle other enforcers. 5. No trash talk if you can avoid it.

Last, Tom showed me how to tear off another guy's helmet and how to use his own jersey against him. If everything went well, I'd grab him by his equipment and yank his face into my fist until the refs stepped in. Then Tom wiggled his pecs at me and dove into the lake.

The lesson had lasted five minutes, but it was an important one. I started playing competitive hockey at age five, which is what you do when you grow up in western Canada. You play until your trajectory stalls or your father allows you to quit—whichever comes first. For a short stint, I played on an elite team. I was a tall kid, which meant that I played defense and was tasked with protecting our goalie. "Protecting the goalie" is a coaching euphemism for "goon." I was given this role at age seven.

This was a loosely defined role but in general it meant that I attacked anyone who bothered our goalie. If it happened, I was supposed to hit him, though my coaches never provided any further instructions. This was confusing for a second-grader: if this was my job, and it was so important, why didn't they teach me how to do it?

Aside from Tom, no one ever actually taught me how to fight. Teaching kids to fight is the single biggest taboo in the minor hockey establishment. With or without instruction, my role was locked anyway. Despite 12 years of junior hockey, no coach ever taught me to stickhandle, deflect a shot from the point, or roof the puck with a backhand. But how to hip-check? How to discreetly break a wrist with a slash? No problem, kid.

Most coaches stop short of fighting lessons because they don't know how or can't bring themselves to do it. Instead, fight lessons are whispered from a deviant uncle, a friend's dad, a neighbor. It's a sort of Talmudic tradition, passed down orally through generations of goons.

So I was shocked to learn, in 2007, that someone had violated that tradition and opened a school that promised to teach kids how to fight each other on skates. The world's only hockey fight camp for children was the brainchild of Trevor Lakness, a franchisee of Puckmasters, a chain of year-round hockey schools. Fight camp was held twice a year, cost $50, and was unadvertised. Players as young as 11 were welcome to attend the one-day clinic, where they learned basic fighting theory, how to throw punches, grapple, defend themselves, and the code of ethics as it pertained to helmetless, bare-knuckle fighting among children in skates.

I wasn't sure hockey fighting could be taught, at least, not in any

kind of codified way. Most fights last less than a minute, and out-
comes appear random. Enforcers are just as likely to land punches
as they are to be punched; to grab jerseys but get separated by refs
before the fight can begin; to start throwing punches only to lose
balance and fall to the ice.

I had to see for myself. When I called Trevor and asked to enroll
in kiddie fight camp, he said no. This was not because I'm about
six-foot-three and weigh 210 pounds. Trevor just thought I'd bring
more negative press attention to his camp.

There had been plenty. *Sports Illustrated* had called it "goon
school"; an ESPN columnist dismissed it as "completely ridiculous";
a *Minneapolis Star Tribune* column claimed the camp was "indoc-
trinating a fresh generation of kids into [a] warped mindset." A
spokesman for Hockey Canada, the organization that oversees all
of Canada's amateur hockey leagues, condemned it on the nation's
largest TV news broadcast. The white-hot media reaction had already cost Trevor his insurance. His provider had learned that
kids were punching other kids and dropped him. Trevor simply
switched to another company and kept on going.

Mostly, Trevor said no because he saw my U.S. area code on his
call display. "I don't need more American media attention," he
said. I knew that some Canadians use "American" as a slur and explained that I grew up in Alberta playing Canada's game. Trevor
warmed up, but not much. So I told him that I play hockey with a
certain dead man's gloves.

That dead man was former Toronto Maple Leaf enforcer John
"Rambo" Kordic, one of the most feared goons in NHL history.
Kordic died in 1992 from respiratory failure. The autopsy found a
stew of steroids and cocaine in his blood. A year before his death,
Kordic gave a pair of his gloves to my uncle Earl, who was the
Leafs' doctor at the time, and Earl gave them to me. I remember
the raw disbelief. Kordic had actually touched these things, had
worn them, played in them, and very likely dropped them. It took
me a year to get over it and actually use them, though I later decided that playing with Kordic's gloves was disrespectful. Now they
sit inside a sealed Rubbermaid container in the attic.

Mentioning the Kordic relic was a desperate move. I did it to
convince Trevor that I understood hockey violence, its history, its
purpose, and its unspoken rules.

It worked. Trevor invited me to the camp's July session in Saskatchewan, where I would be treated like a regular camper. I'd get in on all the drills and instruction sessions and have access to interview any teachers, students, or parents willing to talk to me. Trevor was vague about whether I'd be fighting children or not. I didn't care. I was in.

As we wrapped up the call, discussing the logistics of attending the camp, I asked Trevor how I should transport my fragile, $200 carbon-fiber hockey sticks on an airplane.

"Don't bother," he said. "We don't even bring pucks on the ice."

The Puckmasters rink is housed inside a white cinder-block building in Regina, a small city surrounded by a rural area that approximates Kansas only with more winter and less Christ. Often mispronounced by outsiders, "Regina" rhymes with what no city should. Far from the glittering buildings of downtown, Puckmasters' rink sits in an industrial strip mall between the backside of a Staples and across from Don's Auto Repair & Air Conditioning. The day I arrived, Puckmasters' gravel parking lot was empty except for an abandoned Suzuki Esteem, which someone had cut in half and left to rot on a wooden palette.

Trevor was late. The door to Puckmasters was locked. I waited outside in the July heat while children disgorged from their parents' Cavaliers and Windstars. Some were prepubescent kids already wearing full gear besides the helmets and skates that they carried with them, and some were voice-cracking teenagers in long T-shirts who were just shy of six feet tall. After about an hour, Todd Holt, Trevor's business partner, arrived and let us in. Todd, a short, barrel-chested guy in his mid-thirties, was an eighth-round NHL draft pick in 1993. He never made it to the NHL but bears a striking resemblance to his first cousin, Theoren Fleury, the former NHL all-star. Todd left me to explore the building.

The first thing I noticed was that there is no ice at Puckmasters, just a half-sized rink made from EZ Glide, a high-density plastic surface that behaves like ice, only skates don't glide as far. Each stride feels like 10. Without ice or a building air-conditioner, the room temperature felt close to 80.

In a corner next to the plastic rink, a whiteboard had been hung with two notes written in erasable marker. The first read, "Wall-

sit record Nolan & Cody 25:30," in neat handwriting; the other,
scrawled in a child's writing, declared that "Kyle Sucks." Life-size
vinyl posters of Sidney Crosby and Alexander Ovechkin had been
stuck to the walls. Twelve more vinyl cutouts of encouraging words
were stuck to the far wall above the fake ice: Great! Super! Scintil-
lating! Yes! Fantastic! Excellent! Dynamite! Awesome! Wow! Great
job! Superb! Outstanding! A single hole pocked the drywall below
the words. Inside was a puck.

I left the rink room and walked toward Trevor's office in the
lobby, where I met Brad Herauf, a neckless 26-year-old player with
wide-set eyes and a dark buzz cut, relaxing on a couch. At the time,
Brad, a guest instructor at the camp, was playing center for the
Florida Everblades in the ECHL; he'd later move on to the Albany
River Rats of the American Hockey League. He looked small for
pro hockey but he has a solid reputation as a fighter, totaling 785
penalty minutes over his first three seasons in the ECHL. He had
a deep midsummer's tan from three months off the ice. I made
some small talk about the ECHL but he interrupted me. He'd been
briefed.

"We're not talkin' if you're here to be negative," he said, air-
poking his index finger at my chest. Brad relaxed when I told
him that I was just here to learn, play hockey, and understand the
culture. "Okay, good," said Brad, and he began explaining what
it's like to play pro hockey before an indifferent audience in the
tropics.

Trevor finally arrived. He was in his mid-twenties, tall and fit,
with a cherubic face. He was dressed in red plaid shorts and a hori-
zontally striped shirt, a set of dueling patterns that gave him the
power to induce nausea in others when he moved. On his head was
a *Hockey Night in Canada* ball cap with Oakley sunglasses perched
above the brim.

After exchanging hellos, he walked us to a counter at the entrance while a few more kids bustled through the door. Trevor
launched into a soliloquy that was bookended with "we're striv-
ing to be the best" and "this is a classy school." Eventually his
spiel found its rhythm, and Trevor properly explained himself. "If
you're a high-end prospect at a [tryout], guys are out to get you.
And if you lose a fight, you lose confidence. You could perform
badly at the camp. Then someone on the ice owns you, maybe for

the camp, maybe for your career. Wait . . . have you met your fighting partner yet?" he asked.

I hadn't. Trevor looked past the narrow-shouldered kids loitering in the hall, awkwardly waiting for the school to begin. He pointed at a six-foot-four, 220-pound eugenics experiment wearing a smirk.

"That's Dominic. He's only 16. You're fighting him."

Trevor greeted a few of the latecomers at the entrance and ushered me into a small conference room next to his office. In the room, a few copies of *The Hockey News* were stacked neatly on a long table with foldable legs. A 14-inch television perched on a high shelf. Trevor turned it on and slid a home-burned DVD into the machine. He folded his arms and told me to watch. Onscreen was a shaky homemade highlight reel of Derek Parker, a veteran of three seasons in Quebec's Ligue Nord-Américaine de Hockey, picking fights and finishing them. In 2006, Derek set a league record with 508 penalty minutes in 51 games. After flirting with retirement to train for the Ultimate Fighting Championship, Parker returned to hockey and racked up 145 penalty minutes in 35 games for the IHL's Dayton Gems.

"He's the other guest instructor tonight," said Trevor, who began explaining the three-part structure to the clinic: video analysis, fight theory, and on-ice instruction. He left the room to let me study the clips by myself.

Derek arrived in person a few minutes later and sat down at the table. His nose began near the equator of his forehead and plumbed a lazy arc to the southeast. He too had a buzz cut and stood about six feet tall, his wide shoulders housed under a turquoise track jacket with *Muay Thai* printed on the back. We exchanged hellos, and he immediately began scrawling coaching notes, ignoring both the parents who'd walked into the room and his own highlight reel playing behind him.

Onscreen, Derek and his team skated in a pregame warm-up pattern, arcing a long circle that started behind the goal and notched its widest diameter near center ice. The other team skated the same circular path on the other side. On one pass, Derek lightly whacked one of his opponents on his shin pads with his stick, just a tap, and it sparked a scrum. While the other players grabbed jerseys and exchanged face-washes, Derek and his opponent sneaked out of the fray and skated to center ice, purely for the showmanship of fighting at center ring. They dropped the mitts and removed helmets without taking their eyes off each other. Derek brought his fists up to his temples, weaving each hand as though it orbited a tiny, invisible planet. After 10 seconds of staring each other down, Derek reached for his opponent's right shoulder with his left hand and then threw a right at the other player's left eye. The blow connected, and Derek unleashed three more punches, missing two. Derek's opponent staggered and fell to one knee, but Derek kept punching until the referees intervened. The crowd went nuts.

Derek looked up from the table then, seeming for the first time to notice the parents, whose facial expressions were stuck somewhere between awe and horror. There was a palpable awareness that this man was going to spend the next three hours with their children. The room was quiet.

A few minutes later, Derek excused himself and left the room. I took the opportunity to ask some of the parents why they had taken their children here. Duke Prendinchuk, father of 13-year-old Tyson, told me his son had played tier 1 hockey, the highest level for his age, his whole life. Tyson's participation tonight was "more my idea than his." He was in a transition year between Pee Wee (ages 12 and 13) and Bantam (ages 14 and 15) and it was time to "toughen up." "He's gotten into fights in the last couple of years," Prendinchuk said. "It's for self-protection because people come at him. That's part of the game. He's in games where he gets hacked and one thing leads to another."

One of the mothers, a pretty blonde wearing irony-free acid-washed jeans, wouldn't talk because she was worried the camp might be shut down if I wrote about it. She seemed legitimately afraid for its future. She turned her attention back to the fight reel and resumed ignoring me.

Trevor walked in. I asked him when the video analysis session would officially begin. "You just had it," he said. "Go get changed into your hockey gear with the kids."

Derek and Brad stood in the middle of the dressing room, surrounded by 13 kids and me. We were all wearing hockey pads and sat on a narrow bench that wound around the room. Tall wooden cubbies with hooks were attached to the wall above the bench, a feature typically found in dressing rooms of elite teams. Trevor told me that it was flourish he had insisted upon because he believed it settled players into an elite frame of mind before they went out to skate.

Trevor introduced Brad, who was in full hockey equipment. Then he introduced Derek, who, for reasons clear only to him, was wearing a teal-colored martial arts gi, only one made of terrycloth. Tonight, the terror of the Quebec league would be teaching us to fight in his bathrobe.

"These guys are true experts," said Trevor. "Derek, how many fights would you have in each season? What, about one every other game or so?"

"No. I'd say more than that."

"Like . . . one fight a game?"

"No. About four."

"So you'd spread them out during the game?"

"No. I'd fight all four in the first period."

"So you'd spread them out . . . in the period?"

"No. I'd fight them all during the first minute, though sometimes during the warm-up."

Derek then went around the room and asked each kid why he came to the camp. Most of the kids said they were here to learn how to protect themselves, but one kid, a skinny teenager with a short mop of blond hair, said he had come "to learn how to be a complete player." Derek commended him on this answer.

"That's right. Fighting pumps up your team and gets you in the game," he said. "It's about doing what it takes to win though it's never about hate." Derek then added what he considered the final proof: he and Brad had twice fought during junior hockey and yet here they were, kibitzing. The kids seemed impressed.

The lecture then shifted from motivation to fight theory and rules of engagement. "The number one rule with hockey fighting," Derek said, then pausing for effect, "is don't get hit." Taking a bare-knuckle punch is an unacceptable risk. "I'd rather have a fight where neither of us lands any," Derek added. "In my mind, you still win. You've sent a message."

Though the video portion of fight camp was a disaster and possibly optional to attend, the mood had shifted inside the dressing room. The kids were rapt. All of them watched Derek, except for the eugenics experiment, who was sneaking evil looks at me.

I was being sized up.

Fighting will never return to the levels set during the nightly bench-clearing shitstorms of the 1970s. Still, it will never go away, and for a number of reasons. For starters, hockey fights win hockey games. Unlike fights in football (silly, considering the helmets stay on) or baseball (born of errant pitches) or basketball (rare, but fight-to-injure situations), hockey fights are strategic. Success hinges on a team's will and the liveliness of the crowd. If the home team is down by two goals in its own rink, the fans have essentially paid for a $200 nap. At this point, a coach will assign his designated pugilist to fight, or the fighter will take his own initiative. In theory, the fight should shake the crowd from its slumber and get things loud. The home team will then convert this fan energy into momentum and, ideally, score. In 2008, the Detroit Red Wings fought more than they did the two previous seasons combined and won the Stanley Cup. The year before, the Cup went to the Anaheim Ducks, who had led the league in fighting.

This wasn't supposed to happen. Years earlier, the NHL had attempted to curb violence with the so-called Instigator Rule. Adopted for the 1993 season, the rule adds two extra penalty minutes to the player who starts a fight. The penalty initially dissuaded teams from fighting, but it since has fallen out of favor with referees. In 2007, only 18 instigator penalties were issued—one in 18 fights—while the 2008 season spawned 339 more fights than the previous year.

Moreover, fighting sells tickets. Never mind that I went to college and know which one is the salad fork: when a fight breaks out, I'm on my feet and high-fiving strangers. And I'm aware that fighting makes hockey seem as legitimate a sport as *American Gladiators*. I know that fighting is a zero-sum game for global audience development; that it appeals only to the passionate few while marginalizing the sport to the masses; that fighting has killed a player and injured countless others; that the Montessori/Whole Foods set would sooner let their children watch Glenn Beck before teaching them these values. I and my hockey-loving tribe are supposed to know better. Because there isn't a hockey fan on earth who hasn't been subjected to the dog-pile journalism devoted to the social and physical pathologies associated with hockey brawls. But that's not for us. We dismiss the hysterical nanny-state politics because we recognize excitement when we see it. And more important, we understand that hockey is a momentum game. You have it, you win. And short of scoring a goal, fighting is the surest way to gain momentum. We know that it wins games and Cups. So we tolerate fighting. Love it, even. It's a big part of why many of us go to the rink. In January 2009, NHL Commissioner Gary Bettman, who sought to complete the Disneyfication of hockey into good, clean family fun, admitted it for the first time. "I believe that most of our fans enjoy that aspect of the game . . . It is a part of the game," he said. Paul Kelly, formerly the head of the NHL players union, agreed, stating in a February 2009 television interview that fighting actually mitigated violence in the game and that star players needed protection. Kelly told the Versus network that Gretzky would have played "several hundred" fewer games without Dave Semenko's help. No stars, no face of the game, no product to sell.

Two recent studies support Bettman's and Kelly's assertions that fans like what they see. In a 2009 survey, 63 percent of Canadian fans opposed motions to curb fighting while another survey found that 70 percent of Canadians who identified themselves as "passionate" hockey fans said they supported it. Hockey broadcasts, most notably CBC's *Hockey Night in Canada,* which attracts some 1.8 million viewers out of 30 million Canadians during the playoffs, have embraced hockey fighting. *Hockey Night* features two theme songs prior to the game, one of which is Elton John's "Saturday Night's Alright (for Fighting)," albeit performed by Nickelback to circumvent either royalties, fey association, or both. The song is set to clips of recent fights and especially violent hits. CBC is hardly alone in its fight treatment. Thirty years ago, broadcasters cut to commercial during fights; today, TV crews give every fight play-by-play commentary, reverse angles, and the gratuitous slow-mo treatment.

All of which has fortified the role of fighters in the culture. Derek Boogaard, the Minnesota Wild's designated fighter and the guest instructor at Lakness's first fight camp, has never scored more than six points in an entire season. Yet his replica jersey used to outsell all of his teammates' shirts but one. This fight culture is even stronger in the minors. It has become ironic and cult, and moved far beyond the decades-old shadow of Paul Newman's Charlestown Chiefs in *Slapshot*. In August 2005, organizers held a hockey fight tournament in Prince George, British Columbia, without pucks, sticks, or teams. Most competitors were brawlers from the minors. The tournament was attended by 2,000 locals and filmed by a Canadian documentary crew. Four fights broke out in the bleachers.

This was a one-off, however. The only alternative for fight fans is to attend a minor league game. Minor leaguers scrap partially for the support, but mostly because it can launch a professional hockey career. A 1995 York University study of young hockey players found that "increased levels of violence [fistfights], more than playing or skating skills were seen to lead to greater perception of competence by both team mates and coaches." In some cases, fighting can vault a player to higher levels and higher-paying leagues.

This is true for Jon Mirasty, an enforcer for the AHL's Syracuse Crunch and recipient of a fawning profile in *ESPN The Magazine*. In 2007, Mirasty, who weighs 220 pounds despite standing just five-foot-ten, had retired from low-level pro hockey and was set to coach in an obscure league in northern Alberta. Due to his reputation, Mirasty was recruited later that same year to try out for the Crunch, then a minor league affiliate of the NHL's Columbus Blue Jackets. He made the team and has since played NHL exhibition games for the Jackets. Mirasty, who was well into his sojourn to nowhere, now fights for a decent living. He has a following. He is a staple on hockeyfights.com, a video and chat forum with user posts such as "Guys you want to see get beat up" and "Who's the biggest puss?"—each answered with remarkable wit and sincerity. During the hockey season, the site draws nearly nine million page views each month.

Mirasty's agent, Eric Beman, makes his living as a personal trainer and represents hockey players—enforcers only—as a hobby. Beman's company, One Punch Sports Management, is registered with the PHPA, an agency that represents the professional players in the AHL, CHL, and ECHL. The listed business email address has a hotmail.com suffix.

If there was any question about fighting's place in the sport, especially its lower reaches, consider what happened on December 12, 2008, in the Ontario Hockey Association's top-tier senior league —and what happened afterward. With 2:14 left in the game, Don

Sanderson, a defenseman for the Whitby Dunlops, a minor league team, fought Corey Fulton of the Brantford Blast. Sanderson lost his helmet during the brawl and both fighters fell to the ice. Sanderson's bare head smashed into the ice, and he lost consciousness. Sanderson was rushed to hospital, where he soon fell into a coma. Three weeks later, Sanderson died. In Canada, the incident received as much media attention as the Obama campaign. Shortly after the public outcry, the junior Ontario Hockey League created a rule that suspends any player who removes his helmet to fight. But the OHL took great care not to excise fighting from its game altogether. A ban on fighting in this league, or any other, would be akin to a ban on tackling in the NFL. What the OHL did was merely make fighting safer. It didn't outlaw its savage element; it simply domesticated it.

The stars need protection (Wayne Gretzky so appreciated Semenko's services that in 1983 he gave Semenko the car he won as the all-star game's MVP). The lesser players need a job. The league needs to sell the game. That's why fighting isn't going anywhere — the incentives are too strong to keep it around. Coarse and slapdash as it may have been, fight camp was teaching kids to cope with hockey as it is, not as we might wish it to be.

Brad walked us from the cramped dressing room and onto the ice. Todd threw a bucket of pucks on the plastic ice surface. Some of the smaller kids began shooting against the net while the older kids stood by to the side and talked among themselves while Derek and Brad began rehearsing some fighting moves on the other side of the ice. They seemed to be making it up on the spot. The entire class gathered to watch,

A few minutes later Brad arranged us from tallest to smallest at the blue line. "Turn to your right," he said. "That's the guy you're going to fight." I looked to my right. On skates Dominic stood at least six-foot-five. It still wasn't clear how violent the fights would be, and I was genuinely scared of taking a bare-knuckles punch from Dominic. His size and quiet confidence almost nullified my moral objection to fighting a 16-year-old. Still, I was prepared to play the morality card if he broke my nose.

"Listen up," yelled Derek. "This is how to prevent someone from hitting you." Derek grabbed Brad's jersey, and Brad wadded a handful of Derek's teal bathrobe. "There are three main types of jersey grips," said Derek. "The high shoulder grip, the elbow grip, and the wrist grip." Brad and Derek demonstrated each grip but did not throw any punches. Derek told us that the elbow and wrist grips are not ideal. "These are desperate," he said, "you want to go for the high shoulder grip." Brad took Derek's jersey at the shoulder and told us to watch carefully. Derek drew back his arm and slowly threw a punch at Brad's face. As Derek's fist came closer, Brad pushed his jersey-gripping hand forward into Derek's shoulder. It hemmed Derek's reach. Derek pushed his fist harder, and Brad pushed his shoulder in kind, robbing Derek of range and power to hit him. "The goal here is to take size out of the fight," said Brad. "I've fought guys much bigger than me and they never landed a punch because of this technique."

Derek ordered us to square off with our partners. I grabbed Dominic's jersey and he grabbed mine, though his thumb accidentally clenched a loop of my skin. He twisted the fistful of nylon and flesh and cocked back his arm while I prepared for the inevitable dental work. He threw his first punch. I squeezed my fist around a wad of his jersey with so much force that my finger tendons immediately pulled. I pushed against his shoulder and closed my eyes. When I opened them I saw his fist, six inches from my nose. I could see individual blond hairs on each knuckle. He punched again and I pushed. Nothing. When it was my turn, my punches were similarly stymied. Dominic released his grip. "Wow, that really works," he said, offering a pinched smile that was either polite or deeply condescending.

The rest of the kids were still jostling, and the rink was filled with the sounds of grunting and skates clawing into plastic ice. Brad shouted over the commotion. "If the guy lands a punch with your hand on his shoulder, it's not going to hurt," he yelled. "It's a glancing blow with almost no force. If you looked at the videos in there, it only looks like the other guys are landing punches. But they aren't." That was all we would learn about defense.

Derek then showed us how to break defensive techniques like the high shoulder grab. The two instructors stood in front of us again, grabbing bathrobe and jersey. "The first step is to get your hand on the inside," Derek said, his right shoulder in Brad's grip. "Now punch in an uppercut motion—hard—on the inside. It doesn't matter if you land the uppercut and chances are that you won't." Derek threw an uppercut and didn't come near landing it. "That's only step one," he said. "Now watch." Derek drew his gripped arm back as though he were elbowing someone behind his head. The move not only tore his shoulder immediately out of Brad's hand but left his arm drawn back and ready to punch. Brad was now defenseless. "Now I'm ready to use my weapon," Derek said, looking at his fist. "Okay, now you try it."

The kids looked at each other. A few laughed nervously, as if it were sex ed. Dominic and I took each other's jerseys with mutual shoulder grips. Before we could decide who would go first, Dominic threw the uppercut, slammed back his right elbow, and removed my grip. "I could've killed you there," he said.

I tried the move and was just as successful. My fist was near my ear, and Dominic's head was back, his mouth drawn into a grimace. I was ready to use "my weapon." Suddenly, the class exploded into chaos. Kids traded partners. They used unsanctioned and untaught moves. A pair of 13-year-olds started a playful war. It looked fun. I skated out of the scrum until a 14-year-old wearing G-Unit jewelry grabbed my jersey and challenged me to a fight. I asked him if he was sure. He hadn't finished nodding when I grabbed his jersey at the shoulder and pulled it over his head. I administered three stage punches into the lump inside and accidentally connected one. He stopped struggling, and I let him up, allowing him to poke his head through his jersey collar. "Good fight," he said, and moved on to fight someone else.

Trevor, who was on the ice to supervise, had seen enough. He yelled at us to "smarten up" and arrange ourselves on the blue line again. Our next lesson was the art of the cheap shot. Brad and Derek resumed the now-familiar mutual shoulder grip as we watched. "Fake a few punches," said Derek, feinting toward Brad's face. "Then squat to get under his grab arm, move your head to the right, then quickly stand up tall again." Derek finished the sequence. He'd broken Brad's grip and turned his shoulders perpendicular. "Now unload on his kidneys!" said Derek, stage-punching Brad in the back. "Try it!"

Dominic's first attempt spun me sideways. I struggled against the move but couldn't break it. Then my back caved in. I felt nausea. Dominic had "accidentally" punched me in the kidneys. "Sorry, dude," he said.

"A lot of players discount body shots but they got me some critical advantages," Derek said. "I was able to reset my grip so I could go back to hitting him in the face."

Brad took over the class for the last lesson, on how to square up properly. He told smaller players to engage cautiously. "I like to let the other guy skate around me for a while. If you're smaller, wait for him to lunge toward you. That way you can get on the inside. If you don't get close to him, he'll use his reach to keep you on defense, and you'll get killed. Remember, it's not about size. It's speed and technique and how fast you can grab him and start throwing punches."

Brad and Derek exchanged vacant looks at each other. They spoke to each other, *sotto voce,* until Derek shook his head. "That's it, guys," he said. The session was over. We had spent a total of 40 minutes on the ice.

Trevor thanked the kids for coming out as they began skating off. "One more thing," Derek shouted before we left. "WHAT'S THE MOST IMPORTANT THING IN HOCKEY FIGHTING?"

I wasn't sure. Was it most important to not get hit and send the message? To hijack game momentum and win and protect your star? Was it to launch your pro career, conceal dirty moves, punch your friends, and undermine the legitimacy of your sport while simultaneously enriching it? Or was it just something to give Philadelphians a reason to get up in the morning? But I went with the chorus line on this one.

"DON'T GET HIT," we yelled back in unison.

"That's right," said Derek. "And, uh . . . have fun. That's also important."

The next morning I found blood in my urine. Dominic's kidney punch had turned it a syrupy red. At the meeting of my right bicep and shoulder, where he had grabbed my jersey, I found a deep bruise that was larger than a slice of processed cheese. Still, the damage was light: full set of teeth, face uncut.

Derek, Brad, and Trevor, however disorganized, had taught legitimate techniques that really worked. That the fight camp was as successful as it was became less of a miracle the better I got to know the instructors. After the camp, I had a beer with Todd, Trevor, and Derek. Over chicken wings and pints of Molson at The Press Box, a nearby sports bar, I learned that Trevor was a little shy, Todd a dedicated family man, and Derek, while playing in Quebec, had taught himself to speak French so he could talk to girls.

"So there you go," said Trevor, making one final PR move as I picked up the check. "Fighting can be taught, but we teach them to be responsible."

I didn't catch the responsibility message in any of the lessons. Trevor continued, insisting that he wasn't churning out goons. Of all the kids he'd taught, he claimed that only one had turned into a problem and was now looking for extra action on the ice. It didn't matter; none of the details had made it into any of the media coverage. So he had become a pariah, a sort of Barnum figure minus the self-awareness. I wanted to know: with all the controversy, with the loss of insurance and business, was it worth it?

"CTV news was negative," said Trevor, staring into his food. "But then they interviewed Wayne Gretzky and he said the camp was a good idea. If Gretzky had said, 'That's the stupidest idea ever,' I would look like the biggest idiot in the world. But he didn't."

Epilogue: Trevor has since sold the business and is uninvolved with Puckmasters. Todd Holt remained to help with some of the coaching duties. And fight camp, as far as I know, is on hold.

The Franchise

FROM ESPN.COM

IN THE BEGINNING, there was the word. And that word was no. On a cloudy morning in 1984, three men met in an Amtrak dining car winding through the Rocky Mountains, en route from Denver to Oakland, California. The first was Trip Hawkins, a closet Strat-O-Matic Football junkie and founder of video game maker Electronic Arts (which has a relationship with ESPN to integrate content into its games). The second was Joe Ybarra, Hawkins's lieutenant, a high school chess champ turned pigskin fanatic. The third was John Madden, the former Super Bowl–winning coach, hardware store pitchman, televised NFL evangelist, and poet laureate of interior line play.

Boom! He'll remember that number!

Then, as now, Madden had no use for airplanes. He was nearly as leery of computers. This was before Google, PlayStation, or the Internet. People didn't carry credit card–thin smart phones in their pockets, and video games were quarter-eating diversions for nerdy boys. Madden was a football guy. Intelligent as hell, sure. Unafraid of the telestrator. Once taught an X's and O's class at Berkeley. Yet was totally unmoved by "Pac-Man fever." Honestly didn't know what the heck a PC did. Booming and boisterous, an alpha male to the core, Madden brandished a cigar throughout the meeting—one nearly a foot long with the diameter of a quarter; a veritable kraken of Cohibas to be gazed upon with despair. A chew toy.

Spittle-splattered but unbowed, Hawkins made his pitch, the same one he previously had delivered in a fast-food parking lot outside Madden's Bay Area office: *Help me build a game. Lend your expertise. I'll put your name on the box.*

Madden was intrigued. *Maybe,* he thought, *this could become a coaching tool. Pick a play, run it on a machine, see if it works. No need to scrimmage.*

He sketched formations on paper, lines branching in every direction—little masterworks of unintentional abstract art that Hawkins would later frame.

The onetime Oakland Raiders coach talked philosophy: *Where's my playing field? Below sea level and it rains a lot? Then give me Gene Upshaw. Put the defense on skis and push them all day long.*

Hawkins listened. Ybarra took notes. The duo promised they would create as sophisticated a simulation as home computers would allow. Real football, with seven players to a side . . .

Right there, Madden balked—even though he was technically under contract with EA to endorse a football game. "If it's not 11-on-11," he said, "it's not *real football.*"

"That was a deal breaker," Madden recalled. "If it was going to be me and going to be pro football, it had to have 22 guys on the screen. If we couldn't have that, we couldn't have a game."

The Consummate Video Game

Everyone knows how the story ends. Madden *über alles.* Twenty-two guys on the screen? Try a 22-year-old pop culture phenomenon, a video game once immortalized in a television commercial featuring the apocalyptic strains of "O Fortuna" from the *Carmina Burana* cantata—and the effect was only slightly over-the-top.

You can measure the impact of Madden through its sales: as many as 2 million copies in a single week, 85 million copies since the game's inception, and more than $3 billion in total revenue. You can chart the game's ascent, shoulder to shoulder, alongside the $20-billion-a-year video game industry, which is either co-opting Hollywood (see *Tomb Raider* and *Prince of Persia*) or topping it (opening-week gross of Call of Duty: Modern Warfare 2: $550 million; *The Dark Knight:* $204 million).

You can witness the cultural power of Madden: grown men lining up outside Wal-Marts for the game's annual midnight release;

rock bands, such as Good Charlotte, going mainstream via inclusion on the Madden soundtrack; a pokerlike underground circuit of cash tournaments; the black-cat mojo of the Madden cover curse superseding the *Sports Illustrated* cover jinx; Madden himself being recognized less for his Hall of Fame coaching and broadcasting career than for a game that beat him into Canton.

Alternately, you can listen to Cleveland Browns kick returner Josh Cribbs.

"I used to play Madden all the time with [former teammate] Kellen Winslow [Jr.]," he said. "When Kellen got married, he did it at his house. After the ceremony, he went to play Madden! He just got married. His wife is sitting there. And he's playing. We all made fun of him."

It's a Madden, Madden, Madden world. We're all just playing in it. How did this happen? That's the story you don't know . . . And it's a story that could have starred Joe Montana.

Dreaming of Joe Cool

They wanted Montana. Wouldn't anybody? Think about it: you're Hawkins; a pigskin game is your lifelong dream. As a child, he played wingback on a flag-football squad. He also fell in love with the 1967 edition of Strat-O-Matic Football, a paper-and-dice pigskin game that was, in a rudimentary way, the Madden of its era.

A bright and precocious teenager, Hawkins created a Strat-O-Matic knockoff and attempted to start a business. His next-door neighbor in La Jolla, California, was former AFL president Milt Woodard, which gave Hawkins the opportunity to send a proposal to Kansas City Chiefs owner Lamar Hunt. Hunt wrote back. *Beat it, kid.*

No matter. Hawkins ordered parts. Set up an assembly line in his family's living room. Borrowed $5,000 from his father and took out ads in NFL game programs.

He lost every penny.

The flop was a slap in the face. How could a great football simulation not sell? Around the same time, he got his first computer and, with it, an answer. Strat-O-Matic was too hard. Players had to crunch too many numbers, obliterating the necessary suspension of disbelief. Solution? Put the math inside the computer. Let the machine do the work.

While attending Harvard, Hawkins created his own major in game design. He programmed his first football simulation on a PDP-11 computer, a metal cabinet with flashing lights and tape-reel data storage that spanned two rooms. In 1975, he determined it would take exactly seven years for enough computers to reach homes to support a gaming business.

Eight years later, he was right on schedule. Hawkins was Employee No. 68 at Apple Computer. They called him "junior Steve Jobs." He codified the company's unique, oft-imitated start-up culture. Made millions in stock options, then cashed out. Started Electronic Arts out of his own pocket from a home office, then moved to his first real workspace in San Mateo, California, just north of Silicon Valley. In January 1984, *Time* magazine named the personal computer its "Machine of the Year"; about 20 miles south in Cupertino, Apple was putting the finishing touches on a beige plastic box called Macintosh.

Meanwhile, Hawkins had just shipped his first games, packaged in stylish boxes that looked like album jackets because that's what EA was all about: the artists and the creators. The anonymous guys coding Atari 2600 cartridges were finally getting their rock-star due. Before founding EA, Hawkins went to Los Angeles to study at the feet of record mogul Jerry Moss. What's wrong with a little Hollywood?

Take EA's early basketball game: One-on-One: Dr. J vs. Larry Bird. The real guys—sports celebrities—on the box. On the screen too. Controlled by a joystick. No one had ever done that before. Julius Erving even came to Hawkins's studio and hung out for a day. Shot hoops with Hawkins at a local YMCA. So awesome. Only he was not Hawkins's hero. Not like Montana. Montana was God. Not *a* god. *The* God. Montana played football, as Hawkins briefly did at Harvard, but better. Way better, which is kind of the point. He had already won a Super Bowl for the San Francisco 49ers. Montana-to-Clark. The Catch.

Hawkins was about to make a football game to make up for his failed high school project and show the world everything he had learned. When his dream was ready, when it was coded and debugged and sitting on a store shelf in a stylish box that resembled the cover of, say, Def Leppard's *Pyromania*, it was going to need a face. A mug to move the product, for sure, but also to represent the creators.

Montana. Gotta be Joe Cool. Seriously, who else would even be worth considering?

Plenty of Pain Equals Plenty of Gain

The playbook belonged to the Oakland Raiders, 1980 vintage. There were no pass plays inside, and there were hardly any plays at all. There were calls about formations, blocking schemes, and play-action. There were play names, which weren't actually names but rather alphanumeric combinations indicating pass routes or maybe a particular number telling a particular running back to hit a particular hole. Everything read like programming language — all jargon and technical gibberish.

The playbook came from Madden. One day in the mid-1980s, it arrived at the desk of Ybarra, the EA producer tasked with turning Hawkins's vision into an actual working game.

"I start flipping through," Ybarra said, "and I think to myself, 'These poor people — how the hell do they ever play football if they have to know all this crap?'"

Montana was out. Already had an endorsement deal with video game console maker Atari. Also out was Cal football coach Joe Kapp, Hawkins's second choice, who wanted royalties.

Enter Madden, who was impressed by Hawkins's pedigree and signed on.

"If this guy went to Harvard and made up his own major in games," the former coach said, "I figured he must be a computer genius."

Also enter 22 players on the screen, Ybarra's professional death march. The erstwhile high school chess champ became an office masochist, logging 18-hour days, helming as many as 17 games at the same time. That was doable, par for EA's start-up years. But the Madden-endorsed product was torture.

"All my memories," Ybarra said, "are of pain."

Some of the pain was technical: making a game on a computer, the Apple II, that didn't have enough memory, pixels, or disk storage. No sound chip either, and only one joystick port. The machine could produce four colors, sure, but only if a programmer knew all the dirty tricks. Anything beyond seven-on-seven football caused the on-screen action to slow to a crawl.

"We were trying to model NFL football," Ybarra said, "on a computer with less horsepower than your watch."

Some of the pain was financial. Just as EA brought its first games to market in 1983, the home video game industry imploded. In a two-year span, Coleco abandoned the business, Intellivision went from 1,200 employees to five, and Atari infamously dumped thousands of unsold game cartridges into a New Mexico landfill. Toy retailers bailed, concluding that video games were a Cabbage Patch–style fad. Even at EA—a hot home computer start-up—continued solvency was hardly assured.

"It was like being the newest superhero on a planet that is falling apart and into the sun," former EA producer Don Daglow said. "We didn't know if our superpowers would be enough to defeat those market conditions."

The biggest pain was conceptual: What was a football simulation supposed to look like? How should it play? "Football" on the Atari 2600 console featured three-man teams composed of players who resembled and moved like ambulatory kitchen appliances. Everything was new: play-calling boxes; an "oomph" (read: turbo) button. Ybarra tried a TV-style camera angle. Finding holes at the line of scrimmage proved impossible. He switched to the god's-eye end-zone perspective still used in today's games. The game played better, but it still looked like bleeding Lego blocks.

During the two-day Amtrak ride with Madden, Hawkins and Ybarra quizzed the former coach from dawn to midnight, breaking down passing trees and line stunts and digesting game plans. Ybarra disembarked with blurry eyes, a splitting headache, and a legal pad full of notes.

"We spent hours just learning blocking schemes," he said. "By the third year of the project, I could watch pro football on TV and tell you what was going to happen when the players were still lining up."

Development dragged. A single programmer, Robin Antonick, slaved away on the code. Six months became three years. At the time, the average game took 15 months to make. More than once,

Madden himself figured EA had simply given up. An anxious Hawkins flirted with having an outside developer, Bethesda Softworks, build the game. A short-lived business deal ended in a multimillion-dollar lawsuit, later settled out of court.

"It was like Herbert Hoover," Hawkins said. "Prosperity is just around the corner."

Around EA's offices—a jock-friendly environment, home to Nerf ball fights, weekday golf outings, and the occasional shoving match—the Madden project earned a nickname: Trip's Folly.

"Most games that went as late as Madden and had that many struggles," Daglow said, "they'd take them out behind the barn and do the honorable thing."

Hawkins pressed on. Madden introduced him to Frank Cooney, a football beat writer for the *San Francisco Examiner.* Cooney and Madden went way back, having attended Bay Area high schools just five miles apart. Although the coach was a decade older than the scribe, the two had formed a friendship during Madden's time in Oakland. At heart, both were football nerds. As a side project, Cooney regularly attended the draft combine—unheard of in those days—and supplied scouting reports on college players to NFL and USFL teams. He also designed a figurine-based board game, Grid-Grid, that functioned like electric football, only with numeric skill ratings determining the outcome of player interactions.

"I had an idea," Cooney said, "that was waiting for the technology to catch up with it."

In Madden, Cooney found his tech. Although the game didn't have an NFL license—San Francisco's gold-helmeted digital quarterback was named "Joe Idaho"—it did feature players rated in 10 categories. Thanks to Cooney, Idaho's passing arm had pinpoint accuracy. And that wasn't all.

"For our playbooks, I would say to Frank, 'Go find out what a team's five signature plays are,'" Hawkins said. "He would go up to the assistant coaches, hand them paper. And they would draw up plays! We collected a huge amount of plays that way."

In 1988, John Madden Football was released for the Apple II computer and became a modest commercial success. Ybarra had already left the project to make adventure games. Burned out, he didn't watch real-life pro football for an entire season. Meanwhile, a jubilant Hawkins approached Madden.

HAWKINS: You stayed with me. EA is about to have an IPO [initial public offering]. You can have as much stock as you want.

MADDEN: What do you mean by *have?*

HAWKINS: Well, you have to buy it — at the IPO price.

"Hell, I'm just a football coach," Madden says now. "I pointed with my finger, all knowing, and said, 'I gave you my time. I'm not giving you my money.' I showed him!"

From 1989 to 1999, EA's share price went from $7.50 to $70. Madden laughs. "That was the dumbest thing I ever did in my life."

Eschewing the Literal for the Hyperreal

The stakes were high for a pair of upstart game makers, with a career-making opportunity and a $100,000 development contract on the line. In early 1990, Troy Lyndon and Mike Knox of San Diego–based Park Place Productions met with Hawkins to discuss building a Madden game for Sega's upcoming home video game console, the Genesis. Near the end of the meeting, Hawkins popped a surprise question to the duo: "Are you going to build the game I want to make or the game you want to make?"

"My answer might have been, 'Whatever you want,'" said Lyndon, now head of Left Behind Games, a Christian video game maker. "But before I could open my mouth, Mike says, 'The game I want to make.' I was like, 'Dude, I hope that was the right answer!'"

It was. Because the game that made Madden a phenomenon wasn't the initial Apple II release, it was the Genesis follow-up, a surprise smash spawned by an entirely different mindset. Hawkins wanted Madden to play out like the NFL. Equivalent stats. Similar play charts. Real football.

By contrast, Lyndon and Knox previously had made a well-received Monday Night Football title featuring arcade-style, action-heavy game play. That clicked with Genesis Madden producer Rich Hilleman, whose top design priority was fun — a game with more sacks, more bombs, more tackles in the backfield, and more 60-yard runs than real-life NFL football. Something akin to an episode of *The Hills,* or what philosopher/author Umberto Eco dubbed the "hyperreal"—seemingly authentic, yet more entertaining than the genuine article.

"I came to the game from making flight simulations," said Hilleman, who is now EA's chief creative officer. "If you make an F-16 fighter simulation and it's very accurate, to fire a single missile takes like 20 procedures. Only that's not people's perception of being a pilot. People's perception is Tom Cruise. Push a button and blow something up. With Genesis Madden, we wanted to emphasize what makes football exciting, not perfectly replicate the brutality of a 3.1-yard-per-carry running game."

By 1989, EA had established itself in the home computer market, which was largely a realm of adult hobbyists and $2,000 machines. Game consoles were another story. Thanks to its wildly popular NES system—home to Super Mario Bros. and The Legend of Zelda—Japanese game maker Nintendo enjoyed a near monopoly on American living rooms, using that clout to treat companies producing NES games like feudal serfs, controlling game content, delivery, packaging, and profit distribution.

Hawkins didn't want to play along. But he craved a piece of the $2 billion home console market. Sega, Nintendo's rival in Japan, was preparing to launch the Genesis. Industry consensus held that Nintendo's eventual NES successor would crush the Genesis the same way the NES had swamped Sega's earlier Master System. Hawkins believed otherwise. The Genesis was the future machine: great graphics, fast processor, and two joystick ports. Perfect for sports games.

Secretly, Hawkins assembled a team to reverse-engineer the console—that is, figure out a way to make EA's games run on Sega's hardware without its technology or approval as a way to avoid licensing fees altogether. Publicly, he began negotiations with Sega, once meeting with the company's executives while the reverse-engineering project went on in a nearby room. The gambit was risky: once Sega caught wind of EA's plan, it likely would sue—in part to discourage other software companies from following EA's lead, in part because reverse-engineering without copyright infringement is technologically vexing. Hawkins's team, however, managed to pull it off.

To help write the Genesis Madden code, Lyndon hired high school friend Jim Simmons. Formerly a sound programmer, Simmons approached Hilleman with a far-fetched idea: what if Madden had a pseudo 3-D field?

The EA producer laughed. "Great. So how are you going to do that?"

Simmons turned on a television set. "Kind of like this."

The field was a breakthrough. So was replacing the clumsy Apple II passing interface — on-screen action would freeze — with a still-standard system linking each receiver to the press of a button. The game Ybarra could hardly stand became the game Hilleman couldn't put down. He took Madden home. He took it on vacation. He was hooked.

Meanwhile, Hawkins revealed his reverse-engineering project to Sega and offered a deal. *Let's team up against Nintendo. Share the glory. You can sue, but we did the tech fair and square and have great lawyers. So make us an official licensee. And give us a reduced rate.* Sega normally charged an $8 to $10 fee per game cartridge. Hawkins asked for $2 per game and a $2 million cap. Negotiations stalled.

"Only two times at EA did everyone in my management team pull me into a room and say, 'We all disagree with you,'" Hawkins said. "The first time was about not having private offices. The other time was this."

He stuck to his guns. Ten days later, on the eve of a major consumer electronics show in Chicago, Sega relented, afraid EA would sell its reverse-engineering knowledge to other software companies and torpedo the Genesis's entire business model.

"Over three years," Hawkins said, "that $2 million cap saved us $35 million."

By the late summer of 1990, Genesis Madden was almost finished. Hawkins felt it would be EA's big break: right time, right market, right platform, right game. Meanwhile, Sega was in trouble. The company, like Atari before it, had signed Joe Montana as its North American spokesman but realized it wouldn't be able to complete a planned Montana game in time for the lucrative holiday retail season.

Hawkins received a phone call from Sega's Japanese president, Hayao Nakayama. It was his turn to make an offer: *Trip, you should sacrifice Madden. Give it to us to call it Joe Montana Football. This will save Christmas. We'll both be better off.* Bing Gordon, EA's top marketer, urged his good friend Hawkins to make the deal.

"I said, 'Are you crazy?'" Hawkins recalled. "This is the freaking franchise! This is the turning point. This is everything for us. Then I realized: why don't we do both?"

What followed became one of the biggest secrets in video game history: EA built a Montana game for Sega that was designed to compete with Madden. Sort of.

"We made sure it was totally inferior," Hawkins said.

Working from the Madden code base, EA removed the 3-D field, slashed the pro-style playbook from 113 plays to 13, and added cartoony, big-headed player graphics.

Joe Montana Football was a hit, but John Madden Football was an industry game-changer, spawning yearly sequels and creating a lucrative revenue model that still persists. Robust sales helped Sega pull neck and neck with Nintendo, triggering a second gaming boom—this time around, retailers concluded gaming was here to stay. In 1990, EA had a market cap of about $60 million; three years later, that number swelled to $2 billion.

More crucially, video games were suddenly cool, the province of older teens and college kids, young men who loved competition and talking smack. Escaping the geek world, gaming set course for the center of the pop culture sun.

"Before Madden, jocks did not play video games," Hilleman said. "Somebody playing games was more likely to get made fun of on ESPN than get featured on there."

For Madden (the man), the new world order dawned abruptly. Six weeks after the release of the Genesis game, he arrived in New York to broadcast a Jets game. In a pregame meeting with the team, an agitated New York wide receiver confronted the former coach.

"Three?" the player asked. "Three, old man? You want to see what a three looks like? I'll take you out on the field and show you a three!"

"John had no idea what the guy was talking about," Hilleman said. "We wanted John to rate the players, even gave him a chart. But we added him late to the project. He didn't get it done. So [associate producer] Michael Brook and I sat down and rated them ourselves. Right away, we get a call from John's agent. All he says is, 'John will be doing the ratings next year.'"

Sealed with a Curse

En route from gaming hit to pop culture juggernaut, the Madden franchise has tackled external competition—rival titles such as the NFL 2K series and Mike Ditka Power Football—and the internal division that accompanies any big-money enterprise, with various production studios winning and losing the right to make the game.

Madden's secret weapon? A man named Sandy Sandoval. Officially, Sandoval is the director of athlete relations for EA Sports; unofficially, he's the game's answer to World Wide Wes and Winston Wolf—part fixer, part bon vivant, the guy who helped give the game its inimitable pro football cachet.

Need an in-game ratings boost, what Madden (the man) calls "more juice"? Call Sandoval, as quarterback Byron Leftwich once did. Jonesing for an advance copy of the game? Call Sandoval, as Carson Palmer, Chad Ochocinco, and dozens of other players have done. Need to drop a few pounds, albeit digital ones? Consider it done. Last year, Philadelphia Eagles coach Andy Reid asked Sandoval to slim down his in-game avatar, a little quid pro quo for introducing Sandoval to former Madden cover athlete Brett Favre.

"I just saw Andy at the owners meetings," Sandoval said. "He comes up to me and is like, 'Sandy, thanks for hooking me up. I saw myself in the game. My wife loves it. She loves looking at me skinny!'"

Sandoval came to EA from sports equipment maker Easton, where he canvassed clubhouses and locker rooms across the country, peddling batting gloves and hockey sticks. Each sale was a hard one. Athletes value comfort and familiarity over change. New gear was guilty until proven otherwise.

The first time Sandoval walked into the 49ers locker room with an EA Sports bag, however, things were different. He no longer had to explain himself. Or his product.

"All the young guys were already playing Madden," he said.

Years earlier, a single insight led Hawkins to create Madden: let the machine do the work. To that, Sandoval added a game-selling corollary: let the jocks do the work. His first week on the job, he signed endorsement deals with Barry Sanders and Alex Rodriguez and invited Jerry Rice to visit EA's offices. He then pushed for cover athletes. Madden didn't like the idea; after all, it was his name on the product. In 2000, though, the former coach was off the cover of Madden NFL 2001, replaced by Tennessee Titans running back Eddie George.

Overnight, cover appearances became a status symbol, in pro football and beyond. When New Orleans quarterback Drew Brees landed on the cover of this year's title, he read a Top 10 list on *Letterman*.

"Teams go on the Wheaties box," Cribbs said. "But individually, when you make the cover of Madden, you've arrived."

Of course, not all publicity is good publicity: a string of injuries, performance dips, and off-field trouble for cover athletes such as Michael Vick, Daunte Culpepper, and Shaun Alexander has prompted widespread belief in a Madden cover curse. Sandoval scoffs at the notion. Arizona receiver Larry Fitzgerald does not. Last year's Madden cover featured Fitzgerald and Pittsburgh safety Troy Polamalu. When the latter sprained his knee in the first game of the season, the former freaked out.

"After that game, Larry must have texted me three times before calling me," Sandoval said. "He's the only athlete who has talked to me about the curse. Just getting him on the cover was like trying to get him to walk a tightrope. I texted him the entire season: 'Great game. You made it, dude.' Then one week I was in San Francisco, sitting next to Larry's dad in the press box. Larry's leg got caught underneath him on a catch. I'm like, 'Please, don't let this happen.' Fortunately, he came back into the game. So that doesn't count."

Outsize Success Equals Outsize Expectations

Phil Frazier sighs. A senior producer at EA Tiburon and longtime Madden player, he would love to bring back the comic, still-revered ambulance from the game's 1991 edition—a siren-wailing, red-cross-plastered white van that tore across the field to pick up injured quarterbacks, plowing through other players like bowling pins along the way.

There's just one roadblock.

"We've used the ambulance in presentations," Frazier said. "But with the NFL having to approve [in-game content], that's not the sort of thing we could slip past the goalie."

Football remains football, with 22 players on the screen. But for the current makers of Madden at EA Tiburon, everything else has changed. The suburban Orlando-based game-making studio took over Madden development in the mid-1990s and was acquired by EA shortly thereafter. In 2004, EA paid the NFL a reported $300 million-plus for five years of exclusive rights to teams and players. The deal was later extended to 2013. Just like that, competing games went kaput. The franchise stands alone, triumphant, increasingly encumbered by its outsize success.

Programming teams of two have swelled to 30. Offices that once contained a half-dozen game testers now house more than 100. A typical blockbuster game takes two or three years to program. Madden ships every 12 months, never mind that the effort required to approximate real football keeps rising. Digitally modeling Brees's head alone takes three to four days of work. A game spawned by the idiosyncratic vision of two men has become a popular institution. And, like any popular institution—the federal government, for instance, or *American Idol*—Madden belongs to anyone who expects something of it.

Which is to say, it belongs to just about everyone: an NFL that insists on protecting its brand; corporate suits who feel obligated to meddle with EA's signature title; a mass audience that expects each iteration of the game to be revolutionary, not evolutionary.

Behind the tinted windows of EA Tiburon's five-story office building, Jason Danahy does motion capture for Madden, filming tosses and tackles, blocks and catches, all of which are performed by stuntmen wearing black bodysuits and bright, reflective balls. Generating a single big hit can require up to four takes; an average day encompasses a 100-move shot list. Stuntmen end up with bumps and bruises, sprains and torn Achilles tendons. Mo-cap actor Chris Robin once spent a week in a hospital after rupturing his spleen.

Before a hit or tackle ends up in the game, however, it requires NFL approval. Danahy walks a design tightrope: create violent collisions worthy of the game's "hit stick" control scheme. But keep those same encounters *clean*. "We send everything to the league," he says. "We have problems when the guys get too fired up and shove each other after the play, or jaw at each other."

Ian Cummings is the creative director for Madden. If there's
something amiss in the way the game plays, it's ultimately his fault.
Mike Young is in charge of art. If the style of Pittsburgh's digital
helmet numbers looks wrong, he's probably to blame. Cummings
played his first game of Madden on the Apple II. Young grew up
in St. Louis before the Rams arrived; as a child, Madden *was* his
NFL. In a large corner office adorned with a University of Tennessee flag, the two work side by side, in part to better communicate,
in part to commiserate, as in the following exchange:

> CUMMINGS: Updating player gear is such a pain. Like a guy chang-
> ing from a single wristband to a double. It never stops.
> YOUNG: We have people that just catalog this stuff every week. A
> player will start wearing team-colored gloves. A team will put a special
> logo on the 20-yard line for Week 8. Another team won't wear a special
> patch. And if we don't have that, it ruins the game for some people.
> CUMMINGS: Madden might have the hardest community to please.
> It's painful. It ruins weekends. I've been out to dinner with my wife, and
> I check my phone [for online fan feedback]. It's all, "You suck; you're
> terrible; give up the NFL license."
> YOUNG: The perception among some people is that the game
> doesn't change every year. But I'm here working 16-hour days and
> sleeping in the office. That perception hurts.

To function as its namesake intended, Madden has to invoke
real football. To work as a video game, it has to transcend the brutality of three yards and a cloud of dust. Feel realer than real. Be
fun. This always has been Madden's animating tension—a debate between what avid gamers call "sim" (say, botched virtual long
snaps) and "arcade" (say, throwing 60-yard laser-guided bombs
while scrambling backward)—a split NFL players might recognize
as the difference between training camp tedium and Sunday afternoon's adrenalized rush.

Yet while the game itself grows ever more complex—in-game
playbooks that once came from Cooney's collected assistant-coach
scribbles are now based on actual NFL coaching film—finding a
happy medium remains more art than science. Online data mining can tell Cummings that Madden gamers threw more than 7
million interceptions while playing as Favre. But stat tracking can't
tell him whether those same gamers had a thrilling time doing so.

For Madden NFL '06, EA Tiburon introduced the first major
change to in-game passing since Hilleman's button-to-receiver

mapping on the Genesis. They called it the passing cone. When gamers dropped back to throw the ball, they had to use an analog stick to steer an on-screen cone—imagine light from a flashlight—toward the receiver they wanted to target. The cone was intended to approximate the real-life difference between great quarterbacks and lousy ones: Peyton Manning's cone was nearly as wide as the entire field, Rex Grossman's as narrow as a laser beam. The system worked: the cone made playing QB hard. Gamers hated it, and it was gone by Madden '09.

"Whenever a feature is that polarizing, it ends up being a failure in our eyes," Frazier said. "We have to develop stuff that is pretty much universally liked."

Can Madden itself remain universally liked? That's the larger question keeping EA Tiburon up at night. The franchise has surfed a pair of rising cultural tides: video games and pro football. But the ocean is shifting. Madden was once a disruptive product, a killer ambulance bowling over competitors. Now it's the status quo, established and entrenched, but possibly vulnerable. To wit: Madden NFL '10 sales were lagging behind during the game's August release, usually a prime selling period. For the first time, EA Sports paid for significant television advertising in November and December. The spots helped, but launching into the teeth of a recession still kept overall sales flat. Still, current sales are less of a concern than future growth.

The game's consumers are loyal and legion, good for 6 to 7 million copies sold, year after year. The same gamers are aging, however, guys in their late twenties who are starting families and running out of the free time needed to set the price of hot dogs in franchise mode. Meanwhile, younger gamers have been weaned on Halo and Call of Duty. First-person shooters—not sports simulations—are their default genre. Industry growth is being driven by simple, social gaming—the runaway sales success of the swing-your-arm, even-Grandma-can-play Nintendo Wii; the reported 80 million users of the cartoony, point-and-click Farmville on Facebook.

Scott Orr helped design the original Genesis Madden. He shepherded the franchise through the 1990s. After leaving EA in 2001, he stopped playing the game. He recently gave it a whirl.

"It was so complicated," he said. "It used to be you didn't have to be a video game expert or a football aficionado to have fun with the game. That's why it exploded and resonated. Three buttons. Everyone could pick up and play. Now, unless you practice and have time to devote to it, you'll get your butt kicked. I suspect that on Friday and Saturday nights, guys that used to play Madden are playing Texas Hold 'em."

Jeremy Strauser started at EA in 1995, working for Orr as a game tester. Today, he's the executive producer for Madden, the man in charge of the franchise. He wears a perpetual look of earnest concern. Nobody loves the game more; nobody at EA Tiburon knows Madden (the man) better. On a shelf in Strauser's office are copies of every Madden game he has worked on, neatly boxed and stacked, tangible points of pride and dread.

"There's a lot for us to live up to in terms of history, expectations, the legacy of the franchise," Strauser said. "We're in our 22nd year. I lose sleep over screwing it up."

Forgotten but Not Gone

The sun dips over a distant San Francisco skyline. Hawkins sits in the San Mateo office of his current company, Digital Chocolate, a mobile phone game maker. The place is mostly empty. Now 56, Hawkins still plays Strat-O-Matic; like Orr, he hardly plays Madden anymore. His memories are fond but tinged with regret. Hawkins left EA in the early 1990s to spearhead 3DO, an ill-fated console maker that became a doomed software house. An icy rift between the company and its founder ensued. Detached from the game, and the company, he created, he sometimes feels like the stepfather of his own children — never more so than a decade ago, when he wasn't invited to a 10th-anniversary Madden party. Mention the old coach, however, and Hawkins smiles.

"John and I have a special shared feeling from what got created there, a mutual appreciation," he said. "It wouldn't have been created as well without the both of us. He could have thrown me under the rug. But he knows what we did."

Every Christmas, a gift arrives at Hawkins's office. A three-pound box of chocolates. *Regards, Virginia Madden.* John's wife.

"At the anniversary party, I heard John kept asking, 'Where's Trip?'" Hawkins said with a sigh. "'Where's Trip?'"

Once a Coach, Always a Coach

"I used to say, 'Damn it, you can't go for it on fourth down all the time,'" Madden laments. "But nobody in video games wants to give up the ball."

He is sitting at the far end of a marble-top conference table inside his Pleasanton, California, production studio, a short drive from his family home. There's plenty of food, divided into what Madden terms "floaters" (mixed green salad) and "sinkers" (baked ziti, meatballs the size of cue balls). Chowing down are Madden's son, Joe, who runs the studio's soundstage, and a handful of people from EA Tiburon: Strauser, playbook guru Anthony White, and a few others. They're here to discuss the upcoming Madden NFL '11. That is, when the former coach isn't holding court on gap control and overload blitzes.

"Let me ask," Madden said. "When we get into the spread, the quarterback in shotgun, do the linemen get in three-point stances?"

"In some sets," White said. "But largely in two-point."

"They should all be in two-point stances," Madden admonished.

Madden is 74, a grandfather, and retired from broadcasting. Clad in a black tracksuit and a collared, button-down shirt, he seems smaller in person than on television—voice less booming, movements more ginger. A few years ago, EA removed Madden from in-game color commentary duties. (When Strauser broke the news, Madden replied, "I feel that something is being taken away from me.") Sipping from a can of diet cola, his enormous cigars long gone, he remains an advocate for real football, for art imitating life.

White flips open a laptop. Using "all 11" Detroit Lions coaching film, shot from the same perspective as Madden's original pseudo–3-D field, he demonstrates new in-game blocking schemes. Madden nods his approval.

"The quarterback may fake," White said. "But the guards never lie."

Another nod.

"Anyway, running the ball wasn't Detroit's problem," White continued. "It was passing."

"Once they had Daunte Culpepper in [at quarterback], teams just dared him to pass," Strauser interjected. "He used to be so accurate. What happened to that guy?"

"Wasn't he on our cover one year?" White asked.

Everyone laughs. Madden gets serious. He breaks down upcoming rules changes. He brings up concussions, helmet-to-helmet hits and gimmick quarterbacks. A digression on how the Dome Patrol–era Saints used to frustrate Bill Walsh's 49ers teams with short linebacker drops becomes a lecture on the obsolescence of the fullback, which then morphs into a short aside on player character.

Who, Strauser asked, are the hardest players to coach?

"Single guys," Madden said. "Because they don't have anyone to report to."

When Madden left the Raiders, he took a job at the University of California, offering a course called "Football for Fans." Three decades later, he's still teaching. In a way, so is his game. Current Tampa Bay Buccaneers coach Raheem Morris told game producers that playing Madden has influenced the way he runs his team. Before scoring a game-winning touchdown last season, Denver Broncos receiver Brandon Stokley killed clock by running parallel to the goal line, an unconventional move familiar only to anyone who has ever picked up a control pad. Years ago, Madden wanted his namesake to resemble a television broadcast; by the late 1990s, network producers were flipping the script, deploying skycams and electronic first-down markers, peddling their own brand of hyper-real entertainment. Life imitating art.

Strauser mentions 3-D televisions and the movie *Avatar.* A compatible version of Madden, he said, is already in the works.

Talk turns back to real football. The Super Bowl. Indianapolis versus New Orleans. In the first half, Saints coach Sean Payton went for a touchdown on fourth-and-goal, eschewing a "gimme" field goal. He opened the second half with an onside kick. Madden watched the whole thing from his California studio, incredulous and oddly transfixed. Even now, two months later, the old coach knows exactly what he was seeing.

"I was thinking, 'S—,'" Madden marveled, "'*this guy is playing a video game!*'"

MICHAEL FARBER

Eight Seconds

FROM SPORTS ILLUSTRATED

CONSIDER A MOMENT. Now take that moment—maybe the most significant in sports in 2010—and break it down frame by frame into 100 or so smaller moments. Hit Stop, Rewind, and Play. Now do it again. Follow the traveling puck, the dot that connects four men. Team Canada forwards Sidney Crosby and Jarome Iginla, American goalie Ryan Miller, and referee Bill McCreary. Seated in front of oversized plasmas or small laptops earlier this fall, clicking through a DVD, they watch adjustments, assumptions, decisions, and unadulterated dumb luck. No need for a spoiler alert. The climax never changes. Crosby scores with 12:20 left in overtime. Canada 3, USA 2. Olympic gold. These men know too well what will happen because they were there.

The golden goal in Vancouver is embroidered on the tapestry of hockey, part of a Crosby legacy that will one day veer into legend.

But what if Crosby had not scored to end the most significant game ever played on Canadian ice and an American like, say, Joe Pavelski, who had a credible chance seconds earlier, had?

The same people who still bask in the reflected glow of the goal light would be muttering about a hockey messiah who, other than a round-robin shootout winner, had experienced a middling Olympics.

Canadians would be lining their sackcloth with fur in anticipation of winter.

Hockey in the U.S. might have undergone a dramatic updraft that likely would have made Miller a breakout star, boosted interest among hockey agnostics in NHL cities such as Atlanta and Columbus, and maybe even prodded owners of the 24 American-based teams to look past their wallets and embrace participation in Sochi 2014 so Team USA could properly defend its gold medal.

"If we'd lost to the U.S.," Iginla says, his eyes dancing, "they'd've probably made another *Miracle* movie."

The four men met separately with *Sports Illustrated* and talked through the most memorable goal scored by a Canadian since 1972 and the most deflating one scored against the U.S. since, well, ever. Viewed through the prism of personal experience they deconstructed the kaleidoscopic twists of those last eight seconds, offering explanation but not excuse, hammering happenstance into narrative. As their tales eddied and flowed, it was clear they were not simply reliving how four men came to be in one quadrant of Olympic ice on the last day of February—but telling a universal story of how the regimented and the random blend to make history.

12:28

Crosby barrels into the high slot with the puck on his stick, trying to barge past defensemen Brian Rafalski and Ryan Suter. Their teammates, forwards Zach Parise and Jamie Langenbrunner, apply backside pressure, swallowing Crosby in a deep blue sea of U.S. and A. as the puck skitters ahead toward the American net. He is in jail. Crosby might be Superman, but unless he leaps defensemen in a single bound, his options are limited. The Americans are in control, which appeals to the man on the ice who most craves it.

Miller is a problem solver who likes to muse about the position he has played since age eight; he recognizes the egocentricity innate to goaltenders, wonders if the controlling nature of a goalie has psychosocial implications for a team. This is how he thinks. Sometimes this is how he talks. In any case he derives visceral pleasure from the challenge of denying shooters: Sid the Kid vs. Ryan the Id. During Miller's three years at Michigan State he would drop in at the basketball offices to visit Tom Izzo, not to have the coach help him think outside the box but to expand that box. Izzo, NCAA champion, and Miller, Hobey Baker winner, often would talk about how to meet expectations.

Three hundred fifty-four minutes and 59 seconds into his Olympic tournament, Miller has exceeded expectations. Those in the States who watch hockey once every four years reflexively attach themselves to goalies (Jim Craig in 1980, even Ray LeBlanc during a surprising run to the medal round in 1992) because it is the black-and-white position in a game with so many moving parts. The goalie stops the puck. Or he doesn't. Simple. And Miller has stopped it 138 times on 145 shots at the instant the puck dribbles toward him. In the past 13 days a goalie who plays in the modest market of Buffalo has become a quasi-celebrity, one whose back story—he is dating an actress, he owns a chic clothing store in East Lansing—has become front-page material. He is accustomed to hockey being a cult sport to which people pay attention at their convenience, but now his game is the main attraction at the five-ring circus. The phrase Miller-cle on Ice is tweeted and retweeted. Four years after being left off the Olympic team because of a broken thumb, Miller is at the zenith of the position. The thing making him uneasy is having all the attention lavished on him rather than on his U.S. teammates.

Although Rafalski is deep into his shift, Miller, at the edge of his crease, backhands the loose puck toward the corner to his right.

12:27

McCreary is anticipating that Miller will freeze the puck—he guesses Rafalski is tired—and prepares to blow a quick whistle but then sees the goalie send the puck to the corner. Legs churning, Crosby pursues it as Suter and Rafalski, whose helmet has been knocked askew, sort out who will chase him and the play. Within one second, a benign one-on-four morphs into a one-on-one in the corner.

Iginla, who jumped onto the ice three seconds earlier, ponders his possibilities: he can position himself near the hash marks in anticipation of Crosby slinging the puck up the boards or he can switch positions with his center, allowing Crosby to skate back up the wing on the vacated ice. Judging the angle of Crosby's torso, Iginla is certain his center will keep walking up the wall.

Iginla is an optimist. He can no more help seeing the good in a situation than Miller can help analyzing it. Although his line has so far failed to produce the anticipated stream of goals — Crosby, Iginla, and Eric Staal have nine among them at this moment — he continually reassures them that they will get the Big One. He thinks he inherited his sunshine from his maternal grandfather. Rick Schuchard would drive Jarome to his youth hockey games and, if the team lost, on the ride home would say, "Oh, that other team sure got lucky." Once when Iginla's team finally scored near the end of a trouncing, Schuchard bellowed from the stands, "There goes the shutout!" He built the framework of his grandson's worldview one bromide at a time.

And Iginla pays it forward, at least once by credit card. During the 2002 Olympics, Iginla was introduced to four Flames fans who had driven from Calgary to Salt Lake City without tickets or a place to stay. When he learned they had been sleeping in their car in a hotel parking lot, he excused himself, made a few calls, and booked them into the same hotel where his family was staying. Iginla later would score twice in the gold medal victory over Team USA, karmic proof there is a hockey god. (Crosby will ask only one player for an autographed stick in Vancouver — Iginla.)

As he skates toward the corner, Iginla figures if nothing develops for Crosby, the center might bounce the puck back to him so he will have a chance to roll for a shot.

12:26

Iginla is right. Crosby swivels his head and spots Iginla heading toward the corner, leaving him a path along the boards, a situation that is more ripe with promise than trying to manufacture a scoring chance from the extended goal line. Rafalski adjusts his helmet. Initially unsure whether Crosby or Iginla ultimately will wind up with the puck, McCreary must choose to stay along the boards or dart behind the net, a decision that will ultimately bring him more attention than his old-school mustache.

Some two and a half hours earlier McCreary had flipped the puck like a coin at midfield — the puck flip is the referee's signature; he started doing it fifteen years ago, as a way of saying hello to his five-year-old daughter, Melissa, who had suffered a stroke —

and dropped it to start the match. This is McCreary's third Olympics, third gold medal game. (He called the 2002 final when Iginla scored twice.) NHL director of officiating Terry Gregson approvingly says McCreary "referees from the neck up." This means he knows how to control the flow of the game, understands when to intimidate players in order to lower the temperature of a match, and realizes when he should swallow his whistle. McCreary is confident in his assessment of situations and players. Team USA general manager Brian Burke calls him "one of the best referees in the history of the NHL."

Still McCreary is surprised to be here—in the final, in Vancouver at all, really. He is in the last year or two of his career, "past my time," and he is not certain the International Ice Hockey Federation is as enamored of him as his NHL bosses. He doesn't think he fits the IIHF "style." In a meeting before the medal-round games, an official from Finland tells him that he has to get off the boards and get to the net area more.

Two days before the gold medal game, McCreary learned he would be part of the most watched game in North America since the Miracle on Ice in 1980—another hallmark in a career brimming with them. (He also has worked in 15 of the past 16 Stanley Cup finals.) He will officiate with Dan O'Halloran, another well-regarded NHL referee. Like McCreary, O'Halloran is a Canadian. Even with experienced American-born NHL referees available, two Canadians are calling a Canada-USA final. This would not happen in any other Olympic sport—ever—but the IIHF and NHL make a daring assumption that professional referees are, well, professional.

Gregson, who, with Konstantin Komissarov, the secretary of the IIHF's officiating committee, gave the game to McCreary and O'Halloran instead of force-feeding an American into the mix, is sensitive to the issue of neutrality; 11 years earlier he essentially had been labeled the worst thing a ref can be: a homer. Late in a scoreless Game 6 of the 1999 Maple Leafs–Flyers playoff series in Philadelphia, Gregson, who is from Ontario, called an elbowing penalty on Flyers star John LeClair. When Toronto scored on the ensuing power play to eliminate his team, Philadelphia chairman Ed Snider ranted in the home dressing room, assailing Gregson's impartiality while denouncing the call as "a disgrace to the game."

When the referee supervisors and IIHF and NHL officials convene in Vancouver before the medal-round games, Gregson opens the meeting by saying, "Will we be using the best or are there political ramifications to our decisions?"

McCreary tries to make himself inconspicuous along the boards, trying to guess Crosby's next move.

12:25

Crosby crosses with Iginla, the center lugging the puck toward the hash marks and the right wing dropping to the goal line. There are now crevices in the American defense, a residue of Crosby's determined skating, but he fails to notice an avenue of clear ice from the boards to the middle in which he might have been able to squeeze a pass to Scott Niedermayer or Drew Doughty, the pinching defensemen. The opportunity vanishes. The puck rolls off the blade of Crosby's stick—he hasn't cupped it sufficiently—and ticks the front of his left skate, which pushes it toward the blue line. McCreary thinks about jumping out of the path of the puck but stays planted because if he hops and holds on to the boards, he would hang in no man's land, unable to make it to the net quickly enough to rule on a goal.

In the three seconds since Crosby tried to bully his way past the defensemen, options have been weighed, choices made. Still nothing has alarmed Miller. Rafalski pressures Crosby. Good. Suter wanders to the corner to track Iginla. Well, fine. Parise, a left wing with a mature grasp of positioning, stands sentry outside the crease. In a perfect world Parise would chase the play and a defenseman would take the front of the net, but forwards and defensemen are free to make adjustments. Besides, hockey is an imperfect world.

The kaleidoscope turns. The one-on-four that evolved into a one-on-one is now a four-on-four.

12:24

The puck that glances off Crosby's left skate hits McCreary on the inside of the referee's right skate. (Stuff happens. The ref can be an impediment in any game. There are roughly 17,000 square feet of ice surface in Canada Hockey Place and the four officials—two referees and two linesmen—need to be somewhere.) Although McCreary has no idea it has struck his size eight, his skate has killed whatever momentum the puck had been carrying in the slushy residue along the boards. The puck sits there, inert as Monty Python's parrot.

Crosby overskates the dead puck. If an American corrals it—Rafalski appears to be in position to do so—the U.S. can counter three-on-two. Crosby senses the danger. He must make sure the puck does not slip past him. He must shovel it deep, toward Iginla in the corner, before Rafalski closes.

Crosby plants his left skate, unleashing a geyser of snowy spray that flies waist high—frozen testament to the immense power of his legs. The area along the boards looks as if someone has shaken a snow globe. With only his right hand on his stick, Crosby stabs at the puck.

12:23

The broken play is mended by Crosby's one-handed lunge, which propels the puck down along the boards to Iginla a foot in front of the extended goal line. Iginla originally thought the battle for the puck would be 50-50, a coin toss, Crosby vs. Rafalski, but the situation turns up heads for Canada because Crosby chips the puck before the defenseman can nudge it in the opposite direction to Langenbrunner, who is about six feet up the boards.

This time, Miller will wryly note later, McCreary lifts his skates and the puck slides past.

Crosby notices Rafalski's momentum has carried him away from the changing flow. He sees Rafalski is flatfooted, which prompts. . . .

12:22

"Iggy!!!" Iginla never especially liked the nickname Shane Doan gave him when they played junior hockey in Kamloops, British Columbia. He thought it sounded soft. Iggy. Like Eggy or something. Of course when your full name is Jarome Arthur-Leigh Adekunle Tij Junior Elvis Iginla, you shouldn't quibble. And if you object whenever a teammate uses a nickname that sounds as if it came from the comics section . . . well, that cements it, doesn't it?

Iginla has grown comfortable with his nickname through his 13 years with the Flames. Iginla hears "Iggy" daily. Now he hears "IGGY!!!," ornamented with capital letters and exclamation points. He is planning to spin out of the corner and away from Suter, but the vehemence in Crosby's voice leads him to reconsider. Iginla certainly can differentiate degrees of urgency, and Crosby's yell is imbued with an unmistakable tone of, Get me the puck right now! Iginla's head is down. His eyes are on the puck. But the scream that drifts above the bedlam of 17,748 at Canada Hockey Place— "IGGY!!!" is clearly audible on the replay—demands he shift to a Plan B.

As Iginla suspects, Crosby, pushing off his left skate, has lost Rafalski.

When Crosby was 13 and the best player his age in the world, he met Andy O'Brien, a strength and conditioning coach, at a hockey school in Prince Edward Island. When Crosby was 14, O'Brien moved his business to Halifax. Crosby was his only local client to start. For the past 10 years O'Brien has worked with Crosby on building exceptional core strength. He has trained Crosby to develop hockey-related biomechanical and neurological efficiency. In three sessions over six hours on almost every summer day—90 minutes on the track, 90 minutes of weights, and 45 minutes of targeted muscle work interspersed with recovery periods—they nurtured the key elements of first-step speed: low center of gravity, shin forward, weight distribution on a single leg. They trained on unstable surfaces, like balance boards and Bosu balls, to enable Crosby to move his limbs dynamically while stabilizing his spine and pelvis. The result is Crosby's superb hockey haunches, what O'Brien calls his "massive ass." Crosby's obsession with angles (shin, torso, everything) is Euclidian; he forwards to O'Brien action photos of himself torn from magazines and newspapers and asks, "How do my angles look?" After 2,000 hours in O'Brien's company, and innumerable more hours of training on his own, no hockey player can accelerate from a dead stop to 25 miles per hour quite like the bowlegged Crosby.

Sometimes one moment is 2,000 hours in the making.

From his standing start, Crosby gains the edge of the face-off circle to Miller's right before Rafalski appreciably moves off the boards. He approaches the face-off dot before Rafalski gets to the edge of the circle.

The scoreboard clock still reads 12:22.

The recalcitrant puck is spinning, refusing to behave. Iginla struggles to retain control. He is wearing Suter like a size 42 regular. And as Suter is about to check the off-balance Iginla to the ice, the winger flicks the puck across the face-off circle to Crosby, praying he has not reacted too late.

12:21

Miller, the Vezina Trophy–winner last season, plays for the Sabres, which means he faces Crosby, the Pittsburgh captain, four times a year in intraconference games. He knows Crosby usually looks at the net when he prepares to shoot. Crosby receives Iginla's pass on his backhand, tape to tape, then moves it to his forehand. Studying Crosby's posture, Miller concludes Crosby is not contemplating a shot. Crosby generally releases the puck with his hands in front of his body, and they are now too far back. With the open lane — Parise is perhaps a step high but still in the play — the goalie expects Crosby to take another lateral stride to the front of the net, dip to his backhand, and try to tuck the puck under the crossbar.

Miller shifts his hands on his stick, readying a pokecheck.

Because of his peripheral vision, Crosby knows Miller is relatively deep in his crease. In stories after the gold medal game, Miller's hands are identified as the factors that induce Crosby to shoot. In fact he never sees Miller move them. At first Crosby is not fully aware the goalie even has extended his stick. He rejects the lane to the front of the net not because of the incipient pokecheck but because he expects Parise to cut him off. Unsure of how Miller will play the situation — one pad down? butterfly? — Crosby decides to release a quick shot from the bottom of the circle, aiming low. Five hole or glove side. Either, really.

If Crosby holds the puck for a fraction of a second longer, Miller assumes he can salvage a deteriorating situation. The goalie, who has extended his stick like a man reaching with a broom for a

quarter that has rolled under the sofa, thinks he can drop into his
butterfly quickly enough to force Crosby to change his shooting
angle.

"When he doesn't hold it," Miller says, turning from the computer, "now you know you're screwed."

12:20

Miller is late on his butterfly. Five hole. The puck is in the net. Pan-
demonium. Crosby flings his gloves skyward in a spasm of joy, an
emotion that overwhelms rational thought. He is elated not for
having scored a goal but for having won a game, even if the two are
inextricable. Can you understand? If Crosby can detect the out-
lines of the big picture . . . well, that's all he can see in the blur of
celebrating teammates. He knows this is about something larger
than one player, no matter how prepared or how gifted. What's the
cliché? There's no I in Canada.

Iginla hears rather than sees the goal. He is still on the ice, courtesy of a check by Suter that McCreary considered penalizing but,
six months later, with the benefit of Stop-Rewind-Click, knows was
a legal play. The hike along the Olympic abyss has worn on Iginla
— "We're winning games and everybody's asking, What about Sid?
He didn't get a hat trick, he didn't get two goals," he says—but
now a wave of relief washes over him. He is a sensitive man, aware
of the wide world beyond the Olympic bubble. He knows that no
matter what, the sun will rise Monday morning. He also knows that
now it will shine that much brighter on a country whose identity is
welded to the sport.

Miller, on his knees, hunches over the ice and bows his head.

Epilogue

On a brilliant September afternoon in New York City, after about a
half-hour of DVD to-and fro, Miller is done. Really, he needed no
video prompting. He played the game. Miller had stuffed it into
the file cabinet of experience and moved on, although something
in his eyes hints those eight seconds never will be far away.

"Right when [Crosby] did what I didn't think he would do, I knew the puck was in," he says. "I didn't get angry. Just disappointed. [What I did] was in-between what I should have done: held my net, the safe thing. But I played the whole tournament pretty aggressive. I just thought if he got in that area, that low, I would be on top of him by the time he figured things out. I probably only watched the replay once, until now. Why should I? I lived it. But history happens. Life goes on, and things unfold. You look back too much, you go crazy."

MEGAN CHUCHMACH AND AVNI PATEL

ABC News Investigation: USA Swimming Coaches Molested, Secretly Taped Dozens of Teen Swimmers

FROM ABCNEWS.COM

APRIL 9, 2010—In a sex abuse scandal that some victims compare to what happened in the Catholic Church, at least 36 swimming coaches have been banned for life by the USA Swimming organization over the last 10 years because of sexual misconduct.

The coaches have molested, fondled, and abused dozens of swimmers, according to court records and interviews conducted by ABC News for reports on *World News with Diane Sawyer* and *20/20.*

One coach, Brian Hindson of Kokomo, Indiana, secretly taped teenage girls he coached in two high school pool locker rooms, in one of which he directed girls to a "special" shower room where he had a hidden camera inside a locker.

"It was a sense of betrayal," Indiana swimming star Brooke Taflinger told ABC News chief investigative correspondent Brian Ross for a report to be broadcast on *20/20.*

Taflinger's parents later identified Brooke for the FBI as one of the girls who was taped naked in the locker and shower area.

"I gotta tell you, it hurt," Brooke's father, Bruce Taflinger, told *20/20.* "My wife only had to look at one picture before she turned away in tears," he said.

FBI agents became aware of the pictures after a North Carolina woman bought the coach's computer on eBay and discovered a video clip of a young girl in a locker room appearing to be taped without her knowledge. A subsequent search of Hindson's home turned up more locker room footage and a large selection of child pornography.

"This had gone on for nearly 10 years, without any detection whatsoever," Lt. Don Whitehead of the Kokomo, Indiana, police department's cyber crime unit told ABC News.

Hindson was sentenced in 2008 to 33 years in federal prison. His attorney Gregg Stark did not return repeated requests for comment.

Still, another one of Hindson's victims, Sarah Rutkowski, now 21, said there are many questions left unanswered.

"I'd really like to know how he did it and where the videos have ended up, if they're on the Internet or if he put them through Limewire or if they were just sitting around for his personal use," Rutkowski, who is believed to have been 12 or 13 when she was taped, told ABC News. "That's really disturbing to me, not knowing where those videos are."

USA Swimming

Hindson is one of the 36 coaches banned for life for sexual misconduct over the last 10 years by USA Swimming, the governing body for the sport up to and including the U.S. Olympic team.

Ken Stopkotte, named Indiana High School Boys Swimming and Diving State Coach of the Year for 2009, said the problem is pervasive and has been going on his entire 27 years in coaching.

"It's something that coaches talk about all the time," Stopkotte told ABC News.

The executive director of USA Swimming, Chuck Wielgus, acknowledged the problem, but said, "It's not nearly as serious in USA Swimming as it might be in the rest of society."

"I don't want to be the one to sit here and say 36 is not too many, one is too many, but this is not just a problem that's isolated to one sport," said Wielgus.

In some cases, the swimming coaches found to have been sexual predators were able to move from town to town, one step ahead of police and angry victims and their parents.

"We have a system that does not encourage the reporting," said Bob Allard, a San Jose, California, lawyer representing sex abuse victims suing USA Swimming.

A San Jose swimming coach, Andy King, 62, was sentenced to 40 years in prison in January after authorities discovered a pattern of sexual abuse that stretched over three decades up and down the West Coast and involved more than a dozen teen female victims.

"He was a monster," said Santa Clara County prosecutor Ray Mendoza. "He had almost every conceivable sex act," he said.

Mendoza said King would move out of town once parents or police began asking questions and was stopped only after a 14-year-old girl in San Jose complained to her youth pastor.

King previously worked as a swim coach in the San Francisco Bay Area and in Oak Harbor, Washington, where he was regarded as an excellent coach for aspiring Olympic team swimmers.

"He may have been a good coach, but his goal with these girls ultimately was to molest them," said prosecutor Mendoza.

King's lawyer, Jamie Harley, said some of the responsibility belongs to the swimmers' parents, whose ambition for their children blinded them to the problem.

"I think Mr. King bears enormous responsibility here. But I think the parents were not minding the store," she said. "I think had they been minding the store—had they been watching what's going on with their own children—this opportunity never could have presented itself."

Background Checks for Swimming Coaches

In 2008, USA Swimming gave King a clean bill of health, saying his background screening had been approved.

"Congratulations," read the letter. "Your background screening has been thoroughly reviewed and meets the qualification standards set by USA Swimming."

According to USA Swimming, the organization only checks for criminal convictions and does not include background interviews or investigations with local police.

"It was willfully incomplete," said Bob Allard, a lawyer for families now suing USA Swimming. "A simple phone call to Oak Harbor, his prior stop, or to the East Bay would have revealed much about this man's propensity to abuse and molest kids."

Police later documented at least 15 victims among the teenage girl swimmers he coached over the years, including a woman who said she had an abortion after King got her pregnant at the age of 14.

"We want to have the gold standard and I think we do an awesome job," said USA Swimming executive director Chuck Wielgus. "I don't think we're perfect."

Wielgus says the local swim clubs, not the national organization, bear the responsibility to check the full backgrounds of swimming coaches they hire.

He said the 36 coaches banned by the organization over the last 10 years were only a tiny fraction of the organization's 12,000 coaches in that time period.

"Thirty-six does seem like a whole lot. A hundred is even more. Five hundred is even more," he told correspondent Brian Ross.

Asked if he had apologized to any of the young teen victims, Wielgus responded, "You feel I need to apologize to them?"

He added, "I think it's unfair for you to ask me whether individually or me as the representative of an organization to apologize for something when all we are trying to do is everything we possibly can to create a safe and healthy environment for kids who are participating in our particular activity."

Editorial note: Five months after this story appeared, ABCNews.com published this follow-up:

USA Swimming Votes "Yes" to Athlete Protection Measures After Sex Abuse Scandal

Five months after an ABC News investigation revealed that 36 swim coaches were quietly banned for alleged sexual misconduct with their athletes, USA Swimming has officially passed new legislation that implements athlete protection policies, expands background checks, and enacts mandatory reporting of credible information of sexual abuse.

"Our membership really stepped up today to provide their overwhelming support to this important issue," outgoing USA Swimming president Jim Wood said in a statement.

The House of Delegates, the group in charge of passing USA Swimming bylaws, voted on the new measures by overwhelming majority, which also included enacting new education efforts to inform members of USA Swimming about the issue of sexual misconduct. The measures had been put forth by the group's Board of Directors.

New athlete protection policies now prohibit rubdowns or massages by coaches, audio or visual recordings in locker rooms, and shared hotel rooms between athletes and coaches at swim meets, among others.

Effective January 1, 2011, the expanded criminal background check program will be updated on a "continual basis, to avoid any gap in information," USA Swimming announced. Previously, the checks were only updated every two years since being implemented in 2006.

In the past, the criminal background check program did not check all predators.

San Jose swimming coach Andy King, 62, was sentenced to 40 years in prison in January after authorities discovered a pattern of sexual abuse that stretched over three decades up and down the West Coast and involved more than a dozen teen female victims. Despite allegations against him and a police investigation, as he had never been charged or convicted of a crime, the USA Swimming background screening came back clean in 2008.

"Congratulations," read the letter. "Your background screening has been thoroughly reviewed and meets the qualification standards set by USA Swimming." King went on to molest a 14-year-old swimmer in San Jose, now one plaintiff in a handful of lawsuits against USA Swimming.

Addressing Sexual Misconduct by Swim Coaches

Now, all employees and volunteers of USA Swimming and its local affiliate clubs will be required to undergo background checks as well. And local clubs are encouraged to include further background screenings and employer checks.

Also new, the USA Swimming rulebook will now require members to report any incident regarding sexual misconduct to the organization's new Athlete Protection Officer, former competitive swimmer Susan Woessner.

"Reporting must occur when an individual has firsthand knowledge of misconduct or where specific and credible information has been received from a victim or knowledgeable third party," according to USA Swimming.

Attorney Bob Allard, who is representing multiple alleged victims of abuse by USA Swimming coaches, warned that "the policies and procedures adopted will only be as good as the enforcement and follow-through by USA Swimming."

"We are pleased that after years of neglect, the current leadership group for USA Swimming, albeit only under extreme media pressure, has finally implemented some rules and regulations to protect children from sex abuse," Allard said. "We remain highly pessimistic, however, that real and permanent change can be made with this control group."

Five lawsuits have been filed against USA Swimming, claiming the governing body of swimming in the U.S. failed to protect young swimmers from alleged sexual misconduct by coaches.

WELLS TOWER

Own Goal

FROM HARPER'S MAGAZINE

I.

IT'S THE NIGHT before the 2008 Homeless Soccer USA Cup, in which teams of homeless soccer players from 13 American cities will gather for three days of competition in Washington, D.C., and only a very foolish, and very specialized, bookie would give odds on the team from New York City. Least among the team's impediments is that its seven players, all of them residents at the HELP Supportive Employment Center on Ward's Island, have so far convened for only a half-dozen or so practices and have never so much as scrimmaged together. Yet even for a jerry-built outfit like Team New York, the tournament reportedly includes a couple of easy targets: Richmond, whose goalie is said to have some sort of nerve disorder, and St. Louis, one of whose attackers is a dwarf. In any case, there's something not wholly ingenuous in speculating overmuch about which city's going to take home the trophy, as a good share of the teams are, like New York, squads contrived ad hoc at the eleventh hour for the three days of competition in the capital. The weekend's actual mission, one hears from its organizers at the nonprofit Street Soccer USA, which has orchestrated the Cup each year since 2006, is to instill in the players the virtues of teamwork and sportsmanship and to send everyone home feeling like a winner, while at the same time drumming up ink and airtime for the homelessness cause with a media spectacle too outré and amusing and swollen with human interest to resist.

At the moment, minutes before 8:00 P.M. on Cup eve, it's look-

ing like the weekend's going to be a nonstarter on all counts for
New York, seeing as the tournament kicks off in 12 hours and the
New York players and coaching staff are marooned on the shelter's
parking lot in the middle of the East River because Miss Rose, a
terse and stolid bureaucrat in charge of the shelter's motor pool,
will release only a single Toyota minivan built for six to transport
the seven players, plus driver, coach, media entourage, and gear,
the five hours south.

"This is what you get," Miss Rose explains to Chris Murray, the
team's coach. When Chris proposes that he shuttle three players in
his own automobile, Miss Rose says that this isn't possible either.
Because of legal liabilities, the shelter is permitted to release its
residents exclusively to the guardianship of HELP-SEC employees,
which means that any player departing the shelter grounds in the
unapproved custody of Chris Murray, an unpaid volunteer, would
probably return from the weekend of feeling like a winner in D.C.
to find that his bed had been given away.

"This is what you get," Miss Rose says again, wanding a finger at
the lone small van. An air of mutinous outrage gathers over the
players, who stand scowling by the Toyota.

"For the homeless fucking all-stars, what did you expect, a lim-
ousine?" says Diego Viveros. Diego is a lithe and muscular young
Colombian, who before he was homeless sold subprime mortgages
to Spanish-speaking clients throughout the five boroughs. "They
don't give a shit about us, bro."

Goaltender Leo Lopez, a man built like a Coke machine, is surprised, to near amusement, that HELP-SEC would dare to trifle
with a man like him in such a way as this. "I used to do maintenance here. Doesn't it dawn on them that I know where all the gas
lines are? I was a Navy SEAL. Keep fucking me around, I'll blow
this place to the clouds." What were Leo Lopez's duties when he
was a Navy SEAL? "Suffice it to say that I was the one doing certain
work behind enemy lines between one and four in the morning,
carrying a photograph and a .45 and some piano wire."

The van negotiations remain at an impasse. The team captain, a
brooding man named Quentin, becomes so exasperated that he
walks off in the direction of the East River footbridge, where he
is known to have a favorite thinking spot. Chris Murray ruefully
watches him go.

"He got sick of the BS," explains Jason Moore, a twenty-four-year-old Baltimore native who has been at Ward's Island for eight months. Jason is a religious man, and he is known at the shelter as the Reverend, or as Reverend Pimpin', and is usually seen in a pin-striped suit. "In fact," the Reverend says, "a lot of the brothers are thinking about walking."

But thankfully, before Team New York disintegrates, Miss Rose undergoes a change of heart and astounds everyone by producing a second minivan. She could have released the van a couple of hours ago, but this particular van is brand-new, and so lending it out is, for Miss Rose, an anxious matter of last resort. And so, finally, the motorcade departs, a player and captain short, the remaining six players already feeling not so much like winners, while the ocher leavings of a sunset wane above the Jersey Palisades.

Despite pregame publicity on National Public Radio and local distribution of some very professional-looking programs, when the Homeless Soccer USA Cup gets under way the next day, bona fide audience members tally out at zero. But the media complement—print, radio, and a crew of elfin young men who have secured Hollywood funding to make a feature-length documentary—is dense. At this point, they record the quotations and take photographs of people like Mayor Adrian Fenty, who will not be attending the competition but who has come by to say a few words into a microphone and to have his photo snapped. The players from the 13 competing cities are politely corralled into the background so as to obscure the empty bleachers.

A cursory survey of the other teams reveals that competition will be both fierce and otherwise. Los Angeles promises to be murderous: Latino men in their early twenties, whippet thin, sinewy of leg, betraying not a trace of infirmity. They scamper around the pitch in a precompetition showcase of rainbow and bicycle kicks and other high-bounding feats of ball art. Minneapolis's youthful squad and salon-grade coiffures inspire grouchy conjectures that they are in breach of the rule stipulating that all tournament players must have been documentably homeless within the past two years.

The newspaper photographers are not so interested in the fresh-faced, virtuoso teams as they are in teams like Austin, which includes a trio of men looking recently recruited off the steam grate.

Although Austin will suffer terrible losses on the field, they'll remain uncontested champs in the ambassadorship game, owing to the camera-ready charms of Tad Christie. The only entirely toothless player in the league, Tad, 37, is a versatile subject for portraiture. When he is not wearing his teeth, his face has the collapsed, cronelike topography we associate with long-term methamphetamine addicts, which Tad was, on and off, for two decades or so. With his teeth inserted and his sandy-blond hair combed out, he seems to shed 20 years, appearing as handsome as a 1970s television star. Upon request, he will pose or conduct interviews with his teeth in, or he is glad to remove them, holding them up to reporters' dictaphones and manipulating them, ventriloquist-style, while uttering a rapid, winning patois of inspirational pull quotes and bawdy one-liners.

Q: What position do you play, Tad?

A: My position? I'm pro-choice, and pro-life. My position is forward, though sometimes I do it in reverse, or doggie-style.

Q: So, Tad, how did you get these teeth?

A: My coach bought them for a hundred dollars, and I'm glad to have them, not just because they look good but because they help me advocate for the homeless. They're a little uncomfortable, but you make sacrifices, because looks are important. For example, when I was stripping, I wasn't about to start wearing a change purse just because the coins kept falling through my G-string.

At 10:00 A.M., New York prepares for its first match, an exhibition game against a homeless all-star team from a previous year, under a sun of hot-dog-lamp intensity. Homeless Cup games are played not on a traditional full field but on a cramped, proprietary tennis-court-size arena enclosed by Triton Barriers and tiled in a red and blue plastic milk-crate material capable of delivering the mother of all friction burns. Clock and team structure are miniaturized as well: four-on-four with seven-minute halves. Though the game's rules are presumably tailored to be comprehensible to people who have never really played soccer before, the regulations are in fact knotty and cumbersome. There are complicated offsides stipulations, and rules about where the goalie is permitted to tread, and how he is permitted to throw the ball, and permissible proximities of attackers to the goals. In the last moments before the whistle, Chris Murray—a voice-over man and aspiring actor who coaches Team New York as a favor to the founder and CEO of Street Soccer USA, Lawrence Cann, with whom he played on the Davidson College team—conducts a frantic, muddled explanation of the rules while fielding such questions as "Do we have an offensive strategy? What about defense?"

The next 14 minutes are more or less a hyperventilatory cadenza of whistle-bleatings against the New York players. Jason Moore, the friendly diplomat, plays a friendly, diplomatic game. He does much ardent capering alongside the ball, though he politely refuses to touch a foot to it, even as the attackers bear down on the New York net, which Leo Lopez inadequately tends. Despite Leo's purported lethal grace in enemy camps under cover of night, and despite the way his bulk almost entirely obscures the goal's aperture, he is pretty much incapable of thwarting even the most fainthearted attempts on goal. His huge frame seems to bend space, to draw balls to it like an anvil on a trampoline, only to let most shots roll dawdlingly between his knees or slip into the net from his vast clasping hands. David Cotiere, a tall gloomy Haitian, manages the occasional possession, yet whenever he's forced to give up the ball, the grief of the loss immobilizes him, and he stands in his tracks, arms akimbo, and moans in a piteous way: "We are terrible, the worst team. We will never score even one goal!"

Compared with his teammates, Diego Viveros, the former broker of high-risk home loans, turns out to be an artistic, nimble player, whose feet move about the ball in a deft, lancing embroidery, like a spider swaddling a grub. But his every step, it seems, also draws a penalty for a breach of one or another of the game's obscure rules. By the middle of the second half, Diego has pretty much stopped playing in order to bawl frustrated obscenities at the capricious referee, which compounds the team's penalty woes. At one point Coach Murray turns to me, deflated by the incessant whistles, and says, "It's such a perfect metaphor for these guys' situation. It's like every time they turn around there's some rule they bump up against."

At the end of the first day, drubbed and woeful, the team loiters in a dining tent pitched adjacent to the bleachers, awaiting dinner, courtesy of Papa John's pizza, which will be arriving shortly. The talk turns to women, reportedly common agents in the team members' paths to homelessness. Joey Martinez, a recovering substance abuser, speaks of his lady, who kicked him out of the house he'd shared with her and their two children. Diego Viveros laments that he'd failed to heed his father when he met the first great love of his life. "My father told me to keep my mind on work, not to get too wrapped up in that bitch," he says. "But I was like, 'Fuck you, bro.' And then what happens? I lose my job, and the bitch leave, and I wind up in the shelter."

And here, Glenn Richards, who has been taciturn for most of the trip, puts his spoke in. By his own telling, he is a man of storied sexual reputation, a venereal buccaneer known variously, he says, as the "Hammer Man" and "Ding Dong." Glenn offers the general advice that girlfriends are not a good idea, that enlisting the services of a prostitute is a more sensible, cost-effective method for a trouble-free romantic life. Then someone raises the point that what you save in hassle you may stand to lose in trips to the STD clinic, to which Glenn cries, "Not true!" Glenn has a method. "You take two condoms, and in between you sprinkle Dettol disinfectant. You never have any trouble." He does concede that there was this one time, down in the Caribbean, when he contracted a bad case of biting underlice despite his special system. But he handled the problem in his own way, by dousing himself with diesel fuel, which did indeed kill the crabs but also gave him blisters of a terrible kind.

Later that evening, when Chris Murray and I are heading to Georgetown to eat dinner with Lawrence Cann and his fiancée, we bump into Diego out in front of the George Washington University dorms, where the players are being lodged. He asks where we're going, and before I can think the better of it, I say, "We're going out to eat in Georgetown!" Then I launch into a fit of stammering apologies about how very sorry I am that Diego won't be joining us at the fancy dinner. He pats my shoulder and gives a warm but wounded smile, and says, "It's okay. I'm fucking homeless. What are you gonna do?"

By the time the tournament closes on Sunday evening, New York is pleased to finish 9th in the field of 13, having eked out narrow victories over Austin and St. Louis, the team with the dwarf. New

York owes its modest triumph pretty much entirely to its leading
scorer, Diego Viveros, whose peremptory manner on the field and
lopsided share of playing time have made him an object of resent-
ment rather than admiration among his teammates.

When the trophy-dispersal hoopla relents, Lawrence Cann takes
the microphone to dispatch the more significant business of nomi-
nating players to the U.S. National Homeless Soccer Team, whose
eight members, selected at the discretion of Cann and colleagues,
will enjoy an all-expenses-paid ride to the Homeless World Cup, a
weeklong, forty-eight-nation tournament taking place five months
hence in Melbourne, Australia. Two lean aces from Los Angeles
make the cut, as does Tad Christie, Austin's genial captain. Then
Cann announces Diego's name, and Diego's features, which are
generally tuned to the affective register of a lowered portcullis,
suddenly bloom, his mouth and eyes dilating to beauty-pageant-
finalist diameters. He falls to his knees and presses palms to cheeks,
cooing, "I can't believe it! I'm going to see fucking kangaroos!" It's
precisely this sort of joyous display that the human-interest beat
reporters have been on the lookout for, and Diego is temporarily
obscured by a video crew, a photographer, and a radio man prodding a shotgun mike at his chin, scarfing up breathless, articulate
quotes about Diego's gratitude to the Street Soccer program and
his zeal to be an example to homeless people everywhere, evidently
confirming the soundness of his election to the national team.

The rest of Team New York does not share in his gladness.
"Knowing what I know about Australia, Melbourne isn't all that,"
says Jason Moore. "If it was Sydney, now that'd be something worth
checking out. Sydney's what's *up*."

"They got some beautiful women in Sydney," says Leo Lopez.

"But *Melbourne*," Reverend Pimpin' adds, his face aslant with
scorn. "Melbourne just ain't the place."

Danny Boansi, a squat 43-year-old Haitian, takes the news exceptionally hard. "Why didn't I get picked? I scored four goals. They
should have picked me."

"They went for youth," the Hammer Man consoles.

"You had two blue cards," Chris Murray points out. "That didn't
necessarily look good. But keep training. You were right near the
top."

"Train for what?" says Danny. "I'm done. I have lost hope."

*

The sullen, pugnacious air that settled on Danny Boansi seems to expand into a minor epidemic as the players say their goodbyes. With nothing on the line now, several of the players discard the pretense of sportsmanship and lapse into squabbles and near-assaults. At the George Washington dorms, as we board the mini-vans, the newly nominated goalie for the national team, a large, bald Charlotte player named Tim Cummings, is roaring at a member of the San Francisco team, promising to "bust that ass" for reasons having to do with the San Francisco player's advances on Cummings's Kool-Aid jug.

As we caravan north through New Jersey, the shelter assistant driving our vehicle loses contact with the second minivan, the new and precious one, and presently gets a call from the Hammer Man. We can hear him screaming incoherently through the receiver. We circle back and find the Toyota parked on the shoulder of the highway. The men have spilled out onto a grassy berm, where a gory fistfight is just now exhausting itself. Danny and Joey are howling curses at each other. Both are rinsed in red. Diego, who donned a brocaded white button-down shirt and expensive jeans after the last game, stands between them. He looks as though he's just slaughtered a pig.

We learn that the fight broke out while the van was in transit at fifty miles an hour. The problem was this: one man had wanted to use what was left of the food per diem at McDonald's, while the other was in favor of spending it on cigarettes. Fists and head butts were thrown, and then men rolled into the front seat, spraying quantities of blood and partly destroying the dashboard of the brand-new minivan, fulfilling Miss Rose's bodings that the D.C. trip would not end well for the Toyota.

II.

After returning to New York, I find myself in the habit of reciting Diego Viveros's biography to colleagues and dinner-party guests. I tell of his beginnings as a quintessential American bootstrapper: an industrious immigrant who came to New York from Colombia when he was 13 and valiantly dropped out of school three years later, taking a job at McDonald's on Queens Boulevard to help his parents with the bills. In his early twenties, Diego says, he began a successful career as a salesman. He started with cars, working his way up from Nissans to Mercedes and BMWs, and at last accepting a position as a mortgage broker with a Wall Street firm in November 2006. I tell of the ideal piquancy of Diego's reversal of fortune, the lure of housing-bubble cash leading to him losing his job in late summer 2007. Shortly thereafter, he says, his apartment was burglarized, and his Green Card was stolen; lacking the money for its replacement, he was unable to apply for work or to pay the rent. Too proud to move in with his parents, Diego entered the shelter system and "became homeless," a phrase that makes him grimace with disgust.

During the tournament in Washington, Chris Murray and I had both come to like and admire Diego, and over the course of the weekend we began making him into a receptacle of our unsolicited sympathies. We found his situation painful and especially worthy of remedy because Diego is handsome, intelligent, and charismatic, apparently unplagued by the overt deficiencies of mind, body, or character that grant us the comfort of Erewhonian indifference when on the street we pass an unfortunate person trembling on a flattened box. When Lawrence Cann balked at picking Diego for the national team because of his tendency to fly into furies at the referees, Chris and I mustered a passionate defense, saying that we too would fly into rages were we—perfectly employable Americans —to find ourselves flung into America's lowest caste, and lobbied and pestered Cann until, in the end, he agreed to admit Diego to the team.

As a member of Team USA, Diego will receive far more than a free trip to Australia; he will also get financial and case-management assistance unavailable to his 200 fellows on Ward's Island. Diego says he has foundered in New York's shelter system for nine months for want of the four or five hundred dollars it will take to get his Green Card and working papers in order. Street Soccer USA will now pony up the dough to restore Diego to legal employability, oversee the procurement of those documents, and even advance him the money to rent an apartment where he will not have to claim his bed by 7:00 P.M. or lose it, or submit to surprise drug tests, or pass through a metal detector en route to his shared dorm room, or have as his neighbors the terminal alcoholics and hopelessly insane across the courtyard in the building for "noncompliant" cases. It is a wondrous time for Diego, and a nearly as thrilling time for me, because I have stumbled onto something singular and valuable, the chance to chronicle a species of moment rampantly counterfeited but rarely witnessed in the annals of human-interest reportage, a genuine Life-Altering Correction of Wracking Misfortune.

I am so certain that in Diego's story I've pried up the first rich nuggets of a narrative mother lode, I go to lunch with a literary agent and tell her the events of the weekend, the van, and the exciting business with the blood and the moving *peripeteia* of Diego Viveros. She shares my feeling that this is indeed a golden story, one that ramifies in all sorts of matterful ways: the collapse of the American economy, the immigration debate, the merit of entitlement programs, the mythos of competitive sports in American society, and so on. By the time the bill arrives, we have roused ourselves to the conviction that it's no mere magazine story I've stumbled onto but a cross-platform media gusher with at least two movie angles ("It's the *Bad News Bears* meets *Hoop Dreams!*") and a television angle ("It's like *Friday Night Lights!*") and a plump book contract to boot.

As I plot the payoff of my mortgage with the earnings from his story, I am also heartened that Diego has begun to regard me as both advocate and friend. Through the summer and fall of that year, hardly a week passes when he fails to telephone. Sometimes he calls because he's bored or lonely. Other times he calls in frantic need of help. When the shelter confiscates his possessions, preparatory to evicting him, he telephones me, and I telephone Lawrence Cann, and he telephones the shelter, and Diego is allowed to stay on Ward's Island. When he needs a four-day loan of 50 dollars, he telephones me, and I give him the 50 dollars, which he does not pay back in four days. When it is time to go to the Colombian Consulate to obtain a passport for the first time in 16 years, he calls me to accompany him.

When Diego is contacted by members of the media who find his story through the proud press release on the shelter's website, he calls me in a panic. Although he relishes the special dotings, the cash assistance for his important documents, and the image of himself as a kind of soccer star, the attention also makes him nervous, because he regards his homelessness as the most shameful of secrets, one unknown to his friends, his parents, his sisters, and something he can't discuss with reporters without wanting to throw up.

He agrees, however, to be the subject of a short profile for a television show called *SportsLife NYC*, which offers fitness tips and inspirational true tales that fulfill its slogan, "Sports and human interest stories coming together." I join him for the taping. Diego is still living on Ward's Island, though he has found work with a construction crew, and the shoot commences in front of a building on the Upper West Side where he has been spared an afternoon's toil uprooting a bathroom floor in order to appear on television. The camera rolls. The cable channel's producer, a woman with short bleached hair and a black tunic, asks Diego to state his name and his housing situation.

"My name is Diego Viveros, and I am homeless," he tells the camera, pursing his lips in an embouchure of discomfort.

Then the crew heads indoors to conduct an interview with Kevin Gleixner, Diego's boss, while Diego, in the background, quietly pretends to sweep construction flotsam from the parquet floor. The show's producer asks what it was about Diego that made Gleixner want to give him a job. Gleixner gives a confused sort of smile, because Diego, having been hired only a couple of weeks ago, is more or less a stranger to him, and Diego did not disclose his homelessness until this very afternoon.

"He was well groomed," he says at last.

"You're obviously a person who believes in giving people a chance," the producer observes.

"Absolutely," says Kevin Gleixner.

"I need you to say it," she instructs.

"I believe in giving other people chances," Kevin Gleixner says. "My favorite movie in the world is *Pay It Forward*." And then, apropos of second chances and redemption, Gleixner tells the camera that he is a recovering alcoholic who must remind himself daily to "keep smiling" and that nobody promised him a tomorrow.

"What do you think is going to happen to Diego down the road?" the producer asks.

"Good things," Kevin Gleixner says. "So far, he's done whatever I told him: 'This needs to be cleaned up in this area.' Or, 'This needs to be put somewhere,' or, 'Start stacking this here.'"

With Gleixner's interview wrapped, the crew gets a few shots of Diego savaging a linoleum floor with a pry bar, and the producer and I linger by the living-room window giving onto the sherbet-tinged bosk along the Hudson, whose waters double the extravagant blueness of the sky.

"Diego—what an incredible story," she says with a slow shake of her head.

"It sure is," I say.

"It's hard in everybody's life," she says.

"That's true."

To illustrate this truth, she leans toward me and says in a confidential tone, "My daughter just got off crystal meth."

And I say, "Mm, mm," which comes out less as a sympathetic murmur than as noises betokening erotic pleasure or the consumption of good food.

Nine weeks before Diego is to fly to Australia, nearly all the men of Team New York have been transferred from Ward's Island or have left of their own choosing. Leo Lopez is relocated to a Brooklyn shelter, Joey Martinez moves back in with his estranged girlfriend, and, according to rumor, Danny Boansi is sent to a treatment program after his urine tests positive for marijuana. Only Diego and the Reverend Jason Moore remain. Although HELP-SEC typically ousts even employed tenants after a season or so, Jason has managed to dodge eviction for almost a full year, which he takes as proud proof of his cunning. "I have not shown them one pay stub," he tells me. "No job applications, no nothing"—a dereliction of HELP-SEC's tenant covenant for which he has not been made to suffer because, he believes, of his status as a man of the cloth. "Being a reverend, you kind of learn to be pimpalicious. The way you talk, the way you relate, and you *pimp* them into doing what you want them to do."

Jason has to himself a cinder-block room containing a bed, a tin armoire, a grade school chair-and-writing-palette rig, and a hard-used copy of a book called *The Daily Drucker: 366 Days of Insight and Motivation for Getting the Right Things Done,* by the late management guru Peter Drucker. "I'm getting very deep into Peter Drucker," Jason explains.

I am curious to know what "right things" Drucker is inspiring Jason to get done, and where departing Ward's Island figures in his aims. Perched on the edge of his waferlike mattress, he tells me many things: that he has been corresponding regularly with fund managers via the free computers at the public library and plans to enter the market soon, that he is planning to launch a men's clothing line, and that he not only intends to leave the shelter but is in negotiations to close on a home of his own, six weeks or so from now.

"Where?" I picture an efficiency apartment bought with inheritance hoardings in an unimproved neighborhood in Jason's native Baltimore.

"Trump Tower," he replies. "Eighteen million dollars. Four thousand four hundred square feet, four bedrooms, six bathrooms. There's a bathroom in each room, and the master bedroom has two bathrooms. I'll convert one bedroom into a library, and it's on the 43rd floor, unit 43C. I'm gonna say, just for the sake of being safe, by the end of next month."

Jason says he has spoken to the broker, whom he mentions by name.

"Really? You're going to have 18 million dollars by the end of the next month?"

A sly, luminous smile brightens Jason's face. "It's not as big as it sounds."

Jason's zeal for Drucker's teachings has inspired him to join the Drucker Society of New York City, a group that includes an assistant professor of sports management at NYU, a young woman who works for a hedge fund, and a European whose expertise is improv comedy. For want of a proper headquarters, they meet every other Tuesday at a restaurant or coffee shop in Manhattan, to ponder strategies for bringing the great man's wisdoms to bear on the social problems of the day.

But companionable evenings with the Drucker Society are a rare distraction in the life of Jason Moore. During his days, when he is supposed to be out applying for jobs, he goes instead to the Park Avenue United Methodist Church on East 86th Street, where he tries to make sense of the troubling elements of his own history. He worries over the failed marriage of his parents, who met at Philadelphia Biblical University and who divorced when Jason was six, when it came to light that Jason's father was bisexual and had been conducting affairs with men and had contracted HIV. He worries over his mother, over the early years after the divorce when, lacking money for an apartment, she and Jason lived much of the time in homeless shelters in Mid-Atlantic states. He worries over his father's long and gruesome death, which took the last of the family's money. He worries over his grandmother, a woman he loved and who, in 2001, was choked and then stabbed to death by Vernon Beander—her grandson, Jason's cousin—who, along with several others in the years of Jason's raising, inflicted upon Jason cruelties and savagenesses that we will not discuss here. But let us say that if you yourself had suffered the sorts of things that Jason Moore ponders in the noonday silence of the Park Avenue UMC, you might also be somebody who finds analgesic power in the words of the Bible and Peter Drucker, and who exchanges fanciful emails with stock and real estate brokers, if it affords you, even for an hour, the relief of being someone else.

I receive a succession of urgent messages from Diego, asking in a dire tone for me to call him back. Is some misfortune afoot? No. Diego is simply keen to know if I have a digital camera he can borrow. Next week the team will gather to train in Los Angeles before shipping out to Melbourne, and Diego wants to memorialize the trip in photographs.

"Where's the camera?" is not the first thing out of Diego's mouth when I meet him in California; it is perhaps the third or fourth. And so I tender the camera, along with a craven, murmured speech about how it is my only camera but that we can share it, sure, no sweat. Diego does not appear to be listening; rather, he is absorbed by the camera itself. He tests its heft, twists the focus ring, and then drapes the strap around his neck, where the camera will hang like a talisman for many days to come.

We are sleeping, team and entourage, on a floor and on cots in a Brentwood home belonging to a friend of Lawrence Cann's, where a farting, chaffing camaraderie quickly takes hold among the members of the team. But Diego shows little interest in getting acquainted. He does not take pictures of his teammates, but photographs instead Brentwood's sumptuous homes on walks he takes in solitude. He refers to Team USA as "those people," as in, "I can't sleep with those people; it fucking stinks in there, bro," which is what he announces when he withdraws his bedding from the group dorm in the living room, preferring to camp alone out in the hall.

Diego Viveros, whose light shone so brightly among his New York fellows, looks frail of foot alongside the stronger talents on the national squad. In the first practice match—against a pubescent hockey team at an Orange County rec center—he claims an injury to his toe and broaches the topic of plane fare back to New York. Yet he returns for the second scrimmage, only to quarrel with the coaches and belabor his teammates with unwelcome commands.

The hostility between Diego and the team is increasingly mutual. "I'm starting to suspect that Diego might be kind of an asshole," Tad Christie remarks. "I mean, he can't play soccer worth a shit. All he wants to do is walk around with that camera and tell people what to do like he's some kind of superstar. At least I know *I* suck."

Relations are likewise cooling between Diego and myself. Ours is now a camera friendship, with little friendship to it at that. Every evening the camera is returned to me, and every morning I am visited by Diego, who sometimes says, simply, "Camera." I check the memory card periodically and am surprised to see how few photographs Diego takes each day. My camera's chief function to Diego, it seems, is as an emblem of his distinction from the others, as if he has come to California as a tourist, not as a member of a team of homeless athletes.

It's troubling, Diego's reversal, and maybe it could have been foreseen, if not for my obtuseness and, perhaps, bigotry. After all, it was Diego's hauteur, his handsome face and good clothes, his very difference from the homeless folk around him, his similarity to people like myself, that inspired me to push his nomination on Lawrence Cann. Little wonder, then, that finding himself publicly tethered to a team through the bonds of poverty, misfortune, and error should fill him with abhorrence.

Nevertheless, I begin to withhold the camera spitefully. I run the battery down by snapping flash photos of my hand. I vanish with it at the "magic hour." On Thanksgiving morning, the day of our departure for Melbourne, I go into hiding in a coffee shop while angry messages from Diego accumulate on my cell phone.

When I see him later in the day, he is in a fury and demands to know where I got off to with the Canon. "You promised me you would bring a camera for me, and now you're going back on it."

He puts his face very close to mine. "You want to fight? We'll go right over there. We can fight." He points to a palm glade that, he says, might make a pleasant spot for him to punch my face.

Woozy trans-dateline arrival. Malarial with exhaustion and inadequately braced for the spectacle of Melbourne, a city in convulsive throes of architectural pizzazz, almost every building erumpent with giant plastic blisters, chain-mail mullions, or Mondrian facades. Diego: "This looks like Flushing."

Homeless World Cup proceedings begin in earnest the following afternoon, over at the University of Melbourne, where all the teams will be quartered for the week. The teams assemble in a quaddish area for the Cup's opening rites, and it's thrilling to stand amid the clamor of so many unguessable tongues, to see so many skin tones and skeletal habits and disparate facial structures in a single throng and pretty much everybody out of their minds with happiness— the women's team from Paraguay, chatting shyly among themselves and sporting at least four different styles of straw hats; the Afghans, tall and Harlequin-cover handsome, with gray eyes and dark hair, and not looking even faintly hardscrabble—indicating, one imagines, the rampancy of homelessness in Afghanistan, a place where it probably doesn't require drug addiction or mental illness or exceptional poverty to find yourself without a roof to sleep beneath; the stolid, unsmiling women of Kyrgyzstan; Team Australia ("The Street Socceroos"), one of whose number is running in circles and squawking like a crow; the frighteningly well-muscled Netherlanders; the frighteningly undersized Filipinos, Namibians, and Cambodians. Most of the African teams have shown up with drums and flawlessly rehearsed contrapuntal songs and synchronized dance steps. The Ghanaians are doing this dance where they turn in a slow circle, rising and dropping in a supercool, loose-limbed, jellied piston-boogie, like sand being shaken on the hide of a pulsing tambourine, all the while bellowing a catchy song from the deeps of their throats. Then Namibia, evenly coed, cranks up their song, a call-and-response number with the women going high in a pained and jubilant alto and the guys coming in on the low, harmonious moan, and the melodious riot of the whole mob pulsing in a mass anthem of beauty and force and sorrow.

Tad Christie, who on our first night in Melbourne caused something of a crisis by disappearing on a bender, only to be discovered asleep in a public toilet, has recovered his spirits and is moved by the ascendant mood. "I want to fly back with the World Cup trophy," he declares. "We're gonna get it too, because there is something about our team that no one can touch. There's an aura about it that is untouchable. It cannot be destroyed by anyone." Tad pauses. "Except by Diego."

Yet in the early days of tournament play, Team USA's aura is pretty well ravaged, first by the Irish (11–2), and then the Romanians (7–2). The USA lands its first victory against Cambodia, whose players look like third-graders and most of whom, the team liaison tells me, spent much of their lives in a garbage dump, surviving on 25 cents a day and huffing glue in their leisure hours. The USA win is a 6–5 squeaker that feels tantamount to defeat. "Six–five against those guys?" Jeremy Wisham, a bright and charming reconstructed gutter punk from Atlanta, says after the buzzer. "We got our asses beat. I was cheering for *them*. From the perspective of the universe, it would have been cooler if we'd lost."

In hopes of bettering the USA's 36th-place finish the previous year, in Copenhagen, the coaches have benched the team's weaker players. Strolling along a downtown sidewalk, Tad Christie reflects with equanimity on the strategy. "Tad Christie, on day three, remains remarkably upbeat despite no playing time whatsoever," he says, dictating my notepad jottings. "We must piss-test him immediately to see what's keeping his motor running."

During lulls between matches, the Cup's more ambitious athletes jog the banks of the Yarra River or train in dribbling scrums, but Tad, who entertains no visions of competitive glory, spends most of his idle hours with me, recounting his biography. He tells me of his origins, of his grandfather, who was an off-and-on rich man, a contractor who whizzed a lot of money away gambling and who was also kind of a prick. When Tad would go to visit him, he'd say, "You bring me a whore?" and Tad would sigh and say, "No, Paw, I didn't."

Tad's father was a truck driver. He was once a handsome man, a Golden Gloves boxer in Vietnam who used to have such thick hair in his underarms that when Tad was a child he thought it was seaweed growing there.

Tad's late mother was a biker chick who, along with some of Tad's aunts, maybe hung around with Charlie Manson and all that gang, and in fact there's a rumor that Manson is possibly Tad's real father. June 14, 1971, is when Tad Christie was born in South Oak Cliff, Texas. When Tad's father was off doing long hauls for Frozen Food Express, his mother would sometimes put Tad and his two older brothers in a playpen, and then she would climb out a rear window so the neighbors wouldn't see her get on the back of somebody's motorcycle to ride off to Louisiana or God-knows-where to party and have a good time.

When Tad was eight, he saw his mom after she had been gone a long time. In his memory, his mother was this beautiful, slender, model-looking lady, but when the car pulled up in the driveway an obese woman stepped out, and in a panic Tad turned to his brother and said, "Jim, that fat lady ate our mom!"

Tad was molested a lot when he was growing up. People were always coming and going at the house. He thinks the first time was when he was about two. The perpetrator might have been one of Tad's mother's boyfriends, or maybe one of her girlfriends, a really manly-looking one. Probably half a dozen people molested Tad Christie, but that stopped once he was old enough to swing a crowbar.

By the time he was 12, Tad Christie was allegedly committing felonies and misdemeanors: breaking and entering, grand theft auto, smashing stuff, stealing beer off the beer truck.

Burger King gave Tad a job when he was 12 or 13, and with money of his own he left home to go live under an overpass in Plano, I-35, or maybe I-75, over by Collin Creek Mall. There were no other kids down there, just Tad and two older guys, one named Mr. Vario. Up until that point, all Tad had done was weed and LSD and meth in his Coca-Cola. One night, Tad told Mr. Vario he wanted some heroin, so he turned his head while Mr. Vario administered a dose of black tar, which made Tad Christie feel perfect. That went on for a while, until one night the police showed up because Mr. Vario had overdosed and rolled down the embankment and died facedown in the creek.

Tad got sent to the West Texas Boys' Ranch, which was kind of like a boot camp but also a ranch where you had to work your ass off.

Rough-stock producers would bring in bucking bulls and have the boys buck them out so they could tell whether they had college stock or pro stock on their hands. Tad was good at riding bulls. He got to where he nearly had enough points to start riding in the Professional Rodeo Cowboys Association, and he might have had a career, except he got on this one bull named Airplane. Airplane hooked him in the mouth, and that's what knocked out most of his teeth, which people think he lost because of drugs.

After some time in Louisiana, Tad went to Colorado, where his mother had a job managing a run-down apartment complex, and he started cooking meth. What he would do, he would break open Vicks Inhalers, mix the cotton with muriatic acid in an empty Cuervo Gold bottle, shake it up until it got milky, pour it into Pyrex, and scrape off the white powder when it cooked down. Tad oversaw the theft of thousands of inhalers (hypothetically speaking, allegedly, by the way), and that is how Tad earned the nickname the "Benzedrex Bandit."

So Tad was cooking meth and, a little later, living in a shooting gallery, a trailer owned by a man named Uncle Jesse, who was fairly throwed off. The reason Tad was able to move into Uncle Jesse's trailer was that Tad could give him a bump when nobody else could. Uncle Jesse would be trying to find a vein, going, "Ah, motherfucker, I'm a dartboard. I'm a fucking pincushion." Fat guys would come to Tad to have him find a vein. And usually he found one, and that is how Tad earned the nickname "Dr. Tag-'Em Tad."

But then the Feds got in touch with Tad. They said they knew what he was doing. They had also pulled his rap sheet and read his psych evals and decided he was someone capable of turning his life around. They told him to leave Colorado and to stay gone for at least five years or he'd spend the next 50 behind bars. Tad's father Western Unioned him 50 bucks and told him a Denny's to go to in Colorado Springs. Five or six hours later, Tad's father showed up in his truck.

Back in Dallas, Tad met a girl. He got her pregnant and was kind of relieved that he had. This girl was a churchgoer, kind of snotty and judgmental, but he needed someone like that, you see, a parole-officer-type girl to give structure to his life. She was not bad-looking either, but a big girl nonetheless, with motherfucking facial hair. He married her at the age of 20.

Tad got clean and did the family thing for, like, 10 years. He was making good money as a pressure fitter and a material expediter at oil refineries. Do you know the big tanks you see in oil refineries? Tad put all the internal and external shit on them, and he earned enough to keep a nice home near Shreveport, Louisiana. Everybody would gather there for Thanksgiving and Christmas. He had three children with his wife, a boy and twin girls.

But then Tad got laid off. He had to take a job at a local grocery store, making $300 a week. In his new occupation, the opportunity showed itself for Tad to get back into the meth game. He could steal cough pills, pseudoephedrine, and sell them for $300 a case to a fellow he knew who would also kick him back some dope straight off the Pyrex, which he could take a gram of and turn into a fucking eight-ball, $350 street value. Before long, Tad was bringing home an extra grand a week.

But it got to where one night another employee, a crackhead, took notice. She said, "I know you got something going on, Mr. Tad, come on, hook me up." And Tad was like, "Look, you want a hundred dollars? Take this bag and set it out in the back alley on the cool." Well, that crackhead flat told on him, maybe to try to get promoted. Tad didn't mind getting fired, but he had taken some money too, and he wasn't interested in getting locked up. When his boss called a meeting, Tad said, preemptively, "Oh, I need to talk to you too. I got a drug problem. And I've been taking money."

His boss was a religious guy, and nice. He said, "How much have you taken?"

"About five hundred bucks."

He said, "Since you been honest with me, if you agree to pay back the five hundred bucks and you resign, I won't call the cops."

Actually, Tad had taken closer to $50,000, in money and pills, so he put his Johnny on that motherfucker *real* quick. The crackhead got fired for stealing money out of the Coke machine. She did some time. Thirty days or so.

Basically, that was the end of Tad's marriage. When the money ran out, so did his wife. She wiped out his bank account, took everything. Tad left, and around that time was when he started doing his suicide attempts. He would get in his truck and drive out to the country. He would pick a big thick tree—"There's my bitch!"—

and he would floor his fucking truck, and *wham!* He bashed out a few of his remaining teeth on the steering wheel, busted his nose, split his chin, wrapped barbwire up around the undercarriage, anything *but* kill himself.

One day he took a gun, a Lorcin .380, chambered a round, cocked it, put it to his head, and said, "Fuck you, motherfucker." He pulled the trigger, but the gun didn't go off. He took that bullet out, put another bullet in the chamber. But that one didn't go off either, and that second time, it was a wrap, and he quit doing the suicide attempts.

He fell in with his wife's ex-sister-in-law. She, too, was throwed off, serious bipolar, but his love for her made him feel like a superhero, capable of anything. The reality of it, though, is when you mix drugs and alcohol and mental illness you get what happened next, which was one day Tad and the ex-sister-in-law are riding down the road, and she slams on the brakes and goes, "Get the fuck out of my car." Not a word was said. The radio wasn't on or anything.

Tad said, "What's going on, baby?"

"I know what you were thinking. I heard you. Get the fuck out of my car." And she pulls out a steak knife she kept under the seat. So Tad got out and walked home in his flip-flops, ten or fifteen miles.

Tad moved into a trailer with an old welder buddy of his. The trailer was plagued by wasps, and Tad spent a run of days crying and smacking wasps with his bare hands. Then he checked into the Shreveport-Bossier Rescue Mission, but the problem there was they mixed recovery with God, so you had a lot of people getting jailhouse religion, which was all shit, a fucking lie.

Still, he saw a future there, and was glad to find work sorting clothes at a Salvation Army donation center, where a perk of the job was first pick of the garments that came down the line. One day, Tad found a throwback Dallas Cowboys jersey in the heap, a jersey so desirable that other shelter residents hated him for having it. His ex-wife even heard about that excellent jersey he'd found, which was how his children got exposed to a rumor that Tad had been stealing clothes from the homeless. So he quit the rescue mission. Just walked out and left that jersey there.

Then Tad moved in with his brother, but he had no job and no food and no cigarettes, and when he met a man who wanted to pay 20 dollars for Tad to drive him to the Red River party boats and bring his truck back, Tad agreed. But that old boy went and got drunk and hopped up on methadone, and when he got off the party boat he got it in his head that someone had stolen his truck. The truck's owner called the police, and Tad did ten months in the Caddo Parish lockup for unauthorized use of a vehicle, plus another four at a penal farm for a hot check his wife wrote back in '92.

Jail was not too bad for Tad. He made people laugh, and he was popular because of that. He got in only four fights in 14 months, and one of those was just some psych case whose door was popped open by mistake one morning and he came down to breakfast and for no reason hit Tad with a pillowcase full of AAA batteries.

When he had served his time, they released him. After a while he got back into the meth scene, cooking out in the country near Shreveport, sometimes going to Dallas twice a day to make runs. But later he caught a lift to Austin and got into case management, where if you want to hold a bed in the shelter you have to do 10 jobs a week. You set goals: get an ID, a birth certificate, write a résumé. It was at the Arch, a homeless shelter in Austin, that Tad found out about Street Soccer. He's gotten to go to Washington and now Australia, and it's given him an excuse not to fuck up. His case manager also got him the set of fake teeth and a studio apartment.

The limelight has been good for him. It's given him much confidence, and he can now handle himself in an interview without stammering. But is he maybe going to go out to Barton Springs one day and smoke the fuck out of some weed? Who's to say? But Street Soccer has Tad believing in himself, believing that anything is possible.

But what, I ask Tad Christie, does he imagine will become of him once the limelight goes away?

"I don't think it will go away" is his answer. "For me, I think it'll just get brighter."

As the week wears on, Diego's mood worsens. He shrieks at the coaches. He receives so many yellow cards as to rule out America's chances for the sportsmanship medal. He criticizes his teammates, though Diego is one of the only players who has yet to score a goal. On day five, he announces that he has quit the team.

Near the end of the tournament, he puts his arm around my

shoulders and says, "You've been very nice to me, and I appreciate it. But you better write good about me, or I will kick your mother-fucking ass."

Thanks to late-night beer jags among the U.S. athletes, coaching staff, and media complement the previous evening, the team is tardy in assembling for its final match of the tournament, versus Greece. Oscar Granberry — a willowy fellow from St. Louis who 30 seconds into our first conversation told me he was a member of the mile-high club — to the astonishment of all has been holed up in a luxury hotel with a newfound ladyfriend. He misses the final game entirely. After serial abasements to the coaching staff, Diego Viveros is permitted to rescind his resignation and join the team for the game.

He plays with desperate zeal, steaming hard for every loose ball, confounding his opponents with mad jammings and leggy flutterings. At last, in the second half, Diego traps the ball downfield, with an open channel to the goal. He takes a nervous, faltering shot, lofting the ball straight into the keeper's hands. Diego claps his hands to his head and lows with anguish. On the sidelines, his teammates guffaw uncharitably. Chris Murray, whose relationship with Diego has so deteriorated that they very nearly came to blows a few days back, emits a snort. "Good," he says.

But for all the rearguard glee at Diego's failure, it seems to me that his troubled stint with the team might have been a kind of victory. Thanks to cash outlays from Street Soccer USA, Diego's working papers are in order, and he's moved up from homelessness to his rented room in Washington Heights. He managed to nibble only the sweet side of the deal — the expenses-paid trip to Australia; the cossetings from Chris, Lawrence Cann, and me — while spitting out the bitter end, the proviso that he transform himself into the proud public symbol of something he despises. And his unsettling oscillations between friendliness and pugnacity would cure me of my mercenary plan to auction his story to Hollywood, even of the idea to try to recover his outstanding debt of 50 bucks.

Back on the pitch, thanks to a botched Greek penalty shot, Team USA secures 29th place with a 3–2 win. Medals are draped about the necks of both teams. Snapping shutters chirr beneath the din of the PA system, blaring strains of David Bowie: "We can be heroes, just for one day."

His special lady on his arm, Oscar Granberry arrives well after the final whistle and seems genuinely sorry to have overslept the game. "Man, I was *trying* to get my shit together," he laments. "I can't believe I fucked that up."

"Well, was it worth it?"

He cuts an amorous eye at his friend, a Spanish woman in her forties who looks uncannily like Benjamin Franklin. "*Hell* yes," he says in a low, sensual growl. (Three months hence, incidentally, Oscar will return to Melbourne to marry his Spanish friend. "Who says we don't change lives?" Lawrence Cann will say of the union.)

Strolling back along the Yarra, Tad Christie handles the trophy, a silver plate fixed with a plaque reading HOMELESS WORLD CUP 29TH PLACE. "It's not even etched on there—it's just mirrored plastic with this thing glued on it," Tad says, plucking at the plaque with his thumbnail. "What a cheap-ass fucking trophy. Well, it's all right. They spent a lot of cash on all this other shit." He makes a sweeping gesture, taking in media vans, the Ren-faire skyline of the deluxe players' pavilion, the crowd of hundreds filing in to watch the Cup final.

A brutal, predawn departure for the airport the following morning. The team and entourage, groggy and fragrant from post-tournament celebrations, settles like a heap of spaniels on the terminal's terrazzo floor, napping until boarding time. All except, of course, Diego, skulking at the duty-free. He hasn't uttered a syllable all morning, and I imagine he'll maintain his sour silence for the journey's 16-hour duration.

But shortly after takeoff, Diego's voice rises in the cabin: "We're gonna have a fucking problem!" He is yelling not at his teammates or acquaintances, for a change, but at a perfect stranger in the seat behind his. "I'm serious, you don't know me. We'll have a fucking problem here."

The trouble is that, during takeoff, Diego reclined his seat into the airspace of perhaps the only other passenger on the plane with as ready an appetite for asperity as Diego himself, and the man gave a quick hard fist-jab to Diego's headrest.

"He hit my fucking seat," exclaims Diego as the flight attendants swarm. "What, I'm not allowed to put my seat back?"

"Not during takeoff, you aren't," replies the antagonist, an Australian, early fifties, with head of wiry brindle hair, his upper lip hoisted in a ratlike expression of alert malignity.

Lawrence Cann, a man generally unruffled by roosterish theatrics, turns in his seat, his brow knitted with concern. "Uh-oh," he says. "This could get bad."

An electric silence falls over the cabin. Passengers crane necks and swivel eyes, eager for a glimpse of a thrown punch or the spectacle of an air-marshal rendition. But the flight attendants speak to Diego in cool and reasonable tones, behind which seems to lurk the threat of a tranq gun or chloroform rag. And Diego, sensing the grave unwisdom of initiating an in-flight brawl, sinks into his seat, scowling at the entertainment screen from the depths of his sweatshirt's hood.

Four hours later, descending to our layover in New Zealand, Diego, to the astonishment of his nearby coaches and teammates, turns in his seat and offers the hand of peace to the older man.

"Sir, I want to say I'm sorry," Diego says. "I was very rude to you. I apologize."

"No, no," the other man replies. "I am. Really."

As the plane taxis to the gate, the men trade companionable chitchat. So, what took Diego to Melbourne, asks the man with the rodent mouth.

"I am a professional soccer player. I was there for a tournament," Diego announces to the economy cabin. "We did very well. We came in third place."

"Did you like Melbourne, then?"

"I *loved* Melbourne," Diego says. "It was a great, great experience for me."

SALLY JENKINS

Culture of Silence Gives Free Rein to Male Athletes

FROM THE WASHINGTON POST

GEORGE HUGUELY IS SAID to have been a vicious drunk who menaced Yeardley Love, yet there has been no indication that any of his teammates said anything to police. Ben Roethlisberger seems to be a serial insulter of women, whose behavior is shielded by the off-duty cops he employs. And if the charges are true, Lawrence Taylor ignored the bruises on a 16-year-old girl's face as he had sex with her, never thinking to ask who beat her.

It's a bad stretch for women in the sports pages. After reading the news accounts and police reports, it's reasonable to ask: Should women fear athletes? Is there something in our sports culture that condones these assaults? It's a difficult, even upsetting question, because it risks demonizing scores of decent, guiltless men. But we've got to ask it, because something is going on here—there's a disturbing association, and surely we're just as obliged to address it as we are concussions.

"We can no longer dismiss these actions as representative of a few bad apples," says Jay Coakley, author of *Sport in Society: Issues and Controversies,* and a professor of sociology at the University of Colorado. "The evidence suggests that they are connected to particular group cultures that are in need of critical assessment."

What do we mean when we ask whether there was something in the lacrosse "culture" that led to the murder of Yeardley Love? The Latin root of the word *cultura* means "to grow." It means the attitudes, practices, and values that are implanted and nourished in a group or society.

There's a lot we still don't know about Huguely and his "brothers," but three attitudes and practices of at least some members of the Virginia lacrosse team seem obvious: physical swagger, heavy drinking, and fraternal silence.

In 2008, a drunken Huguely was so brutally combative with a female cop that she felt she had to Taser him. Last year, he assaulted a sleeping teammate who he believed had kissed Love, several former players say, and this year, he had other violent confrontations with Love herself, witnesses say.

We can argue about gaps in the system, but one constituency very likely knew about Huguely's behavior: his teammates and friends, the ones who watched him smash up windows and bottles and heard him rant about Love.

Why didn't they tackle him? Why didn't they turn him in?

Undoubtedly, many of the young men on the Virginia lacrosse team are fine human beings. I don't mean to question their decency. I don't mean to blame them.

But I do mean to ask those who knew of Huguely's behavior an important question. Why did they not treat Yeardley Love as their teammate too?

Where were *her* brothers?

Why was she not deserving of the same loyalty as George Huguely? She played lacrosse. She wore a Virginia uniform. She was equally a champion. And yet because she played on the women's team, she seems not to have been accorded the same protection that Huguely was.

That doesn't just break the heart. It shatters it into a thousand pieces.

The allegations against Huguely, Roethlisberger, and Taylor share something in common. In all of these cases, the alleged female victims were treated as undeserving of inclusion in the protected circle. They were "others" rather than insiders.

Sports Illustrated's profile of Roethlisberger and the men who look after him is utterly damning. According to the magazine story, on the night that he allegedly accosted an overserved undergrad in a Milledgeville, Georgia, restroom, Roethlisberger held up a tray of tequila shots and hollered, "All my bitches, take some shots!" He exposed himself at the bar. He forced his hand up someone's skirt. Yet police sergeant Jerry Blash described the alleged victim as "this drunken bitch," and Roethlisberger's bodyguards apparently blocked off the area. Protecting Roethlisberger, being "in" with him, took precedence over ethics.

"Who needs the bodyguard here?" Coakley asks incredulously. "What is the role of bodyguard? It's not to maintain male hegemony and privilege. It's to maintain order."

The charge of third-degree rape against Taylor prompts another question. Police allege that a 16-year-old runaway was beaten by a sex trafficker and brought to Taylor's hotel room, where, according to the police report, instead of protecting her, he allegedly protected himself with a condom. If Taylor is guilty, how could he have acted in such a depersonalizing way—unless he viewed her as more object than person?

According to Coakley, the data is clear: certain types of all-male groups generally have higher rates of assault against women than the average, and their profile is unmistakable. They tend to include sports teams, fraternities, and military units, and they stress the physical subordination of others—and exclusiveness.

Common sense tells me that "sport" in general is not the culprit in all of this so much as excessive celebration and rewarding of it: binge drinking, women-as-trophies, the hubris resulting from exaggerated entitlement and years of being let off the hook. We are hatching physically gifted young men in incubators of besotted excess and a vocabulary of "bitches and hos."

What has happened to kindness, to the cordial pleasures of friendship between men and women in the sports world? Above all, what has happened to sexuality? When did the most sublime human exchange become more about power and status than romance? When did it become so pornographic and transactional, so implacably cold?

The truth is, women can't do anything about this problem. Men are the only ones who can change it—by taking responsibility for their locker room culture, and the behavior and language of their teammates. Nothing will change until the biggest stars in the clubhouse are mortally offended, until their grief and remorse over an assault trumps their solidarity.

SELENA ROBERTS

High School Dissonance

FROM SPORTS ILLUSTRATED

THE FIRST LINK you see on the Silsbee (Texas) High School web page, right under a photo of its main building with a proud *S* on the facade and a sign that proclaims TIGER COUNTRY, sends you to the Spectator Rules of Conduct, which prohibit insults, ridicule, and chants that taunt. It's an antibullying code for athletic events. But does it protect anyone from offensive behavior off the gym floor—in, say, the foyer next to a concession stand? And what if the "mean girls" are school administrators?

On February 27, 2009, in a *Glee* moment with a few real-life Sue Sylvesters, a Tigers cheerleader—one of the popular people— found herself surrounded at halftime of a basketball playoff game. "It was the administrators against me," she recalls. As fans walked by, the cheerleader, dressed in her maroon-and-white uniform, was reduced to tears by a powerful posse: Silsbee superintendent Richard Bain, principal Gaye Lokey, and cheerleading coach Sissy McInnis. Voices raised, they issued an ultimatum to the 16-year-old: cheer for Rakheem Bolton or go home. "It wasn't right," she says.

Four months earlier the cheerleader, known in court documents as H.S., had told police that at a house party where beer flowed to minors, she had been cornered in a room by three young men —Bolton, 17; another athlete, Christian Rountree, 18; and a 16-year-old unidentified in legal records—who locked the door and sexually assaulted her. Her screams were heard; the police were called; charges were filed. In a town whose population is 7,341 and whose high school football stadium seats 7,000, the tale of that October night spread from Avenue B to Avenue R along the main drag of Silsbee. The alleged assault prompted two questions: How would it affect the girl? And how would it affect the team? H.S. saw a therapist, who urged her to resume her routine to help deal with the trauma. The alleged assailants were barred from campus, and she chose to cheer again. Then, in January 2009, a Hardin County grand jury decided there was not enough evidence to pursue charges.

Bolton, a football and basketball star, was back on the court by February, but the wheels of justice would continue to turn. In November 2009 another grand jury, convened because of renewed interest in the case, would indict Bolton and Rountree on charges of sexual assault of a minor. (Bolton would plead guilty to a lesser offense, simple assault, in September; Rountree is awaiting his arraignment.) But in the meantime Silsbee officials had to heed the decision of the first grand jury. Bolton could play. While school officials did not return *SI*'s calls, Tanner Hunt Jr., the attorney for the district, notes, "They followed the law." Fair enough. But the law wasn't in question during the basketball game that winter night. It was kindness and common sense that were on the line.

By custom Tigers cheerleaders support any player at the foul line by shouting his name. In the first half Bolton was fouled twice. H.S. had been cheering as usual, but each time Bolton went to the line, in a peaceful protest, she folded her arms, stepped back, and remained silent while her squad cheered, "Go, Rakheem!" After the halftime buzzer, H.S. was scolded "in front of God and everybody," says her father. H.S. had not "abided by the Cheerleader Constitution," according to Hunt. The code requires cheerleaders to shout equally for all. Rather than cheer for Bolton, she chose to go home.

The violation was apparently so egregious that as H.S. walked into cheerleading class the following Monday, McInnis met her with this hello: go to the principal's office. H.S. was kicked off the squad. Within an hour her father was in Bain's office. "I asked him, 'Are you telling me that my daughter had to cheer for her [attacker]?'" recalls the father. "He told me that if it means she had to cheer for Bolton or be removed, then that's what I'm telling you."

Though H.S. was later permitted to rejoin the cheerleading squad if she would follow its rules, the family filed a civil suit against the school district, and on September 16 the Fifth U.S. Circuit

Court of Appeals ruled that H.S.'s silent protest was not protected speech under the First Amendment. However, the court wrangling distracts from the bottom line: a school is supposed to be an emotional safe haven for all students, and educators should help, not harass, students in vulnerable positions. Why force H.S. to do something that made her uncomfortable? Why not err on the side of compassion? "For all anyone knew," Hunt says of the protest, "it was a girl mad at a boy." By this rationale a rape charge is no different from a text-message breakup.

"They chose to support the athlete," says Larry Watts, H.S.'s attorney, who last week asked the court to rehear the constitutional case. "They chose to support the male. It's just good ol' testosteronic East Texas."

The students involved in the controversy are gone now. H.S. graduated and has college plans. She vows to keep pressing ahead legally to "make it easier for other girls if they have to go through this." Bolton is on probation and entering an anger management program as part of his plea deal. He is also trying to enroll in college. However, lessons remain to be learned—by the educators. "If there was something to apologize for, we would," Hunt says. This is not *Glee*. This is sad.

STERRY BUTCHER

Gentling Cheatgrass

FROM TEXAS MONTHLY

THE MUSTANG HAS EYES that are large and dark and betray his mood. His coat is bright bay, which is to say he's a rich red, with black running down his knees and hocks. He has a white star the size of a silver dollar on his forehead and a freeze mark on his neck. He cranks his head high as a rider approaches, shaking out a rope from a large gray gelding. The mustang does not know what is to come. His name is Cheatgrass, and he's six years old. In May he was as wild as a songbird.

The little horse belongs to Teryn Lee Muench, a 27-year-old son of the Big Bend who grew up in Brewster and Presidio Counties. Teryn Lee is tall, blue-eyed, and long-limbed. He wears his shirts buttoned all the way to the neck and custom spurs that bear his name. He never rolls up his sleeves. A turkey feather is jammed in his hatband, and he's prone to saying things like "I was out yesterday and it came a downpour," or, speaking of a hardheaded horse, "He's a sorry, counterfeit son of a gun." Horse training is the only job he has ever had.

Teryn Lee was among 130 people who signed up this spring for the Supreme Extreme Mustang Makeover, a contest in which trainers are given 100 days to take feral horses from the Bureau of Land Management (BLM), gentle these creatures, and teach them to accept grooming, leading, saddling, and riding. Don't let the silliness of the contest's name distract from the difficulty of the challenge. Domestic horses can be taught to walk, trot, and lope under saddle in 100 days; it's called being green-broke. But domestic horses are usually familiar with people. The mustangs in the Makeover have lived on the range for years without human interaction, surviving drought, brutal winters, and trolling mountain lions. The only connection they have to people is fear. Age presents another challenge. A domestic horse is broke to saddle at about age two, when it's a gawky teenager. The contest mustangs are opinionated and mature. The culmination of the contest is a two-day event in Fort Worth in August, where the horses are judged on their level of training and responsiveness. The top 20 teams make the finals. The winner takes home $50,000.

For Teryn Lee, however, there's more at stake than money. Most of his clients bring him horses that buck or bully, horses that have developed bad habits that stymie or even frighten their owners. Teryn Lee enjoys this work, but his goal is to become a well-known trainer and clinician who rides in top reined cow horse and cutting horse competitions. To step up to that level, he'll have to do something dramatic. Transforming a scruffy, feral mustang that no one wanted into a handsome, gentle, willing riding horse would make people take notice. Winning would get his name out there, he says.

How does that work, gentling a wild thing? How do you convince a nomad that a different life is possible? Teryn Lee picked up Cheatgrass on May 8 from a BLM facility in Oklahoma and hauled him to his training operation near Marfa, a 50,000-acre ranch leased by his father and managed by Teryn Lee and his wife, Holly. Two days later, standing in a round pen, Cheatgrass looks runty and ribby, like a cayuse from a Frederic Remington painting, still wearing the BLM halter.

Teryn Lee rides a gelding called Big Gray. The mustang eyes them. Horses are prey animals that are vulnerable by themselves; as social beings, they seek out friendship. They feel safe with another horse, even if it's a stranger. Cheatgrass allows Big Gray to step close. Teryn Lee leans down from his saddle and drops the halter off the mustang's head.

"There," he says. "Now he's a wild mustang."

Teryn Lee begins swinging a rope behind the mustang, who zips frantically around the perimeter of the round pen at a dead run, mane streaming. As Cheatgrass flies past, Teryn Lee occasionally flicks the tail of the rope into the horse's path to make the mustang change direction. Cheatgrass nimbly tucks his knees and wheels away, deft as a cat, fleet as a thought.

"I want him to move around," Teryn Lee explains. "Breaking a horse is all about controlling his feet. If I can control his feet, I've got him. Later I'll try to touch him all over, but we'll see. You can't hurry a horse."

Cheatgrass's adrenaline slows down a tick as he considers his options. Thousands of generations of flight instinct course through a mustang, but he is also a survivor who comes loaded with a keen ability to adapt. Running away isn't working, so Cheatgrass slows to a fast trot. He is small but spring-loaded, muscles bunching and jumping under his coat. His inside ear and white-ringed eye never leave the man deciding where he can go and how fast. With a swing or two of the rope over his head, Teryn Lee sends a loop and catches the horse around the neck. As the loop tightens, the mustang roars and rears, his hooves momentarily striking the sky. He faces Teryn Lee, sides heaving and nostrils flaring. They stare at each other. There is the sound of the horse's breathing and the wind sliding by. Moments pass. Teryn Lee asks the gray gelding to step forward, his hand moving up the rope until the two horses are neck to neck. The loop loosens. Neither slow nor fast, Teryn Lee's hand reaches forward and lightly rubs the star on Cheatgrass's forehead. The first touch. The mustang is canted backward, every muscle straining, but he stands. His world has just changed.

The ranch where Cheatgrass lived this summer is high and remote, an hour from Marfa and deep within Presidio County. Great treeless hills roll and fold to the mountains on the horizon: Chinati Peak, humped and blue, not far from the ranch house; Mount Livermore and the Davis Mountains in the north; Haystack, Paisano Peak, Twin Sisters, Goat Mountain, Santiago to the east. Summer monsoons carpet the desert with grama. From most points on the ranch, no homes or roads are visible. No power lines, no vehicles, no buildings for mile upon mile — just grass, rocks, and the impassive, tenantless sky. On a high hill, with the chorus of mountains and wind all around, it's possible to imagine these unsettled plains as they were 200 or 400 or even 1,000 years ago: open, ancient, and achingly beautiful.

Bountiful land like this nurtured the mustang. Horses were native to North America until about 11,000 years ago, when evidence of them tapers out. They didn't return to the main continent until 1519, when Hernán Cortés famously flummoxed the Aztecs with

16 horses that landed with his men on the Mexican coast. More
Spanish explorers, missionaries, soldiers, and settlers came, and
they all brought horses. Animals that escaped or were loosed onto
the prairies multiplied and changed the lives of Plains Indians,
whose culture would become as fully integrated with horses as it
was with bison. During World War I, ranchers responded to war-
time's increased need for horses by turning their well-bred stallions
onto the range to better the native herds, which were later gathered and exported to the European front. It's from this array of
purebreds and mongrels that mustangs are descended.

   J. Frank Dobie wrote the history of America's wild horses in his
1952 book, *The Mustangs.* Wild horses tramped across the plains
and the western United States, but Texas was their true home. "My
own guess is that at no time were there more than a million mustangs in Texas and no more than a million others scattered over
the remainder of the West," he wrote. The mustang's history and
our own are inextricable. Mustangs galloped in Comanche raids
on the Llano Estacado, pushed Longhorns across the Canadian,
busted sod at immigrant farms in central Texas, bore Texans into
war. Their glory stirred souls.

   Among those who chronicled the mustang in Texas was Ulysses
S. Grant, who in 1846 served as a lieutenant under Zachary Taylor
in the U.S.-Mexican War. Grant rode a $5 mustang. He was a few
days outside Corpus Christi when word came of an immense group
of mustangs near the head of the column. "As far as the eye could
reach to our right, the herd extended," he wrote in his memoirs.
"To the left, it extended equally. There was no estimating the number of animals in it; I have no idea that they could all have been
corralled in the state of Rhode Island, or Delaware, at one time."

   No one seems to have recorded when the last wild horse in Texas
was roped and put to work. It might have been a horseman named
Ben Green, who trailed a wild band from Big Bend into northern
Mexico and Arizona during the Depression. Dobie closes his book
by musing that the mustang's days were over.

Well, the wild ones — the coyote duns, the smokies, the blues, the blue
roans, the snip-nosed pintos, the flea-bitten grays and the black-skinned
whites, the shining blacks and the rusty browns, the red roans, the
toasted sorrels and the stockinged bays, the splotched appaloosas and
the cream-maned palominos and all the others in shadings of color as

various as the hues that show and fade on the clouds at sunset—they
are all gone now, gone as completely as the free grass they vivified. Only
through "visionary gleam" can any man ever again run with them, for
only in the symbolism of poetry does ghost draw lover in hope-continued
pursuit.

The book is a wonderful balance of scholarly research and folk-
lore, but on the utter demise of the mustang, Dobie was mistaken.
A federal law passed in 1971 protects feral horses on public lands.
Today the BLM oversees nearly 34,000 wild horses and several
thousand burros that graze across 26.6 million acres in ten western
states. For most of his life, Cheatgrass was one of them.

Have you studied a person who can do something well? Have you
seen how effortless the work appears? Teryn Lee has that with
horses. He never hurries. He never seems indecisive. He never becomes angry or worried that he's messed up. One action to the
next flows like water.

"A horse has all the qualities I'd like to possess as a human," he
said more than once this summer. "They're curious, not corrupted.
They only know what they're taught. They're a mirror of the person riding them." That's not necessarily how horse gentling has always gone. There's a reason it's called "breaking." Dobie wrote that
"one out of every three mustangs captured in southwest Texas was
expected to die before they were tamed. The process of breaking
often broke the spirits of the other two."

Teryn Lee doesn't follow those old, brutal ways. "Every time
Cheatgrass has seen men, he's been poked with a needle, been
freeze-branded, or been castrated," he said. "If I were him, I don't
think I'd like people very much. Horses are the most forgiving animal there is."

On day two, not long after the sun has crested Goat Mountain,
Teryn Lee walks into the pen, catches Cheatgrass by the lead rope,
and rubs him steadily all over with one hand.

"Here's where he'll get mad," he says, and his hand makes its way
along the horse's belly. Cheatgrass bugs his eyes and begins to
quiver. His ears swivel furiously, and Teryn Lee gives him a moment. Every time the horse does what he asks—or tries to—he
gives the horse a release, whether it's a momentary rest, a stroke,
or allowing it to slow. Once Teryn Lee starts an action, he carries it

through very deliberately. He lets Cheatgrass sniff the saddle pad and smoothly drapes it onto his back. He rests the saddle on his hip and allows the horse to go over it with his nose, then carefully sets it on the mustang. The horse's head is jacked up and his nostrils flutter. Slowly, the cinches are tightened. Teryn Lee slips off the halter and backs away.

Cheatgrass is frozen for two beats and then, *bam,* he jams his head to the earth and his shoulders to the clouds in a series of see-saw bucks. Time slows into freeze-frames: the C-shaped horse suspended in air, the hip-high dust, the rigid-legged horse pounding the ground. Just as suddenly as he starts, Cheatgrass stops and looks at Teryn Lee, his ears tipped forward.

"That wasn't too bad!" Teryn Lee exclaims.

"We've had domestic colts that buck for much longer," Holly says.

Teryn Lee leaves the horse to get used to the saddle and returns in an hour, pointing to the dust in the pen.

"You can see where he got down and rolled on the saddle a few times," he says. "Horses can move left, right, forward, backward, up, and down. I'd like to get him comfortable moving in all those directions. He went up and down. Now I'll have him go forward and backward."

Teryn Lee uses his body and the flicking of a rope to move Cheatgrass around the pen: more pressure and a kissing sound from Teryn Lee means lope; stepping into his path makes the mustang change direction; turning away from the horse makes him slow or stop.

"A large part of training is feel," Teryn Lee says. "I can feel what they'll do before they do it. If you can't feel it, you can't fix it. You have to move with a purpose but be sensitive about it."

Within a few minutes, he's at the mustang's side. He puts a foot in the stirrup and bounces a couple of times before standing up in the stirrup for a second or two. There's no preamble to this—he just does it, on both sides. The horse's mouth is clamped in a prim line.

"He's pretty tight, but he's taking it real good," says Teryn Lee. "Confidence is a big thing. If he's confident, everything else will take care of itself."

*

Wild mustangs forage on land that is populated by antelope, deer, and elk and share food and water sources with domestic cattle owned by ranchers with grazing leases on public land. Nowadays they live mostly in Nevada. According to the BLM, mustangs can double in population every four years, and when there are too many horses for the available acreage, the herds must be periodically thinned.

"The land can only support what it will support," said Sally Spencer, the head of marketing for the BLM. "The land needs to stay healthy, and the animals need to stay healthy. We want to make sure the mustangs are there for all Americans to see forever and ever."

From BLM holding facilities, captured mustangs are carted across the country to different public adoption events. Horses in unusual colors—pintos, buckskins, palominos—are likelier to get adopted than a plain bay or brown horse. Older horses aren't typically adopted either. Those that are deemed unadoptable are shipped for long-term holding to private ranches primarily in the Midwest, which contract with the BLM to maintain the horses for the rest of their lives.

But the BLM has received biting criticism for its gathering practices, which sometimes result in injury or death to mustangs as they're rounded up. Mustang advocates argue that the horses are pushed off the range in favor of cattle that ranchers run on land leased from the government. Advocates also say there are too many horses in holding facilities. Cheatgrass, for instance, lived 15 months at a Colorado short-term holding facility before being picked for the Makeover.

And none of this is cheap. The wild horse and burro program cost $63.9 million to run in 2010, 57 percent of which went to keeping horses in holding facilities. Adoption rates have fallen in recent years. "The program we have is not sustainable," Spencer said. "We need to figure out another way the horses can be managed on the range."

Madeleine Pickens, the wife of oil billionaire T. Boone Pickens, is among the people working on solutions. "The horses that are in short-term holding cost the taxpayer $2,500 per year, which is very costly," she said. "The conditions are pretty severe, when you consider they're animals that roamed freely and they're suddenly put in a temporary corral. They're only supposed to be there three months, and some are there for three years."

Pickens is passionate about mustangs. She's been in talks with the BLM since 2008 on her proposal to place as many as 30,000 mustangs on more than 600,000 acres of public and private lands in northeast Nevada. In the plan, her foundation, Saving America's Mustangs, would oversee the ranch and develop it into an ecotourism facility. In return, the foundation would receive $500 per year per horse, which is about the same rate contractors receive for horses that live in long-term holding ranches on private property. According to Pickens, the deal would offer transparency that the privately run holding sites do not.

"The government has a fiscal and moral responsibility, since they've moved horses off of public lands," she said. "Let's fence it in, have a nonreproductive herd, and let the public come and enjoy it."

Pickens sees the mustang ranch as nothing less than preserving an emblem of America.

"One hundred years ago there were two million horses on the range," she said. "If we're down to the last thirty thousand or so, as the BLM says, we're getting closer to extinction, and that's when people start to pay attention."

That's where events like the Supreme Extreme Mustang Makeover come in. "The research shows that if a mustang is gentled, the odds of it getting adopted jump," said Patti Colbert, the executive director of the Mustang Heritage Foundation, which puts on the Makeover. "I figured we could take talented people and turn wild horses into something that was viable as a riding or working partner. It's a piece of Americana that you're taking into your home."

The Makeover grew from a single event in Fort Worth in 2007 to eight contests held all over the country this year. The previous contests offered prizes, but mostly the winners got bragging rights. Teryn Lee earned third at last year's Makeover in Fort Worth and walked away with two grand. Fifty thousand dollars, though, is a different story.

"I say not to think about the money," Holly told Teryn Lee one day in the first week of training. Holly has round blue eyes, yellow braids, and an Oklahoman's practicality. She's an ace cutting horse rider, but she leaves the training to Teryn Lee. At any given time, he has 20 horses in training, and he rides each of them every day.

While he's riding, Holly bustles around the pens, feeding, filling water troughs, saddling her husband's next mount, and bathing the one he's just finished with.

"Nothing would be different if we won," Teryn Lee said. "We'd just have more operating capital."

"Still," she said, "you shouldn't count on things before they happen."

On the third day of training, Cheatgrass is saddled and tense, pawing in frustration. The action of his circling foot is too fast for the eye to follow. He rumbles a snort.

"The third day is the worst day," Teryn Lee says cheerfully. "They're sore and tired of being messed with, but I think I can talk him out of bucking."

He introduces the bridle, and there are several long minutes while he holds the bit to Cheatgrass's mouth until the horse takes it. After a one-two-three bounce from the stirrup, he swings a leg half over Cheatgrass and then steps off. He does it again, but this time he settles in the saddle.

Cheatgrass pauses, trembles, and jettisons into bucks that roll like a current in a river. Teryn Lee sits still and yielding at the same time, his hands well in front of him and the reins not tight. The bucks decelerate into a ragged lope. At Teryn Lee's instruction, Holly waggles a plastic flag to keep Cheatgrass going forward, because a horse moving forward is less likely to also go up. They trot and lope until Teryn Lee allows him to walk and uses the reins to gently guide Cheatgrass a few steps to the right and left. He gets off. Cheatgrass sighs.

"He got scared when I swung my leg around, but he wasn't scared at the end and that's what's important," says Teryn Lee. "That wasn't too bad. Tomorrow we'll ride outside."

The next morning Teryn Lee hops twice in the stirrup before landing lightly on the mustang's back. Holly waits on Big Gray as the gate swings open. Cheatgrass follows the gray at a lope down a ranch road and up a draw. Ten minutes later, they appear on a hilltop, picking their way through the rocks at a walk. Cheatgrass jigs and his tail flags behind him.

"Today he understands what is going to happen to him," Teryn Lee says. "It's fine for him to accept that he's going to be doing this for the rest of his life."

Cheatgrass was ridden nearly every day during the summer. By day 10, he moved free and soft, with simple changes in direction. By day 20, he was loping long, straight paths across pastures. He was bathed, brushed, and shod. He was taught to back, circle, and stop. He sidestepped and snorted during bridling and saddling, but after he was ridden and turned loose, he'd follow Holly around and sidle up for a pat. He grew accustomed to ropes and squealed with excitement at the sight of cattle.

"For a six-year-old with less than forty-five days on him, he gets working cattle," Teryn Lee said. "I didn't think he'd enjoy it, but he enjoys the heck out of it." In June and July, when Teryn Lee was hired to work on other ranches, he used Cheatgrass. They negotiated rocky hillsides, stepped through thorny brush, and forded water. Cheatgrass loaded into trailers and stood tied in the warm-up arena while Teryn Lee and Holly competed at shows on other horses. Word got around that Teryn Lee had entered the Makeover. Railbirds watched him trot the mustang around the fairgrounds after a show in Las Cruces, New Mexico. Cheatgrass had been in training about 80 days.

"What will he do?" one of them called out.

"He'll tie and work off a rope," Teryn Lee replied.

"Was he ever handled?" another asked.

"Nope."

"How'd you get into that deal?"

"You've got to be willing to ride a wild mustang," Teryn Lee said.

Kevin Hanratty, a working cow horse competitor from Lincoln, New Mexico, stood off to one side and watched too. Little Cheatgrass, with the BLM freeze mark on his neck, looked out of place next to the bulldoggy quarter horses around him. Despite the clanking, hollering clamor of the showgrounds, the mustang blinked happily as Teryn Lee chatted. Hanratty, with his jeans tucked into his stovepipe boots, was riveted. "That horse, his blood goes back to the old Spanish vaqueros," he said. "Right there is the little bit of us that's still wild, a remnant of the Old West. There's not much of it left, but it's still alive with Teryn Lee and that horse."

Three weeks later the warm-up ring at the Will Rogers Memorial Center, in Fort Worth, swarmed with shiny-hided mustangs: red, yellow, brown, black, and gray. The challenge of training them had taken a toll. Of the 130 trainers who had signed up for the Makeover, only 83 had made it to the contest. Trainers came from 23 states. One of the top contenders was Mark Lyon, a Nebraska trainer who won the contest in 2008. He wore his red mustache waxed, like a friendly Snidely Whiplash, and a flat-crowned black hat. "They were once wild, and they've decided to become willing partners," he said. "They're the forgotten horse."

Many of the animals showed little evidence of their wild days. Day campers visiting the horse barns lined up to meet a black mare. Three months earlier, she had never felt human touch. Now she lowered her head and half-dozed as little hands patted her all over. Nearby, Victor Villarreal waited for his next class with his blaze-faced mustang, Cochise. Villarreal lives in Fairfield and works at a power plant. Unlike Teryn Lee, he's not a professional trainer. "I'm just a regular joe who has a passion for it," he said. "How many people can say they've trained a wild mustang?"

In the two-day contest, the horse and rider teams qualified for the finals by competing in four preliminary classes, where the difficulty of what they'd attempted became clear. Some horses trotted through cones but refused to go through the gate obstacle in trail class. Some docilely lifted their feet on their trainer's cue but freaked at the sight of a flag. Others didn't stop too well. There were horses that jerked, stamped, and said no. Several riders very nearly got dumped.

There were also successes, teams like Cheatgrass and Teryn Lee that demonstrated an abiding understanding of each other and traveled the classes on a loose rein, relaxed. Cheatgrass did everything he was asked, stopping and turning and accepting commands despite the indoor spaces he'd never seen before, the crowds, the noise. Teryn Lee's strategy was simple. "I don't have to win every class," he said. "I just have to make the top 20."

Amid the thrill of competition, the BLM made sure to get its message out. Not far from the vendors selling halters and miracle supplements, Don Glenn, the director of the wild horse and burro program, sat behind a table laden with mustang trinkets and promotional materials.

"We can't allow the wild horse to expand and let nature take its course," he said. "They'll destroy their own habitat and die from lack of food and water. Congress has passed laws to allow for livestock grazing and mandated for multiple-use management not just for horses, not just for cows, not just for wildlife or oil and gas but for all those things."

It was late in the afternoon of the contest's second day. In a few minutes, judges would announce the 20 finalists, who would compete that evening, including Teryn Lee and Cheatgrass.

"This has been the highlight of the wild horse and burro program," Glenn said. "This effort gets more horses adopted. The last thing we want is for the mustang to disappear."

There is something that happens when horses travel loose together. The finals began with the national anthem in four-part harmony. The gates of the coliseum opened and eight mustangs of eight colors flowed out, followed by a cowboy snapping a bullwhip. They moved in unison as seamlessly as birds in flight, necks arched, manes floating, shifting speed and direction by some unseen communication known only to them. It was hokey, it was sentimental, and, reader, it was beautiful.

Each finalist had four and a half minutes to show off his or her horse to music. Judges looked for horses with the basics of walk, trot, and lope, along with several other maneuvers. They also judged the riders' horsemanship and the overall presentation of the performance. Props were encouraged. Several contestants dressed as Indians, complete with braided wigs, one of whom leaned over at a lope and snatched up what appeared to be a blow-up doll dressed as an Indian maiden. He set the stolen maid on the back of the horse, where she flapped gracelessly against the horse's rump at every stride. One rider, dressed as a firefighter, did a tribute to U.S. service members and first responders. This got big applause. Another finalist eschewed music and rode to an original spoken-word piece from the point of view of her buckskin horse, Tucker. At one point in her routine, she laid the horse down on the arena floor in front of all those thousands of people. She got on her knees, leaned against him, and prayed.

"I am the creator's gift to you," the voice-over said earnestly. "I am mustang. I am Tucker the mustang."

Shooting was popular in the finals, the extremely loud *ka-pows* apparently demonstrating the animals' tolerance for the unpredictable array of human antics. But a few routines were less scripted, and these unadorned performances best highlighted the achievements the teams had made. Horses chased calves with all the speed they had. There were riders who stood on their horses' backs or rode without bridles. One mustang docilely carried the young daughter of the trainer at the end of her performance.

Under the blaze of Will Rogers's lights, very far from the deserts of Utah, where he was born, Cheatgrass the wild horse loped out and stopped neatly at the end of the arena. He turned in a careful spin, collected himself, and loped large, even circles. Teryn Lee gunned him a bit, then Cheatgrass made a long, sliding stop. When a calf was sent into the arena, the mustang's ears stood at pert attention. He dodged when it dodged and skittered when it skittered. He tracked the calf as Teryn Lee built a loop and caught it with a minute to go. Other finalists had done this much, but Teryn Lee dropped off the side of the horse and ran down the rope to the calf, flipping it onto its side and tying its feet as it flopped and struggled. Cheatgrass backed up and kept the rope taut, as a little calf-roping horse should. His eyes never left Teryn Lee and his feet did not move. People in the stands thundered applause and rose to cheer until the music was hard to hear; the mustang stayed at his job until Teryn Lee mounted, slacked his rope, and tipped his hat to the stands as they walked away. It's not what horses with a hundred days of handling are supposed to be able to do.

When Teryn Lee's name was called, he dropped his head and rubbed his mustang's neck. A colored sash was thrown over Cheatgrass. Teryn Lee, looking a little stunned, gripped the $50,000 cardboard check as he was mobbed by well-wishers. Photographers posed him with judges and rodeo queens in spangled suits.

"He has a home with us forever," he told anyone who asked.

They had won the highest purse ever awarded in a wild horse competition. Cheatgrass stood quiet amid the flash and hubbub, his eyes dark and soft. He's a mustang. He does not know what is to come.

S. L. PRICE

Pride of a Nation

FROM SPORTS ILLUSTRATED

THE WOOD IS ALIVE, they say. Yes, a good stick talks to you when it's finished and agleam: begging to be picked up and cradled, demanding that you rake the nearest ball into the cow-gut webbing that with time becomes so sensitive, so responsive, that it can feel as if you're carrying an egg in the palm of your hand. But Alf E. Jacques can hear the wood long before that, when what will become a lacrosse stick still resembles a shepherd's crook, and the drilling and sanding and shellacking are yet to be done. This one? He can all but feel it breathe beneath his blade.

But then, Jacques expected as much. A master stick-maker whose workshop squats behind his mother's house on the Onondaga reservation, just outside Syracuse, New York, he selected, steamed, bent, and began air-drying a prime batch of hickory poles 28 months ago. Usually a year is long enough to make a good lacrosse stick, but Jacques was taking no chances; he wanted these poles cured to perfection for this mid-June afternoon, when he would sit at his cooper's bench, take a draw-shave in hand, and begin shaping the six-foot defensive sticks for the competition to come.

"This is for the Iroquois Nationals," the 61-year-old Jacques says. "Nobody else gets one. Every four years I make at least six D-sticks for them." He laughs. "And they usually save them for when they play the Americans."

On July 15 the Nationals are scheduled to open the 2010 lacrosse world championships against host England in Manchester, but that's no sure thing. For 27 years the team representing the Iroquois—the confederacy of Mohawk, Oneida, Onondaga, Cayuga,

Seneca, and Tuscarora nations—has been the sole Native American entity to compete internationally, traveling on Iroquois (or, in their language, Haudenosaunee, meaning People of the Long House) passports and balancing lacrosse's prep school vibe with an aura of history and mystery and loss. But last week, just days before their scheduled departure, the Nationals were told by officials of the U.S. State and Homeland Security Departments that they would not be allowed to exit and enter the country on those documents.

The Iroquois in turn rejected an offer to travel on U.S. passports. "We are representing a nation, and we are not going to travel on the passport of a competitor," said Tonya Gonnella Frichner, an Onondaga lawyer and a representative to the United Nations Permanent Forum on Indigenous Issues. As of Monday night neither side had budged, raising the possibility that for the first time since 1990, the world championships would be contested without the game's inventors.

This might seem like a mere bureaucratic snafu, but it represents a serious threat to both the tournament and the Iroquois nation. Despite drawing from a population of only about 125,000 people scattered across northeastern North America and despite lacking the financial clout of lacrosse's international powers, the Iroquois have finished fourth in the last three world championships, and they figured to enter the 30-nation 2010 competition as true contenders. The Nationals are also the Iroquois's most public expression of sovereignty, of their long-held belief that they are an independent people. Beating mighty Team USA or defending champion Canada in Manchester would be sweet, of course. But the mere hope that the Nationals would enter the United Kingdom on their own terms, bless the tournament with a traditional tobacco-burning ceremony, and then take the field against the world's best would make claiming the championship almost beside the point. "Winning is not the end-all," says Sid Jamieson, who coached the first Nationals team in the early 1980s. "Just being there is a victory."

Let 'em know you're there, they say. Having a presence, showing the world that they still exist, is a constant theme with the Iroquois, and few things express it more memorably than a jab with a wooden stick. "I remember getting checked, and my arm would go numb, just go limp," says former Syracuse player John Desko, who now coaches the Orange and who coached Team USA at the 2006 world championships. In the Nationals' match against host Canada that year, defender Mark Burnam, now a Nationals assistant coach, says he used his pole to "slash people on purpose and let them know that they were going to get slashed every time. I'd throw poke-checks, and that thing don't bend. [Opponents] would shy away from me. I don't blame them. The thing is like a friggin' weapon. It nearly kills you."

The advent of the aluminum-shaft, plastic-head, nylon-web stick in 1970 might have been the single greatest spur to lacrosse's growth, but it marginalized the wooden shaft; leagues now ban it, coaches discourage it, parents see one and complain. Native American or not, every player in NCAA lacrosse uses what Oren Lyons, a member of the Onondaga council of chiefs, calls "Tupperware." And if the Nationals play in England, most of their stickheads will be plastic too.

Yet the wooden stick remains central to the Iroquois religion and culture: males are given a miniature version at birth, sleep with their playing sticks nearby or even in bed, and take one with them into the grave. In international field lacrosse the Iroquois are the only players who still use wood, and while the sight of it might be unwelcome to their opponents, it gives even victimized apostates a thrill. During a hotly contested game between the Nationals and Team USA at the 1999 under-19 world championships in Adelaide, Australia, players from Australia, Canada, and England began chanting, "Bring out the woodies!" Three Nationals defenders swapped their Tupperware for hickory to roars from the crowd.

"When those six-foot wooden sticks come out," says Iroquois attackman Drew Bucktooth, "they know we're there." That's why, a month before the start of the 2010 world championships, Sid Smith felt compelled to make his way to Jacques's workshop. Smith, a 23-year-old defender from the Six Nations reservation in Ontario, led two NCAA championship teams and was a onetime All-America at Syracuse; he capped his college career by stripping the ball and setting up the game-winner in overtime of the 2009 title game, against Cornell. Smith grew up playing almost exclusively with plastic and has never used a six-foot wooden stick in competition. But he wants one now.

Jacques isn't ready for Smith's request: each stick is different, and players always want a batch from which to choose. But Smith is less patient than most Nationals ("I want to win all the championships I can," he says), and this year's roster is coming in thin and disorganized. He's going to need help.

"I'm here [again] next Thursday," Smith says to Jacques. "Will you have it done by then?"

"I'll try," Jacques says. "I'll get done as many as I can—maybe four. I got other work too. I was thinking, like, July. I wasn't thinking now."

"Even one," Smith says. "I'll take whatever one you finish."

The game is older than the country, they say. It goes back 900 years, maybe more; what's certain is that Native Americans in the Great Lakes region invented lacrosse, began the massive gatherings involving anywhere from 100 to 1,000 men playing one game over days on a field with goals spread as far as two miles apart. But the ceremony known as Dey Hon Tshi Gwa' Ehs (To Bump Hips) was less a substitute for war than a way to honor the Creator. When an Iroquois dies, the first thing he does after crossing over is grab the stick laid in his coffin. "You'll be playing again that day," says Lyons, an Onondaga faith keeper, or protector of Native traditions, "and you will be the captain."

In the late 19th century a Montreal dentist named William George Beers, following the usual white man's practice of appropriating all things Indian, codified the modern rules of field lacrosse, giving it a time limit and replacing the leather ball with a rubber one. By 1880, after it was discovered that some Native Americans had accepted pay to play the purportedly amateur sport, all Natives were banned from international competition by the sport's governing body. Shut out from the 10-on-10 field game at the highest level, Natives competed in obscurity until box lacrosse —a faster, more violent, six-on-six version invented in 1930 to take advantage of unused hockey rinks—swept across the reservations.

What ensued over the next decades is one of sport's shadow tales, unseen by a world entranced by Ruth and Unitas and Ali, played out by hard, proud men steeped in privation. Their names are famous only on reservations in New York and Canada: unstoppables such as Oliver Hill, Ross Powless, Edward Shenandoah. The Mohawk great of the late 1940s, Angus Thomas? He had a shot so hard, they say, that it killed two goalies. Banned from box leagues for more than a year after one of the deaths, Thomas played his first game back against the Onondagas in the old Akwesasne box near St. Regis, New York—with 19-year-old Lyons between the pipes. Lyons, armored with two chest protectors and a wad of sliced fan belt, saw Thomas wind up and heard the ball sizzle just before it cracked into his midsection, snapping three ribs, leaving him down and breathless for 20 minutes. But Thomas didn't score. "There was no way the ball was going to go in," Lyons says.

Some non-Natives tried coming over from their elegant, wide-open field game to slum in the dusty outdoor box on the Onondaga reservation, where cross-checking was legal and anyone lingering along the boards was begging to be hurt. "I wanted to play their game their way, but I wasn't tough like that," says Roy "Slugger" Simmons Jr., who played for Syracuse in the 1950s under his father, the legendary Roy Simmons Sr., and later coached the Orange to six national championships.

The scene at Slugger's first box game was cockfight crazy: Native women ringing the boards, shaking the chicken-wire fencing as he passed with the ball, stopping their unnerving screams just long enough to spit at him. After a line change Simmons dropped to the bench and was approached by an old Indian named Percy Lazore, who had played against Simmons's dad in the 1920s and '30s. "Roy, you mad," Lazore said.

"Yeah, Percy, look at all the gobs of spit on me," Simmons said. "What the hell's wrong with them?"

"Roy, they spit on good players. What you worry about is if they don't spit on you."

To the wider world, NFL legend Jim Brown is the most famous Syracuse lacrosse player, often deemed the greatest of all time, supposedly never knocked off his feet. But on the reservation they remember the pickup game in 1957 in which the 155-pound Irving Powless, a future chief, sent the 230-pound, new-to-the-box Brown tumbling with a brutally precise hip check. "Brown never left his feet the rest of the day," Simmons says. "He just destroyed them."

By then Lyons had become one of the trailblazers of the route from the rez to Syracuse. He co-captained the Orangemen's undefeated 1957 team with Brown and Simmons, earning All-America honors in front of the net with his deft hands and sawed-off goalie's stick. He graduated, worked in New York City as a greeting-card illustrator, and was inducted into the Lacrosse Hall of Fame. He became a faith keeper in '67, moved back to Onondaga in '70, and taught U.S. history at SUNY Buffalo. In 1977 he designed the Iroquois passport and verified its acceptance on a group trip to Switzerland.

The Iroquois's independent streak and their players' lack of field experience earned them a cool reception when they tried out for U.S. or Canadian teams. A few Iroquois became stars in the college game, but as a group they "were kind of snuffed out," Simmons Jr. says. Decades in the box had cut the nation off from its own game; generations of Iroquois had never learned team defense. When, in 1983, Simmons asked Lyons to bring a squad to Baltimore for a series of international friendlies, he heard one of history's saddest replies. "We don't have a field team," Lyons said.

Still, along with Tuscarora stickmaker Wes Patterson, Lyons cobbled together a disparate mix of box, high school, and college players for the inevitable thrashing. Syracuse crushed the first Nationals 28–5, and Hobart handled them 22–14. But a spark caught. "The guys didn't like to get beat," Lyons says. The Iroquois hosted a special tournament in Los Angeles before the 1984 Olympics and earned their first victory, over the English national team. They went to England the next year, won several more games and lost only one. Two years after that Lyons got a 3:00 A.M. call from England: the century-old ban was lifted. The international federation had accepted the Iroquois as a full member nation. "It was our game," Lyons says. "So here we are 100 years later, back up again."

Box lacrosse remains the game of choice for most Iroquois, so it's no shock that their best international result has been indoors: second place, ahead of Team USA, in the last two world box championships. But a growing stream of Division I stars, such as Loyola's Gewas Schindler and Syracuse's Sid Smith, Brett Bucktooth, Cody Jamieson, and Jeremy Thompson, has made the Nationals an increasing threat on grass, and it's not as if outdoor play had been excised from the Iroquois DNA. Throughout the year "medicine" games are played for the health of all players, the traditional way: two poles are jammed in the ground on each end to serve as goals, an unlimited number of males from ages seven to seventy ranges about, and the first team to score a certain number of goals—

sometimes three, sometimes five—wins. Any male can call for a
medicine game to deal with personal strife; a runner goes out to
contact the players, and the food is gathered and a deerskin ball
obtained that day. The caller doesn't play, but he keeps the ball.
"The ball is the medicine," Lyons says.

The Iroquois don't like talking in detail about the medicine
game, at least not with outsiders. But 20 years ago Nationals offensive coach Freeman Bucktooth called for a medicine game on The
Greens at Onondaga to help him and a friend fight an illness. "It
helped," Bucktooth says, so he renews it each year. "Whatever illness you have, it pushes it away. It's amazing how well it cures you."

Only wooden sticks are allowed in medicine games. Familiarity,
the long break-in time, and the sheer beauty of a prized lacrosse
stick partly explain why some Iroquois cry when one splinters. But
a deeper reason for their grief is the belief that the stick is a gift
from Mother Earth, that a living thing died to make it, and that its
spirit has been transferred to the Iroquois player, who honors the
tree's sacrifice by playing humbly, calmly, "in a more spiritual manner," Jacques says. "Nobody likes a dirty player, and the energy from
that tree is transferred to that player who knows how to use it."

One evening last January, Lyons, soon to be 80, stick in hand,
hustled along the darkened hallways of the Onondaga Nation
Arena. A $7 million facility that opened in 2001, Tsha'Honnonyen-
dakhwa' (Where They Play Games) is the modern centerpiece of
the Onondaga reservation and a far more practical statement than
the tattered billboard on I-81 whose faded message reads, WE THE
INDIGENOUS PEOPLE OWN THE WESTERN HEMISPHERE!

Not that Lyons doesn't believe that. Two 1794 treaties, one of
them brokered by George Washington—the one that still pays
each Iroquois descendant five yards of calico yearly—are the Iroquois's legal basis for sovereignty and the reason Syracuse police
have no jurisdiction on the reservation. Casinos? Establishing a ca-
sino would entail asking the U.S. government's permission. Oren
Lyons, for one, has never asked the U.S. permission for anything.

He stopped in the lobby, at the trophy case, and pointed at its
most eye-catching display, a lone blue warm-up jacket with red-and-
white piping on the shoulders, hanging on a wire hanger. There's
no placard, no list of accomplishments, no explanation. "Here's
Lee," Lyons said.

*

He was one of the best ever, they say. That mattered to Leroy "Lee" Shenandoah; whether he was doing ironwork or playing lacrosse or serving in the Army, nothing less than excellence would do. "I used to be afraid to fry him an egg—everything was perfection," says his sister, Beulah Powless. "And his temper: If [his wife] Deena didn't iron the pants just right? He'd rip them in half. She didn't get upset. She knew."

From the late 1950s through the '60s, Shenandoah put his ferocity and skill to work in the box for the Onondaga Warriors, precursors to today's Senior B Can-Am Lacrosse League entry, the Redhawks. Shenandoah was a lean and fast force who could shoot, dodge, pass, and defend. He could power or slash to the goal. "He was like [Alex] Ovechkin: he could score, he could run you over," says Freeman Bucktooth. "And when he spoke, you listened."

It was easy, once he was dead, to make Shenandoah a symbol of the tragic Native experience, illustrating all the bad that could befall an Indian who ventured off the rez. After dropping out of high school at 16 and becoming a high-iron foreman on construction sites at 17, Shenandoah joined the Army and became so accomplished a Green Beret that he marched in the honor guard at President Kennedy's funeral. Less than a decade later, in March 1972, he died at 32 after being shot five times and kicked by Philadelphia police, who claimed he had attacked them and resisted arrest —until film of the incident surfaced that raised questions about the police version of the events. The two officers responsible were never charged with a crime.

"The war's not over," Lyons says with a smile. "Not by a long shot."

These days Shenandoah's legacy burns most fiercely with the Iroquois Nationals. He had a way of looking out for people, sometimes even white opponents in the box. "He knew I was naive and a target, and many times he could've leveled me," Slugger Simmons says. "But he'd come up and say, 'Roy, I'm doing you a favor: keep your head up.'" Shenandoah was close to the Bucktooths and kept an eye on young Freeman, first babysitting him, then teaching him all he knew about the game. Nobody, Freeman says, had better all-around skill, and from Shenandoah he learned most of what he knows about winning face-offs, the subtleties of stickhandling, the value of spying on the opposing goalie during warm-ups. "And he could fight," Bucktooth says. "Nobody would mess with him."

No wonder, then, that fisticuffs became Freeman's trademark too. For a decade he led the Senior B League in scoring; he once rang up 19 goals in a game. But ask about him and the first thing everyone mentions is how he brawled in the box as a teenager, cutting through other teams' enforcers, leaving a line of 25-year-old men facedown, needing stitches. Bucktooth played two years at Syracuse for Slugger Simmons, who knew the effect that Freeman's "Geronimo look"—high cheekbones, shock of black hair—could have on nervous whites. Whenever the team bus rolled onto a new campus, Simmons made sure that Bucktooth was the first man off. "I'll scare 'em," Freeman would say.

College life didn't take, but Bucktooth carried Shenandoah's perfectionist bent into adulthood. He put in 80 hours a week climbing poles, repairing high wire for Niagara Mohawk Power. He dragooned his sons into helping him build their log-cabin home with 140 precisely notched timbers—no nails. He overhauled the structure of kids' leagues at Onondaga to expose hundreds of young Iroquois to more and better competition and coached them at every level from Peanuts to Juniors, traveling with the six-year-olds into Canada one year, taking the U-19s to Australia another, making his voice heard on the Nationals' governing board.

Knowing that college lax was one sure route out of the rez, Bucktooth insisted on teaching field techniques in the box, guiding all the Iroquois boys to cradle and pass and shoot off both wings. And always in his mind he would hear Shenandoah's voice, preaching toughness, a hunger to win every ground ball. "We could never get through a scrimmage, couldn't go three minutes without the whistle stopping and him instructing us: *It should be done right. Practice how you play in the game,*" says Freeman's third son, Brett. "And if you're playing against your best friend and you don't cross-check him or you let him pick up a ground ball, he said, 'I don't care if he's your best friend: go hit him.' The game's meant to be tough."

Of course, all four Bucktooth boys and their countless cousins —"Go out in the woods," says Jacques, "and you'll step on one"— lived Freeman's philosophy. This year, with Freeman coaching the offense, Brett at midfield, and 29-year-old Drew at attack, the Nationals will again have Bucktooth marks all over them.

The family's influence is pervasive; any afternoon at Onondaga Nation Arena, Freeman can still be found roaming the box during youth practices, even down to the Peanut division, where four- to six-year-old boys pump their little legs up and down the floor. Brett and other Nationals vets will be there too, coaching their own sons; every few minutes another kid will be sent sprawling by a vicious slash. The men give each boy a moment to lie there, then tap a foot with a stick: That's enough. Let's go.

One June day Beulah Powless is sitting out in the lobby, waiting for her six-year-old great-grandson, Gabe, to finish Tykes practice. She's speaking about her brother, Lee Shenandoah, nearly 40 years gone: how his two children have scattered, how the family received a small settlement from the city of Philadelphia but no apology, how Lee came to their mother, Gertrude Shenandoah, in a dream. But then Gabe runs up asking for snack money, and she recalls a moment from two weeks before, when he got leveled by a shot to the neck in a game against Allegheny. She went over to the team bench where Gabe sat stewing and asked if he was okay, and he gave her a look that was so pure, so Lee, that for just a second it was as if her brother were still living.

"I'm going back in," Gabe said, "and I'm going to fight."

There's no team like it, they say. When the Iroquois Nationals travel, overseas especially, they carry a mystique born of Hollywood imagery and pure novelty. So English schoolkids ask Nationals coaches, "How does the smoke get out of your house? Do you still hurt people?" and Japanese opponents treat the players like rock stars and reporters flock to see the exotics in action. Thus is delivered the only message that matters. "We're still here," Smith says.

"The Nationals are showing the world that we are on the map," Jacques says, his voice rising. "When you say Indians, Native Americans, what pops into mind? Out west, in a tepee, on a reservation, alcohol, drug abuse, drain on society, poverty, uneducated — beaten down. How many negatives can they put on this group of people? So to have a positive there on the world stage is such a big thing for us."

But the Nationals' singularity stems not just from their role as standard-bearers for all Native Americans; there are three roster spots for players from any other tribe, and this year's squad includes a Cherokee goalie and an Ojibwa defender. The Nationals also operate in ways that can mystify their own staff, let alone sympathetic outsiders. "They're an extremely funny group, sarcastic, love to talk and have fun and compete," says Roy Simmons III, Slugger's son, director of lacrosse operations at Syracuse. "But every time I walk away, I'm always scratching my head, wondering what happened."

As the youngest member of one of sport's enduring coaching dynasties, Roy III grew up proud of his family's 50-year relationship with the Iroquois and couldn't have been more honored when the Nationals asked him last summer to join the coaching staff. But in early June, he and Bill Bjorness, the 2006 Nationals coach, who had been a member of the coaching staff since 1994, resigned because of frustration over management moves that had reduced training time, paralyzed the selection process, and left the team scrambling on the eve of the worlds.

The Americans have beaten the Nationals in the last five world championships, Smith says, because they're "usually bigger, in a little better shape, [have] a lot more players to choose from—and [are] a lot better organized." This year the contrast has been starker than usual. Team USA set its 23-man roster last November and scheduled five tough exhibition games. The Nationals didn't announce their roster until June 20, by which time they'd had only two scrimmages, none since February. They finally held another training camp in the first week of July.

The delays didn't allow newly appointed general manager Ansley Jemison much time to arrange airline tickets and visas to Great Britain; when the U.S. dropped its passport bomb, there were only three days left before the Iroquois's planned departure, and what could have been a challenging problem became a crisis. But long before the travel mix-up, the Iroquois's concern with self-definition had taken a toll on their lacrosse program.

An imperative to include players representing all Six Nations increased political maneuvering during the Nationals' selection process, and last December—*after* months of tryouts—the Iroquois Traditional Council made a devastating decision: for the first time in Nationals history, a player's Native lineage would be a major issue, decided strictly through his mother. Once-acceptable adoptees, players with only small traces of Indian blood, and offspring of mixed marriages involving non-Native mothers were rejected. The Nationals' midfield was gutted when five players were cut loose for reasons of lineage.

Just as curious, some prime Iroquois players didn't try out for this year's team, opting to devote themselves to family, work, or their box teams. "There are players who should be on this team who aren't," Freeman Bucktooth says. "[Defender] Marshall Abrams—an All-America at Syracuse—chose not to play. I'm upset that some didn't try out, and I'm upset that some guys got cut. I told everybody: there are three guys who should be on the team because they add speed, and that's something we lack."

For someone like Roy Simmons III, who comes from a white, win-at-all-costs culture, such decisions seem inexplicable. "Here I am stupidly thinking we're going to send the best team," he says, "and it's not really going to happen." But though many of the coaches—such as Mark Burnam, who saw his brother bounced from the squad—share Simmons's frustration over the Traditional Council's ruling, they don't have the luxury of walking away. "I have to respect that," says Jemison. "That's the stance of the coach and the entire staff: we respect our tradition, and that's what we're going to go by. We can't bellyache, because then we're cutting our own throats."

What he means is, at a time when the Iroquois are struggling to protect their language and culture from the enticing encroachments of American life, when each Iroquois lacrosse player who goes to Syracuse represents, yes, a success story but also a flight risk —a man in danger of losing his Native ways—things such as lineage do mean more than the world's biggest lacrosse tournament. Iroquois tradition requires that chiefs make each decision with an eye on its impact seven generations from now (hence the N7 logo on Nationals gear); there's a reason Lyons calls Nike the team's *partner*, not sponsor. Today's Iroquois fear being subsumed, fear Culture USA more than Team USA, and the message *We are still here* will mean little if the *we* is allowed to grow fuzzy.

"There's a lot more weighing on us," Jemison says. "It's our identity." Which, not by accident, dovetails with the larger Iroquois lacrosse paradox: spiritually and socially the game is central in ways inconceivable for any sport in any other culture—but winning isn't. Some players, such as Smith and Cody Jamieson, may indeed be motivated to win titles, but the typical Iroquois sees lacrosse as the place to present himself to the Creator, not prove himself number one.

Desko, the Syracuse coach, understands this, at least enough to make allowances. Last fall his dazzling new midfielder, Jeremy Thompson, announced that he would miss more than a week of training because he had to fast for four days—no food, no water —in an Onondaga cleansing ritual that leaves participants weak and sometimes delirious. "And I'm sitting here going, Whooo. Interesting," Desko says. "But another coach? 'Screw that, fast on your own time! Miss practice and you're done!' But Jeremy's not doing it to take the day off. He's doing it because he wants to be a better Iroquois."

Thompson feels many of the pressures facing young Natives who try, as he puts it, to "live in two worlds." His great-grandfather was a chief, and Jeremy grew up steeped in tradition. "We weren't allowed to have the girls touch our wooden sticks; it's a medicine game for men, not women," he says. "If it was on the ground, my mom would leave it there."

With his summer job tutoring Onondaga kids in their Native tongue and his plans to resurrect the adolescent rite of passage known as vision quest—not to mention the long ponytail trailing down his back—Thompson, 23, seems the picture of Native American piety. But living according to his ideals has been a struggle. When his family moved from the Mohawk reservation to Onondaga, he was in the fifth grade and could barely read or speak English; he struggled in school and by 15 began bingeing on alcohol. Why not? That's what many of the men on the rez do.

Only 11.5 percent of Native Americans graduate from college. "We're always thinking back home is more important," Thompson says. "That's the problem we have nowadays in getting kids off and going to college. They don't want to leave the family or the reserve, and another big part is the drugs and alcohol. They have no way of finding themselves. We don't have that connection, the role models, somebody there to direct them the right way."

After poor grades derailed his dream of playing for Syracuse, Thompson won two junior college national titles at Onondaga Community College and beefed up his transcript enough to gain admission to Syracuse last fall. But he also boozed plenty, and his dream of playing for the Orange with his younger brother, Jerome, died when Jerome ran into academic trouble. "He quit," says Jeremy. "He couldn't handle school." Then Jeremy's longtime girl-friend, whom he had planned to marry this summer, broke up with him.

"I'm a better person because she did that," he says. "I'm thank-ful. I realize what I put her through all those years I was out drink-ing, doing what I wanted to do. She's a good woman, traditional, Long House, had all those qualities that I want in a woman. And I shot that out the door."

Thompson started to get clean 18 months ago, but last fall the constant toggle between all-Native life on the rez and all-American college life sparked a short relapse. After that, however, he learned that negotiating both worlds, working toward a degree but not forsaking his traditions, was actually doable. "It's not like the old days," he says. "We have to go out." Loneliness helped him see it clearly: *he* could be the example he never had. This fall he'll be a senior at Syracuse, on track to earn a degree in communications.

"I'm on the verge," he says. "I found out these things are always going to pull at you, but I'm really digging in now; I feel like my days of fooling around are done. I'm down to business with learn-ing our ways, our ceremonies, and lacrosse started to help me out. It's a sport I can always go to for medicine, for relief, to have fun.

"Another thing I found out about lacrosse: I'm doing it for the younger ones behind me now. I look at my life—how it was taken, where I fell off my track—and I want to be there and have a pro-gram for kids to find themselves, their spirituality, and find what they were put here for. That way, they're ahead of the game."

He's still young, they say. Quick of mind, light on his feet, zipping around town in a Prius, Oren Lyons begins his ninth decade ut-terly unimpressed by his own stature. One morning last January a teenager walked into a Syracuse restaurant carrying a defender's stick and, when introduced to Lyons, clearly didn't know that the man in front of him was a chief, a caretaker of the Iroquois way, a voice on indigenous and climate issues who has been heard by the United Nations General Assembly and Bill Moyers and the bright lights who gather each year in Davos. That was fine: Lyons had more important things to talk about.

"Don't forget to pokecheck," he said. "Any ball on the ground is yours, you know."

Because before he was anyone, Lyons was one of the best goalkeepers ever, and even old goalies can't help bossing defenders around. In 1996 he traveled with the U-19 Nationals to Edogawa, Japan, for the world championships. He was in the locker room before an exhibition against a college team when coach Freeman Bucktooth jokingly suggested he suit up. Lyons didn't laugh. He borrowed some equipment, grabbed his wooden stick, and headed for the goal.

He was 66 years old. The day was witheringly hot. Though manning the larger field net, Lyons positioned himself with one hand on his stick, box style. And then they started to come, the shots: breakaways, one-on-ones, rocketing in after every fake and juke the young athletes could muster. But for one half Lyons stood in, erasing four decades until he was at Syracuse again, with Jim Brown and Slugger Simmons ranging upfield. Lyons whipped his stick around like a nunchaku, deflected ball after rock-hard rubber ball, stuffed one point-blank missile after another as sweat poured down his back.

"I've never seen a goalie play like that, with one hand on his stick in a six-foot net," says Drew Bucktooth. "Jumping up with his elbow, making saves? And he didn't have arm pads, so he's making saves with bare arms. He had to have 12, 15 saves and gave up just one goal. Had to be 100 degrees that day. I've never seen anything like it."

So, yes, Lyons is nearly evangelical when he speaks of the Onondagas' new partnership with a Swedish firm to make vertical greenhouses for cities, and dead serious about the Iroquois's role as a ravaged planet's prime steward. "The Haudenosaunee are the ones who give thanks to the earth," he says. "We take care of it, and we're doing it very well here. When you look around the world today and see what's going on? We're in deep s—. People have no idea. But we know."

Lacrosse is the Creator's game, a way to show gratitude for this same earth, and Lyons expects progress there too. The passport problem only energized him, made him sure that "either way, we still win," he says. If the Nationals are forced to stay home, they become a rallying point for indigenous rights; if the U.S. clears them to travel on their own documents, Lyons says, "it's going to be a recognition." And if the Iroquois play in England this week, Lyons is sure their days of finishing fourth will end. "We will medal," he says. And for anyone who figures the recent turmoil makes the Nationals ripe for defeat, he serves up a challenge.

Like Thompson, Lyons wears his hair in a long braid. But now he brings up an old Iroquois warrior style, a shaved head with a small patch of hair on the back. Asked the native term for it, he says, "Scalplock. To make it easier for them to scalp you." As his guest's bewildered, sputtering reply stalls at "but why would . . . ?" his eyes gleam. Lyons grins and nods as the trap snaps shut.

"You want it?" he says. "You come and get it."

The Crash

FROM 5280

THEY ALL HEARD IT: the buzz of the propellers, like a swarm of angry bees flying low over U.S. 6 through the central mountains. The plane was so low that it cast a gigantic shadow across the pine-covered landscape, and made people stop what they were doing and stare. The plane went right up to where that asphalt ended and 12,000 feet of rock stretched to the sky.

That was the plane that changed John Putt forever.

It was October 2, 1970, and the perfect, crisp fall morning had given way to an afternoon of endless blue sky. A snow had fallen earlier and the tree line around Evergreen was touched with spots of white. It was one of those Rocky Mountain days that made you glad to be alive. *Thank God for Colorado.*

And thank God for a reason to cut class early. Wasn't that what 12-year-old John Putt thought when that voice boomed over the loudspeaker at Evergreen Junior High School? *Members of the Alpine Rescue Team, you're needed. Now.* There was a mission, and Putt was determined to be in on it.

Anticipation, excitement. That's what Putt felt. The joy of the moment. Whatever had happened, it must have been big. The folks at Alpine didn't call the youngest members out of class when grandma got lost hunting mushrooms in the woods. No, this was special—momentous. He could feel it.

He'd trained six months for his first call to action, for an opportunity to prove himself to the roughly 50 teenagers and adults who made up one of Colorado's only mountain-rescue outfits. Putt had tied knots behind his back in dark closets, searched for water, slept in snow caves, hiked until his feet bled.

Putt shot out of the classroom door. He was just a kid, really, a prepubescent boy heading to . . . well, who knows what? Honor? Glory? Yes, that's what it felt like to Putt—all five feet three inches and maybe 100 pounds of him, a sliver of a boy with a tuft of unkempt brown hair sticking from his head. He headed down the hallway proud, his head held high.

He pushed open the school doors. It was nearly two miles to his house, and Putt ran the whole way. It was as hard and as fast as he'd ever run before. He reached home, but no one was there. *Mom won't understand this,* Putt thought to himself. He called his dad at work. I'm going on a mission, he said. I don't know when I'll be back.

Stay safe. That's what Putt's dad told him over the phone. But what did that mean? He grabbed his pack, and soon he was back on the road, running again. Three minutes, five minutes. A car passed and Putt waved it down. He hitched a ride to the Shack, the shed attached to an Evergreen church where the Alpine crew was mounting up. The last vehicles were blazing out of the lot. A National Guard helicopter had taken off. What about me? Putt asked, desperately. There was room in the back of a Suburban. Putt's heart leapt. Hop in, someone called to him.

March 26, 1969. The *thump-thump-thump* of the propeller blades boomed across the Spanish Peaks northwest of Trinidad, Colorado, as the pilot lowered his helicopter onto a windblown patch of earth.

Chuck Burdick, a 17-year-old from the Evergreen-based Alpine Rescue Team, was aboard, along with a handful of other rescuers, including Alpine members and several from a search unit based in Boulder. The early-morning fog had lifted, and Burdick found himself 200 miles from home, prepared for the worst.

Sturdy with thick shoulders and blond hair, Burdick was a senior at Thomas Jefferson High School in Denver and the burgeoning leader of Alpine Rescue—an all-volunteer mountain-rescue unit founded nearly a decade earlier. Among the younger members, Burdick was an unparalleled mountaineer. Although he wasn't from Evergreen like most of the other teenagers, he was a folk hero of sorts to the kids in the group. His technical knowledge was unmatched: he could tie any knot in seconds; he could read the most complicated topographical maps; he could rappel like a spider fetching its prey. One time, he zipped 70 feet across Bear Creek, just to show the newbies how it was done.

Burdick lived Alpine Rescue. When Alpine called in the middle of the night, his father would ring a doorbell attached to Burdick's room to wake him up. His Toyota Corolla was a rolling rescue unit, packed with a rucksack, a sleeping bag, a tent, extra batteries, and all sorts of radios. On those nights when he left home, his parents knew better than to ask if he'd be back for breakfast.

And now here he was, flying among the Spanish Peaks on a helicopter heading toward a narrow ridge. Atop one of the peaks was a Cessna 308 that had crashed five days earlier and killed everyone aboard. The recovery squad approached the wreckage. An hour or two later, someone found the Cessna's tail 300 feet below. Some of the men hustled down and found a gruesome scene. Burdick saw part of one man's frozen torso. None of the remains were recognizable.

The teenager worked quietly for the next few hours, removing remains and loading them. He hiked back eight miles with the rest of the team to the dirt road where they'd parked their cars. By the time Burdick was on the road home, it was early the next morning. Six bodies, only 250 pounds of remains. The road signs zipped past. Burdick was certain it wouldn't be the last tragedy he'd see.

The Suburban cruised along U.S. 6, which ran from Denver to the Continental Divide, past the old gold-mining towns of Georgetown and Idaho Springs. John Putt sat on the squad's equipment in the back of the SUV. There was chatter up front, a crackle on the radio. Ahead, he could see a column of smoke growing as they neared Mt. Trelease, one of the smaller mountains near Loveland Pass. The teens drove until it seemed the smoke column was right on top of them. The driver pulled off the road to where a makeshift command post had been set up.

The boys raced out of the vehicle. Putt followed with his 30-pound pack on his back. He was ready. It was just past 4:00 P.M.

Putt could see that Burdick had a map stretched across the hood of a car. A gaggle of people surrounded him: Lindon "Woody" Wood, Alpine Rescue's training director and head of the team's youth program; the Clear Creek County sheriff, Harold Brumbaugh; a number of Colorado State Patrol officers; and 18-year-old

Bob Watson, another of Alpine's young leaders. They were swapping information.

Employees of the Loveland Ski Area and construction workers building the Straight Creek Tunnel—later named the Eisenhower Tunnel—saw a twin-engine propliner fly into the mountains three hours earlier. There was fire and lots of smoke. The workers ran up the highway and then hiked toward the crash, where they helped 11 victims off Mt. Trelease and got them to a doctor about 30 minutes away in Idaho Springs. Some were badly hurt; a few looked like they might die. Already, one body had been recovered at the crash site, but there had been an explosion and a fire was burning —beyond that, the information about what was going on at the scene was spotty. The Alpine team didn't know the plane's exact size or the number of passengers. Earlier, some survivors had told first responders there was a football team on board. At the crash site, football pads and gold helmets were strewn everywhere.

The information was relayed to Watson, who absorbed the news like an accountant. Bespectacled and skinny, with a mustache and scruffy hair, the high school senior was designated the team leader on the mission. He would be Burdick's number two and one of the more senior Alpine members heading up the mountain. Calculated, confident, and tough, Watson was a walking contradiction —a hippie who was one of the most fastidious and safety-conscious of the Alpine members, the kid who wanted to work in medicine, but only after he spent a summer working on an oil rig in Alaska.

In all, there were 18 or so kids, many of whom were on their first mission. There was Putt and 16-year-old John Baroch—a boy who'd been hiking these mountains for as long as he could remember. There was 14-year-old Kevin Dunn and his 13-year-old brother, Mike. And there was 19-year-old Steve Greene, a devout Catholic who was studying physics at the University of Colorado Denver.

Watson lined up the teenagers along the mountainside, a rocky slope that ran a few dozen feet up then opened onto a ledge that extended into a thick forest. With their boots and packs, the teenagers looked like troops preparing to storm an enemy position. *We are looking for survivors,* Watson told them. *Watch your step.*

And then they were gone, a mass of knees and elbows up that mountain, rocks crumbling underfoot. Putt was among the last to go. He could hardly contain his anticipation. He was filled with anxiousness and something else. Was it joy? Maybe. On perhaps Alpine Rescue's biggest day, Putt would play a role. It would be his chance to prove himself—and to prove *to* himself that he could hang with the older boys. That he was worthy.

Putt couldn't wait to touch that mountain. As the other teens clawed their way toward the trees, Putt finally placed a hand on the rocky mountainside and looked up.

The Martin 404 aircraft was a 40-seater, and there were 36 people associated with Wichita State University's football program on the plane on October 2. They were bound for Logan, Utah, and a Saturday football game against Utah State University. The players were excited to get out of Kansas, even if it was only for a couple of days —excited to see the Rockies from the air. So far, the schedule had given them one home game and two away games in Texas. The latest road trip would be another chance for the players to prove themselves on the field—especially after more than a month of practices in the stifling Midwest heat.

When the nearly 20-year-old twin-engine plane took off from Kansas, it carried 14 Wichita State starters, the head coach, team staff, administrators, wives, and boosters. N464M—its tail number —was one of two chartered planes flying from Wichita to Utah that day. (A larger DC-6 jet was supposed to ferry players that season but had been damaged in a windstorm.) The planes were code-named "Black" and "Gold" for the university's colors.

The trip was straightforward: the two planes would leave Wichita, refuel at Denver's Stapleton International Airport, and arrive around 2:00 P.M. in Logan. The flight path would take the team on a route that looked a bit like an elongated zigzag line, a north-by-northwest path to Laramie, Wyoming, then a turn west to Logan, in the northern part of Utah. It was hardly a straight shot, but circumnavigating the central Colorado Rockies was far and away the safest way to get to Logan. The route was favorable for Ron Skipper —the first officer in the Gold plane carrying the starters—who'd logged approximately 30 hours flying the Martin 404 and was unfamiliar with the terrain of the Rockies.

Though he only weighed 165 pounds, Skipper was full in the face, with slicked reddish-brown hair and thick glasses he was required to wear when he flew. The 34-year-old Oklahoman was also the CEO of the flight crew–leasing company, Golden Eagle Aviation, which contracted with the planes' owner to carry the Wichita players in 1970.

Somewhere between the takeoff in Kansas and the refueling stop in Denver, Skipper told his passengers that he'd deviate from the flight plan and take the group through the mountains, maybe show them some ski resorts. The Black plane would follow the original flight path toward Laramie and then on to Logan.

As the plane refueled on the Stapleton tarmac, it exceeded its maximum-certified gross takeoff weight, an especially dangerous oversight considering Skipper's limited knowledge of the aircraft and the revised route. Even if the plane lost 200 gallons of fuel per hour, typical for a Martin 404, the plane would remain overweight throughout the flight. And there was perhaps an even bigger concern: neither Skipper nor the 27-year-old captain, Dan Crocker, had an aeronautical sectional chart of the new route. Skipper excused himself, left the plane, and bought a map inside the airport terminal.

In the cabin, wide receiver John Duren couldn't wait to get in the air. The lanky 19-year-old had worked hard that offseason, running sprints, flipping tires, catching hundreds of balls. The discipline paid off: a few days before the trip to Utah, he learned he'd be riding the Gold plane with the first team. Now he was less than 24 hours from starting his first game for the Shockers. He'd never seemed happier.

Seated near Duren were Kansas state representative Raymond King and his wife, Yvonne. The couple had left their seven children behind in Kansas. Near them was 19-year-old Carl Krueger from Chicago, a defensive lineman who turned down an offer to attend the United States Naval Academy just because he liked the down-home feel of Wichita: to fit in, Krueger bought a cowboy hat and wore it around campus. There was 30-year-old Tom Reeves, the team's trainer, whose wife had just given birth to their second child, a son named Brad. And there was head coach Ben Wilson, who was in his second year of rebuilding a football program that had won only a dozen games from 1964 to 1969. It would be a tough job, he knew. His crew already was off to an 0-3 start, and Arkansas and Louisville still loomed on the schedule.

When Skipper returned to the plane with a map, he set it aside and talked to the passengers. About 15 minutes passed, and then the plane was ready to go, but it was more than 5,000 pounds overweight. Skipper and Crocker fired up the propellers, and the plane lumbered down the runway. N464M finally lifted off, but it was nearly a half-mile past the usual departure point on the tarmac. It was 12:29 P.M. A puff of smoke belched from the right engine.

An air traffic controller called to the plane's cockpit to see if everything was okay.

We're just running a little rich is all.

The plane climbed a few thousand feet and headed northwest. With Crocker giving heading directions, Skipper turned west toward the mountains. Minutes passed, and city neighborhoods, and then the suburban developments, disappeared behind them. The route loosely followed U.S. 6. Skipper maneuvered into the Clear Creek Valley, just outside of Idaho Springs, and powered down the engines. He was going to impress these kids. While the engines buzzed, Skipper and Crocker could see the highway. The plane was flying among the Rockies, not above them. As they moved west, the plane barely kept up with the rise of terrain. Strips of mountainside extended on each side of them. Players, dumbstruck by the beauty, took off their seatbelts and wandered the cabin, their faces close to the windows. They were on a sightseeing tour—at 161 miles per hour.

Toward the back of the plane, Bob Renner, the team's 21-year-old quarterback, lounged with his friends and marveled at the sight while two flight attendants passed out sandwiches, potato chips, and apples. Glenn Kostal, one of the linebackers, was three rows from the back of the plane, seated by junior cornerback John Taylor. While his teammates milled around, Taylor nudged Kostal and pointed out the window: *If I had a .22,* he joked, *I could shoot some rabbits down there.*

At 10,000 feet—less than 1,500 feet above the highway—people on the ground below began to take notice, first in Idaho Springs, then 13 miles away in Georgetown, then from trails in the mountains. Some had to look down to see the plane. People pulled their cars over to watch. No smoke. No fire. So why was the plane so low?

Twenty-five minutes into the flight, Rick Stephens, a 22-year-old offensive lineman, thought the mass of trees outside the windows was unsettling. He got up and walked to the cockpit, where he saw Crocker and Skipper studying maps.

After Georgetown, it was less than five minutes to Dry Gulch, a piece of land about 10 miles from the Continental Divide. Skipper pointed to a mountain. *What's that elevation?* he asked.

Thirteen-five, Crocker said.

They were in a box canyon, and the highway they'd been following was about to end. It looked like there was no escape. Skipper banked right, a wide swing in a futile attempt to make a 180-degree turn to safety. The turn tossed a flight attendant, and the passengers hollered. Crocker yelled to Skipper: "I've got the airplane." He made a sharp left. The plane began to vibrate like a speedboat slapping water; the engines stalled. As the plane lost altitude, Crocker nosed up, and the first trees thwacked against the plane's wings. There was a low rumble. Then darkness.

Skipper awoke to a haze of smoke. He was still buckled into his seat. His nose was smashed and bleeding; there was no skin left on his knuckles. Crocker was no longer in the cockpit. A ball of fire was advancing toward the front of the plane. Skipper blacked out.

The smell. That's what they'd all remember. At first it smelled like unwashed socks left to rot in a gym locker. But it grew into something more. Eventually, it became stomach-turning, gag-inducing —a pungent funk, one difficult to explain in any human terms. Later, when the boys from Alpine Rescue would get together, they'd find that there was only one word to describe that smell: death.

As the Alpine crew pushed farther up the mountain on October 2, the odor wafted toward them and nearly froze John Putt in his hiking boots. The excitement he'd felt unloading gear 20 minutes ago drained from his body.

It was a rifle-straight shot uphill through smoke. The landscape grew hazy, darker, more ominous, as they ascended the mountainside. Boulders, stumps, rescuers—they all turned into shadows in the dimming light as the sun slipped behind the trees. Branches snapped and crackled as the teenagers headed up the mountain: 100 vertical feet. Two hundred feet. Putt was losing ground. His legs burned.

Baroch, a high school junior, distracted himself by repeating the contents of his pack, over and over: *batteries, compass, freeze-dried food, map, water. Batteries, compass, freeze-dried food, map, water.*

Three hundred feet.

Thirteen-year-old Mike Dunn couldn't wait to hit the crest. Along with Putt, he was one of the youngest on the rescue team, another eager-to-please junior high kid ready to prove himself to the older boys. The smoke and the smell didn't discourage him.

Four hundred feet.

Dunn's brother, 14-year-old Alpine rookie Kevin Dunn, couldn't believe his luck. *What kid gets to do this?* he asked himself.

Four hundred and fifty. There was still plenty of ground to cover.

Greene, the college freshman, wondered if this was what war looked like. Of all the scenes Alpine Rescue had given him over the years—finding lost hikers in a blizzard, recovering bodies fallen from cliffs—this one would stay with him. He'd see this scene once more—30 years later when he was a nuclear physicist in New Mexico. His house would burn to the ground in Los Alamos, and as he'd stand among the smoldering remnants with his wife, he'd remember climbing this mountain on this day, and what he saw when he reached the crash and looked around.

No matter how bad the scene was, the boys were trained to remain focused. *This is your job,* Greene thought. *Do it right.*

As they approached the crash site, the boys funneled into a line and walked silently, one by one. They could now hear small fires crackling. Trees were scorched, bent, and broken; bolts and rivets and pieces of the plane's wing surrounded them, like someone had tipped over a massive garbage can. Ahead, more broken trees. The teenagers inched closer to the hill, and the smell became even more intense. And then, there it was, the mangled propeller and landing gear. They paused. Greene crossed himself and began to pray.

Get out! That's what the Wichita boys thought. *Get the hell out now! Run!*

Rick Stephens, the offensive lineman, had been behind the cockpit a few moments earlier, and now he was waking up on the side of a steep mountain with a cut on his forehead. Both of his legs were fractured, his hip was dislocated, and his sternum was crushed. The sky was turning black.

Fuel sprayed everywhere and doused the passengers. Taylor, the cornerback, crawled out of a hole in the aircraft, but found himself standing in a puddle of jet fuel and caught fire. So did Reeves, the team trainer. His body was badly burned. The survivors were now running on adrenaline: they started gathering others who were clawing their way out of the plane. Skipper, the first officer, regained consciousness and crawled to safety, then began pulling passengers away from the wreckage. One by one, they came: Mike Bruce, an offensive lineman. Randy Jackson, the team's star running back. Dave Lewis, a defensive end. Others were coming.

We've got to move back! The plane could explode! Bruce volunteered to get help and scooted down the mountain.

Inside, the plane was a mess of broken seats: the players' heavy, unrestrained bodies had plowed into them like they were tackling dummies. People were alive, but they were pinned between seats, struggling to free themselves. Of the passengers, nine were accounted for. Renner, the quarterback, was stuck beneath one of the seats. He freed himself and then turned his attention to three teammates. No one could move. Renner stood above his friends, his roommates, and tried to pull them from the wreckage. "Bobby!" one of them shouted to Renner, "I'm burning! Get out of here!"

It was getting cool on the mountain. The boys from Alpine Rescue saw the flames and smoke and broken-up plane. They looked right and saw snapped pine trees, sawed off at perfect angles, the white wood glowing like porch lights. In a small valley to the left, it looked as if a section of the forest had been clear cut.

Less than 20 yards away, in the dimming light and hazy smoke, Steve Greene saw the remains of bodies in seats and in the center aisle of the aircraft. One wing stuck out perpendicular to the mountain's slope and was buried under a thicket of broken tree limbs. A small fire glowed orange near the middle of a metal pile, a few feet from an engine and what appeared to be landing gear; a fireball had ripped through the wreckage earlier. *My God,* Putt thought, *it's like witnessing the apocalypse.*

In reality, it was a smallish disaster area—a strip of land no bigger than a couple hundred square yards, a scab on the elbow of Mother Nature. John Baroch, thin with a long face and tousled hair, marveled at the site. In its last maneuver, the plane had eased into the mountain to avoid a direct hit. It was as if the pilot were attempting to ride the trees like a kid on a sled.

Near Baroch, Bob Watson scanned the damage and wondered

how anyone would have been able to get out alive. Burdick, the 19-year-old mission leader manning the radio from the roadside, didn't have any new information from the sheriff. As far as anyone knew, they were still looking for survivors. To the group of teenagers overlooking the crash, though, it was oddly quiet for a rescue.

Theirs was a daunting task. Not only were they looking for survivors, but they'd also have to do it among spot fires, thick smoke, boulders, gasoline-slicked pine needles, and pieces of broken wood that stuck out like daggers. Baroch heard an order to turn on their helmet lights and flashlights.

Brothers Mike and Kevin Dunn popped their lights on, and the yellowish glow cast shadows across the trees. Watson ordered the group into a search line about 50 feet long. They'd sweep the crash site. The line was organized with the older boys like Watson nearest to the crash. They'd need to stay straight the entire way; Watson didn't want any stragglers. *Look deep into the trees and search the ground for bodies,* Watson ordered. The area was now a crime scene, and the rescue squad was careful not to get too close to the plane. Anyway, if anyone were still alive, Watson said to the team, they would be dazed and wandering far away. Someone spoke up: the force of an airplane slamming into the ground might have sent bodies into the treetops.

Putt grimaced. The last thing he wanted to do was look up. He kept his eyes toward his boots and wanted to disappear. The others began to walk; Putt moved forward about 10 feet and then stopped, afraid to move. No one looked back at him.

Mike Dunn was sure there would be at least one survivor of the crash, and he was certain he would find him or her. His brother Kevin couldn't believe that anyone survived the impact and fire. The reality of the situation had finally hit him. How were they, a bunch of kids, going to help someone injured in a plane crash?

Closer to the wreck, the heat was tremendous, and Greene felt it despite the cool evening air. Around them were scraps of metal ripped and bent like crushed soda cans. Gold helmets and shoes had spilled onto the forest floor. Watson could see the front of the plane—a molten mess, liquefied pieces of metal dripping and bubbling and already hardening like concrete onto the charred grass. A gaping hole split the fuselage into two distinct pieces; the plane's rear was more intact. Greene scanned the mountain slope. Every time he turned around, his eyes caught the wreckage.

There were larger pieces of debris—a door, part of a wing—and fallen trees stacked like Popsicle sticks around them. As the search team made a ring around the crash, first below the site, then above it, the late-afternoon light had given way to darkness. The boys' headlamps and flashlights gave off an eerie glow. If they were growing weary, none showed it. It was a few hours into their work, and still only part of the area had been searched. No survivors had been found.

As the others worked their way around the site, Putt remained frozen, his eyes focused on the ground. The boy was afraid to sit down on the logs felled around him, afraid of what might be under them.

And then his headlamp caught something. The black leather reflected back at him; it was a shiny square atop a charred pile of pine needles. He bent down and picked it up carefully. It was a wallet, still smooth and in nearly perfect condition. The boy stretched his thin fingers out and opened it. He saw a photo: a man and a woman and kids. Kids, just like him. A family, just like his.

Putt gulped for breath. His chest tightened. He felt sick. He'd come here to prove himself, but now he only felt fear. He dropped the wallet and wanted nothing more than to rip off his pack and run away. He thought of his fellow teammates: *Please come back soon. Don't leave me here.*

It was around 10:00 P.M. when the Alpine team headed back to the makeshift base. They hiked down the mountainside in silence, and when they reached the road, the asphalt was aglow in police lights and flood lamps. Next to a small ditch, Burdick, Wood, and a few others were waiting. Watson approached. After nearly five hours of searching, he told the waiting men, the team hadn't found anyone alive.

The group huddled for a few minutes as the rest of the team made its way down the last stretch of mountain. When Putt arrived, he'd gathered himself. The others around him didn't seem overly affected by what they'd just seen. Putt, however, was still terrified and kept quiet. In the biggest moment of his brief existence, he'd crumbled under the pressure.

The teens met with the other Alpine adults. The older kids who wanted to stay the night could, but it wasn't mandatory. There'd be work in the morning, perhaps to remove bodies. Burdick, Greene, and Watson agreed to spend the night there.

The kids were dismissed, and Putt found a ride home with the same teenagers who'd brought him up the mountain. It was nearly midnight when the SUV rolled up to the two-story house Putt lived in with his parents and six siblings. The front porch light was on; Putt rang the doorbell and his father let him in. Putt crept up the stairs to his room and changed his clothes. He fell into bed, exhausted, but he couldn't sleep. As the night's light cast shadows throughout his bedroom, Putt lay on his back, staring at the ceiling, thinking about the photo in the wallet. He felt sick again.

The boy got up and sneaked down the hallway to his parents' room—they were both asleep when he entered. Putt lifted the edge of the bed sheets and slid in between his mother and father. He could hear their breathing, and for the first time all night, he felt safe.

By the time the sun broke and ran a trail of light through the valley, Burdick, Greene, and Watson were already up. Slowly, the government types began arriving: the National Transportation Safety Board (NTSB), the Federal Aviation Administration, the Federal Bureau of Investigation, the sheriff, the coroner. Ambulances parked along the highway.

The adults confirmed to the boys what had happened: the wrecked plane above them was carrying the Wichita State football team, and they now were presiding over the worst collegiate air disaster in the nation's history. Twenty-nine people were presumed dead. Another 11 were injured—some terribly—and were being cared for at Denver-area hospitals.

Plans were made: Burdick and Watson would remove bodies with two members from another rescue team. The four would be the only ones allowed to touch the remains. Greene would be one of the lead runners on the "litters," light frames that held the remains and were belayed along a series of ropes that led from the crash site to the road.

A bulldozer was called in from the Straight Creek Tunnel construction site and began cutting across the forest to pick up the broken engines.

Around 8:00 A.M., Burdick, Watson, and Greene began the trek to the crash site. Watson was hoping the crew would not find any more body parts.

Click. The front of the plane had burned hottest, and Burdick and Watson found the first skulls. The teenagers—wearing gloves, boots taped at the shins to keep the dust out, and bandanas and ripped-up T-shirts as makeshift masks—backed away so a photographer could take a photo of the remains.

Click. The two collected bones and put them in bags.

There were remains near the middle of the plane. Some looked mummified. Burdick and Watson stopped seeing them as humans. The intense smell of death permeated the site.

Click. The pair lifted one body out of a seat. It broke apart in their hands.

Click. There was another body at the back of the plane, face down, with an arm stuck above its head, as if it were reaching out, trying to escape the danger. Watson situated himself over the body and tried to figure out how to put it into the black bag. He turned the body over and pushed the arm down. The body belched trapped air in his face.

A few feet away, Greene said prayers as he ushered the bags down the mountain. He made sure the remains didn't bounce on the way to the ambulances. Just because their souls had gone to heaven, Greene thought, didn't mean that these hadn't been people a day earlier.

Nine. That's how many people survived the crash. There were 31 dead, including the head coach, the athletic director, the state representative and his wife, the boosters, the plane's captain, the student equipment manager. Taylor. Reeves. Those two made it out after the crash, but their injuries were too severe. Reeves's wife left the maternity ward so she could be with her husband, who eventually died. In all, 13 children were orphaned.

Not long after the accident, the investigations and finger-pointing began. No one wanted to be responsible for the tragedy. The plane's owner told the NTSB he wasn't running the show—the plane was chartered by the university and the school should have taken more precautions, should have had sole authority over the flight. The university disagreed, but the agreement didn't spell out who was in charge of the flight. The man who'd made the agreement died on the plane.

Skipper lived. The first officer told the NTSB that the school was in charge. He testified that he was taking the shortest route to Logan, that the decision to change flight plans wasn't part of a sightseeing trip. It didn't matter anyway, he said, because his pilot was calling the shots. The dead captain had put that plane into the ground. An "act of God," Skipper called the crash.

In the end, Skipper would be punished: he was forced to temporarily give up his pilot's license, and Golden Eagle Aviation lost its air-taxi certificate. The pilot-leasing business went belly-up.

The team took a vote nine days after the crash and decided they'd play the next six games with freshmen and reserves. They called it the Second Season. And so, 22 days after they lost their head coach and 14 starters, the Shockers took the field at War Memorial Stadium in Little Rock, Arkansas. The crowd rose to its feet, and the fans stomped and clapped and cheered for their opponents. Arkansas won the game 62–0.

The Shockers would play a few more games before another news story swept them from the front pages of even their own newspapers. On November 14, 1970, a plane carrying Marshall University's football team went down in West Virginia and killed all 75 people aboard.

August 23, 2010. The rain has just passed overhead, casting cool, gray clouds over Mt. Trelease. John Putt squirms into his pack — the litter, the massive piece of metal that unfolds into a stretcher — as he stands along a road at the mountain's base. The pack is crammed with 400 feet of bagged climbing rope, brake plates, and other gear. All told, the metal contraption extends a foot above his head and weighs more than 80 pounds. He'll need none of this equipment today, but he needs to feel all of it.

Fifty feet.

He scrambles up this mountain because it is what he does now to chase the ghosts from his mind. And when he goes up now and the memories still don't go away, he returns. Again and again. Five times up Mt. Trelease. And when those memories still haunt him, he returns once more, this time with 80 pounds strapped to his back because that weight is both his punishment and his redemption.

One hundred feet.

Coward. That's what he'd thought of himself for nearly 40 years after the crash. On that night in October 1970, he froze and he failed his teammates. And he failed those folks from Wichita State, even when there was no one alive for him to fail.

One hundred and fifty feet.

Friend. That's what the people from Wichita State call John Putt when they ask if he can take families to the site these days. That's what they call him when a dead player's niece stands among that debris and shakes Putt's hand and tells him that he must have been a brave boy to go up that night. *Twelve years old.* Putt does not respond. But in helping these people, he knows he is helping himself, and perhaps giving final comfort to those who died on that plane almost a half-century ago.

Two hundred feet.

But until he no longer feels as if he's let himself and others down, he will climb. He will climb until those ghosts no longer follow him back down that mountain. So on days like this, when cool air sweeps through the valley and clouds shadow the sun from the pine trees below, Putt will climb and he will suck for air and sweat will run down his face.

Two hundred and fifty feet. There is still a ways to go.

He stops along a trail and leans against a tree. Putt takes off his glasses. His eyes are red and teary. He wipes them and looks up that mountain. And then he starts to climb again, hoping that one day when he comes down, he will feel a peace he hasn't felt in 40 years.

JOHN McPHEE

The Patch

FROM THE NEW YORKER

YOU MOVE YOUR CANOE through open water a fly cast away from a patch of lily pads. You cast just shy of the edge of the pads—inches off the edge of the pads. A chain pickerel is a lone ambush hunter. Its body resembles a barracuda's and has evolved to similar purpose. Territorial, concealed in the vegetation, it hovers; and not much but its pectoral fins are in motion. Endlessly patient, it waits for prey to come by—frogs, crayfish, newts, turtles, and smaller fish, including its own young. Long, tubular, with its pelvic fins set far back like the wings of some jets, it can accelerate like a bullet.

You lay a kiwi muddler out there—best white or yellow. In the water, it appears to be a minnow. Strip in line, more line, more line. In a swirl as audible as it is visible, the lake seems to explode. You need at least a 12-pound leader, because this fish has teeth like concertina wire. I tried a braided steel tippet once, of a type made for fish of this family, but casting it was clunky and I gave it up in favor of monofilament thick enough to win the contest between the scissoring teeth and the time it takes to net the fish. I've been doing this for more than 30 years, always in October in New Hampshire with my friend George Hackl, whose wife owns an undeveloped island in Lake Winnipesaukee. Chain pickerel are sluggish and indifferent in the warmer months. In the cold dawns and the cold dusks of October, they hit like hammers, some days on the surface, some days below it, a mass idiosyncrasy that is not well understood.

Thoreau understood—more than most, anyway—this "swiftest, wariest, and most ravenous of fishes . . . stately, ruminant . . . lurking under the shadow of a pad at noon . . . still, circumspect . . . motionless as a jewel set in water." He said he had "caught one which had swallowed a brother pickerel half as large as itself, with the tail still visible in its mouth," and he noted that "sometimes a striped snake, bound to greener meadows across the stream, ends its undulatory progress in the same receptacle."

Men who pass us on the lake in bass boats, sitting on their elevated seats and sweeping the water with spinning gear, are less impressed. They think of chain pickerel as trash, call them names like "slime darts," and actually laugh when we tell them what we are fishing for. They also tend to thank us. They want bass in their nets, not pickerel, and pickerel can not only outrace bass to their lures but also wreck the lures with their teeth. We are out there neither to trash them nor to admire them but to catch them for breakfast. A sautéed young pickerel is more delicious than most fish. The paradox of pickerel fishing is that a pickerel's culinary quality is in inverse proportion to its size. The big ones taste like kiln-dried basswood, and are also full of bones. The Y-shaped, intermuscular bones of the very young ones go down soft. Pickerel grow like bamboo. Ichthyologists have watched them grow an inch in two days.

As far as I know, my father never fished for chain pickerel. When I was three years old, he was the medical doctor at a summer camp on the Baie de Chaleur, and he fished for salmon in the Restigouche with his bamboo rod. He fished with grasshoppers in a Vermont gorge, and angleworms in Buzzards Bay, taking me with him when I was six, seven, eight. And across the same years we went trout fishing in New Jersey streams. On Opening Day, in April, we would get up in the pitch dark in order to be standing beside a stream at the break of dawn. One time, as dawn broke, we discovered that the stream was frozen over. On the way home, he let me "drive." I sat in his lap and steered—seat belts an innovation not yet innovated. These are my fondest memories of my father, his best way of being close, and I therefore regret all the more that my childhood love of fishing fell away in my teenage years, and stayed away, in favor of organized sports and other preoccupations.

The dormant angler in me remained dormant until he woke up in Arctic Alaska for the purpose of eating grayling, salmon, and char. After that, I took fishing gear on other canoe trips—down the Allagash, down the St. John—but seldom used it until the October of my 48th year, camping with the Hackls on the New Hampshire island, watching the colors fall into the water, and looking around for things to do.

Sometimes when chain pickerel are hovering high they see your moving fly from a distance, and come for it, come right toward you, etching on the surface a rippling wake, like a torpedo. It takes just one such scene to arouse you forever. Across an open channel from the New Hampshire island lay a quarter-mile of sharply edged lily pads, and soon we were calling it not a patch but The Patch. We scouted the lily pads of other bays, and fished every one of them, but always came back to The Patch. It was the home shore, running from a sedge fen off the tip of a neighboring island and along a white-pine forest on the mainland to the near side of another island. Our wives—Ann and Yolanda, each the other's oldest friend —were absolutely uninterested in pickerel except with their toast and coffee, but from year to year George and I grew better at fishing for them, each of us standing up and casting from his own canoe, anchored or drifting, sense of balance as yet uneroded. At the end of the seventh October, after Yolanda and I had driven home to New Jersey, we came up the driveway and the telephone inside the house was ringing as we approached the door. My brother was calling to tell me that my father was in a Baltimore County hospital, having suffered a debilitating stroke.

His room had a south-facing window. My mother, in a flood of light, 87, looked even smaller than she was, and space was limited around her, with me, my brother, my sister, and a young doctor together beside the bed. I was startled by the candor of the doctor. He said the patient did not have many days to live, and he described cerebral events in language only the patient, among those present, was equipped to understand. But the patient did not understand: "He can't comprehend anything, his eyes follow nothing, he is finished," the doctor said, and we should prepare ourselves.

Wordlessly, I said to him, "You fucking bastard." My father may not have been comprehending, but my mother was right there before him, and his words, like everything else in those hours, were falling upon her and dripping away like rain. Nor did he stop. There was more of the same, until he finally excused himself to continue on his rounds.

During our second day there, my mother, brother, and sister went off at one point, and I was alone for an hour in the room with my father. Eyes wide open in a fixed stare at the ceiling, he lay motionless. I wondered what to do. I wasn't about to pick up a book and read. I looked out the window for a time, at Baltimore, spilling over its beltway. I looked back at him. Spontaneously, I began to talk. In my unplanned, unprepared way, I wanted to fill the air around us with words, and keep on filling it, to no apparent purpose but, I suppose, a form of self-protection. I told him where I had been — up in New England on the lake in the canoe, casting — and that the fishing had gone well despite the cold. One day, there had been an inch of ice on the water bucket in the morning. My fingers were red as I paddled and cast. Water, coming off the fly line as I stripped it in, froze in the guides that hold the line close to the rod, and so jammed the line that it was uncastable; so I went up the rod from bottom to top punching out little disks of ice with my thumb until I could make another cast and watch a fresh torpedo come out of the vegetation.

I went on in this manner, impulsively blurting out everything I could think of about the species, now and again making comparisons and asking him questions — did he remember the sand sharks off Sias Point? the rainbows of Ripton? the bullhead he gutted beside Stony Brook that flipped out of his hand and, completely gutless, swam away? — to which I expected no answers, and got none.

With those minutely oscillating fins, a pickerel treads water in much the way that a hummingbird treads air. If the pickerel bursts forth to go after prey, it returns to the place it started from, with or without the prey. If a pickerel swirls for your fly and misses, it goes back to the exact spot from which it struck. You can return half an hour later and it will be there. You can return at the end of the day and it will be there. You can go back next year and it will be there.

In an acreage of lily pads, their territorial haunts are not always far apart. I have laid a fly on the water and seen three wakes converge upon it. Where Genio C. Scott, in *Fishing in American Waters* (1869), describes chain pickerel at such a moment, he says, "You will find cause for surprise that will force you to ejaculate." For my part, I'll admit, I damned near fell out of the canoe. An acreage of lily pads is not entirely like a woven mat. There are open spots, small clear basins, like blue gaps among clouds. By no means all the pickerel in The Patch are close to the edge as if looking out from beneath a marquee. They are also back among the gaps, and some are in acute shallows very close to shore, in case a mouse slips on something and falls into the water. To fly-cast among the gaps is much more difficult than along the edge of open water. Typically, you are trying to drop a long throw into six square feet of clear space, and if you miss you will be stuck fast to nymphaeaceous stems and cursing. Yanking on your line, you will bomb the territory and retrieve a pound of weed.

This family—*Esocidae*—is not popular with aesthetes, with people who torture trout. Put a pickerel in a pond full of trout, and before long all that's in there is a larger pickerel. There are people who hunt pickerel with shotguns. In Vermont, that is legal. Two other members of the family—pike and muskellunge—are quite similar in pattern, configuration, color, and appetite but are, of course, much and very much larger. Under each eye, chain pickerel have a black vertical bar, not unlike the black horizontal bars that are painted under the eyes of football players, and evidently for the same reason: to sharpen vision by cutting down glare. A pickerel's back is forest green, and its sides shade into a light gold that is overprinted with a black pattern of chain links as consistent and uniform as a fence. This artistic presentation is entirely in the scales, which are extremely thin and small. On a filleting board, a couple of passes with a scaler completely destroy the art, revealing plain silver skin.

On the filleting board, evidence is forthcoming that chain pickerel are as voracious as insurance companies, as greedy as banks. The stomachs, usually, are packed and distended. A well-fed pickerel will readily strike, the fact notwithstanding that it already has in its stomach a frog, say, and a crayfish and a young pickerel, each in a different stage of decomposition. I have almost never opened a pickerel and found an empty stomach. I have caught pickerel, slit their stomachs, and watched crayfish walk out undamaged. I put the crayfish back in the lake. Stomachs of pickerel have contained birds.

Pickerel have palatal teeth. They also have teeth on their tongues, not to mention those razor jaws. On their bodies, they sometimes bear scars from the teeth of other pickerel. Pickerel that have been found in the stomachs of pickerel have in turn contained pickerel in their stomachs. A minnow found in the stomach of a pickerel had a pickerel in its stomach that had in its stomach a minnow. Young pickerel start eating one another when they are scarcely two inches long. How did I know all this that was tumbling out? I was mining a preoccupation. I am the owner of not one but two copies of *An Annotated Bibliography of the Chain Pickerel*, E. J. Crossman and G. E. Lewis, the Royal Ontario Museum, 1973.

In uncounted millions, they live in the lakes, ponds, streams, and rivers of the Atlantic watershed from the Canadian Maritimes to the whole of Florida, and across to the Mississippi, and up it to the Current River in southern Missouri. They seem about as endangered as mosquitoes. In midwestern states and elsewhere, walleyes are often called pickerel and sometimes walleyed pike. A walleye is not a pickerel, nor is it a pike; it's a perch. A bluegill maneuvers better than most fish do. Blue sharks and tunas are ultimate cruisers. In the department of acceleration — the drag race of the deep — almost nothing comes near a pike, pickerel, or muskellunge. A pickerel's body is 60 percent muscle. Undulations move along the body in propulsive waves that culminate, like oar sculling, in straight-line forward thrust. A particularly successful tuna will catch about 30 percent of the fish it goes after. A trout catches half the fish it strikes at. A chain pickerel, on a good day, nails 80 percent. The last time a frog escaped a pickerel must have been in Pliocene time.

The young doctor returned, 24 hours exactly after his earlier visit. He touched the patient with fingers and steel, and qualified for compensation. He said there had been no change and not to expect any; the patient's comprehension would not improve. He went on as he had the day before. My father, across the years, had always seemed incapable of speaking critically of another doctor, perhaps, in a paradoxical way, because he had been present in an operating room where the mistake of another doctor had ended his mother's life. Even-tempered as he generally appeared to be, my father could blow his top, and I wondered, with respect to his profession, to what extent this situation would be testing him if he were able to listen, comprehend, and speak. Silent myself now, in the attending physician's presence, I looked down at my father in his frozen state, 89, a three-season athlete who grew up in the central neighborhoods of Youngstown, Ohio, and played football at Oberlin in a game that was won by Ohio State 128–0, captained basketball, was trained at Western Reserve, went into sports medicine for five years at Iowa State and thirty-six at Princeton, and was the head physician of U.S. Olympic teams in Helsinki, Rome, Tokyo, Innsbruck, and elsewhere. The young doctor departed.

In a small open pool in the vegetation, about halfway down The Patch, there had been, this year and last, a chain pickerel that was either too smart or too inept to get itself around an assemblage of deer hair, rabbit fur, turkey quill, marabou silk, and sharp heavy wire. The swirls had been violent every time, the strike consistently missing or spurning the fly, and coming always from the same place on the same side of the same blue gap. In the repetitive geometries of The Patch, with its paisley patterns in six acres of closed and open space, how did I know it was the same gap? I just knew, that's all. It's like running a trapline. You don't forget where the traps are; or you don't run a trapline. This gap in the lily pads was 30 yards off the mainland shore between the second-tallest white pine and a granitic outcrop projecting from Ann's island. As I was getting back into the story, again speaking aloud in the renewed privacy of the hospital room, I mentioned that I had been fishing The Patch that last morning with my father's bamboo rod, and it felt a bit heavy in the hand, but since the day he had turned it over to me I had taken it with my other rods on fishing trips, and had used it, on occasion, to keep it active because it was his. Now—just a couple of days ago—time was more than close to running out. Yolanda was calling from the island: "John, we must go! John, stop fishing! John!" It was time to load the canoe and paddle west around some islands to the car, time to depart for home, yes; but I meant to have one more drift through The Patch. From the northwest, a light breeze was coming down over the sedge fen. I called to Yolanda that I'd "be right there," then swept the bow around and headed for the fen. Since I had failed and failed again while anchored near that fish, I would let the light breeze carry me this time, freelance, free-form, moving down The Patch like the slow shadow of a cloud. Which is just what happened—a quiet slide, the light rustle on the hull, Yolanda calling twice more before she gave up. Two touches with the paddle were all that was needed to perfect the aim. Standing now, closing in, I waved the bamboo rod like a semaphore—backcasting once, twice—and then threw the line. Dropping a little short, the muddler landed on the near side of the gap. The pickerel scored the surface in crossing it, swirled, made a solid hit, and took the tight line down, wrapping it around the stems of the plants.

"I pulled him out of there plants and all," I said. "I caught him with your bamboo rod."

I looked closely at my father. His eyes had welled over. His face was damp. Six weeks later, he was dead.

P. J. O'ROURKE

Fetch Daddy a Drink

FROM GARDEN AND GUN

I HAVE THREE badly behaved children and a damn good bird dog. My Brittany spaniel, Millie (age seven), is far more biddable and obedient than my daughters, Muffin (eleven) and Poppet (nine), and has a better nose than my son, Buster (five). Buster does smell, but in his case it's an intransitive verb.

My dog is perdition to the woodcock and ruffled grouse we hunt hereabouts and death itself to the pen-raised Huns, chukars, and quail she encounters at the local shooting club. Millie hunts close, quarters well, points beautifully, is staunch to wing and shot, and retrieves with verve. My children . . . are doing okay in school, I guess. They look very sweet—when they're asleep.

As my family was growing, I got a lot of excellent advice about discipline, responsibility, respect, affection, and cultivation of the work ethic. Unfortunately this advice was from dog trainers and was directed to my dog. In the matter of child rearing there was also plenty of advice, all of it contradictory—from family and family-in-law, wife, wife's girlfriends, pediatricians, nursery school teachers, babysitters, neighbors and random old ladies on the street, plus Dr. Spock, Dr. Phil, and, for all I know, Dr. Pepper: Spank them/Don't spank them. Make them clean their plate/ Keep them from overeating. Potty train them at one/Send them to Potty Training Camp at fourteen. Hover over their every activity/ Get out of their faces. Don't drink or smoke during pregnancy/ Junior colleges need students too. And none of this advice works when you're trying to get the kids to quit playing video games and go to bed.

It took me years to realize that I should stop asking myself what I'm doing wrong as a parent and start asking myself what I'm doing right as a dog handler.

The first right thing I do is read and reread *Gun Dog* by the late Richard A. Wolters. This is the book that revolutionized dog training in 1961. (Of course, the dogs are now 49 years old and not much use, but the book is still great.)

"Start 'em young" is the message from Wolters. And that's why, if we have another child, he's going to learn to walk pushing on the handle of a Toro in the yard instead of teetering along the edge of the sofa cushions in the living room. Wolters, along with a number of other bird shooters, had realized that waiting until the traditional one-year mark before teaching a puppy to hunt was like carrying your kid in a Snugli until he was seven. Wolters was sure he was right about this, but he wasn't sure why. Then he came across the work of Dr. John Paul Scott, a founder of the Animal Behavior Society. Dr. Scott was involved in a project to help Guide Dogs for the Blind, Inc. Seeing Eye dog training was considered almost too difficult to be worthwhile. Using litters from even the best bloodlines, the success rate for guide-dog training was only 20 percent. Dr. Scott discovered that if training began at five weeks instead of a year, and continued uninterrupted, the success rate rose to 90 percent.

It goes without saying that the idea of Seeing Eye kids is wrong — probably against child labor laws and an awful thing to do to blind people. But I take Dr. Scott's point. And so did Richard Wolters, who devised a gun-dog training regime that had dogs field-ready at as early as six months. That's three and a half in kid years. My kids weren't doing anything at three and a half, other than at night in their Pull-Ups.

The Start-'Em-Young program turns out to be a surprise blessing for dads. Wolters writes in *Gun Dog* of a puppy's first 28 days (equal to about six months for a kid), "Removal from Mother at this time is drastic." That's just what I told my wife about the care and feeding of our infants — *drastic* is the word for leaving it to me. According to Wolters, I'm really not supposed to get involved until the kid is one (equivalent to a 56-day-old pup). Then I can commence the nurturing (Happy Meals) and the "establishing rapport" (sitting with me on the couch watching football).

Next the training proper begins. "Repetition, more repetition, and still more repetition," enjoins Wolters. I've reached the age where I'm repeating myself all the time, so this is easy. "Commands should be short, brisk, single words: SIT, FETCH, WHOA, COME, NO, etc." In the case of my kids the "etc." will be GETAJOB or at least MARRYMONEY.

"Keep lessons short," writes Wolters. And that must be good advice because notice how all the fancy private schools start later, end earlier, and get much more time off at Christmas and Easter than P.S. 1248. Wolters also points out that body language is important to the training process. "Your movements should be slow and deliberate, never quick and jerky." Martinis work for me.

"Don't clutter up his brain with useless nonsense," warns Wolters, who is opposed to tricks such as "roll over" or "play Dick Cheney's lawyer" for dogs that have a serious purpose in life. Therefore, no, Muffin, Poppet, and Buster, I am not paying your college tuition so you can take a course called "Post-Marxist Structuralism in Fantasy/Sci-Fi Film." And, meanwhile, no, you can't have a Wii either.

Wolters favors corporal punishment for deliberate disobedience. "Failure to discipline is crueler," he claims. I do not recall my own dad's failure to discipline as being crueler than his pants-seat handiwork, but that may be my failing memory. In any case, a whack on the hindquarters is a last resort. Wolters prefers to use psychology: "You can hurt a dog just as much by ignoring him. For example, if you're trying to teach him SIT and STAY, but he gets up and comes to you, *ignore him*." When I was a kid, we called this dad working late every day of the week and playing golf all Sunday.

According to Wolters, the basic commands for a gun dog are SIT, STAY, COME, and WHOA. With no double-entendre intended concerning the GIT OVER HERE directive, those are exactly the four things my boy, Buster, will have to learn if he wants a happy marriage. My girls, Muffin and Poppet, on the other hand, seem to have arrived from the womb with a full understanding of these actions—and how to order everyone to do them.

"The last two, COME and WHOA," writes Wolters, "are so important that if a dog had good hunting instincts and knew only these two commands he would make a gun dog." It's the same for accomplishment in every other field, among people and pooches alike. If you had to give just two rules for success in business, politics, family, friendship, or even church, you could do a lot worse than SHOW UP and SHUT UP.

Wolters begins, however, with SIT and STAY. And these are important too. Kids today are given frequent encouragement to STAND UP FOR THIS AND THAT. But SIT TIGHT 'TIL IT BLOWS OVER is wiser counsel. Wolters employs a leash to pull the head up as he pushes the rump down. I've found that the collar of a T-shirt works just as well. Wolters uses praise in the place of dog biscuits; he writes, "I do not believe in paying off a dog by shoving food into his mouth." I, on the other hand, try to make sure the kids eat their green leafy vegetables once I've got them seated.

Wolters teaches STAY by slowly moving away from the dog while repeating the command and making a hand signal with an upright palm. But I've found that if your kids get Nickelodeon on cable TV, you don't have to say or do anything. They'll stay right there in front of it for hours.

Once SIT and STAY have been mastered, you can go on to COME. Wolters lowers his palm as a signal to go with the command, but a cell-phone signal will also work if your kids are properly trained. Mine aren't. Getting a kid to come when he's called is a lot harder than getting a dog to, probably because the dog is almost certain that you don't have green leafy vegetables in the pocket of your shooting jacket. Wolters suggests that if you're having trouble teaching COME, you should run away, thereby enticing the dog to run after you. This has been tried with kids in divorce after divorce all across America, with mixed results.

The command that's the most fun to teach using Wolters's method is WHOA:

"The dog," writes Wolters, "is ready to learn WHOA as soon as he will STAY on hand signal alone and COME on command. When he has this down pat, my system is— *scare the hell out of the dog*. Put the pup in the SIT STAY position. Walk a good distance away from him. Command COME. Run like hell away from him. Make him get up steam. Then reverse your field. Turn, run at the dog. Shout WHOA. Thrust the hand up in the STAY hand signal like a traffic cop. Jump in the air at him. *Do it with gusto.* You'll look so foolish doing it that he'll stop."

Personally, I don't have to go to this much trouble. Just my morning appearance—hungover, unshaven, wearing my ratty bathrobe and slippers Millie chewed—is enough to stop my children cold. I reserve the antics that Wolters describes for commands to this idiot computer I'm writing on. *Gun Dog* was authored in the days of the simple, reliable Royal Portable. Thus Wolters has nothing to say about computers. Besides, dogs don't use computers. (Although, on my Visa bills, I've noticed some charges to rottenmeat.com.)

Children don't need computer training either. Muffin, Poppet, and Buster—who can't even read—have "good computing instincts." When the Internet says COME, they come. Mom and Dad try WHOA on certain websites, but whether that works we can't tell. I'm the one who should be taught some basic commands, to make this darned PC . . .

"What's the matter, Daddy?" Muffin asks. With one deft flick of the mouse thing, she persuades the balky printer to disgorge all that I have composed. I see her frown. "Daddy, Millie chews everybody's shoes. She bit the teenager that mows the lawn. She killed Mom's chickens. And every time you come home from hunting, you're all red in the face and yelling that you're going to sell her to a Korean restaurant. And . . ."

And here is where my Richard A. Wolters theory of parenting goes to pieces. There is one crucial difference between children and dogs. You can teach a dog to lie. DOWN.

YONI BRENNER

Trick Plays

FROM THE NEW YORKER

The Quadruple Play Fake

The quarterback receives the snap from the center and fakes a handoff to the running back. Then he pivots right and fakes another handoff to the fullback. Then he fakes two more handoffs in quick succession: to a wide receiver, and then, once again, to the running back, who looped back behind the line of scrimmage during all the faking. Pretty soon, the defense catches on and goes after the quarterback, at which point the actual trick is revealed: the first fake handoff was real.

Musical Chairs

The offense arrives on the field with a two-receiver, two-end package. The receivers bunch to the left and the first tight end splits out wide to the right. Then the quarterback starts patting his pockets and looking around anxiously, as if he can't find his keys. Meanwhile, the second tight end—who has a beautiful singing voice—drifts into the backfield and croons selections from *A Little Night Music.* This continues until the referee blows the whistle for delay of game.

This play will not yield any yards, but it will get the defense thinking.

Double Trick Inside Stunt

Essentially, a well-disguised variation on the strong-side blitz. For the first trick, the strong-side linebacker "stunts" inside the defensive tackle to confuse the blockers. The other trick is that they're all on steroids.

The Open-Source Sweep

A week before the big game, team officials engineer a "chance encounter" between the opposing quarterback and the actor Jake Gyllenhaal. The pair become fast friends, attending a number of folk concerts and rummage sales together. As their relationship blossoms, Gyllenhaal inculcates the quarterback with progressive ideas about transparency and freedom of information, and by the end of the week he convinces the quarterback to post his team's playbook on WikiLeaks. The team loses five of its next six games, and the quarterback is benched. As for Jake Gyllenhaal, he is eventually cleared of any wrongdoing, and is hired by Fox Sports to join Howie Long and Michael Strahan on the Sunday NFL pregame show.

Last Man Standing

In a single-back, four-wideout formation, the quarterback accidentally sends the receivers on identical crossing routes, causing a spectacular collision at midfield. The defense seizes the advantage: they overpower the offensive line and pancake the quarterback for a substantial loss, leaving only the running back to tell their stories and sing their songs and pass on their proud traditions of hunting and leatherwork.

The Sleight of Hand

The quarterback lines up behind the center and takes the snap. But as he drops back we see that he's holding not a football but a basketball. This causes the defense to hesitate, and the quarterback lobs the basketball deep to the wide receiver. The receiver catches it in stride for a touchdown—at which point the ball turns into a bouquet of roses. If, however, the ball is intercepted, it turns into bees.

Buried Treasure!

After sacking the quarterback, a defensive lineman "accidentally" leaves behind a tattered parchment scroll that turns out to be a sixteenth-century treasure map. In the second half, the quarterback is consumed with visions of rubies, silver coins, and gold bullion. He recruits a party of his most trusted offensive linemen and together they embark on a two-week journey to a forgotten island off the coast of Guadeloupe. They return, bedraggled but successful, bearing a treasure worth nearly $80,000—only to discover that the combined lost salary for the weeks they missed added up to $4.3 million. The season ends badly, with the team slipping into last place and the starting left guard succumbing to wounds sustained in a cutlass fight.

West Coast Misdirection

During the offseason, the opposing quarterback is again approached by the actor Jake Gyllenhaal. The quarterback warns Gyllenhaal to keep his distance, but Gyllenhaal tells him that it isn't like that—he wants to offer the quarterback a part in an independent film he is producing, called *The Quarterback and the Dame,* about an unlikely romance between a gridiron hero and the English stage legend Judi Dench. The quarterback reads the script, and he has to admit it's pretty good, so he signs on. The quarterback arrives on the set for the first day of shooting, only to find Gyllenhaal costumed in shoulder pads and eye black. The quarterback goes berserk, believing that he'd been promised the part.

"No, no," Gyllenhaal coos, "you're playing Judi Dench."

The End of Days

In the waning seconds of the first half of the NFC championship game, the pious visiting quarterback leads a masterly 80-yard drive, culminating in a 15-yard touchdown strike. As his teammates celebrate, the quarterback drops to one knee to thank Jesus. Just then, the Rapture comes, and the quarterback is instantly beamed up to Heaven, leaving only his cleats behind. The visiting team is forced to play the second half with the inconsistent journeyman Billy Joe Hobert, who throws three interceptions, and they end up losing the game, 42–10. The home team advances to the Super Bowl— only to lose in heartbreaking fashion, when what would have been the winning field goal caroms off an apocalyptic horseman and falls wide right.

MARK PEARSON

The Short History of an Ear

FROM SPORT LITERATE

THE KNEE HIT HARD, crumpled the vinyl halo, not much in the way of ear protection, but enough to pass the safety standard. The full force of the knee brought to bear upon the ear inside the halo. The bruised ear echoed with pain, skin separated from cartilage, and blood filled the space between. Within moments, the ear transformed itself into an overripe plum, split and dripping thick red nectar.

Weeks later, the doctor said: "I can still get a few milliliters of blood out of there."

His hypodermic needle poised on the examining table like a massive mosquito. I had seen ears, drained again and again, only to refill and harden, moonscapes, pocked with craters, rimmed with ridges. This ear was mine, earned, and paid for; he would not deflate it with his hungry hypodermic. On purpose, I waited too long, a week, maybe two, as the sharp twinges of my heart beat in my ear. When I walked outside, the midwestern winter wind felt good, iced the skin, and numbed the pain. The ear, once soft, a pliable blood balloon, overflowed its rim then it shrank like a receding flood and hardened. Fissures formed like drying mud flats.

"That's okay," I said. "Leave it."

He looked at me. Slightly amused, he asked, "Where are you from?"

"Pennsylvania."

"A tough guy from Pennsylvania, huh?"

We weren't quite from coal country, but we were close enough. Twenty-five minutes away they fired the Bethlehem Steel mills with the coal that was mined a little farther north. Next town over, Allentown, they bent and shaped steel into Mack Trucks. An hour away they were ripping slate and shale from the mountains and turning the hillsides into black stick forests of dead trees and mud. I grew up wrestling against the sons of the men who worked in those places, tending the furnaces, shoveling the coal, and bending the steel.

My father worked with steel in a different kind of factory. He was a furniture designer for Knoll International. He made sculptures in his spare time, and our living room was filled with his plaster, plastic, and wood found-object sculptures. His Pearson Chair was in the Louvre in Paris in a Knoll exhibition. The Pennsylvania Dutch kids, whose fathers were farmers and factory workers, thought we were weird, but they liked to look at my father's creations, filled with branches and plastic action figures caught in plaster like some abstract re-creation of Pompeii.

To add to it, we lived in what they called a modern house. It was more than 100 years old. What was modern about it, I wasn't sure. When my parents bought it, it had no plumbing and its heating system consisted of black potbelly stoves. They bought the house from an old man who used to shoot deer from the living room window. He would come back to the house sometimes to pick wild mint to make tea. My father gutted it before we moved in. He and a friend took an electric saw to the outhouse, then kicked it over and it rolled down the hill. He knocked a hole in the three-foot-thick stonewalls to put in a kitchen window. He rounded the corners of the new window instead of squaring them. This was apparently modern to the neighborhood kids.

We lived in the middle of the woods on the side of a steep hill that ran down into a narrow valley split by a trout stream where I spent most of my springs fishing for rainbows.

One time when I was six or seven, I made a model chair like the ones I saw him make. I used scraps of leather and balsa wood. It was covered in white glue and crooked. My father looked at it and said, "It looks like a dancing chair." It hurt when he said it. Later, when I wondered if I should follow him into design, he just said, "It's too hard to make a living at it."

Growing up, we didn't have much more than dreams. Knoll shut down its design department and my father found another job.

When that company closed down, he tried to freelance. It didn't work out. That winter we had a cold snap and our electricity was shut off. I'd shower in the gym each morning when I got to school. When I got home, I would carry tin buckets in the dark to the top of the hill behind the house to get water from the spring. The water line had frozen and we had no running water in the house. I'd fill 10 one-gallon buckets and leave them in the living room, so my brothers and sister could take baths the next day. The hillside was frozen over and the spring looked like a miniature glacier.

Years later, it was still with me. "Your ear doesn't bend," the barber said. One finger pressed the back of it, scissors snipped hair, and each cut exposed it more. There is not much hair to hide it anymore and just as well. I never wanted it hidden.

"Cauliflower ear," I said.

She nodded and said: "I don't like people playing with my ears." She held the ear gently between her thumb and forefinger, and trimmed the hair around it. The electric razor hummed in my ear as she worked. She was unfazed, not like the girl at the coffee shop, who stared, and asked: "Is it a birth defect?"

"No."

"Does it hurt?"

"No."

"Can you hear okay?"

"What?"

She looked down, counted the change into my palm, made eye contact with the next customer.

The folds of skin and cartilage that make up the external ear are what got damaged. The external ear is there to protect the eardrum, collect and guide sound waves into the ear canal to the eardrum. It's an intricate system designed to catch sound waves. It did its job of protecting the middle and the inner ear, those delicate internal mechanisms where the eardrum passes its vibrations to the middle ear (ossicles), then on to the hammer (malleus), then the anvil (incus), and then on into the labyrinth where eventually the sound passes through a liquid chamber where nerve impulses transmit to the brain.

The internal mechanisms of my ear are intact.

I can hear just fine.

People ask: Can you get plastic surgery?

I ignore it.

In Japan where they have a cultural respect for martial arts it is seen as a badge of honor. Here, people just think it's ugly.

Medical sources refer to it as a deformity, prescribe treatments: ice, drain, and pack tightly.

What I hear is my father's story about wrestling in the national finals in Laramie, Wyoming. It's 1958—a year before I was born. Thirty seconds from the end of his final match, he's winning and he has a vision of himself stepping to the top of the awards podium and accepting the national championship plaque. The image floats there for a moment and then it's gone. A last-second takedown erases his lead and he loses 7–5.

The vision, born in the old gym on the high desert plateau of Wyoming, blew east, across the western plains, and midwestern cornfields, and caught up with me when I was a boy in the Appalachian foothills of eastern Pennsylvania. It hovered above me until it became my dream. One day at my elementary school, the principal announced that the youth association was starting a wrestling team. I couldn't wait until the end of school. When I got off the bus that afternoon, I ran all the way home, clutching a sign-up sheet, and sat on the front door step until my father got home.

It took me a long time to learn that wrestling was nothing but a fight with some rules to make sure nobody gets killed. It's a painful lesson, not just physical. I want to make my father proud, but early on, I get beat, and beat badly. I'm on my own.

My father made a wrestling mat out of vinyl and foam rubber and vinyl tape he got from Knoll's design and development department. We rolled it up against the wall in our living room. We would unroll it twice a week to practice, my father putting my younger brother, Eric, and me through drills. He was an expert at the side roll and bottom wrestling in general, techniques that were nearly lost as American folkstyle later got closer and closer to freestyle— an international style. One night I got angry because I felt he was unfairly using more strength on me while letting Eric, who was younger and smaller, execute his moves with ease. I was about 12, a skinny kid. I weighed 75 pounds. We got in a flurry and I caught him off balance and shoved him into the wall, then I jumped up and threw a wild punch that grazed his head. He shook it off and then launched me into the air—my head skimmed the ceiling and my legs were moving before I hit the ground, and they didn't stop moving until I was up the stairs and in my room. A few minutes later, I was back on the mat, finishing the drill. *Don't lose your composure* was all he said. My ears burned with anger and the constant abrasion from the vinyl mat.

It was just the beginning. From the time I was nine years old, wrestling hijacks my imagination. I dream of moves in my sleep. I walk through the days picturing my next match. I wrestle through elementary school and junior high school. Eastern Pennsylvania was a hot bed of wrestling and every weekend I faced opponents who went on to successful college wrestling careers. I got better, and then I got good. I started winning, but I was never a dominating wrestler, never did someone say: Man, that guy is great. That sort of notoriety eludes me, but it doesn't matter. I loved it. At first, I would make the finals of local tournaments, but end up second. Finally, I started to win.

All that mat time primes the ear. It's a matter of repetition: a head butt, an elbow, bang, bang, bang, agitate the skin and the cartilage. All it will take is one solid hit and then: the big blowup. The ear as it was previously known will disappear.

The ear isn't the only body part that takes a beating. I break my nose at least four times, tear ligaments in both ankles, snap my ACL, and tear cartilage in my knee and rib cage. I break my thumb —the same thumb I also dislocate—a dislocation so bad that when it happened all I could see of my thumb was the end of it with the fingernail sticking out of the other side of my palm. I almost puked. I held my hand up and my assistant coach snapped it back into place. Then my palm blew up to the size of a baseball. At the medical center, they shot my hand full of painkillers, and then a doctor cranked my thumb around in a full circle like it was the hour hand of a clock. "Yeah, I'd say you're done for a while," he said casually.

One night freshman year, overheated and starved from trying to cut to 129, I stick my head out of my dorm window into a starless Michigan night and open my mouth to catch the snowflakes that sift silently to the ground.

I once told my father I was going to Paris because I wanted to write and Paris was the place to go if you were young and wanted to write. He looked up, and squinting his eyes as if he was sighting a distant object, said: "If you want to write, go to Bayonne, New Jersey." Then he picked up a shovel and returned to tending his garden.

His words have stayed with me all of these years although he had forgotten them long ago. At one point in the intervening years, I asked him if he remembered them; he said no. Clearly, he never gave the significance to those words that I did. They were a kind of sphinx's riddle to me, and I sensed that if I could grasp their meaning, I would have unlocked the secret to artistic success. I worshiped my father in the way that some sons do, so his words—not frequently or carelessly issued—had the gravity of important things.

My wife, who is studying acupuncture, has a poster of an ear with all its acupuncture points hanging on a wall in our home office. In another picture in one of her textbooks, the image of a baby—a curled-up embryo—is superimposed over an ear. All the acupuncture points in an ear apply to the rest of the human body. Picture the image of a tiny baby tucked in your ear with its head nestled in your earlobe. There are hundreds of acupuncture points on the ear. You can treat the whole body through the ear. The ear is like some mystical spiral that unfolds into an entire body, everything flows through it.

"Ear" is even part of my name—Pearson. I've seen it spelled other ways too, Pierson, and Pehrson, the Swedish version. The name made its way from its Nordic roots to Scotland, down through England, and then on to the States when my father's parents immigrated here from the border of Scotland and northern England in the 1930s.

The lights flash in my eyes and leave spots. I blink, blink, blink, bridge, bridge. I'm skidding across the black mat on my face. The arena is upside down. I see feet, legs of chairs, then people sitting in them, my coaches. They're screaming something at me, but all I hear is my heart pounding in my ears, intermittent yells, thuds, my own strained breathing, an opponent clamped tight to my chest, breathing in my face. I'm wrapped tight, fighting off my back. It can't end here, I think — in a pigtail match at the Big Ten's.

How'd I draw the pigtail? Loser is out of the tournament, no chance to wrestle back. I twist, arch, drive with my feet, punch my hand across my chest, and I'm on my stomach, but two minutes have expired. A minute to go in the first period and I'm already down by five. 0–5. No time to waste. What happened? He was in on my legs. I tried to throw some junk move, but not the way I usually did it. I hipped to the side instead of rolling straight back and kicking him over me.

Five years of my coach yelling: "Don't throw that crap," so I went a different route. Bad time to experiment. I should have known. I get a one-point escape at the end of the first period to cut the lead to four. In the second period, I start to score, first an escape, then a takedown, but he escapes for one point. He has riding time from the eternity I fought off my back in the first period, and he scores just enough to stay ahead by 5–4 going into the third. He escapes in the third, to go up 6–4. He still has riding time, but I rode him enough to cut it down.

I get over-aggressive, as the clock winds down, and he scores a takedown, I'm down by five again, but I escape, score a takedown, run down his riding time. He's too hard to turn, so I cut him loose, but before I can score, time expires. I lose 9–7, and my college career is over.

Walking down the hall one day to teach a class at the University of Georgia, a middle-aged man, gray hair, squat, crushed nose, paused as I passed and asked: *Where did you wrestle . . . what college?* I had been lost in thought, reviewing the day's lesson, and his voice sounded alien in the polished corridor.

As he spoke, I heard the familiar singsong dialect of the Pennsylvania Dutch — the rising inflection at the end of the sentence. Living in the South, I had nearly forgotten it. He was a coach from the athletic department, arranging a tutor for an athlete. When I told him I wrestled at Michigan, he said: *You don't see many ears like that around here.*

I go to the acupuncture clinic for the pain in my hips and knees, residual effects from wrestling. The Chinese doctor sticks a needle into my hardened, thickened ear. It burns and I flinch. "Your ear is very special," she says. She seems to think it's congenital, some miraculous sign from a blessed birth, not from a violent blow to the head.

"It's from an injury," I say.

She nods, but I'm not sure she understands that there are wrestlers, boxers, rugby players, and others walking around with the same injury caused by some similar brutal collision. There's nothing miraculous or strange about it. It's a brutal trademark of a sport I sometimes love and sometimes hate. For days after the treatment, I can feel the place where the needle punctured my ear. It's a vague burning that makes me reach up and rub it. It feels too thick, almost alien, and reminds me of the past.

One day, I see a Knoll sign in the window of a furniture store. I turn the car around at the next intersection and go in. Max Pearson is my father, I said to the store manager. She seemed mildly amused. *We sell lots of your dad's chairs,* she said.

I look around the store and see the furniture we grew up with. We had prototypes from the different designers in our house. Saarinen's pedestal table was our dining room table. At some point, the works of Pollock, Shultz, Platner, and the other icons of modern furniture design drifted through our living room.

It feels strangely like home—the hillside home in Pennsylvania, where I heard the names of the other designers nearly every day. The same living room where we wrestled on the wrestling mat my father made out of vinyl and foam and rolled up against the wall, so we could practice whenever we wanted. In the humid, urban Houston environment, I realize how far I am from those cold winters in rural Pennsylvania. In the end, when it was clear I wasn't there to buy, the manager seemed to care that I was Max Pearson's son as much as those kids I wrestled against when I was a boy.

Another barber sees the ear. *You've got a broken ear,* he says with an accent that sounds Middle Eastern, Iranian, or perhaps Turkish. "Me too," he says pointing to a pair of flattened ears.

Broken ear, I said to myself. I'd never heard it called that before. I liked it. The name seemed so simple, so true—much better than cauliflower ear. I'd always thought of it as more stone—fossil even

—than vegetable. We talked about the sport that deformed our ears. He was from one of the places where it was an honor to have a broken ear and he spoke fondly of his days in the sport.

My father doesn't remember anything these days. He's deep in the throes of Alzheimer's. The last time I saw him, he didn't know who I was. For a while he used to take out his old wrestling scrapbook, and look over and over at the pictures and the headlines. "Did you see what they gave me?" he said once about his outstanding wrestler award from the Big Ten's. "I must have been pretty good."

But he's stopped doing that now. He spends his time running his fingers over chairs and fabric. In his mind, he must still be designing furniture. I read somewhere that in his final years, when he was suffering the final blows of Alzheimer's, they used to put Willem de Kooning in front of a canvas and he would go to work just like he always did.

My father isn't designing furniture anymore. The little workshop that he built out of trees that he felled in the backwoods of our house has fallen into chaos. He lives in a nursing home now. It's painful to see him that way. He'd always striven for independence. He always had a copy of *Walden* nearby. For a long time, he kept exercising. When my oldest daughter was seven, he raced her up the hill behind his house. When he was well, he used to bike and run, hike, and paddle his kayak on the Susquehanna River. One day he walked off into the woods and they found him in the darkness eight hours later, walking across a field at three o'clock in the morning. There were 125 people and a helicopter looking for him. When the paramedics checked him out, they said he was in amazing physical condition for a man his age.

But the exercise has stopped now. The last time he got lost in the woods seemed to take more of his life out of him. Even in his emaciated physical state, it seemed his body wouldn't quit on him. It compelled him forward, just like it had done 50 years before in the NCAA championships, pushing his opponents purposefully into overtime, where he knew he had an advantage. There was no advantage now, just some stubborn impulse to keep moving, to stay alive.

The mice are scratching at the insulation in the air conditioner in my father's studio. It's December and cold air whistles at the windows. Drafting tools and sketches of chairs that no one will ever sit in are piled on his desk. A router sits on the floor. He built the studio himself out of trees from his property, framed it up, put a roof on it, and nailed some sheetrock inside. He installed a wood-stove designed by a former colleague of his. The windows face the forest. I lift a torn piece of paper with notes on it. He has distinct handwriting. Strong lines. When I was a boy, I used to imitate his signature. The paper says: *Sculptures that move by air pressure; Random patterns of raindrops on a ceramic plate.*

The only wrestling I do anymore is with my daughters on the living room rug. They think it's great fun to jump on my back and get caught in the bear trap of my legs. They scream, *Let's wrestle, Daddy, come on, get down on your hands and knees. Let's go!*

We roll around on the floor in a knot of arms and legs. It's two on one, and I lose every time. When I pick up my three-year-old daughter, her small fingers find my ear. She hangs on to it as if it is a handle that keeps her from falling. She runs her fingers over it and it almost tickles. She looks at it, and then checks my other ear, her fingers pinch lightly, like tiny calipers, measuring the thickness of each ear. I can see in her eyes that she has noticed the difference between the two ears, but she doesn't say anything. She just holds the damaged ear.

I'm 50 now, and I'm glad I have two daughters. I grew up with two brothers and a sister, but I have no sons of my own to teach wrestling the way my father taught me. But that's all right with me because the thought of teaching a young boy to wrestle at my age seems much too painful. My knees and hips ache after a long walk. I have screws and staples in my knee from a wrestling injury. But the truth is, as much joy and pride as there is between a father and a son, I don't know that I could endure much more of the unspoken pain that marks the lives of fathers and sons. It never ends.

If You Think It, They Will Win

FROM THE LOS ANGELES TIMES

THE MOST CURIOUS FIGURE to emerge in the Dodgers' drama answers the door with a kindly smile and a hearty handshake. He motions toward the living room, where his wife has put out a spread of chocolate and fruit, coffee and tea.

Vladimir Shpunt, 71, lived most of his life in Russia. He has three degrees in physics and a letter of reference from a Nobel Prize winner.

He knows next to nothing about baseball.

Yet the Dodgers hired him to, well, think blue.

Frank and Jamie McCourt paid him to help the team win by sending positive energy over great distances.

Shpunt says he is a scientist and a healer, not a magician. His method could not guarantee the Dodgers would win, he says, but it could make a difference.

"Maybe it is just a little," he said. "Maybe it can help."

In the five years he worked for the Dodgers, he attended just one game. Instead, he watched them on television in his home more than 3,000 miles from Dodger Stadium, channeling his thoughts toward the team's success.

Shpunt's work was one of the best-kept secrets of the McCourt era. The couple kept it hidden even from the team's top executives. But from emails and interviews, a picture emerges of how the émigré physicist tried to use his long-distance energy to give the Dodgers an edge.

The McCourts, who are embroiled in a contentious divorce, declined to be interviewed about Shpunt. Through their representatives, Frank said it was Jamie's idea to hire him and Jamie said it was Frank's.

Shpunt lives in suburban Boston, in a community he insisted not be named. He sits uneasily for an interview, joined by his wife, Sofya, and Barry Cohen, an executive leadership consultant who worked with the McCourts and who introduced Shpunt to Jamie.

Shpunt is wary of publicity, disappointed in the loss of his anonymity, concerned about being caricatured. He speaks reluctantly, in halting English, about a commitment to the Dodgers that he said often required up to four hours a day.

"It's very big work. My blood pressure may be 200," Shpunt said, with a hint of a smile. "I like this team to win."

Shpunt could not transform a bad team into a good one, Cohen said, but his energy could increase the chance of winning by 10 to 15 percent.

"The team has some level of capacity," Cohen said. "What we're talking about is optimizing that capacity."

It is unclear how much Shpunt was paid. Cohen, who negotiated on behalf of Shpunt, would not say. Dodgers attorney Marshall Grossman said he did not know and could not find a copy of the contract.

But Bert Fields, an attorney for Jamie, said the Dodgers paid Shpunt a stipend, plus a bonus of "certainly six figures and even higher," depending on whether the Dodgers won the National League West title and how far the team advanced in the playoffs.

On September 26, 2008 — one day after the Dodgers clinched the National League West championship and their third playoff berth in five years of McCourt ownership — Frank was jubilant.

"Congratulations and thanks to you and vlad," Frank emailed Cohen. "Also, pls pass along a special 'thank you' to vlad for all of his hard work. . . . This organization and this community will benefit a long time from our continued success. Thanks again."

The discoveries that led to whatever energy flowed to Dodger Stadium originated in a laboratory halfway around the world.

Shpunt said he led a team of Russian scientists that in the 1970s found that heat could travel beneath the skin and through so-called "gap junctions" between cells, increasing blood flow and promoting healing by directing energy to ill cells without harming healthy ones.

He worked at the same scientific academy in St. Petersburg as Zhores Alferov, a future Nobel Prize winner in physics. In 1998, in support of Shpunt's application to emigrate to the United States, Alferov wrote that Shpunt was an "eminent scientist" and "outstanding inventor."

Igor Sokolov, a Russian-born professor of physics and chemistry at Clarkson University in Potsdam, New York, said Shpunt had done "world-class research."

Yet his experiments have rarely been replicated in the West. William Parker, chairman of the physics department at UC Irvine, said Shpunt published his research in "second-tier Russian journals" not widely circulated in the international physics community.

"That doesn't mean he's not any good," Parker said. "He's just not a leading figure."

At one point, as Shpunt's research team studied how medical devices transmit electrical current through the human body, the devices malfunctioned. Yet energy was measurably transmitted, and Shpunt concluded he must have been the source.

Shpunt, who said his grandfather was a village healer in Russia, said he subsequently discovered that his hands generated much more energy than the average person's.

In the 1980s, after doctors had ordered a conventional treatment for a 14-year-old girl with leukemia, Shpunt said he tried to heal her and she responded to the energy from his hands.

"I don't know why," he said. "My energy might be 10 or 15 times higher."

Shpunt began to use touch therapy with clients whom modern medicine could not help. He would place his hands on various places on the body, believing his healing energy would be transmitted to the source of the illness.

Charles Shang, an assistant professor of medicine at Baylor College of Medicine in Houston, has cited Shpunt's work in his own research and said the concept of gap junctions is "fairly established." The theory that ill cells can be treated with touch therapy, he said, is not.

Shpunt said he redirected his efforts from research toward treatment, working with sick people in China, Germany, Russia, and Vietnam.

In the mid-1980s, he said, he heard a girl complain about hip pain after her legs had been amputated. He said he left her room and thought about how he might help resolve the discomfort, then returned to hear her say the pain had diminished.

That episode, he said, revealed that he could channel that healing energy not just through his hands but over distances.

"It seems like praying, or a magical way," Shpunt said. "There is no magic."

In 2004, not long after the McCourts bought the Dodgers and moved to Los Angeles, Jamie contracted an infection in her right eye so severe that doctors warned her she might lose vision in that eye.

Shpunt had met Cohen through a mutual friend and later worked with his family. Cohen referred Jamie to Shpunt in the hope that his unconventional methods might help.

Shpunt treated her in person and via long distance, and the eye was saved, Cohen said.

Jamie said through a spokesman that she could not definitively say Shpunt's treatment preserved her vision.

At the time, however, she urged Frank to consult Shpunt regarding an undisclosed health issue, according to Cohen and Fields, the attorney for Jamie. Grossman, the Dodgers' lawyer, declined to say whether Frank sought treatment from Shpunt.

In any case, the McCourts debated whether to add Shpunt to the Dodgers' training staff but decided against it, according to their representatives.

Instead, they hired him to direct his energy to benefit the team. "Dr. Shpunt and others believe that he has the gift of providing positive energy," Grossman said.

Shpunt most often dispatched the energy from his home office, in a room that included a television, chair, bed, and computer, watching the Dodgers late into the evening. If the Dodgers played on the West Coast, the game usually started at 10:00 P.M. in Boston.

He would concentrate, sometimes with his eyes closed, as if meditating, Cohen said.

Shpunt could transmit the energy at any time and from any place, Cohen said, but watching the games provided him with immediate feedback on its effects and intensity.

At one point, Shpunt also tried to heal a player. In 2005, Jamie referred outfielder Jayson Werth to him for treatment of a wrist

injury, after Werth had told her of his interest in alternative medicine, according to Cohen and representatives for Frank and
Jamie.

Werth had one in-person healing session and one distance healing session, apparently not successful. In 2008, as he emerged as a
star with the Philadelphia Phillies, Werth said Dodgers doctors had
misdiagnosed the injury and that he did not get proper treatment
until he went to the Mayo Clinic on his own. He made no mention
of Shpunt.

More recently, Werth appeared startled when asked whether he
had worked with a healer named Vladimir while with the Dodgers.

"Where'd you hear about that?" Werth said. He declined to talk
about it.

On October 2, 2004, Steve Finley capped the first season of Mc-
Court ownership by hitting a walk-off grand slam, clinching the
Dodgers' first playoff spot in eight years.

"The miracle finish . . . was the result of V energy," Cohen wrote
in an email to Jamie. "Frank was privileged to actually feel the energy."

Cohen sent that email during the final week of the 2005 season
to reinforce Shpunt's value to the team. The Dodgers lost 91 games
that season, their worst in 13 years.

"V believes without his help this team would have lost about 15
more games," Cohen wrote, adding: "It would be a giant error to
take V off team."

Cohen also wrote that Shpunt had "diagnosed the disconnects"
among manager Jim Tracy, general manager Paul DePodesta, and
the team's pitchers and catchers.

"Your general manager destroyed last year's team," the email
read, "and put together a group of players that could not be a team
and could not win."

Cohen further conveyed Shpunt's critical assessments of out-
fielders Milton Bradley and J. D. Drew and said Shpunt had identified Tracy as the "final reason for failure."

Grossman said Shpunt had been "introduced to the Dodger organization as someone who had the ability to observe the team,
observe opposing teams and provide evaluations of performance
of areas and strength and weakness."

McCourt fired DePodesta after the season, three weeks after publicly backing him when Tracy and the Dodgers parted ways. Grossman said Shpunt's evaluations did not persuade McCourt to fire DePodesta or to cut ties with Tracy or any player.

"I doubt that one or more decisions were based just on what he had to say," Grossman said. "I'm confident what he had to say was put into the mix of opinions."

The relationship between Shpunt and the Dodgers lasted through the '08 season, after which Jamie asked him for help with matters separate from the team, Cohen said. That would have required Shpunt to move to Los Angeles, and he declined, Cohen said.

Cohen would not say what kind of work Jamie had asked Shpunt to do, and Jamie would neither confirm nor deny she had asked for his assistance.

By then, Shpunt thought his results with the Dodgers had been so successful that he started to work with amateur and professional athletes, sometimes with hands-on treatment, sometimes trying to will them to victory from a distance.

Would he say which athletes? He said he would, well, think about it.

JASON FAGONE

The Dirtiest Player

FROM GQ

A PRAYER IN THE CITY, four words long: *I ain't seen nothin'*.
It was a lie, of course.

Robert Nixon had seen everything. He had seen more than
enough to put a rich and famous man, an NFL superstar, in prison.
But this is what you tell the police unless you're a fool. You can't go
wrong if you say you ain't seen nothin', and you can go very wrong
if you say otherwise. And as far as Robert Nixon is concerned, what
happened to the fat man with the Muslim beard is proof.

Nixon didn't know the fat man with the Muslim beard when the
fat man was still alive—that is to say, before he was perforated with
bullets. But he'd seen him around. More than a year before the
murder, Nixon stumbled upon the fat man lying in the street, in
front of a water-ice stand, getting the crap beaten out of him by
Marvin Harrison and Stanley McCray, one of Harrison's employees.

It was a scene* to make anybody stop and watch. Broad daylight
in North Philadelphia. April 29, 2008—a Tuesday. The corner of
25th Street and Thompson, about seven blocks north of the Philadelphia Museum of Art and the steps Rocky climbed. A block of
brick row houses, a church with a rubbed-out sign, a Hispanic grocery, a vacant lot. In one sense, the presence of a future Hall of
Famer at this seedy vortex of the city—Harrison, eight-time Pro
Bowl wide receiver with the Indianapolis Colts, then at the tail end

---

* Recreated from interviews, court filings, and police reports, and told through the
eyes of Robert Nixon.

of a 13-season career and a $67 million contract—was incongru-
ous. Especially given that Harrison, who is usually described as
"quiet" and "humble," was noisily stomping the fat man in the face
and gut.

To Nixon, the fat man looked semi-conscious.

After several minutes, Harrison and McCray walked away. The
fat man slowly picked himself up. Shouting epithets, he staggered
to his car. Nixon watched as Marvin Harrison got into his own
car, parked to the west of the fat man's. The fat man put his car
into reverse. Thompson Street is one-way going east. The fat man
backed up the wrong way until he was smack in front of Chuckie's
Garage, a car wash Harrison owns. The fat man was now blocking
Harrison, who was trying to drive away.

Nixon saw Harrison get out of his car and exchange words with
the fat man. He couldn't hear the words, but he could see the ges-
tures of threat and counterthreat. The fat man stayed in his car.
He called somebody on his cell. Harrison got back into his car and
called somebody on *his* cell. After a minute or two, Harrison got
out of his car for the second time.

Marvin Harrison is six feet tall and 185 pounds. He has a neatly
trimmed mustache and the body-fat content of an Olympic swimmer. He became the dominant wide receiver of his era not by out-
leaping or outwrestling defenders but by exploiting an almost su-
pernatural talent for getting open: for feints, fakes, jukes, dodges,
bluffs, stutter steps, sudden bursts of sick speed. But at this moment, Nixon says, Marvin Harrison did not run. He stood on the
sidewalk and calmly raised his wiry arms. In each hand, Nixon
clearly saw, was a gun.

Nixon froze.

"YOU A BITCH-ASS NIGGA!" Nixon heard the fat man scream
at Harrison. "YOU AIN'T GONNA SHOOT. YOU AIN'T GONNA
SHOOT. DO WHAT YOU GOTTA DO."

Nixon was across the street and thirty yards away when Harrison
started shooting. *Pop pop pop pop pop pop*—a great staccato gust of
bullets. Steadily, Nixon says, Harrison unloaded both guns into the
fat man's car, stippling the red Toyota Tundra with bullet holes
as the fat man ducked in his seat. Eventually, the fat man sat up
and sped off, heading straight toward Nixon's position as Harrison
darted into the street and continued to shoot.

Now Nixon was in the line of fire. He turned and ran. He ran as fast as he could with his belly and his smoker's cough as bullets slivered through doors and lodged in walls.

Behind him, unbeknownst to Nixon, a bullet ripped through the fat man's hand. Another bullet shattered the glass of a car containing multiple adults and a two-year-old boy. The adults instantly bailed, abandoning the little boy in the car, the glass flowering into razor-sharp petals and bloodying the boy's eye.

And yes, Robert Nixon was also hit. Once, in the back. He didn't realize it at first. Too much adrenaline. Then he scraped his left hand against his right shoulder. He felt a hole in his black T-shirt. His fingers came back stained with blood.

By this time, Marvin Harrison and the fat man had both fled. But Nixon needed to retrieve his car, which was parked on Thompson Street. As Nixon sprinted back to the scene of the crime, the police pulled up. An officer spotted Nixon running and thought he might be the shooter. *Hey, c'mere.* The officer patted him down for weapons. Nixon was clean.

The officer didn't notice Nixon's gunshot wound, and Nixon didn't volunteer that he'd been shot.

I ain't seen nothin'.

The smart call.

So the officer moved on.

Marvin Darnell Harrison was not supposed to be this guy, the black athlete with a gun. Insecure, obnoxious, prone to acts of catharsis —that was Terrell Owens, Michael Vick. But Marvin?

Marvin drank juice.

He was a worker. Marvin was the guy who never wore his gloves in practice because the gloves were sticky and made catching balls easy, and he wanted to practice the hard way. He was the neat freak who sat with his back to the press at a locker that would make a drill sergeant swoon. Marvin, who juked my repeated requests for an interview, was the perfectionist who evolved an ability to communicate almost telepathically with his quarterback, Peyton Manning, but barely at all with mere English. If he left any trace of his existence in the league, it was only in the record books: second (to Jerry Rice) in all-time receptions, third in all-time 100-yard games, first in receptions in a single season. Through all this, his teammates claimed they didn't know him in the slightest. "He's like Bat-man," linebacker Cato June told *Sports Illustrated*.

Think about the discipline it would take to make a living as an elite star of a multibillion-dollar entertainment juggernaut without ever once being truly *seen*. In this sense, Harrison's football career is not only historic; it's also a sort of miracle. The dude skipped like a flat stone across a rancid pool and emerged, 12 years later, dry as a bone.

And when he stood up and looked around, he went right back to the place his heart had always been, the place he had never really left: Philadelphia, the city of his birth. His family was large and close, and although some members had been violent criminals, his inner circle struggled to protect him from those influences. His uncle Vincent Cowell was a respected anesthesiologist at Temple University Hospital. His mother, Linda, and his stepfather, Anthony Gilliard, were modest businesspeople who worked hard and fed needy families when they could. (Just like Marvin did: in 2006 at Thanksgiving, he donated 88 turkey dinners to the poor of North Philly.)

They had taught Marvin to value family above all else, certainly above mere dollars. Yes, he had splurged on a couple of large pur-chases—a house for his mother in a leafy enclave of Montgom-ery County, and for himself a four-bedroom, five-bath 7,600-square-foot stucco home in Jenkintown, a quiet village to the north—but otherwise he was so conservative about money (he favored low-risk mutual funds, according to a 2006 newspaper profile) that if you started asking Philly people about Marvin Harrison, one of the first things you heard about the man was that he was, well, cheap. Whenever you went looking for Marvin, you tended not to find him sipping Venti lattes in Jenkintown. You found him on the streets of North Philly, tending to the unpretentious businesses he was either too detail-oriented or too stingy or too authentically modest—too *something*, anyway—to let other people run: his car wash, his sports bar, the soul-food kitchen he had bought for his aunt and his mother, and more than a dozen rental and invest-ment properties he had snatched up at bargain prices.

From up high, Marvin appeared to be a millionaire athlete like any other; at street level, he was a businessman cobbling together a mini-empire in the hood. It was an iconoclastic way to reconcile his money with his roots—a tricky thing for any athlete flung from poverty into wealth. Many simply flee to suburban McMansions. Some, like Allen Iverson, go the other way, keeping questionable company and giving shout-outs to "my niggas back home." But Marvin didn't run and he didn't flaunt. He just sort of *hid*. His life was exquisitely controlled—an extraordinary man's attempt to become a ghost in his own story. For a long time, it worked. And then, for reasons that go well beyond Marvin Harrison—reasons having to do with race, class, jealousy, politics, and the problems of American cities—it didn't.

"Fuck you," the fat man said. "Fuck the bar, and I'll fuck you up."

It was mid-April of 2008, two weeks before the shooting. The fat man, aka Dwight Dixon, age 32, was standing with a friend at the front door of Playmakers, Harrison's bar, demanding to be let inside.

Playmakers is about a half-mile southwest of 25th and Thompson, on a side street of a gentrifying neighborhood; a block to the east is North Star Bar, where you can see indie bands like the Mountain Goats. From the press coverage of the Harrison case, you'd think Playmakers was some kind of ghetto shithole. But once you get past the bouncers and their pat-downs, you find yourself in a warm, upscale black bar. There are two pool tables and an old-school Galaga arcade console. The walls are covered with framed jerseys (Donovan McNabb, Jerry Rice) and photographs (Charles Barkley, a Negro League baseball team)—but no Harrison jersey, no Harrison photos. Who needs memorabilia when you've got the hero himself? Odds are good that if you go to Playmakers on a weekend, you'll see Harrison adjusting the thermostat, checking the taps, peering out the front door.

Or if you're Dwight Dixon, you get to watch him pat you down, and pat your friend down, and lay a hand on something gun-shaped and concealed on your friend's person, and tell you both to get lost.

Dixon—everyone called him Pop on account of his size—was not welcome at Playmakers, Harrison made clear that night in April. And Pop was not the sort of person to let this insult slide. Three hundred pounds of swagger squeezed into expensive Gucci and Polo shirts, he was a finely tuned instrument for the detection of disrespect. "I call him a straight-up hustler," says Fishay Bryant, one of Pop's cousins. "Like, he didn't take any handouts. He was very proud."

Pop saw himself as Harrison's equal. After all, they'd both grown up in the same North Philly neighborhood. They knew each other as kids. They'd both been born in the city's worst modern hour — when it was grimy and vegetal, when it stank, when gangs ruled the neighborhoods, when the old industries were dying and the white ethnics were hightailing it to the suburbs, when the notorious Black Mafia was flooding the streets with heroin of unprecedented potency and the newly elected mayor was a skull-cracking cop who promised to be so tough on crime he'd "make Attila the Hun look like a faggot." And they both had chosen to hawk their products — car washes and liquor for Harrison, drugs for Pop — in a part of the city that remained, even in April 2008, profoundly fucked.

If Harrison had moved to some better place, Pop would have understood. Hell, Pop wanted to leave Philly himself. *Dreamed* of it. Took his girl on vacations every weekend he could — Texas, Florida, California, Arizona. They flew Southwest. Super-saver fares. But Harrison had stayed, digging his roots deeper and deeper. In 1994, Pop had gone to state prison for dealing crack. When he came out six years later, he was a Muslim, but otherwise he was the same prideful Pop — and Harrison was *still there,* a king among paupers, distributing small-scale charity to needy supplicants beneath the media's radar, his wealth creating a gravity that warped the physics of the neighborhood. "Everybody sucks up to him, and I don't," Pop told a close friend. "I'm gonna see you in your place of business, and I'm gonna buy drinks."

A week after Pop was barred from Playmakers, he drove to Chuckie's and demanded a car wash. He was denied. That Friday he went back to Playmakers. He was turned away — again. The next Tuesday was his confrontation with Harrison. Harrison describes it in detail in his statement to police:

> I walked down and asked him why he was continually threatening me and coming to my businesses and harassing my employees. He said, "I'm a grown man, I can do and go wherever I want and say what I want . . . and like I said, I will fuck you up and fuck your bar up . . . NOW

WHAT!" He put his hands up and swung at me. He grazed me on my left shoulder and chin. I swung back and I missed. We wrestled and threw punches a little bit . . . I then walked up the street back to my garage, I guess like five minutes later he backs up the street to in front of my car wash. Gets on the phone and is saying, "get your guns . . . you know what you gonna get STAN [McCray] . . . I'm gonna fuck you up MARV . . . you ain't no Gangster." I told him that I wasn't a gangster but that he couldn't keep coming back to my place of business and threaten me and start trouble. He drove off down the street. I was inside the garage. I heard gunshots like right after that.

Three years before Marvin Harrison was born, there was another man on the streets of Philly who faced a similar sort of fight-or-flight decision. His name was Marvin too.

Marvin Greer was a 16-year-old gang member. He lived in a high-rise housing project in South Philly. On January 15, 1969, Greer and three friends spotted a boy from an enemy gang. The boy ran. Greer and the others chased him. When Greer caught up to the boy, he pulled out a four-inch pearl-handled knife. He stabbed the boy in the back, killing him, and threw the knife into the sewer. He pled guilty to second-degree murder.

About five years later, in 1974, Marvin Greer died suddenly at age 22; there was no mention of his death in the newspapers, and the cause remains a mystery. Before he died, Greer fathered at least three boys with different mothers. (Back then in Pennsylvania, juvenile felons were furloughed for good behavior, affording them a certain freedom of movement.) The eldest boy was Marvin Harrison.

The next was Markwann "Coots" Gordon. From 1995 to 1997, Gordon participated in a string of seven armed robberies in Philadelphia. According to a 1999 account by Kitty Caparella, the dean of Philadelphia's crime reporters, Gordon was one of "the Philadelphia Mob's two top associates in the African-American underworld," an enforcer with the Junior Black Mafia. Gordon is currently serving 140 years in a federal prison in White Deer, Pennsylvania.

After Gordon came Marvin "Back to Back" Woods. On September 3, 1991, when Marvin Woods was 17, he was playing in the championship game of a schoolyard hoops league when his coach took him out of the game, subbing in another boy. Woods got angry. He left the game. When he rode back on his bike, 20 minutes later, he was carrying a Tec-9. He sprayed his substitute with bullets, killing him, and rode off. Marvin Woods is currently serving a life sentence for first-degree murder at the State Correctional Institution in Dallas, Pennsylvania.

So those are Marvin Harrison's half-brothers. In more recent years, Marvin Harrison's cousin Lonnie Harrison, age 41, has been convicted of robbery, drug possession, and possessing an illegal firearm. And in 2000, another cousin, Isa Muhammad, was murdered in the aftermath of an eight-man shoot-out that also wounded a 10-year-old girl. The police described the murder as a revenge killing.

None of this proves, of course, that Marvin Harrison shot Dwight Dixon and Robert Nixon. It just shows that he has a strikingly violent family history. It also suggests that Harrison's NFL career is an even greater triumph than commonly understood. He was able, for all those years, to reject the logic that claimed the life of his cousin and the freedom of his father and his half-brothers—the same street logic that allows only one sort of response to a challenge like Pop's.

After the shooting, Pop got a ride to Lankenau Hospital, five miles west of Chuckie's Garage. The hospital staff called the cops, as they're required to do when they see shooting victims. The cops arrived and asked Pop for his name.

Malik Tucker, he said. It was one of his many aliases: Demetrius Bryant, Swight Dixon, Donte Jones, Dwight M. Mobely.

The cops asked how he'd been shot.

Pop said that he'd been robbed at 62nd and Lebanon—again, several miles west of the shooting.

Soon, the cops at the hospital got a call from the cops back at 25th and Thompson. A red Toyota Tundra full of bullet holes was being towed there. The person who had called the tow truck was Pop's girlfriend.

The cops now knew that Pop was lying. They told him he'd better come clean. Pop grinned and told them to fuck off. The mood around Pop's hospital bed was relaxed, jovial; the cops had a professional appreciation for the purity of Pop's bullshit. "*You* know who shot me," Pop said, toying with them.

Why didn't Pop blurt out the truth? He might have been scared. To be a witness in Philadelphia is no small thing, even if you're a 300-pound drug dealer. In December the *Philadelphia Inquirer* reported that 13 witnesses or relatives of witnesses have been murdered in the city since 2001.

But there are two other theories. The most likely one is that Pop lied to the cops because he had shot back at Harrison with a gun of his own. If this was true, then Pop was potentially on the hook for an attempted murder charge, same as Harrison. No gun of Pop's has ever been found, but casings were recovered from three types of guns: a five-seven, a nine-millimeter, and a .40-caliber. And two fired nine-millimeter casings were found in the cab of Pop's truck.

The second theory is that Pop lied to the cops simply because he didn't want them to get in the way. He was planning to resolve the dispute himself, in his own fashion.

The police kept Pop in custody overnight to give him time to cool off and rethink his story. The next day, Wednesday, they began gathering evidence. Acting on a tip, they plugged Harrison's name and DOB into a state database of gun licenses. A long list of guns came up, including two Fabrique Nationale (FN) five-seven pistols. The cops already knew that some of the casings recovered at the scene came from this type of gun.

The five-seven has been described in newspapers and on ESPN as "custom-made" and "a collector's weapon." Wrong. A five-seven is a lightweight, low-recoil, high-capacity, semiautomatic tactical pistol made by a Belgian arms manufacturer. NATO uses it for peacekeeping missions, and the ersatz jihadist Nidal Malik Hasan allegedly used it to massacre 13 at Fort Hood. So it's not unique, but it's hardly your average urban drug dealer's piece; the Philly officer who recovered the casings, which have a distinctively long and skinny shape, had never seen anything like them before.

Later that day, about a dozen plainclothes and uniformed officers, including several guys from the state attorney general's Gun Violence Task Force, drove en masse to Chuckie's Garage in search of the five-seven. Harrison seemed to know they were coming. He was lounging in a cheap aluminum beach chair before a full-size cardboard cutout of himself. He looked serene. A detective asked him if he was carrying a gun. Yes, he said. He swung his right foot

up onto a pool table—he had bruised his left knee the previous
season and had trouble bending over—and the detective reached
down and removed, from an ankle holster, a loaded .32-caliber
handgun.

But the .32 was irrelevant. It had nothing to do with the crime.
At this point, a lieutenant disappeared into the car wash's office
along with Harrison and Anthony Gilliard, Harrison's stepfather.
Fifteen minutes later, they emerged. Gilliard said, "Detective, I
know what you've come for. It's right over here." Gilliard led the
detectives to a filing cabinet. In front of the cabinet was a trash
bucket. Behind the bucket, lying on the floor, was the five-seven. It
too was fully loaded: 19 bullets in the clip, one in the chamber.

This was suggestive, but not necessarily incriminating. Harrison
still had a number of plausible alibis, even if the gun hammer
were to exactly match the markings left on the recovered casings
(and ballistics tests would eventually prove that five of six casings
did match). For instance, Harrison could have been acting in self-
defense—maybe Pop had barged into the car wash with his own
gun blazing. Whatever the alibi, Harrison was under no obligation
even to provide one; he wasn't under arrest.

But then—and even the cops couldn't figure out why—Harrison answered questions at the Central Detectives Division for about
an hour, accompanied by his lawyer, Jerome Brown, and his stepfather. When it was over, he signed each page of a typed seven-page
statement: a single M for "Marvin," its points like the peak of a
crown.

In the statement, excerpted here for the first time, Harrison admits that his fight with Pop took place "five to ten minutes before"
the shooting. He says that immediately before he heard the gunshots, he was "sitting in the doorway of my garage." The detectives
ask him if Pop had a gun that day. Harrison says "no." In his own
words, then, Harrison establishes his motive, puts himself at the
scene of the crime, and eliminates any possible self-defense defense.

The real doozy, though, is that Harrison admits to *continuous and
unbroken custody of the gun.*

Q. When was the last time you or anyone else fired your FN 5.7-caliber
handgun?
A. Probably the day that I bought it.

Q. What day was that?
A. In 2006 or 2007.
Q. Where do you store this weapon?
A. In a safe at my home in Jenkintown, Pennsylvania.
Q. Today, you had it at the car wash? Do you know how it got there?
A. I brought it today, 20 minutes before you came.
Q. Are you saying that the 5.7-cal. handgun that you own was in the safe at your home up until today, when you decided to bring it to your shop in the 2500 block of Thompson Street?
A. Yes.

That *yes* is the sound of a trap snapping shut. Harrison says his gun hasn't been fired since 2006 or 2007. That's impossible. Fresh casings exist, so the gun had to have been fired. But by whom? Harrison says he doesn't know. All he knows is that the gun couldn't have been lent or stolen, because it was locked away the whole time in his suburban safe. Only it couldn't have been in the safe either, because it had to have made an appearance at the corner of 25th and Thompson.

Harrison's story makes no sense.

On May 2, three days after the shooting, Robert Nixon contacted the police. It went against his instinct, but he felt he was out of options. He was scared.

According to Nixon, who spoke to me in November—his first interview with a reporter—he was scared because he had been contacted by intermediaries of Marvin Harrison. The intermediaries offered to pay for surgery to remove the bullet. And if Nixon stayed away from the police, he says, they might also compensate him. He was ready to make a deal: "I really wanted it to be over." Then, according to Nixon, he was summoned to a meeting in West Philly—specifically, in the woods across from the Philadelphia Zoo—at 2:00 A.M. Nixon shut off his phone. The next thing he knew, news of the shooting was all over the papers, and his voice mail was filling with threats: "You think you slick. We gonna kill you."

There was no way for Nixon to know if the threats were serious, he told me. That was the problem. Nixon was a low-level hustler. He was overweight and shuffling, with eyes hidden behind heavy glasses and a low, scratchy voice. Even his transgressions were small-time: weed, cough syrup, pills. He was a nobody, and he knew it. But now he had a Very Important Bullet in his back. The gap in wealth and stature between Marvin Harrison, a pillar of the community, and Robert Nixon created an inherently unstable situation. Harrison wouldn't have to say a word for something bad to just . . . happen. "The streets pick it up," says Malik Aziz, a North Philly activist who spent 10 years in jail for dealing drugs. "Some a-hole, he's puttin' pressure down there? You'd be surprised how many people would take care of it, just on general principle."

On May 3, then, Robert Nixon sat down with detectives and prosecutors at the office of the Philadelphia district attorney and gave a formal statement. He told them about the fight in front of the water-ice stand, Harrison and his guns, and the aborted meeting at the zoo. Afterward, he was placed in protective custody in a downtown hotel, and detectives started to kick the tires on his story.

There were a few discrepancies. For one thing, Nixon claimed that Harrison had two guns — same as Pop had eventually claimed, despite his initial stonewalling — but the neat, even spacing of the recovered shells along the street convinced the cops that the shooter had been gripping a single gun with two hands on the stock, keeping it steady. Then there was the tale of the zoo meeting. According to one source close to the investigation, it didn't happen the way Nixon claimed. It wasn't Harrison's people who asked to meet Nixon at the zoo at 2:00 A.M. It was *Nixon* who asked *them,* in a ploy to suss out their intentions; thugs from North Philly never go to West Philly, and vice versa, so Nixon only suggested the meeting spot in West Philly because he thought they'd never agree. When they said yes, that's when he knew he was in trouble and panicked. (Nixon denies this.)

The cops, however, saw these as minor flaws in a largely truthful tale. The crucial story beats were 100 percent verifiable. Through hospital records, detectives verified that Nixon sought treatment for the bullet wound on May 1. They talked to the cop who had originally patted Nixon down, and the cop remembered him, placing him at the scene. Overall, Nixon's story proved "incredibly consistent," according to one detective who interviewed him multiple times. It also matched up well with the statements from the other witnesses. "They all had different pieces of the same story," the detective says. "And here's a case where you don't need to believe *anybody.*" You have a gun. You have casings. You have ballistic tests. You have Harrison's own words. You have probable cause for an arrest warrant.

But the prosecutors saw the case differently. They had been burned before by witnesses who changed their stories between the interview and the trial. (Their last big case against a Philly athlete, a 2002 gun charge involving Allen Iverson, blew up when a key witness recanted his story.) During "balls-out fuckin' arguments" with cops, the Philly prosecutors fixated on the criminal records of the witnesses and slight discrepancies in their statements. They thought it would be hard to win the case on the backs of such blatant pieces of shit.

Piece of shit is a versatile bit of law enforcement slang. It can mean something as specific as "hustler with a record" or it can mean something rounder, like "person who won't cooperate with us" or "person who lied to us" or "person who will not be trusted by a jury." All of the witnesses, for various reasons, could be grouped under this same heading. Nixon was a piece of shit. Pop was a piece of shit. The father of the wounded boy was a piece of shit. McCray was a piece of shit, albeit an intelligent piece of shit, because he never signed a statement. And Harrison, although he had no record, was a piece of shit too. The prosecutors and cops were in agreement on the piece-of-shit front; the only difference was that the cops believed that there were degrees, with Robert Nixon being what one of them called "the least piece of shit."

The cops also thought it was wrong to drop the case just because a piece-of-shit famous person might be guilty of shooting a piece-of-shit unfamous person in a piece-of-shit part of the city. If prosecutors required every witness to have a pristine record, one detective says, "most of the cases in the city wouldn't be solved." None of the cops doubted for a second that if Harrison was a plumber or a UPS driver instead of a famous athlete, he'd have long since been arrested. "Everybody has their career-anticipation light on with this," says veteran Philadelphia detective Michael Chitwood, now a police chief in Florida. "'If I go forward with this and this guy's found not guilty, I may not get promoted' . . . and I just think that's wrong."

In the end, though, it wasn't the cops' call. It was Lynne Abraham's. After investigating the Harrison case for more than eight months, the veteran Philly DA called a press conference on January 6, 2009. A diminutive woman with frosty white hair, Abraham has built her career on making life miserable for "punks with guns." Toughness is her brand. But at her press conference, at which no detectives were present, she spent much of her time impugning the credibility of the witnesses who had cooperated (Nixon, Dixon) and lamenting the ones who had not (the father of the two-year-old boy, who never spoke to police; anyone else who may have seen the broad-daylight shooting). The case would not be going forward, Abraham said, due to "multiple, mutually exclusive, inherently untrustworthy, and sometimes false statements by the people present." (Abraham declined to be interviewed for this story.)

As for Nixon, he was back on the street. The DA had apparently forgotten to pay his hotel bill after a month, so he wandered off.

"I'm gonna get Lynne Abraham if it kills me." This is Pop's mother, Pearl Bronson, a middle-aged woman wearing gray Nikes and her braided hair back in a bun. "I truly believe that because Lynne Abraham did not arrest that son of a bitch, my son is dead," she tells me, eyes aflame. "Just like she pulled the trigger herself."

On January 28, three weeks after Abraham's press conference, one of her deputies prosecuted Pop for making a false report to the police. It was surreal, carnivalesque — like when Dick Cheney shot his friend in the face and the friend apologized for getting in the way of Cheney's bullet. The judge imposed six months' probation. Pop was already on probation for another case, and the conviction meant he had to go to jail; he was briefly handcuffed, then immediately released pending appeal.

Before that day, Pop seemed willing to let the system give him some measure of justice. He was suing Harrison in civil court for damages. Pearl overheard him one night talking on the phone; he mentioned Harrison's name, then said, "I'm gonna let it go, let my lawyer take care of it." But to be shot *and* prosecuted? Especially while Harrison walked the city a free man and the street was abuzz about how Pop had been punked? They were *laughing* at him. He told a friend, "He's not gonna run me out of my neighborhood."

Pop made it a point to eat breakfast every day at the Chopstick & Fork, a diner on 28th and Girard, half a block from Playmakers. Pop didn't live anywhere near the Chopstick & Fork. Even to sit down over some eggs and pancakes was an act of defiance.

On July 21, 2009, according to surveillance video captured from a nearby convenience store, Pop emerged from the Chopstick &

Fork and walked to his car. He looked over his shoulder, then got into his car and made a phone call. Three minutes later, a six-foot-tall man in a black hoodie and white sneakers ran up to the driver's side and shot Pop multiple times through the window. Then the man sprinted around the hood to the passenger side and shot Pop again. The shooter fled.

Pop spent the next two months in Hahnemann Hospital, a tracheostomy tube jammed into his windpipe, able to communicate with his family only by blinking. He died on September 4, 2009.

According to multiple sources with knowledge of the investigation, the primary suspect in Pop's murder was initially Lonnie Harrison, Marvin's cousin. Acting on a tip, police searched Lonnie's apartment, looking for a gun. The apartment was a tiny room above Deborah's Kitchen, the soul-food restaurant on Girard run by Marvin's mother and aunt. But Lonnie hadn't been living there for a year. There was no gun or any other evidence to tie him to the murder, and no witnesses have ever come forward to identify Lonnie or anyone else as the shooter. On the convenience-store video, the shooter's face was obscured by shadow, making a positive identification impossible.

The cops recovered a second surveillance tape, but it, too, was inconclusive. It came from Playmakers. This tape, according to police, showed a man crossing in front of the bar on 28th Street just below Girard. Detectives felt certain that it was the same man they had seen on the convenience-store tape: the shooter, walking toward the scene of the crime. But just as the man got close enough to the camera to bring his face into focus, the tape went blank—and skipped the next three minutes. "There are no coincidences," says one police source. "For the previous hour, that camera picked up every movement, and then it happens to go blank just at that moment?"

In Indianapolis, when Marvin was still playing football, he ate most of his meals at a small cluster of fast-food joints off the highway. There was a Wendy's, a McDonald's, a sub shop, and a Chinese buffet. "This is me, right here," he once told ESPN's Suzy Kolber, who was riding shotgun in his car. "If Wendy's has a long line, I go right across the street to Mickey D's." He smiled, rubbed his hands. "That's how it works."

The Kolber clip is on YouTube, and it's an amazing thing, because you get to see Marvin in a rare affectionate mood. He's talking about the perfect order of his world, from his mealtime routine to the way he keeps his favorite snack foods secreted around his condo. "Pillsbury Doughboy," he sighs, hefting a tube of cookie dough in the freezer. "Me and him get along just fine." Everything is in its right place. He seems so *happy*.

How, then, did such a careful man end up making such a mess? What happened to him back home in Philly?

It's a sunny afternoon in November, and I've gone to see a man I hope can give me some answers. I'm sitting in a white room in a prison I'm not allowed to name. I'm not allowed to name the prison because the man I've come to interview says he fears his fellow inmates might assault him if they knew he was the guy who snitched on Marvin Harrison.

Robert Nixon's jeans are scuffed. His hands are folded in his lap. His glasses give him a sort of professorial, beatnik vibe — a pudgier version of Cornel West. He calls me "sir." In fact, Nixon is deferential to the point of meekness until the moment I ask him about Pop's murder. Does he think it was meant to send a message to any other potential witnesses? "Are you kidding?" Nixon says, startled. "Do *you* think it was a message?" Nixon shoots a look to his attorney, Wadud Ahmad, a powerfully built black man who is sitting in on our interview, and the two of them explode into howls of laughter, as if I just asked the dumbest question in the history of white people.

Nixon is here on a misdemeanor drug conviction. Perversely, he says he's glad for it. "That's probably the best thing that happened to me. That's how fucked-up my life is with this. [Jail is] the safest place for me." Nixon says he would move himself and his family to another city if he could afford it, but he can't. He's now suing Harrison in civil court, claiming damages from the shooting.

Nixon's civil suit is only one of several dangling threads in Marvin Harrison's life. There's also the civil suit filed by Pop, which is still alive even though Pop is not. If the lawyers in the two civil suits get a chance to depose Marvin Harrison, Harrison's words could, in theory, be used against him by prosecutors down the line. In January, Lynne Abraham stepped down after almost 20 years, making way for the incoming DA, Seth Williams, a young, passionate reformer with a grassroots political base. (Williams, who is black, has not commented on the Harrison case.) Harrison could avoid the depositions by settling the cases. As of press time, though, he hadn't done that. Nor had he announced his definitive retirement from football, though no team has demonstrated much interest in his services, given his declining stats and aging knees.

Say this for Marvin Harrison: he tried to be his own person. He succeeded on a level that most of us can only dream of reaching. But he either never realized or flat-out denied the destabilizing effect of his presence in a poor and desperate part of the city. Much as he insisted that he was a normal working person like any other, he was never going to be seen that way. He was always going to be a target for the hopes, resentments, and ambitions of other people, a reality that rippled and swirled around him in unpredictable ways. And the proof is still there, scattered across the city, for anyone who cares enough to look.

"Can I see it?" I ask Robert Nixon.

There in the prison, Nixon pulls up his shirt. I spot it immediately. A dark bruise, oval-shaped. Remarkably clean-edged. Dark-bordered and slightly lighter in the center. Six inches from his jugular. I press my index finger into the bruise's soft center. I can feel the bullet. So close. So lightly embedded. As if I could pop it out with the slightest scrape of my fingernail. Not a hustler's tale, not a prayer uttered and revoked, but a truth awaiting a seeker.

TOM FRIEND

Old College Try

FROM ESPN.COM

THE RIM AND DARRYL DAWKINS used to have a relationship. They would meet at night, in crowded gyms across America, and each time, young, crass, muscle-bound Dawkins would beg the rim to go home with him. He'd taunt it, attack it, and swing on it, but the rim always had the last laugh—until the 1979 night in Kansas City when he tore a backboard to a thousand pieces.

The closest witness, Bill Robinzine (God rest his soul), had to have his head checked for glass. Dawkins's 76ers teammate Steve Mix rushed to the locker room, dug out a camera, and snapped pictures. Their coach, Billy Cunningham, bitched and moaned about the 90-minute delay. Dawkins, thrilled to see the rim fractured on the floor, did what he does best: he gave his slam a formal name.

If You Ain't Groovin' Best Get Movin'—Chocolate Thunder Flyin'— Robinzine Cryin'—Teeth Shakin'—Glass Breakin'—Rump Roastin'— Bun Toastin'—Glass Still Flyin'—Wham Bam I Am Jam!

It was a night the earth moved, just a little, and the NBA was never the same. The league ushered in breakaway rims later that season, and hanging on to the basket became taboo and/or a technical foul. It was the Dawkins Rule—he would live in infamy now —and young Darryl celebrated the moment by crowning himself "The Master of Disaster."

But time moves on, ruthlessly, and 30-odd years later, 53-year-old Darryl Dawkins is standing in an obscure Pennsylvania gym, glaring at a basket, thinking the strangest, damnedest thing:

I'm not sure I can dunk.

The Man from Lovetron

You evolve. Your body and mind change. A lot of players, coaches, and writers made predictions about "Chocolate Thunder," about how his life would turn out—and it's crazy how many were dead wrong.

They thought he'd never wipe that impish grin off his face. They thought he'd never get rid of his harem. They thought he'd never stop rhyming. They thought he'd make his name off Bill Robinzine forever. But the hell with them—he's nothing like they remember. In fact, they'll never believe what's in Darryl Dawkins's pocket as he's staring up at that Pennsylvania rim: a whistle.

It must be difficult to be stereotyped from the age of 14, to be serially labeled a Baby Huey, a man-child, the next Wilt, a coach-killer, a cutup, a bust. You can laugh or cry about it, but for the longest time, Dawkins chose denial . . . and moved into an imaginary world. He called it Planet Lovetron, a place where critics, coaches, and refs were not permitted. He invented this planet in high school, brought it with him to the pros, and Lovetron was how he got through the scrutiny and ridicule.

In other words, it was all a show, an act. The Philadelphia 76ers took him fifth overall in 1975—the first high school player to be drafted and go directly to the NBA, a year after Moses Malone made the same jump to the ABA—and he signed his contract wearing a cream suit, a top hat, and a bow tie. By training camp, his hair was greased back, à la James Brown, and his dress suits were fire-engine red and Chiquita-banana yellow and even fuchsia. The veterans considered him a nut job—better that than have them think he was scared—but the team's second-round pick, Lloyd B. Free out of Brooklyn, was dying to know more.

"I said, 'Darryl, what's all that stuff in your hair?'" Free remembers. "And he said, 'No, I'm cool, I'm cool, I'm from Lovetron.' So I wondered where that place was. I said, 'Darryl, we're going to a party; you want to go?' He said, 'Yeah, bro, let's go, let's do this thing.' I said, 'Yo, I'm going to come get you in three hours,' and he had on a lime green outfit. Looked like a big leprechaun. I'm like, 'Wait a minute, Darryl, I'm not going to the club with you looking like that,' and Darryl said, 'No, I'm cool.' And he had on green shoes! I couldn't believe it. If you turned the lights out, you'd still see Darryl walking around."

Dawkins was 18 at the time, and this was back when 18 was really 18—no YouTube or Internet or 256 TV channels. He was 6-foot-11, 255 pounds, and naive, and when he saw veterans such as George McGinnis smoking cigarettes at halftime, he figured it was okay to walk over and grab a beer. They wagged a finger at him, so he just wagged one back. He always carried a gigantic boom box on his shoulder—on the bus, to the team hotels—and woke up one morning with a sore rotator cuff. He thought he had tweaked it in practice, so he went to see a doctor.

"Doc, my shoulder hurts."

"Is that your radio, Darryl?"

"Yes."

"How much does it weigh?"

"Seventy pounds."

"There's your problem."

He barely played as a rookie because his coach, Gene Shue, didn't trust him. How could he? Dawkins was eating chocolate bars on the bench.

If his coaches thought he was a fool or uncouth, it was because they knew nothing about him. They didn't know that, growing up in Orlando, Florida, he hadn't had indoor plumbing until he was in middle school. They didn't know he turned pro to buy homes for his mother and grandmother. They didn't know he was planning to send all seven of his brothers and sisters to college. They didn't know that after a Sixers home game, he saw a disheveled kid standing in the rain and drove the kid home to the slums. They didn't know that after the next game the same kid showed up and invited him back to the slums for dinner. They didn't know Darryl Dawkins had heart—and, problem was, Dawkins didn't either.

Disenchanted, Undereducated, and Self-Destructive

The players and coaches would talk among themselves: *If only he'd gone to college . . .*

The kid, at 19, already was maybe the strongest player in the league, and they'd dream of the possibilities. They would see him hold the ball like a grapefruit, drain a 15-footer, and run the floor

in four steps, and they'd expect him to abuse Wes Unseld, Bob La-
nier, and Kareem Abdul-Jabbar. But he couldn't—he wasn't technically sound—and they all wondered what he would have looked
like if he had gone to Kentucky like he was supposed to.

Dawkins heard the whispers, and they pissed him off. By his second season, he was the Sixers' backup center, averaging five points
a game, and he was sick of being bashed. His peers around the
league knew he was a beast, and in one particular game in Denver,
he dunked the ball with such force that the net whipped, knotted,
and sent the ball spinning back out of the basket. While the refs
were deciding whether the bucket should count—which it did—
Nuggets forward Bobby Jones smelled smoke.

"This is the truth—I'm smelling smoke," Jones says. "I'm smelling something burning. The nets weren't on fire or anything, but
as I looked up there, because of the friction his dunk had caused, I
could see these tiny little silk strands sort of drifting through the
air. I thought, 'Boy, I'd like to have a guy like that watching my
back.'"

That same season, 1977, the Sixers reached the NBA Finals
against Portland and were cruising to a second straight victory in
Game 2 when Dawkins and forward Bobby Gross exchanged words.
There was some clenching, and Dawkins sucker-punched Gross,
starting a melee. Portland enforcer Maurice Lucas went charging
at Dawkins from behind, and when Sixers rookie guard Mike Dunleavy rose to help his teammate, guard Henry Bibby said, "Where
you going, rook?"

"They're about to fight," Dunleavy said.

"We don't go anywhere until *he* gets involved," Bibby said, pointing to the team's uber-star, Julius Erving, who was standing like a
statue at midcourt.

As a result, Dawkins was blindsided by Lucas, and when he was
tossed from the game and banished to the locker room, he tore a
toilet out of the wall. He felt none of his teammates had had his
back, so he dislodged a seven-foot wood-paneled locker stall and
barricaded the door. "We couldn't get in," Dunleavy says. "We had
to ask him to open up." The Sixers lost the next four games, and
everyone under the sun said the brawl changed the series. Dawkins
got much of the blame—along with Shue, who couldn't solve the
Blazers' backdoor cuts—and it cemented a leaguewide perception
that the kid was too infantile to count on.

Shue was replaced a full season later by Cunningham, and Dawkins entered camp fat and disinterested. Screw everyone, he thought. Billy C's rule was that every player had to run a six-minute mile before the first practice, and that first day, Dawkins ended up clomping in with a time of 15 minutes. Cunningham ordered him to keep running the mile every day until he could trim his time to six flat, and on the second morning, assistant coach Jack McMahon took Dawkins back out to the track. "They came back in a few minutes later, and Jack said he made it," former teammate Mix says. "But we all knew he didn't."

Cunningham kept hounding Dawkins, kept making him run suicides, and during a practice, he blew his top at him for loafing. He told him he needed to be serious, and Dawkins said, "Yep, coach." He told him he needed to hustle, and he said, "Yep, coach." And as Billy C walked away, Dawkins tripped him.

"And he's laughing his tail off," Cunningham says. "I just looked at him and said, 'I give up.' And you had to laugh yourself. I mean, here's this big kid laughing. It was hard to be mad at Darryl Dawkins. I mean, he would drive you crazy, but then he was a little boy inside. A little boy."

His first three years under Cunningham, Dawkins averaged 11 points and 8 rebounds, 13 and 8, and 15 and 9. He played major minutes off the bench. One game, he went off for 30 and 15, but when owner Harold Katz said, "Good game," Dawkins said, "I hope you don't expect me to do it every night."

He felt Katz was disingenuous with players, which was part of it, but the other part was he didn't want to be Chamberlain. "He could've been the next colossus of pros," former 76er Fred Carter says, "and there's only been one colossus of pros, and that's Wilt. But Darryl did not want that pressure to dominate every night. See, he had no expectations of himself. He was having fun. Because again, it's not his fault—he did not go to college.

"He missed those years of college—those teaching years, those dreaming years. Dreaming about being something special. Coming out of high school, you can't quite dream it. College helps you . . . because you learn to grow. You learn to govern yourself, the dos and don'ts. You learn to put yourself to bed at a certain time. You learn what to say and what not to say. Don't get me wrong, Darryl was a lot sharper than what people realized. But, unfortunately for Darryl, he had to learn on the fly."

Instead of working on his deficiencies, he just kept dunking harder and harder, kept joking more and more. He kept retreating to Lovetron, and the idea was to distract everyone. He drove a Corvette that was painted so many colors Dunleavy said it looked like a meteorite. "Either that, or it looked like someone puked all over it," Free says. Dawkins also wrote a rap saying he was "bad as I want to be"—20 years before Dennis Rodman—and, in '79, he became a household name when he shattered that Kansas City backboard.

Now it was official: he was a sideshow. He didn't need to play inspired, fundamental basketball to be famous. Three weeks later, against the Spurs in Philadelphia, he demolished another backboard, just to see whether he could do it again. And as the public waited with bated breath, he named this dunk:

The Chocolate Thunder Ain't Playin—Get Out of the Wayin'—Backboard Swayin'—Game Delayin'—Super Spike!

All Billy C knew was that the Sixers lost both backboard games, and—even though the team had become the biggest draw in the NBA—he and the league office gave Dawkins a scolding. "I was uncoachable," Dawkins confesses now. "I should have been sent to Cleveland because that is where all the uncoachables went at the time."

As the '70s morphed into the '80s, the Sixers continued to tolerate him, largely because they were on the brink of a title and he had a way of kneeing Lakers star Abdul-Jabbar in the kidneys. In fact, Philly faced off against Abdul-Jabbar and a rookie named Magic Johnson in the 1980 Finals, and as usual, Chocolate Thunder created mischief. Cunningham says he took a call, midseries, from a sneaker executive who said Dawkins was wearing a Nike shoe on one foot and a Pony shoe on the other. He had signed deals with both—because there weren't any noncompete clauses back then—and Cunningham told the exec there was nothing he could do.

The series eventually was locked at 2–2 when Abdul-Jabbar severely twisted his ankle in the Lakers' Game 5 victory. Even though the Sixers now were down a game, L.A. would have no one to deal with Dawkins for the rest of the series, giving Philly a clear edge. Abdul-Jabbar didn't even make the trip east for Game 6, and when Magic ambled out to jump center, the Philly fans expected a runaway. But Magic went for 42 points, 15 rebounds, and 7 assists in L.A.'s title-clinching win, and the common perception was that he had embarrassed Dawkins. Of course, Dawkins had barely guarded him; Johnson had done most of his damage in transition or outside. But, again, the fingers were pointed Dawkins's way. If only he'd gone to college . . .

At least the Sixers' players had his back now. They knew Dawkins, deep down, was smarter and more team-oriented than the rest of the basketball world realized. In fact, they thought he was brilliant, always so quick-witted. Bobby Jones, by then a teammate, remembers an early morning wake-up call, when the team was walking trancelike to the bus at 5:00 A.M. Trainer Al Domenico was wearing a checkered jacket no one had seen before, and Dawkins piped up, "Rook 3 to Pawn 4 . . . checkmate." He was too good.

Something was in him, something generous, something hopeful. When his buddy Lloyd B. Free—an eccentric himself who later would change his name to World B. Free—needed a place to stay as a rookie, Dawkins rented a cot and planted Free in his living room. When Free suffered a collapsed lung during the '77 playoffs, Dawkins scooped him up and carried him off the court like a six-month-old. When Bill Robinzine, of shattered backboard fame, committed suicide, Dawkins felt guilty for dunking on him. In one of Dawkins's final years in Philly, Cunningham mailed Mother's Day cards to all the players' moms, and a week later, the coach received a warm, appreciative reply from Harriette Dawkins—"the most beautiful note I got back."

He couldn't coach him, but Billy C liked Dawkins. He saved the note. He thought to himself, "Darryl has good genes. He's got a chance. A chance."

Loved Kids, Hated Refs

Cunningham hit the nail on the head: Harriette and Darryl's grandmother, Amanda Jones, must have done something right.

When Darryl was a teenager in Orlando, he had a job picking oranges, earning $20 a week, and he siphoned the money to two places. Half of it went to his mother to help pay the phone bill, and of his remaining 10 bucks, $4 went to kids in the neighborhood so they could buy ice cream.

Darryl soon was the king of that neighborhood and a bevy of others. Later, because of the broken backboards and his raps, he'd be mobbed everywhere by kids who would beg him to rhyme. And as an NBA player, he ended up working as many as 85 basketball camps a summer.

He and his brother Chico would drive to the Poconos and Connecticut to work with the children—he trusted them more than adults—and when the 76ers traded him to the New Jersey Nets in August 1982 for a first-round pick (used on Leo Rautins), he started the Darryl Dawkins Basketball Camp.

Almost every little kid had the same request: pick me up so I can dunk. And Free swears that's why Dawkins always looked so ripped —from picking up 100 kids, one by one by one.

"Sometimes you don't want people to know that side of you," Dawkins says. "You want people to know you for the guy you are on TV. They see you knocking a couple guys around on the court, and they say, 'Oh, he's mean, look at his face; look how he's sweating on the foul line.' I wanted them to think of me as that guy."

In other words, he was a faux bad boy—intent on being insufferably macho—and his battles with referees only reinforced his image as a screwup. As soon as his minutes went up in New Jersey, so did the foul calls, and Dawkins purposely never censored himself. He felt he was too manly to take a charge—preferring to stay on his feet and let players bounce off him—and after almost every whistle, he'd say, "Yo mama," which pretty much disintegrated his relationship with the refs.

By the 1983–84 season, he could sneeze on a guy and the officials would call a foul on him. "I'm not kidding," Free says. "Darryl was so big, he could go up to block your shot, and the actual wind from him swinging down would knock a guy over. They'd see a guy come out of the lane like he'd been shot out of a cannon, and the refs would just figure, 'Darryl.'"

By season's end, he had set the NBA record for fouls (386, or 4.7 a game), a record that still stands. Carter and Dunleavy say if he'd gone to college—and learned how to respect authority, or how to flop or scream out on contact and get to the free throw line—he would have been an All-Star. As it was, he averaged a career-high 16.8 points per game that season, so imagine his numbers if he hadn't been forced to wither away on the bench in foul trouble.

After he averaged 15.3 points in '85–86, his back went bad and he needed two disk surgeries, which was the beginning of the end. He lost much of his explosiveness and played a total of only 12

games over the next three seasons, as he was peddled from New
Jersey to Utah to Detroit. He probably had more NBA games left in
him, but he was so high maintenance that general managers didn't
want him if he was going to be only a 10th or 11th man. He was out
of the league by 1989, his legacy a confounding one. He never became Wilt, but he was as popular as any All-Star, and he finished his
14 seasons with a .572 shooting percentage, fifth-best all time. He
showed NBA execs it was feasible for a high school kid to go pro,
setting the stage for Kevin Garnett, Kobe, and LeBron. According
to Dunleavy, he was a mini Shaq. But all of that didn't alter the perception of him — fair or unfair — as an underachiever, and he was
forced to conclude his career overseas, out of the spotlight.

He spent five seasons in Italy, then a year with the Globetrotters,
which appealed to him because of the yuks and the kids. He'd be
introduced with "From the Planet Lovetron . . . Darryl Dawkins!"
He conducted children's clinics all over the world. But, eventually,
he returned to the States in the late '90s, lonely and thinking of
trying something new: coaching.

When he heard the news, Billy C fell down laughing.

Three Marriages Before He Finally Got It Right

His mantra, as soon as he found his first coaching job, was: do like
I say, not what I did.

He had played for every kind of coach — Shue stressed offense,
Cunningham stressed defense, Larry Brown just stressed — and
knew what to use and what to throw away. He knew, from personal
experience, how to yell at the refs. He'd played with one of the
greatest offensive players of all time (Dr. J) and one of the greatest
defensive players of all time (Bobby Jones). He had a remarkable
résumé. Of course, despite this, nobody in the States would hire
him. So he coached in Canada.

In April 1999, he led the Winnipeg Cyclone of the International
Basketball Association to a 22–12 record and a playoff berth, and
he was on his way. He was mentoring 22-year-old wannabes and
29-year-old has-beens, and although the work was rewarding, he
was still lonely, still missing something. He'd been married three
times, but none of the relationships had stuck. He had fathered a
daughter, Dara, with his first wife, Penny, but this was early in his

NBA career when monogamy was not in his vocabulary, and they eventually had the marriage annulled. His second marriage, to Kelly Barnes, lasted longer, but while they were estranged in 1987, Barnes overdosed on prescription medication and died.

Her death left him inconsolable — he says he lay around for nine months getting fat, living off deferred payments from the Nets — before he ended up leaping into another marriage, in 1988, with a former Nets cheerleader, Robbin Thornton. That relationship ended in divorce 10 years later while he was in Winnipeg, and it was good ol' basketball that came to his mini rescue. He landed a new coaching job at the tail end of 1999 with the Pennsylvania Val- leyDawgs of the United States Basketball League, who played their games in Allentown during the summer. No one from the 76ers could have ever imagined Chocolate Thunder bunkered down in small-town America, but something about the place appealed to him — especially after he met a woman named Janice Hoderman at a trade show in April 2000.

She was bubbly, warm, and the single parent of a four-year-old child with Down's syndrome. At the time, little Tabitha was barely two feet tall, and Janice was raising her with the help of her parents after giving birth to her in high school. Dawkins invited them to his ValleyDawgs games that summer, and although he and Tabitha had not been formally introduced, he'd wink at Tabitha in the stands, make goofy faces, the same corkscrew faces he used to make at Cunningham.

He asked Janice whether he could say hello to her daughter, but Tabitha was her entire world, and she was not going to let Dawkins meet her until she trusted he was in the relationship for the long haul. She knew he was fabulous with kids, but she still made him wait six months. "I wasn't going to introduce him and then have it not work out between us," Janice says. "It wouldn't have been fair to her."

When he and Tabitha finally formally met, they were instant buddies. After Dawkins and Janice married in 2001 — "My final wife, finally got it right," he says — little Tabitha would sneak into their bed at night to snuggle with him. Janice wanted to cry. Dawk- ins was comfortable with this; he had coached special-needs kids with the Nets, and his daughter Dara had a significant hearing impairment. And it wasn't long until Tabitha had him wrapped around her finger.

She likes ketchup on all her food, so she'd ask him to get the bottle and pour the ketchup for her. He'd rush to do it, of course. She'd then say she needed him to put the portable straw in her juice box. He'd rush to do that, as well. Janice walked in on them one day and told him, "Please stop waiting on her hand and foot. She can do all these things. She's conning you."

He smirked a little smirk and wagged his finger at Tabitha. And from then on, he let her pour her own ketchup.

Darryl Dawkins was getting coachable.

The World's Biggest Househusband

Nine years later, Darryl Dawkins was a family man, an absolute homebody. Nine years later, he and Janice were the parents of a seven-year-old son, Nicholas, and a six-year-old daughter, Alexis — not to mention a flourishing 14-year-old Tabitha.

He'd coached the ValleyDawgs to two USBL titles, in 2001 and 2004, and when the team folded in 2005, he was recruited to do nonprofit work for the NBA. With the Nets, he had always signed autographs until his wrist fell off, so the league asked him to be an "ambassador," doing what he does best: shaking hands, hamming it up, saying, "Yo mama." He couldn't have been more domesticated. Every morning, it was his job to get Tabitha out the door for school. Janice could never rouse her, but he knew all the tricks. He'd say, "I'm goooooing to geeeet youuuu," and Tabitha would swing into motion.

After that, their routine was priceless. Tabitha had a habit of secretly taking Janice's necklaces and earrings to school, or bringing in family photos or a radio. "If Tabitha could pack up her whole bedroom and take it to school, she'd do it," Janice says. So it was Darryl's assignment, each morning, to check her pockets. He'd turn this into a game. He'd pat her down, then she'd pat him down. She'd say, "Stick 'em up." Then he'd take Tabitha to the bus stop.

He also was heavily involved in her Special Olympics events, in which she was something of a prodigy — 120 medals in soccer and swimming. When Dawkins would show up at her events, she'd come running up to him shouting, "Daddy!"

"You should see people's faces," Janice says. "I mean, who's going to believe a little white Down's syndrome kid who says Darryl Dawkins is her daddy."

He still would talk periodically with World B. Free and Bobby Jones, and they both were overwhelmed by how this little girl had changed their old friend's life. "Tabitha does not need anyone to have pity on her," Dawkins says. "If you show her love and you be who you are, she can accept that. And through that, it's helped me to mature and grow also."

By 2009, he seemed to have everything—except basketball. He'd help a local AAU team and conduct an occasional clinic, but he didn't have a daily hoops fix. And then, this past summer, while Janice was scanning a careers website, she saw a want ad for a basketball coach.

At a college.

And Introducing the Head Coach of L-Tri-C . . . Mr. Chocolate Thunder

The phone rang at Lehigh Carbon Community College, in the Allentown suburb of Schnecksville, Pennsylvania, and athletic director Jocelyn Beck picked up.

"Hi, this is Darryl Dawkins. I'm interested in being your basketball coach."

"Who is this?"

"Darryl Dawkins."

"Okay, just send me your résumé."

"What do you mean?"

"I need to have a résumé. Thank you."

Beck honestly thought it was a crank phone call, a joke, which was why she rushed him off the line in 14 seconds. Beck, the former women's coach at Lehigh University, was a longtime Sixers fan who remembered Dawkins busting those backboards. To her, he was a legend. Why would he want to coach at L-Tri-C? How did he even know about L-Tri-C?

She told her boss she might have just spoken to Chocolate Thunder, but her boss didn't believe her. "Nobody on campus believed me," she says. Two days later, the résumé arrived. Janice had typed the thing up, and Dawkins's references weren't Billy C or Dr. J; they were local Allentown business leaders. Beck phoned one of the men, who said: "Darryl has only one fault that I can tell you about."

Beck felt a panic attack coming on. In her mind, she had already hired him.

"What's the problem?" she asked.

"His wardrobe. It's like Skittles. He has a lime green suit."

"I can deal with that," she said.

Beck formed a committee and invited Dawkins in for an interview. He barely fit through her door, and his first words were, "Hi, I'm Darryl Dawkins."

"I know."

"So ask me anything."

"Okay. First of all, why? Why do you want this job?"

"Why not?"

"You're hired."

They both burst out laughing, but then the questions grew serious. She asked him what his goals were, and he told her he would stress school first, basketball second. He told her education meant the world to him. His daughter Dara already had earned a degree from Temple University. He'd sent five of his brothers and sisters to college. He told Beck's committee that he valued staying in school—even though he'd never spent a day in college—and that he wanted his players doing good deeds in the community. He said at least he'd been to the college of hard knocks—and that qualified him for the job.

She had to hire him; it was a no-brainer. The school offered him a salary similar to a high school coach's—"By the time he recruits and all that, he's probably making five cents an hour," Beck says—and Dawkins jumped at it. He then took a stroll around campus.

"So this is what college looks like," he thought.

Never Try to Con a Con Man

He scheduled a team tryout for the fall, and some of the kids who showed up didn't even go to L-Tri-C.

They had come to see Chocolate Thunder, and when he walked

in, characteristically late, all 35 players stopped dribbling and just stared. There wasn't a sound.

After Beck chased out the impostors, Dawkins began to run the kids into the ground. Billy C would've been proud; Dawkins, who used to eat 3 Musketeers bars on the bench, whose mile runs used to be timed on a sundial, had finally seen the light.

When the roster was posted a few days later, some of the players who had failed to make the team wept in the parking lot. These were kids who didn't want to lose their *dreaming years,* and that was the reason Dawkins liked the job so much. He couldn't bear to see them cry. So he told some of the kids who got cut that he probably would hold another tryout midseason.

Most of these players were born in the early 1990s; they were 18 and 19, the same age the coach had been in 1975. But, curiously, they knew his whole story. They'd YouTubed him. They'd watched his old Wheaties commercials; they'd seen the Robinzine dunk. And if they weren't certain how legendary he was, imagine their faces when President Barack Obama visited L-Tri-C for a town meeting in December and bum-rushed their coach.

"Chocolate Thunder!" Obama exclaimed.

"Yessir, Mr. President," Dawkins responded.

At first, his players assumed they'd get to hear some of Dawkins's raps, but they found out fairly early that wasn't happening. The team's leading scorer from the previous season, Jake Waylen, finally mustered the courage to ask, "What's up with Planet Lovetron?" But Dawkins's reply was, "Maybe when you're out of school, I'll tell you."

He wasn't playing around. He wanted the team to push the ball 100 miles an hour, and he figured now wasn't the time to tell them tales of his boom box. He'd run them so hard, he'd put trash receptacles all over the gym in case they lost their lunches. He was a taskmaster. Thirty-five years later, here he was in college, even threatening to take a class or two. Lovetron was unnecessary now. In the old days, Lovetron was his escape from reality; now, he preferred reality.

"Lovetron is temporarily shut down for repairs," he says. "It may be shut down for the duration. I'm on the coaching planet right now."

From the minute the season began in December, Beck kept wait-

ing for a lime green suit that never arrived. Dawkins harangued
the refs, ran a tight ship, and realized, when he looked at his starting center, that he had come full circle.

The kid's name was Carlos Pujols, and he was a cutup, just like
Dawkins used to be. He hated to run, just like Dawkins, and he had
some con in him, just like Dawkins.

"You got to box out," the coach said one day.

"What?"

"You got to box out, man."

"What?"

"You can't hear me?"

"What?"

Dawkins had made a career tuning out his coaches, so he knew
what Pujols was doing. "You can't pull anything over on me," he
said. "I've seen it all."

They began to talk, daily. Dawkins found out Pujols worked with
at-risk kids after school, kids who'd been arrested for drugs, stealing cars, or fighting. It was like looking in the mirror. Dawkins
would stop practice and scold the guards for not rewarding Pujols
with the ball when he ran the floor. This was big man sticking
up for big man, goofball sticking up for goofball. Tabitha, who
watches every practice, loved it.

The more questions Dawkins asked, the more engrossed he became in his players, and he found out most of them worked part-
time. Pujols was manager of a company that sold kitchen cutlery.
Waylen was a part-time counselor at the YMCA. Another was a construction worker, and another mowed grass. Another waited tables
at Ruby Tuesday, and another was a movie usher. Another got to
try out again in early January, as Dawkins had promised, and quit
his job at Ross Dress For Less when he made the squad.

By late January, the team's record was hovering around .500, and
Dawkins invited the guys out to a local diner, to finally give them a
glimpse of 1975. He rapped the Robinzine dunk and told them
about a phrase he used to use: "Yo mama." The act is still in there.
He still calls himself "Charming Chocolate" on his voice mail; he
still has his fire-engine red and fuchsia suits in his closet. He still
says his birthday is January 11, 12, and 13—because he's so big he
needs three days to celebrate.

"He's still Chocolate Thunder at home and with the refs," Janice says. "But he's grown up. We all grow up. He just took a little bit longer. Age, children, stability, it all changes out. It makes you a better person if you allow it, and he embraced it."

Says Fred Carter: "No one would've thought, including myself, that Darryl Dawkins would be a college coach. Darryl was never serious . . . that's the picture I had of Darryl in my mind. But all this time, Darryl was absorbing knowledge. He's telling these kids, 'Meet your expectations—because I didn't.' Never saw it coming."

At various times this season, Beck, the players, and the media have asked Dawkins to dunk a ball for them for old times' sake. And that's why, two days after his 53rd birthday, he is standing under an L-Tri-C basket, trying to reopen his relationship with the rim. It's not something he is enthused about. He has that bad back of his and needs to see a chiropractor at least once a week. He hasn't been stretching or working out. So as he eyeballs the basket, he isn't convinced he can rise up there. Is this payback? Is this the rim getting even for Robinzine?

The only people in the gym are Beck, the women's basketball team, and a camera crew. "Anyone know mouth-to-mouth?" he says, laughing. After measuring and strategizing for 10 minutes, Darryl Dawkins finally grunts, jumps—and slams it. The breakaway rim snaps back into place as he walks away.

He doesn't name the dunk. He doesn't need to.

HOWARD BRYANT

Dusty Baker a Symbol of Perseverance

FROM ESPN.COM

"LIGHT A CANDLE," Dusty Baker says, his lone voice softly skimming the looming silence of the empty church. "I'm sure there's someone out there you want to pray for."

He lights a candle, points the flickering matchstick downward in his large hands, the athlete's hands, dousing it into the cool sand. It is here in the solitude of St. Peter in Chains Cathedral—funded by Ohio Catholics who donated 12 cents per month toward its construction in 1841—where Johnnie B. Baker, born Baptist in California, raised in the traditions of the southern black church, kneels alone among the long pews and nourishes his spirituality.

After several moments of prayer, he rises and walks gingerly toward the altar, marveling at the Greek architecture, the Corinthian columns and stained glass mosaics, comforted, despite its bruises, by the sanctuary and the ritual of the church.

"I come in here before home stands, sometimes a couple of times a week during the season," said Baker. "I pray for my family, for my team, and for Barack Obama, because I've never seen people try to take a president down like this, never seen such anger. I mean, what did he *do* to anybody?"

History surrounds Baker this morning, as it does every morning. He is humbled by its density, energized by its lineage and his place in it. The ghosts are touching him. History is not something that happened to others a long time ago, but alive as the river upon whose banks his team plays. His baseball team, the Cincinnati Reds, the original professional ball club in America, proud but down and dowdy in an era of big money, is on the cusp of a first playoff series since 1995, revived by a man who has won three Manager of the Year Awards but was run out of two big jobs in San Francisco and Chicago, and out of baseball in 2007.

Thirty-eight years ago, Baker had just completed his fifth season in the major leagues when Jackie Robinson threw out the first pitch before Game 2 of the 1972 World Series between the Reds and Oakland A's at old Riverfront Stadium.

Robinson would be dead nine days later, but before he passed, he said famously he hoped there would one day be a black third-base coach or field manager in the major leagues. The National League, first to integrate, would not integrate the managerial ranks until 10 years after Robinson's death. Robinson died in 1972, and Baker, 36 years after, became the Reds' first African American manager.

"I think about that. He said that here," Baker said of Robinson. "Imagine being able to win a World Series in the place where Jackie Robinson made his last public appearance, where he said that."

Baker lurches his silver Toyota Tundra along West Eighth Street south, toward the Ohio River and the Great American Ballpark. The river stirs more ghosts. In September 1841, when the region's Irish Catholics donated their pennies to build St. Peter's, where moments earlier Baker's hands waded through holy water, black and Irish dockworkers engaged in three days of rioting, quelled only when the city dispatched the military.

The fighting took place above ground ("Riots and Mobs, Confusion and Blood Shed," wrote the September 6, 1841, *Cincinnati Daily Gazette*) but under the streets, at the grass roots, whites and blacks conspired to subvert the system. Baker—known since his playing days as a bridge between black, white, and Latino players—feels these ghosts too, understanding that he, as the poet Maya Angelou once wrote, is the dream of the slave.

He points directly in front of him, at the Underground Railroad Freedom Center, situated next door to the ballpark, a museum that displays portions of the original Underground Railroad. He mentions that behind him, in the deep basement of the watering hole O'Malley's in the Alley off of Vine Street, just under his feet, remnants of other tunnels that weaved from the south to Canada, to freedom, still remain.

"You have to remember that Ohio was a free state and Kentucky was a slave state," Baker says. "The Underground Railroad was right here. Sometimes I close my eyes and think about that, about what that must have been like. 'Just get across the river and you're free. Just get across the river.'"

The Survivor

Forget all the details of everything that happened in San Francisco to turn a baseball renaissance into the bitterest memory: from former Giants managing partner Peter Magowan attempting to diminish Baker's achievements (as the walls closed in, Magowan once said that Baker's Manager of the Year Awards had less to do with him and more with the organization), to the 5–0 lead and nine outs from the first World Series championship in San Francisco Giants history to the runaway envy that led club executives to privately refer to Baker derisively as their "celebrity manager." Forget Chicago 2003, when Baker was a hair from taking the Cubs to the World Series, up three games to one on the Florida Marlins, coming home with Kerry Wood and Mark Prior on the mound to close out the National League Championship Series. Forget Steve Bartman.

"Chicago wasn't good to me at the end, but it was good for me," Baker said. "You don't want it to end like that, because everybody wants to be the one to do it, to win the World Series. I *still* think I was the one to do it. Didn't happen."

Think instead first about him being a kid, and the promise of having your entire life in front of you, 19 years old, protected by the great Henry Aaron. It was Henry who promised Johnnie and Christine Baker back in 1967 to always look out for their son. It was Henry who introduced Dusty to the world, jazz clubs and civil rights and the big leagues. It was Dusty who was on deck when Henry hit home run number 715 that night in April 1974. It was Dusty—oldest child, Marines platoon leader, big league manager but always heir to Aaron and his dad and the dreams of Robinson —who was always the prodigy.

Today, the prodigy is gone. Only the adult remains. Dusty Baker is 61 years old and the hell of aging conflicts with his boyish fire for baseball. His dad, Johnnie B. Baker Sr., always a signature presence in the dugouts pregame where his son managed, died in 2009 at the age of 84 from, as Dusty says, "diabetes, high blood pressure, dementia, everything."

To be the adult means looking ahead and seeing no one ahead of him, no one leading the way. It means walking to the mound to remove a pitcher while talking to your father, who is gone physically, as Baker has done this season.

In November 2001, after a routine checkup, he was diagnosed with prostate cancer. The doctors were aggressive, immediately removing the prostate—no radiation treatments, no chemotherapy.

"They told me I had to have a PSA [prostate-specific antigen]. They had been charting me, told me it was 1.0, 2.1, and then they told me I spiked to 4.0 [PSA levels under four nanograms per milliliter generally indicate the absence of cancer]. It wasn't a huge surprise because all the Baker-Russell men died early," Baker said. "They took out the entire prostate."

The 242 home runs he hit as a player, the three World Series appearances, all the years he walked into a bar and the place—the women, especially—went wild, all those years in the clubhouse as a member of the world-class athlete fraternity, all disappeared in the face of his mortality. Baker was the leader of a group of men whose identities are forged on the physical, and accepting the withering effects of cancer—being unable to maintain an erection, for one—was a difficult reality to confront.

"It changes your idea of your own manhood. You think you're this macho cat, but you're not," he said. "With some patients, the nerves never come back and you lose your erection permanently. With others, it can come back on its own. I was lucky, some of the nerves returned. Luckily, they have those blue pills these days, knock on wood. People may laugh, but these things mess with your head, make you rethink how you see yourself. You question your whole sense of being.

"Some of the guys used to make fun of me back then—I'm not ashamed to say it—because one of the side effects is incontinence. I was walking around wearing a diaper because I couldn't stop peeing all the time. The guys would see those things in my office, look at me and say, 'Are these your diapers?'"

Still, don't forget the slights because they are unimportant. Forget them because they are today, in the face of disease attacking his body and age taking his family from him, unimportant gnats to be brushed aside. Still, Baker remembers them all, and at times in his office, hours before the Reds will clinch a division title, it requires enormous concentration for him not to think about the member of the Giants ownership team who once sat him down and told him he needed to learn to be "more of a company man." To not think about the fact that he has taken three different teams to the postseason, could win a fourth Manager of the Year Award, and yet finds himself constantly hounded by the criticisms of what he supposedly cannot do, that he cannot win with young players or handle pitching staffs.

More painfully, Baker still believes Magowan and the Giants showed a complete lack of compassion regarding his cancer.

"I was diagnosed in November 2001 and cleared in February 2002. I thought that was pretty fast, and yet there were people who were saying that I was asleep, incapable," Baker said. "And I made some choices. Everybody remembers my son Darren being on the field during the World Series and everyone saying that having him on the field was proof that I had gotten too big, that I was a 'celebrity manager.' They said I wore wristbands because I wanted to keep playing. I wear wristbands because I've always worn wristbands. They said I kept a toothpick in my mouth so I could be noticed. I chew on a toothpick to try and quit tobacco. My daughter dumps it out. My son wants me around. He wants me alive until I'm 130.

"But during that year, when every night I wasn't sure if I was going to wake up the next day, I wasn't going to miss an opportunity to see his face. I didn't know how much time I really had left. He was going to be with me at every opportunity, for every day that I had left."

A Surprise for Everyone

July 8, Philadelphia: the Reds are ranked 21st with a $68 million payroll and before this season hadn't enjoyed a winning season since 2000, when they won 85 games. With most winning clubs living on the margin, seasons are made and broken at critical junctures. The Reds enter Philadelphia for the final four games before the All-Star break with 11 more wins than losses, and the two-time defending National League champion Phillies represent a great test.

"When you're a manager, you have a pretty good idea if you have a shot, and a pretty good idea if you have too many holes," Baker said. "That weekend was the low point."

When it was over, the Phillies—whom the Reds will play in the National League Division Series, beginning on Wednesday—had swept the Reds, each game more excruciating than the last. In the opener, the Reds led and lost in 12. In the next game, the Reds led 7–1, gave up six runs in the ninth inning, and then Ryan Howard ended it with a two-run homer in the 10th.

The next night, rookie Travis Wood pitched a perfect game into the ninth against Roy Halladay. The Reds lost 1–0 in 11 innings. And in the finale, the Reds lost 1–0 again, swept into the All-Star break.

It appeared to be a nice story, the Reds hanging in contention until the season wore them out. But then Cincinnati won 15 of 22 games after the break.

"It wasn't one moment. It was a series of moments when people thought we were going to crack and we didn't," said Reds outfielder Jonny Gomes. "We went on the road in Seattle, [and] got swept. Those games in Philly were rough. Getting beat by the Cardinals at home was embarrassing, but then we won seven straight. Every time there was a fork in the road, we took the right turn."

Even in September, the Reds closed unimpressively. Against rivals and contenders (St. Louis, Philadelphia, San Diego, Colorado, San Francisco, and Atlanta), the Reds were 17–33 on the season. Outside of Cuban phenom Aroldis Chapman, the Reds don't expect to scare anyone—and yet Cincinnati won more series than any team in baseball.

"I think we did sneak up on a lot of people, especially after St. Louis," Reds general manager Walt Jocketty said, referring to the August 9–11 disaster, when the Cardinals swept the Reds at home. "This is a resilient team. The more we were tested, the more we came back and won. I kind of believed in July, after the All-Star break."

The Reds finished September 12–15, adding suspense to a division race that watched the defending division champion Cardinals finish August and September with a 25–30 record. Still, on the day Baker prayed for his team, Jay Bruce won the division with a first-pitch home run in the bottom of the ninth later that night.

"Now *that's* how you make the playoffs!" Baker cried during the clubhouse celebration.

That night, awash in victory, the manager drove to a local restaurant, where he was feted as the savior of what had been a moribund franchise. In stopped traffic, revelers noticed the manager and Baker bathed in the evening with the fans—hugs, handshakes, drinks, and pictures with one caveat: that none ever showed up on Facebook.

"A Heck of a Life"

Away from the champagne spray, the kaleidoscope of influences is apparent on the walls of Baker's office: a commissioned painting of the Native American warrior Tecumseh, photographs of Miles Davis, Henry Aaron, Junior Gilliam, and two of Jackie Robinson. On the far wall is a misty and dreamy drawing of guitar legends Duane Allmann, Stevie Ray Vaughan, and Jimi Hendrix. Closer to his desk is a photograph from the film *Easy Rider*.

The prodigy is long gone and the adult is left. One of his larger paintings is of a healing center in Kauai, Hawaii, from his cancer recovery. The photograph resembles a Mayan temple with beams of rainbows darting through the windows of the shelter.

"That one," he says, "told me everything was going to be all right."

"It changes your outlook. And I want to win the World Series. I hate the question of 'how much longer do I want to do this?' Why would I sell myself short? Joe Torre managed much longer than I. So has Bobby Cox. This is a heck of a life. I've never stopped aspiring, never stopped learning to do this job better. I take pride in being prepared. I take pride in having faith, in myself and in my players. I'm happy.

"Since cancer and my dad, all that other stuff, I try to leave it. This is a life much more fulfilling," Dusty Baker says. "The stars are brighter. And the birds sing louder. I hear them more now than ever."

CRAIG VETTER

Icarus 2010

FROM PLAYBOY

LIKE ICARUS, the brave and foolish bird-boy of Greek mythology, Dean Potter lives to fly. He has already set the world record for height, distance, and duration in a wingsuit, a nylon outfit that allows BASE jumpers to soar like flying squirrels over great distances and to land by deploying a parachute. Potter's record flight was from a 9,000-foot drop off the Eiger, a 13,000-foot-high Swiss alp. Reaching a speed of roughly 120 miles an hour, he landed nearly four miles away and was in the air over fields and towns almost three minutes before he glided in safely under his chute. It was an astounding flight, but it was just a first step in Potter's audacious ambition, the dream he is working toward, which suggests that, had he been Icarus with his feathered wings melted away by the sun, he could have survived a landing. Potter intends to fly his body in jeans and a shirt—without a wingsuit, without a parachute—and walk away from the landing.

"Part of me says it's kind of crazy to think you can fly your human body," he has said. "Another part of me thinks all of us have had the dream that we can fly. Why not chase after it?"

Nothing about Potter seems crazy on sight. He's a wire-taut six-five with brown eyes on an open and friendly face under shaggy brown hair, and he speaks in a way that is somehow intense and laid-back at the same time. He weighed 190 pounds when we met last spring but works himself down to 175 for his flying projects. "One hundred ninety is fine for climbing," he said, "but the difference between that and 175 is like carrying two gallon jugs of water on your back."

We met on the deck of a Yosemite Valley cabin with a view of El Capitan, more than 3,000 hulking feet of sheer granite shoulder, and beyond that the dish-flat face of Half Dome — two of the valley's emblematic cliffs, both of which he has climbed, one after the other, in a single day. Before Potter began flying he was one of the most accomplished rock climbers in the world.

He climbed into his red-and-purple wingsuit and spread his arms. The suit was sewn of parapac, a strong waterproof fabric, and had flaps to catch the air under the arms and between the legs. "There's elegance to it," he said, standing in the wings-out position. In fact, it had the look of ecclesiastic robes, as if he ought to have been the bishop of something, His Insane Excellency, perhaps.

As he began to describe his record-setting flight, he arched his shoulders and held his arms in a parenthesis to demonstrate the wing shape he has to achieve and hold as he soars. While he spoke I remembered the Internet video I'd seen of the amazing event.

He is standing in his flying-squirrel suit on a finger-shape outcrop on the craggy face of the Eiger. The shot is from an overhead helicopter. By the time he stands at the edge he has meditated and is thinking about contorting his body in the perfect flight shape, which he describes in "Embracing Insanity," an article he wrote for *Alpinist* magazine:

> When I step off the edge dozens of thoughts come together for the perfect wing shape. Eyes on the horizon, arms to the side, chin down, head poking forward, angle of attack, concave the chest, arch the back, feel the air, listen for the wind speed, point the toes, concentrate on the suction lifting off my back and reach for the pilot chute before impact.

As he leaves the rock he seems to hesitate in an almost upright position, leaning slightly forward.

"The moment you take off there is this hyper-alert awareness that takes hold," he said. "Your first feeling is to stay in control, not tumble and not hit the walls, which at the beginning are close on both sides."

As his body pitches forward his arms extend into a full wingspan; he hunches his shoulders and becomes what looks like a big red bird but is really a flying human seen from above, sailing over jade-green fields and farmhouses.

Once you start flying you loosen your body and take this wing shape, which is okay for a while, but when you get up to about 150 miles an hour it becomes an endurance and power game because it's hard to hold your body in that unnatural way, scooping your underside and bulging your back. Then your arms get pushed back, which is not too bad at one minute but after two minutes starts to burn and you begin to question your ability to reach back and pull the pilot chute. Then it's a big head game. At the end you're trying to match the slope of the ground, and you want to be at least 300 feet up when you pull because the chute could snivel or be slow on deployment. A lot of people die in those last critical seconds.

Then, after almost four miles and two minutes and 50 seconds in the air on his record-setting flight, his parachute blossoms and he touches down—safely this time, but in the hundreds of flights he has made developing his technique, he has crashed and hung himself from trees more than a few times.

"I've had a lot of close calls," he said, "usually when desire was stronger than reason. One time off the Eiger I was pushing to reach farther down this seven-kilometer gully than I ever had. I was about three minutes into the flight, going 150 miles an hour, really tired, and I saw the ground about 300 feet below me—which isn't that much—and trees right there. I said 'Fuck!' then opened the chute, and I was having these super-slow-motion thoughts. My body turned exactly as I didn't want it to, and a second later I was *boom* —50 feet up in the trees. But I wasn't hurt and got down okay. So lucky."

Potter tells his stories without the whooping bravado that seems to be in the DNA of most edge athletes, though his history on the edge was long and full even before he began flying.

He grew up an Army brat. His father was a colonel in the paratroops, his mother a yoga teacher, and they lived around the world until settling in New Hampshire, where Potter went to high school. In what he calls "magic days," he ran cross-country, played basketball, baseball, and soccer, and began climbing a small nearby cliff with a friend. After hanging on academically for three semesters at the University of New Hampshire, he dropped out to become a dedicated climbing bum and eventually fell in with the lost-boy climbers in Yosemite.

"My first time here," he remembered, "these cliffs scared me. I climbed pretty well by then, but these climbs with their off-width cracks were just kicking my ass." He stayed four months that first trip, sleeping in Camp Four, the climbers' camp, then staying among the boulders that border the camp. He has lived in Yosemite off and on ever since.

I've gone into the valley many times over the years, writing stories about the legendary rock climbers, learning to climb, learning to fall all over this cathedral of stone. I was here this time hoping to watch Potter climb into his wingsuit and soar like a falcon from the top of El Capitan. The weather was looking chancy: rain was forecast for all but one of the days I would be there. And that wasn't the only problem.

"I'm not sure this is a good idea," said Potter, who had suggested that although BASE jumping was illegal in Yosemite, he might make a clandestine flight. He seemed to be changing his mind. "I'm already on the edge with the rangers, and the penalties if I get caught are serious."

BASE jumping (BASE stands for the takeoff points: buildings, antennas, spans, and earth) has a deadly history.

The sport came to wide attention after the 1977 James Bond movie *The Spy Who Loved Me,* in which Roger Moore's stunt double, Rick Sylvester, skied off a high cliff, took several seconds of free fall, then opened a parachute with a Union Jack on it. There are no official figures, but it's estimated that since the early 1980s about 150 people have died BASE jumping.

The history of the sport in Yosemite is typically bloody. The first jump off El Capitan, an ideal BASE-jumping cliff because of its sheer face, was in 1978, and the Park Service quickly banned the sport. It did, however, allow limited hang gliding off the cliff under certain conditions and at certain times of day and in 1980 relented and allowed BASE jumping under similar restrictions. But because BASE jumpers tend to be an ornery, free-swinging bunch, they flouted the regulations, and the sport was banned again later that year. To date, as if to validate the rangers' concerns, at least five BASE jumpers have died in Yosemite.

I knew one of the dead. His name was Frank "the Gambler" Gambalie and he was one of the most experienced BASE jumpers in the world, with 600 jumps, including New York's Chrysler Building. He'd been part of a story I'd written years earlier about a different kind of jumping death in Yosemite. Dan "Dano" Osman, another Yosemite climber, had begun jumping from great heights tethered only to climbing ropes that he rigged to catch his falls just before he hit the ground. In November 1998 he called Gambalie on his cell phone as he jumped from the top of Yosemite's 1,100-foot Leaning Tower. His rope broke, the phone went blank, and Osman died on impact with the forest floor. Potter, a friend of Osman's, was working with search and rescue that day and was called to sit alone with the body through a rainy night so bears and coyotes wouldn't get to it before rangers retrieved it in the morning. While covering that story I talked with both Potter and Gambalie, who by then were good friends. In fact, years earlier Gambalie had introduced Potter to BASE jumping.

"I was kicking hacky sack in Camp Four," said Potter, "when Frank and a guy known as Randy Ride approached me, saying they were photographers and wanted to take an early morning picture from the Rostrum, a pillar with an overhang and about an 800-foot drop straight down. You can walk down to the top from the road, but there's about a 50-foot climb to get to the overhang. They wanted me to guide them up there at first light. I was broke, so I said sure. When we got to the top they said, 'We're not photographers. We're BASE jumpers, and we want to huck this thing.' It was amazing to watch. They landed on a sandbar in the Merced River and made a getaway in a white pickup truck that was waiting for them."

If you're caught BASE jumping in a national park the punishment is a $2,000 fine and confiscation of your gear, which can cost more than $1,000. In 1999, seven months after Osman's death, Gambalie made one of his many illegal El Capitan jumps. He was in the air for 16 seconds, made a safe meadow landing, scrambled his equipment together and took off running. Two rangers chased him to the banks of the Merced River, which was roaring with spring snowmelt. He jumped or fell in and drowned. His body was recovered 28 days later.

Yosemite climbers going back 60 years have had a traditionally snarky relationship with park rangers. Potter's antipathy has been sharpened by rangers "dropping Osman's body and making jokes about it as they carried him out of the woods" and by the fact that he believes BASE-jumping rules in the valley led to Gambalie's death.

"I mean, what sense does it make to chase him into a river for jumping El Cap?" he said. "This is supposed to be the land of the free. I'm sick of playing cops and robbers with the rangers. I'm a hero in Europe, where it's often legal to BASE jump, but I'm an outlaw in my own hometown."

"I think of BASE jumping as the most dangerous of risk sports," I told him. "Many of the best in the sport have died doing it."

"BASE jumping is very dangerous," he said. "The best guys who died were putting too much pressure on themselves to be on the cutting edge. The wingsuiters and BASE jumpers who have died made poor decisions because they were pushing themselves beyond a safe pace of practice and experimentation. People misunderstand BASE. They think it's just leaping off something and falling. They have no idea that if you have the skill and technique you can leap in just a pair of jeans and a jacket and can fly forward two feet for every one foot you drop. It's really human flying."

Our view down the valley was in full sun, maybe the last of the week, so I asked again about an El Cap jump.

"I'm on the edge with the rangers as it is," said Potter. "We're not friendly, and I don't want to go to jail. But maybe we can go over to the Lodi Parachute Center and I'll make a flight out of a plane."

We met that afternoon at the Rostrum, the partly attached leaning pillar on the west end of the valley. I found his car on the road above and adjacent to the rock top and made a 15-minute walk across smooth granite slabs to the sheer edge of the cliff. The angled slabs reminded me of a fall I'd taken on the valley climb called Royal Arches. Trying to cross an open, featureless slab set on a very steep angle, my shoes lost friction near the top; I slid and then bounced 50 feet or so before the rope I was belayed by became taut and stopped me. Potter told me he had taken one of his worst falls on a similar Royal Arches slab somewhat lower on the climb. The difference in our falls is that he was climbing free solo, meaning he was alone and without rope or any other protection, a dangerous and potentially deadly style of climbing.

"I decided I could run across the top of the slab," he said. "After the first couple of steps my feet slipped out and I slid 80 feet and hit a ledge that saved me from a death fall. I was super bloody on my hands and my feet, and I was in shock. I walked down the trail to the grocery store, went in looking like a disaster, and bought a can of Band-Aids. They were really concerned at the checkout counter and asked if I was okay. I said yes, but I really wasn't okay. I was messed up for a good month."

Potter and I sat talking on the cliff's edge. His fingers were heavily taped so he could jam them into small cracks when he moved under the overhanging top of the pillar 900 feet up. It was like watching a spider cross a ceiling. He protected himself with a rope anchored on top of the rock.

"It's really my favorite place to climb," he said as we sat on the precipice. "We used to have huge parties out here, climbers, waitresses from the valley, other friends." He pointed down the face to the treetops along the Merced. "This is where Frank and Randy made the first jump I ever saw. Back then I wasn't in any particular hurry to try it."

In fact it was seven years before he made his first skydive. His hesitation was born of the fact that by then, to the astonishment of the climbing world, he'd been completing long and dangerous routes alone and with no protection in Yosemite, Patagonia, and other risky locales.

"When I began jumping I was more nervous than most people because I'd been climbing free solo, and falling meant dying," he said. "I'd seen friends die. On my first free-fall skydive I was a mess, very unstable. I had a coach with me. I went out at 13,000 feet and was potato-chipping around. We got down to 5,000 feet—time to throw the pilot chute—but when I reached back I grabbed my leg loop by mistake. I started yanking, and my mind froze. I panicked, and my coach had to grab my hand to put it on the pilot chute before I could pull it. It was very intense."

His first BASE jump was in Twin Falls, Idaho, from a bridge over the Snake River.

"Of course it was huge to stand on a 500-foot bridge and drop a rock that falls for six seconds before it hits ground. But a whole new world opened for me, from being a solo climber for 15 years, where falling meant death, to falling for fun. Then I started highlining and climbing with a parachute on my back, which no one had ever done before."

Highlining evolved out of slack lining, a Camp Four climbers' exercise in which a one-inch-wide length of nylon webbing is strung between rocks or trees and then walked like a tightrope. In highlining the web is rigged across chasms between high rocks or across deep canyons. Potter learned it from a climbing hobo named Chongo, and with a parachute on his back he eventually pushed it to a crossing of Utah's Hell Roaring Canyon, 180 feet across, 900 feet high. "If you fall, you just fly away," he said in a way that made me picture a bird lifting off from a telephone wire.

About a year into his BASE-jumping career Potter nearly killed himself. He was in Mexico being filmed highlining across one of the country's deepest open-air pits, known as Cellar of the Swallows: 1,200 feet deep, 170 to 300 feet across at the top.

"Every morning 50,000 swallows would fly out of the hole, then return in the evening," Potter told me. "It was raining, so the highline broke as we stretched it. Meanwhile I was making as many BASE jumps into the pit as I could, and when we finally gave up on walking the line, I decided to make one more jump. I'd been rigging and jumping, rigging and jumping, and I was frantic, trying to do too much."

His parachute had been in the rain and was half wet, making it asymmetrical.

"I knew it wasn't safe, but I ignored it and rushed—another mistake. I was breaking too many rules. I took off, held the free fall for five or six seconds, threw my pilot chute to deploy my main and immediately started spinning out of control. The parachute wrapped around my head, and I knew I was dead. We'd fixed a static line from the top to the bottom for rigging and ascending, and at about 300 feet from the ground—two seconds—the parachute lifted from my face and I grabbed the rope. At first I couldn't hold tight enough to stop the fall, then I used every muscle in my body and stopped myself for just a second. My hands were shredded, and I couldn't hold it. I heard a friend yell that I was near the ground. I slid the last six feet and collapsed, safe, on the bottom. It was some time before I could use my hands, and I'd torn a lot of muscles in my body."

Before we left, Potter used his cell phone to check the weather at the Parachute Center, a skydiving training center in the central valley outside Lodi where he often practiced jumping from planes in his wingsuit. "Rain tomorrow," he said, "just like here."

We hooked up that afternoon in the boulders around Camp Four: a field of house-size rocks containing short, difficult routes that need no protection, where climbers test themselves and polish their moves. There is a boulder here called Midnight Lightning that went unclimbed for years of trying until valley legend Ron Kauk was able to string 12 moves together and reach the 25-foot summit.

Kauk, a 40-year valley resident and an old friend of mine, was there that afternoon, sticking to the side of a 30-foot boulder.

"Yeah," he said as we talked about Potter's accomplishments and ambitions, "there's just something about this valley that makes people want to do extraordinary things."

Potter was on a rock of his own. "What we do bouldering is not that different from what I'm doing on my way to landing without a wingsuit and parachute. No matter how impossible the route looks, you just take it one step at a time, fall off, get back on. These days I'm bouldering toward my ultimate flight."

As the sun set, smutty clouds were lowering over the valley.

Potter saw his first wingsuit flight in Yosemite while he and his then-wife, Steph Davis, a renowned climber herself, were climbing Half Dome. The two were married for more than seven years. Their divorce became final the week we met.

"That day we were near the top of the route on the northwest face. It was sunset, and there was a beautiful red light. Two guys came to the edge, looking really calm. They jumped, opened their wings, and it was magical. They were in the air 60 seconds or so, long enough that Steph started crying because she thought they were falling to their deaths. That's what crystallized it for me. I knew I had to do it to fulfill a dream I had when I was five years old."

Potter gestured with his gnarled hands as he described the dream he had had many times since childhood.

"It's one of my earliest memories. I was probably about four or five, maybe younger. I was falling out of control and some beings were flying next to me. They were human. They didn't have any wings, but there was a bright light around them, and they were smiling and gesturing but not speaking. I was freaking out, really scared, and they showed me how to arch my back. When I did it I felt the sensation of flying, as if I was being grabbed by the back and pulled up. When I did my first skydives they were again teaching me how to get forward movement, showing me where to put my hands and hunch my back. And when I did it right I could feel the vacuum form on my back like someone was grabbing my shirt and pulling me up. That's when I really started believing I was meant to fly. It was too powerful to have had this dream since I was a baby and then to feel it in reality."

The next morning we sat out a heavy rainstorm in a small valley café. Several locals stopped by to congratulate Potter on his record flight.

"You know that stuff is insane," said one of them. Potter smiled, shrugged, and nodded yes.

In fact, he often muses on the sanity of his ambition to ultimately fly and land without wingsuit or parachute. He wrote about it in the "Embracing Insanity" essay. It's a long story, well written, that talks about the death of his father some years earlier, about his time waiting out summer rainstorms in a cave on the Eiger between jumps, about exactly how to put his body into the perfect wing shape to solve what he calls "the landing problem."

"My brain is flawed," he writes.

> I have compulsions I cannot control . . . Defects veil creativity. Minute glitches displace us from the norm. Innovation or insanity, blue sky or buoyant liquid, infinitesimal changes in the [body] curve turn impossible to reality . . . Maybe I'd watched too many cartoons, but ever since I saw Randy and Frank on the Rostrum, I truly believed I would one day fly like Superman.

Writing about the landing, he remembered his two dead friends.

> Frank also believed the landing problem could be solved. He named it the ultimate stunt. He dreamed about controlling his rate of descent by tracking, subtly re-forming his mass and modifying his angle of attack and body position in the air until he could slow enough to glide down on the perfect slope, without ever deploying his parachute. Our mutual friend Dano Osman laughed and called it "wicked rocket scientry." Neither of them ever got a chance to try.

Six months after Potter started BASE jumping he bought his first wingsuit, for $1,200. He made his first flights out of an airplane at the Parachute Center outside Lodi.

His first BASE jump in the wingsuit was off an illegal cliff.

"I remember being at the top sweating profusely, barely able to get into my suit, but when I got into the air this calm feeling took over. That's true to this day. I almost crashed into a hillside on one of my first jumps. I was barely 100 feet above the ground when I pulled my chute."

He returned to Lodi and the airplane wingsuit flights, then went back to jumping off cliffs. "For that first year I sucked at it. I was dropping like a rock. I could never reach what I was shooting for. I kept landing in trees. I needed to push my head down to increase my angle. It's counterintuitive, but if you want to fly forward farther, you have to point your head toward the ground. It took hundreds of flights, but I eventually got better and better, improved my technique. And the wingsuits got better when I started working with designer Tony Uragallo. We designed the one I have now, and it's radical."

"I'm his tailor," said Uragallo when we talked. He's a transplanted cockney whose company, Tony Suits, has been making about 300 wingsuits a year for four years. They cost from $650 to $1,500.

Uragallo flies wingsuits himself, including in European competitions. "Wingsuit flying is very popular in Europe," he said. "For the competitions you jump from an airplane carrying a GPS and are judged on distance, time, and speed over the ground. I placed first in a distance competition last year with a glide ratio of 3.588 meters forward for every one meter I dropped."

He estimates there are 3,000 to 4,000 wingsuiters flying today.

"Dean's a delightful guy, full of ideas," Uragallo said when we talked about Potter. "I'm going out west to fly a big cliff with him next month."

When I asked about Potter's ultimate goal of flying without a wingsuit or parachute he said, "No, you mean with a wingsuit and without a chute."

"No wingsuit," I said.

"Really? I'd get confirmation on that. What if he misses the landing? I've never seen him fly except on Internet video, but he's still alive after doing all that crazy stuff, so somewhere in among the madness he must be careful."

An almost biblical rain was still coming down as we finished lunch, and I was trying to accept the probability that I would have to settle for watching Potter fly on video. He checked a connection to the weather in Lodi that he had programmed into his phone. It was storming there too and was forecast to be storming the next day as well.

He left to spend the afternoon at what he calls his "ups." To keep his body grisly and his mind sharp he does a total of 700 sit-ups, chin-ups, push-ups, crunches, and back arches. That afternoon he ran seven miles down a hill and seven miles back up. In the rain.

My last morning in Yosemite I woke to the sound of frogs. I heard the croaking as the final song of despair for any chance of seeing Potter fly. In person, anyway.

His videos are all over the Internet: climbing, highlining 3,200 feet up with no tether or parachute, and wingsuit flying, including his record-setting flight.

We met on the deck of my cabin during a brief letup in the rain. The view down the valley to El Cap was slowly getting lost in lowering clouds.

He was coming from the small rented house he calls a shack. He makes a good living from half a dozen equipment and clothing sponsors, including the Five Ten shoe company, which had just bought him a Mercedes van. Over the years he has made several hundred thousand dollars—extraordinary for a climber, highliner, and BASE jumper. "I'm happy with what I make," he said. "I'm not superrich, but I have a lot of free time."

"Dean's not cheap, but he's well worth the money," said one of his sponsors.

Just before I left, I asked him, "How can you possibly imagine making a flight without a wingsuit or a parachute, in jeans and a shirt, and land without killing yourself?"

"It doesn't seem that big a leap to me," he said. "You have to remember that with the right body position you can not only fly fast, you can fly slow. I can fly with a 25-mile-an-hour down speed and a 60-mile-an-hour forward speed in a wingsuit. Then what you do is match the angle of the slope as you come in, and if I can find the perfect snow slope I can survive the hit. Speed skiers wipe out at over 100 miles an hour and are fine. It's just a matter of taking little steps forward and putting them together in a breakthrough. All the breakthroughs happen that way. It's just a matter of taking one thing at a time and creating a hybrid. I think it's the same with landing the human body. I'm not going to do anything where I think I'm going to die."

I sat trying to imagine him standing up unhurt out of a violent splash of snow somewhere on his perfect slope.

"Do you wonder why some people think you're crazy?" I asked.

"Insane or enlightened," he said, "it's all pretty close. But something in me has the will to stay alive, which is stronger than anything else."

BRET ANTHONY JOHNSTON

Danny Way and the Gift of Fear

FROM MEN'S JOURNAL

The End, Which Is Always Something of a Beginning

Twilight inks the hills of Vista, California. A murder of crows caw in the trees. Danny Way, arguably the world's greatest skateboarder, is trying to catch his breath atop the monolithic MegaRamp. The Mega stands taller than an eight-story building and stretches longer than a football field; it looks like a plywood ski jump, and after each run, Danny is driven back to the starting point in a golf cart. He's alone and battered, exhausted and punch-drunk and discouraged. His odds of riding away from the trick he's trying, a trick that's never been done, are, at best, equal to those of him slamming so hard he has to be rushed into his 14th surgery. That he's more afraid of not riding away than of getting hurt is unquestionable; Way has been appropriating what scares him since childhood, weaponizing it.

At 36, Way resembles Clint Eastwood — if Eastwood were young, blond, and dressed like a skate rat. He's wearing a Plan B Skateboards shirt, DC shoes and baggy shorts, and full protective gear: heavy plastic-capped knee and elbow pads, a helmet. On the Mega he looks like a gladiator — one who's losing.

Here at the world's only permanent MegaRamp, built on a 12-acre swath of land owned by fellow professional skateboarder Bob Burnquist, a film crew is shooting footage for an upcoming documentary about Danny's 20-plus-year career as a pro, and he's intent on finally landing a trick he's been attempting obsessively for months. We're going on eight hours, and for most of that time, Danny's been wrecking himself. Technically, what he's after is a switch backflip revert. In English, *switch* means he's doing it back-ward, with his right foot forward instead of his left (think switch-hitting in baseball); *backflip* means an honest-to-God backflip, grab-bing his board with his left hand and soaring upside down over a gap the length of two school buses parked end to end; and *revert* (pronounced RE-vert) means that at the absolute last moment, he will twist himself around 180 degrees so that he lands riding for-ward. It's ridiculous.

Now, without looking at me, he says, "Sometimes it can just go sideways, you know?"

I think he's talking about his hopes for this filming session or maybe about how he's been landing, the revert not coming around a full 180 degrees. And maybe that's all he's saying, but maybe not. Earlier this morning, before giving a motivational talk at an ele-mentary school, Way mentioned how there's no television in his house, how his two sons go to a Waldorf school, how his infant daughter will too, and how he and his wife allow very few plastic toys and maintain an all-organic diet. He described, in other words, the exact opposite of his own childhood. Tricks can go sideways, but so can childhoods, so can whole lives, unless you work tirelessly, ruthlessly, to keep them on track.

Absolutely, I say, it can all go sideways.

"But it's good to sweat. It's like there're vaults in your nervous system, where you store whatever pain and stress and bad memo-ries you have," he says. "My theory is to fight fire with fire. You have to dive back into that trauma, go back and do the same tricks that hurt you, in the same place. If you don't process it out, those trau-mas will find homes in your body, hold you back."

"Whenever you're ready, D," Jacob Rosenberg, the director of the documentary, shouts from the Mega's landing pad.

"Okay," Way says, adjusting his pads and helmet. "Okay. Okay."

And then, seconds later, he's riding away from the trick so cleanly that it looks like he's coasting along on a wave as it peters out. The kinetic beauty, the velocity and power and precision and sweep of it, is magnificent—imagine the sound of a basket swooshed from half-court, the arch of a ball before it becomes a hole-in-one, the muscular symmetry of a horse storming to the Triple Crown. But beauty isn't even the most interesting thing about what Way has just done. More interesting is how, in watching him land a trick that's never been landed before, a trick that until he nailed it no one even knew was possible, you can see the full arc of his career. What is genius or art or excellence if not the ability to transcend time, the capacity to encompass the past, present, and future in a singular and fluid movement?

But, finally, what's most interesting about him riding away from another trick chased straight from his imagination into reality is that once he's done it, once the cameramen have confirmed that they shot a winner, Way doesn't celebrate or review the video or do anything except limp toward the golf cart. The switch backflip revert is behind him now, perfect and perfectly useless, an artifact of air. He tells the cart driver to go faster, tells the cameramen to keep rolling. He's got an idea for a new trick. He thinks there's still a little light left.

Then, He Disappeared

That session on the MegaRamp was two years ago, and what followed was actually one of the darkest, most complicated stretches in an already exceedingly complicated life. A few weeks after the session at Burnquist's, he crashed on a botched warm-up air, knocked himself unconscious, and had to be rushed to the hospital in an ambulance. A month later, at X Games 14, live on ESPN in 2008, he suffered what is widely considered one of the worst slams in skateboarding history (more on this later), losing the gold medal to Burnquist. That September, at a MegaRamp contest in Brazil, he came up short on a jump and fractured two vertebrae, taking himself out of the competition; Burnquist won again. Over the next year, Way's marriage dissolved. Then, at X Games 15, he decided against trying to reclaim his Big Air title, focusing instead on a new Mega competition he helped create, the Rail Jam, wherein the skaters launch themselves over the gap and slide or grind on a rainbow-shaped steel rail before dropping onto the bank ramp. He won the contest, but broke his ankle in the process. The injury took him out of commission for months, and then, for all practical purposes, he disappeared.

There were rumors: He'd retreated to Hawaii to build an ultra-private skate compound. He was strung out, addicted to morphine lollipops, and retired from skateboarding. He was reinventing himself as a street skater, riding alone and exclusively at night. He was on TMZ partying at a club. He was spotted in Las Vegas doing reconnaissance at the Luxor hotel, figuring whether he could skate down the side of the onyx pyramid and launch over the Strip. He was in Germany undergoing an experimental surgery not approved in the States. He was flying around the world in Tommy Lee's private jet.

No one knew anything for sure except that Way had dropped out of sight. The documentary went into hibernation. He missed interviews. Photo shoots were scheduled and rescheduled. When I called to check in, his voice mail was full and wouldn't accept new messages. On those few occasions when I could leave a message, he never called back.

And then, in early May, Way finally started returning my calls. He asked if I was going to make it to X Games 16 in July. When I told him I didn't know, he said, "You should definitely try. I'm working on something big. Like, huge."

"What?"

"Oh, man," he said.

"Tell me."

"I don't want to, you know, ruin the surprise. But remember the tricks we filmed at Bob's a couple years ago? The switch back revert? And everything else? Those were nothing compared to this."

"Those were pretty heavy," I said. "No one else has done them since."

"They were nothing," he said. "I was just clearing my throat."

A Short but Telling Incident from Earlier That Day Two Years Ago

Danny Way was tardy for his motivational speech at the elementary school. He'd hit traffic on the drive from his home in Encinitas to Carlsbad, California, and then the parking lot was full. After circling twice, he said, "Fuck it," and steered his BMW M3 into a faculty-only slot.

Inside, the principal cleared his desk so Way could unload the skateboards he'd brought; they were autographed for two students battling cancer. The inscriptions read FEAR IS AN ILLUSION and MAKE YOUR DREAMS COME TRUE. Way's signature is spiky, like the logo of a heavy metal band.

"Very cool," the principal said. Then he inhaled sharply and asked, "Have you ever done drugs?"

A bewildered expression crossed Way's face, as if he'd misheard the question. "Well," he replied, "I mean, I've tried—"

"We had a pro skater visit last year," the principal interrupted, "and when a student asked if he'd done drugs, he said yes. Our parents were none too pleased."

"Not a problem," Way said.

"These kids need role models. Tell them you've made positive choices and you've followed the golden rule. Tell them you can't get where you are by doing drugs."

"I've got good things to say. I grew up in a pretty dysfunctional home," Way said matter-of-factly. If he elaborated, if he laid out exactly how dysfunctional his childhood was, the principal would likely cancel the speech.

"Very cool," the principal said again. Then he noticed I was holding a skateboard and asked if it was mine.

"No," Way answered sheepishly. "That's the board I used to jump the Great Wall of China."

The principal studied the board, possibly expecting Way to admit he was joking. He wasn't. If nonskaters know of Danny Way, it's because of this: in 2005 Way became the first person to jump the Great Wall on a nonmotorized vehicle, soaring across a 60-foot gap, and he did it with a fractured ankle from a previous crash. (The last person to try used a bicycle. He died.) Way has never courted the celebrity that Tony Hawk or MTV reality star Ryan Sheckler enjoy, but after images of him spinning a backside-360 over the wall appeared everywhere from the *South China Morning Post* to *The Daily Show,* the door to mainstream culture swung wide open. And yet he promptly and politely closed it. Had he walked through that door, the stunt might have defined him. It might even have controlled him, relegated him to a world of daredevil sideshows, and the progression of skateboarding—which for Danny carries the weight of religion—would have been waylaid, if not completely thwarted. The religion thing is apt. He wants neither a pulpit nor a stage; he wants a monastery. He wants neither an audience nor disciples; he wants fellow believers. Jumping the Great Wall of China doesn't define Danny Way. The days alone on his MegaRamp do.

Early on, Way used the MegaRamp to set world records for

height and distance, records he still holds. It served as the canvas for his impossibly progressive part in the landmark DC-sponsored skateboarding video. (In 1993 Danny's older brother, Damon Way, cofounded DC shoes. In 2004, a year after *The DC Video* debuted, Quiksilver bought the brand for $87 million.) Within a year, the X Games had adopted the MegaRamp into its competition schedule, and like that, the landscape of skateboarding was, literally and symbolically, forever transformed. Today, among vert pros, there are two groups of skaters: those who ride the Mega and those who don't. The first group is much, much smaller.

"Tell the kids that if they make positive choices, they'll be able to fly too," the principal told Way.

"We're all good," Way said. Then the bell rang.

Dysfunction: Part One

I first met Danny Way in the early '90s, when his skating career was just taking off and my own was both beginning and ending. At 19, I was a decent skateboarder, good enough to tour the country with a very low-level professional skate team for about half a minute. I'd been scheduled to skate in a demonstration with Way, but an injury kept me sidelined. I made a show of acting despondent and pissed, when really I felt spared. He was an undersized towheaded kid with a concave chest and braces, and he scared the bejesus out of me. He had inhuman focus when he dropped in on a ramp, a kind of desperate and almost violent grace. He skated with an authority and poise and aggression that reminded me of a young Mike Tyson — how he would charge across the ring just as the first bell sounded, gloves tucked under his chin and eyes locked on his poor, unsuspecting opponent. Watching Way skate, I sensed that, like Tyson, he had more at stake than everyone else. Which he did.

When Danny was eight months old, his father was arrested for failing to pay child support to his previous wife, and after just nine days in jail, he was found hanged in his cell. (It was ruled a suicide but the Way family remains skeptical.) After her husband's death, Way's mother, Mary, plunged into heavy drug use. Coke. Meth. You name it. With the drugs came a long string of boyfriends who physically and emotionally abused her and her two sons, cruel men who bolted once the mirrors were snorted clean. After a couple of chaotic and traumatic years, however, a good and stable man named Tim O'Dea came along. He introduced Danny and his brother, Damon, to surfing and skateboarding, buying them boards and safety gear and memberships at the world-renowned Del Mar Skate Ranch, near their home in San Diego. (At six years old, Danny was too young to skate the facility, but O'Dea lied about his age.) O'Dea married the boys' mother, but within a few years the marriage went bust. Danny and Damon were devastated. The only reliable thing left in their world was skateboarding—in many ways, their stepfather's legacy. "I felt this connection with my board that I've never felt with anything else in my life," Danny says. "Skateboarding is like therapy for me."

"I remember him as this tiny, tiny kid rolling into these huge bowls at Del Mar," recalls Damon Way, now 38. "The rest of us were scared, but he'd just go for it. That's the blueprint for who he became."

By age eight, Danny's innate talent and obsession with skateboarding became a source of friction. He'd gotten so good so quickly that he intimidated everyone, including famous pros. Older skaters ridiculed him, ostracized him; one soon-to-be-famous pro actually beat him up. At 13, he trounced Tony Hawk in a skater version of the game Horse. (Even in the mid-'80s, Hawk was considered unbeatable, the Michael Jordan of skateboarding, but Way's repertoire—executing complex street tricks while soaring above the ramp, spinning and flipping his board in ways no one else had yet conceived—blew everyone's mind, including Hawk's.) Danny always wanted to be the first to try a trick, even if it meant getting hurt, and he was starting to develop an edge in his personality, a cockiness born of youth and loneliness and physical ability. When older skaters taunted him, Danny refused to back down. "I had to stand up for myself," he says, "because I didn't feel like there was anyone around to do that for me." Even Damon started bullying Danny when he could no longer keep up with his younger brother's rapid progression. "[Damon] was always taking swings at me," Danny says. "It was just typical older-brother stuff, but my only weapon against the physical and mental abuse was to be better than him at what he loved: skateboarding."

At a time when Way felt "lost, confused, sad, unloved," he entered his first two contests on the same day—and won both. Industry sponsors immediately glommed on, offering endorsement deals and a version of the acceptance he'd long craved from his family. He signed with Powell Peralta, which was then something of a corporate empire and, not coincidentally, Tony Hawk's sponsor.

Meanwhile, his brother had started skating with a rougher crew. When Damon was 15, during a scuffle in the school parking lot, he was sucker-punched in the temple, leaving him with a career-ending hematoma, and the family had to file lawsuits against his assailants and the school district to cover his medical expenses. Eventually a settlement came through and Damon bought the Rainbow, California, home that he, Danny, and their mother were living in. But Mary's habit threw the household back into chaos. "My mother had so many boyfriends," Danny recalls, "dealers who'd beat the shit out of her and my brother and me." By the time his mother finally moved out, Danny himself had begun drinking and experimenting with drugs. (Mary has been clean for the past two years.) He was also starting to make real money and was able to buy dirt bikes and four-wheelers and guns—pistols, rifles, shotguns—that he and Damon would shoot when they hosted parties. And they hosted a lot of parties. "My friends at the time were on a pretty destructive path, and I was a sponge," Danny says. "The easiest thing to do was to emulate the things that were going on around me. I stepped out of my own skin because I didn't have anywhere else to step." Although inherently shy, Danny noticed that the more recklessly he behaved, the more attention people paid him. He'd jump from the second-story roof and land on the trampoline. He'd ride a motorcycle on his backyard halfpipe, full tilt. One afternoon, with nothing more exciting to do, he yanked his braces off with a pair of pliers.

Something Revelatory Danny Way Said After Suffering What's Widely Considered One of the Worst Slams in Skateboarding History

After boosting a 540-degree rotation 20 feet over the 27-foot-tall MegaRamp at the X Games two years ago, Danny clipped his shins on the deck upon reentry, did a front flip, and rag-dolled onto his back-head-neck at the bottom of the ramp. His eyes rolled back in their sockets. He lay motionless. It looked career- (if not life-) ending, and is nauseating to watch on YouTube. The on-site doctor called the ambulance and banned Danny from returning to competition. While no one was looking, though, Danny hobbled through the bowels of the Staples Center and made his way back to the top of the ramp in time for his next run. He nailed the trick he'd slammed on earlier.

As Danny awaited the judges' score at the bottom of the ramp, an ESPN reporter asked if he'd be able to take his next few runs, given the fall.

"I'm taking every run," Danny said. His voice was slurred and his eyes were glazed and he couldn't really stand up straight because inside his shoe his foot was swelling to the size of a football.

Then he said: "It's about how much abuse the body can take and come back from."

He thought he was talking about skateboarding.

A Brief Interlude About Fear

Although I'd been hiding the fact that I still skated, I'd long entertained delusions of skating the Mega. But once I was there, I saw the sheer absurdity of my thinking. It wasn't the scale of the ramp that intimidated me. It was Danny. Failing to land even the most basic aerial would've been an insult, like he'd offered me a gift and I chucked it into the trash, bow and all, right in front of him. I was afraid to let him down.

And yet he's a man who strives to put you at ease. In his car he asks if you're getting enough air, if you like the radio station. In restaurants he asks about your food allergies—he has many—and then suggests dishes. He gives extremely thorough driving directions, spells out the street names, and then repeats the spellings, and you get the sense that he'd take your getting lost personally. Which is how I felt on the Mega—afraid not of embarrassing myself so much, but of embarrassing Danny.

All of which got me thinking about fear, so after his next attempt —where he barely made the full flip and kind of landed on his spine and all of the cameramen nervously looked to each other—I asked if the Mega in any way scared him.

"I was more scared talking to those students this morning," he said.

He did look uncomfortable giving his speech, like an awkward groomsman making a toast.

"It's weird," he said. "Onstage I can't get hurt, but here, where I could get maimed or killed, I feel totally relaxed. I have a lot of things in my memory that I can dig into and unlock to propel my motivation. Skateboarding is my tool for processing emotion and energy. I try to use it that way. It's easier said than done."

Then he dropped in again, slammed again, and just lay at the bottom of the ramp for a long, long time.

Dysfunction: Part Two

In 1989, when he was on the verge of being expelled from 10th grade for truancy and his home life was increasingly unstable, Way quit school altogether to skate full-time. Powell Peralta, however, wasn't ready to offer him a professional contract, so when he was approached about riding for H-Street, a new and edgy skater-owned company, Danny accepted. The move would prove significant and prescient. Soon, the few titanic companies that had long monopolized the industry would fall to smaller, grittier upstarts that appealed to skaters' insubordinate sensibilities. The break with Powell epitomizes what would become the defining traits of Danny's personal and professional experience, a pathological need for upheaval and an occasionally sadistic aversion to moderation. He feels most safe, most at home, when he's risking everything.

No one recognized how predisposed toward self-destruction Danny was better than Mike Ternasky, H-Street's cofounder. Ternasky was only 22, but he'd also grown up largely fatherless and saw that Danny's recklessness and the way he punished himself daily wasn't unrelated to the tumult at home. He knew taming Danny wasn't an option, but he also knew that the wildness, coupled with Danny's talent and obsessive nature, could be more than a liability. Ternasky earned Danny's trust not by asking him to share his feelings, but by pushing him to float higher airs and land more technical lip tricks, to channel his anger and confusion into his skating. Again, think Tyson. With Ternasky's guidance, Danny won his first pro contest, beating veterans and newcomers alike, and he began collecting monthly royalty checks in the neighborhood of $20K. He was 15.

And then, when everything seemed golden, Danny quit H-Street. He thought the team was getting too big and losing its edge. He couldn't abide such softness, even though he himself was making $80,000 a year before he could legally drive. For a short period, he skated on the Blind Skateboards team (with eventual *My Name Is Earl* star Jason Lee), but he never found the footing or inspiration he'd had with Ternasky. He placed poorly in contests and his board sales faltered. Any savings he had from the H-Street gravy train were gone. Once, while filming a skate video for his wheel sponsor, he was so broke he jumped off a 150-foot cliff into a lake for $200. And, like his brother, he started gravitating toward a more dangerous crowd, skaters who would fight the security guards who tried to run them off and then reconvene at the Way compound to drink and shoot guns. "Have you seen *Mad Max Beyond Thunderdome*? That was Danny's house when he was 16," says Colin McKay, one of Danny's closest friends, his business partner, and a pro skater himself.

"I look back on that time," Way says now, "and I think, How stupid were we?"

Which was maybe what Ternasky was thinking when he called Danny in 1991 and asked him to skate for a new company he was launching called Plan B. Danny, 17 at the time, signed on immediately, and Ternasky assembled the most advanced and influential team in skateboarding around his star athlete. Ternasky intended to build a skater-centered company that he could eventually bequeath to the elder skaters, ensuring that the nonconformist spirit of the enterprise would endure. Plan B became the shadow version of Powell Peralta, an unvarnished and unrivaled group of skaters that seemed both dangerous and soulful, and nowhere was that paradox more present than in Danny. Reconnecting with Ternasky ushered Danny into one of the most productive and creative periods of his career—even today, there are only a handful of pros who can land the tricks he invented in the early '90s, and no one skater can do all of them.

Then the bottom fell out from under Danny again. In 1994, on his way to the Plan B offices, Ternasky was T-boned at an intersection and died of head trauma. He was 27, and with the exception of Ternasky's wife, Danny was the last person to see him alive. The loss gutted him (the initials MT are tattooed under Danny's left arm, a tribute to his mentor). Even skateboarding, the only shelter he'd known since his stepfather introduced him to the sport, could do little to fill the hollowness he felt. The sport was itself dying, as it had a decade before, the result of increased overhead for skate parks and dwindling sales throughout the industry—board shops closed, ramps were torn down, countless pros sulked into more reliable careers or did humiliating demonstrations at amusement parks to pay the bills. Plan B closed its doors in 1995.

Then, while surfing near San Diego, Danny dove into a shallow break and snapped his neck.

Danny's Plan B

After he broke his neck—which he describes as "my face pretty much hitting me in my stomach"—Danny was partially paralyzed for more than a year. He went in and out of the hospital, bouncing from one doctor to another, and made no progress. He was afraid to lift a carton of milk, convinced that even minimal exertion would cause more damage. He suffered severe depression and spent most days lying on his floor to ease the pain. He was an invalid at 20. Imagine going from jumping off huge cliffs to being scared of something in your fridge. "It's like being in jail," he says. "You lose all your freedom."

Doctors said he'd never skate again. Danny refused to listen. He read everything he could about spinal injuries and experimented with different treatments. Each failure fueled his obsession. Finally he flew to Hawaii and lived with a spiritual healer who guided him out of his "superdepressed" state not with pharmaceuticals, but with meditation and a holistic focus on mind-body synergy. He made slow progress over the course of a few months, exacting the same determination on his recovery that he long had on his skating. When Danny returned to California, he endured months of brutal physical and psychological therapy. Nearly every day, he thought about giving up, but what kept him going was a vision of a ramp so unprecedented, massive, and jaw-droppingly gnarly that it would forever change the face of skateboarding.

As Danny returned to skating—he won a major contest in 1996, shocking the industry that had written him off as a lost soldier—

he began experimenting with the size and design of ramps, testing both the physical limitations and the possibilities he'd dreamed up during his long recuperation. "There were no engineers or mathematicians involved," he says. "It was all human trial and error." Which means that until he hit upon a design that worked, he'd try out the biggest ramp in history, destroy himself, then build a bigger one. Between 1999 and 2002, he underwent seven major surgeries. Then, in 2002, the prototype of what's now called the Mega-Ramp was erected in the desert. Before the weather eroded it, Danny invited other pros to ride the ramp, but only a select few had the requisite skills—and balls.

Danny's high-profile stunts eventually gave him enough cachet and cash to resurrect Plan B Skateboards in 2005. He called back most of the original team members and scooped up prodigies like Paul "P-Rod" Rodriguez and Ryan Sheckler. This March, Plan B partnered with Billabong to increase its market value and visibility. "The partnership will allow Plan B to go bigger and stay true to its core," Danny says. "We aren't going to make girls' clothing. We're going to make the best boards and wheels. We're going to be the modern-day Powell without selling ourselves short." In other words, he's doing exactly what Mike Ternasky had hoped he would. And it was probably because Ternasky would have wanted him to that Danny went to China and built a MegaRamp beside the Great Wall. For Danny, though, it was the means, not the end. He wants to make sure he's given the sport everything he can, everything it will need to flourish in his wake. His concern isn't his legacy, but the future of skateboarding.

As Danny was showing me clips of the new Plan B skate video on his iPhone, he said, "With the window of time left in my career, I'm not interested in proving I'm better than somebody else. I want to push skateboarding into another paradigm."

The new video is called *Superfuture.*

Project Lee-Way

Some of the rumors hewed pretty close to the truth. Way did go to Germany—not to have surgery, but rather an experimental treatment where doctors inject bone marrow into the joints to rejuvenate them; it worked. And he had been considering a stunt that involved skating down the Luxor in Vegas, and he had been doing a lot of street skating, but he put everything on the back burner to train for X Games 16, which could be the defining moment in his career. He wants to build an ecologically sound skate facility in Hawaii, but that's a ways off. Right now he's concentrating on erecting a MegaRamp with a foam pit at the Woodward West Skate Camp in California. The foam pit will help him practice his top-secret new trick, but more important, the Mega at Woodward West will make Big Air skating available to anyone who goes to the camp. It will democratize the genre of skating that has, in Way's opinion, been too exclusive. He wants kids who spend afternoons at small municipal skate parks to envision themselves on the Mega, and he wants to hit upon a Mega design that skate parks around the country will adopt.

Since his marriage ended in 2009, he and his ex-wife have been negotiating how to raise their three kids in two different houses. There were rough patches, but they're in the past. Way says, "Everything is chill. No one's right and no one's wrong. We're great friends on different paths, except with the kids. We're walking with them, together."

As for the rumors about him being strung out and jet-setting with Tommy Lee, Way laughs. "I am friends with Tommy, and I've been in his plane, but he's sober and laid-back. Partying wouldn't complement my life right now. What we usually talk about is our kids and our new band. He's a really wise, spiritual dude."

"He's got some stubborn bull in him," Lee says. "We keep each other going in the right direction. I'm on the Danny Way program and he's on the Tommy Lee one. It's all positive. We should brand it, call it 'Lee-Way.'"

Way tells me that the documentary is back on track, slated to hit theaters in early 2011, and he says he thinks he can take X Games gold in both Big Air and Rail Jam this year, if he can avoid injury. Just as the conversation seems to be wrapping up, he says, "If I tell you the trick I'm working on for X, do you have to print it? Can I just tell you for your own information?"

He sounds keyed up and nervous, like a kid with a secret. Then I realize it: he's not just worried that I'll spill the secret to the world; he's worried that I won't be impressed, worried that what he's trying to do won't be enough.

"We can go off the record," I say.

"Cool," he says.

Then he tells me. I ask him to repeat himself because I'm sure I've misheard him. I haven't. And he's right; everything he's done before seems like a warm-up, a throat-clearing.

"Is that really possible?" I ask.

"I'm optimistic," he says.

And then our connection drops. The line goes dead. When I call back, I'm dumped to his voice mail. His outgoing message is addressed to his sons: "Ryden and Tavin, leave a message and Daddy will call you back. Okay, I love you guys. Later."

Where This Has All Been Leading

I've left a lot out of this article. I haven't mentioned how Danny has twice jumped from a hovering helicopter into a halfpipe, or how one of those times, the first time, he did it with a dislocated shoulder. I've not mentioned his four ACL reconstructions, two of which were done while he was awake. Not the fact that he holds the land speed record on a skateboard. I left all of this, and tons more, out because finally it's irrelevant, which is the definitive difference between Danny Way and, well, you. And me. And most everyone else on the planet. When you add up all of Danny's accomplishments and trespasses, his loves and losses and the times when he's been lost, there's still something missing. And what's missing—it's not fear, but maybe fearfulness—is what the rest of us have an awful lot of. We cling to our fearfulness as tightly as we do our triumphs and traumas; we envision these things as the perimeters of our identities, the irrefutable evidence of our capabilities, and Danny simply, emphatically, doesn't.

Think Picasso, Hemingway, Dvorak. Think Laird Hamilton, Chuck Yeager. And, yes, think Tyson. Consider the likelihood that these men don't possess qualities the rest of us lack, but instead have within them intense voids, empty and expansive chambers of possibility. Maybe these voids—which the men fill with what can only be called art—are innate, or maybe they're the result of damage or sacrifice or failures the artists have endured. The origin doesn't matter. Nor does the medium. True, this is a story of how much abuse the body can transcend, but it's also the story of pushing not merely the limits of skateboarding but the boundaries of the human spirit, the soul. What's most inspiring—and intimidating—about Danny has little to do with his greatness or resilience or the sheer ballsiness of his life; rather, it has everything to do with his ambivalence toward those things. While the rest of us stand in awe, rooted in the past and arrested by timidity, he climbs back to the top of the ramp. He adjusts his pads, hangs his wheels over the edge, and drops in. He throws his weight forward, leaning into gravity again and again, trying to gather the speed he needs.

DAVID DOBBS

The Tight Collar

FROM WIRED.COM

The Collar

Late in May 2008, perched in superb seats a few rows behind home plate at Chicago's Cellular Field, I took in a White Sox–Indians game with Sian Beilock, a professor of psychology at the University of Chicago who studies what is surely, other than serious injury, the most feared catastrophe in sports: the choke.

Beilock, who not long ago played some high-level lacrosse at University of California, San Diego, traces her own interest in choking back to high school, when she discovered that during the tense, game-beginning face-offs, she more often gained control of the ball if she sang to herself, "to keep me from thinking too much." Later, in grad school, it occurred to her that if you could avoid choking by engaging your brain with singing, it followed that choking must rise from what neuroscientists like to call mechanisms — that is, systematic, causal chains of brain activity.

She has spent much of her time since then exposing and exploring those mechanisms. Her labs include a putting room where she can find a way to make virtually anyone screw up putts that were easy just moments before. Her work has brought her absurdly early tenure, a rain of prizes and grants, and a flashy book contract. She is a kind of queen of choke.

Which is what brought us to Cellular Field. I'd hate to say we were *wishing* for someone to choke; more like waiting. And given that baseball offers a hundred openings for pressure's effects, and that this was a tense game between teams vying for first place — the

White Sox led their longtime division rivals, the Indians, by a game and a half—we could wait in confidence, knowing that at some point a player would "suffer," as Beilock politely phrased it, "a decrement under pressure."

The game did not disappoint. Through seven innings the pitchers dominated, and the pressure slowly rose. Then, in the eighth, the White Sox, leading 2–1, got a chance to put the game away when the Indians' pitcher C. C. Sabathia finally tired and was replaced by Jensen Lewis, a rookie, just as the White Sox were sending up their best hitters.

Lewis, perhaps suffering a bit of a decrement himself, walked the first hitter and then surrendered a double that left runners at second and third. When White Sox slugger Jim Thome, who had already homered once, came to bat, Lewis, on orders from the bench, walked him intentionally to get to the next batter.

A certain weight—the weight of great opportunity—falls upon any hitter who steps to the plate with the bases loaded. It falls heavier when the pitcher has just intentionally walked the previous batter.

Feeling this weight now was Paul Konerko, the Sox first baseman. Konerko generally hits well with runners in scoring position, batting a few points higher than his lifetime average, and he could do so in big moments: he had won Game 2 of the 2005 World Series, in fact, by homering with the bases loaded.

But Konerko was also a streaky hitter, and lately he had run cold. In fact he was having a terrible season. He was hitting just .212, and he had not homered in weeks. Now, however, he had a chance to break open an important game.

Though I was there to see a choke, I was pulling for the guy. But he had a horrible at-bat.

It was one I could relate to, for I had endured an at-bat remarkably similar to his the week before. (I play in what my wife calls "geezerball," an amateur league for those over 35.) With two runners on and my team trailing by a single run, I had done everything wrong: I took a hittable fastball for strike one, chased an unreachable curveball outside, and then stood frozen as strike three —another fastball, which you should always be ready for with two strikes—split the plate.

Now I watched with amazement as Konerko did much the same.

He had enough sense to swing at *his* first-pitch fastball, only he missed it. But after that it was carbon copy: he chased a curveball outside, then stood frozen as a heater blew by for strike three.

Now, I don't want to say Konerko *choked,* because (a) he was facing major league pitching, which is incomprehensibly nasty, and (b) I met Konerko later, and he's a tremendously likable guy, and I'd hate to hurt his feelings. Yet it seemed clear that if the tremendous pressure of this crucial at-bat had not exactly destroyed Konerko, it had affected him enough to produce a subpar performance. So I don't want to say he choked. But he gagged.

But what, really, did this mean? What had transpired in his skull to make this feared major leaguer bat like an amateur?

Useful Distraction

Even the greatest athletes sometimes choke. Take Derek Jeter. Jeter's hitting generally holds steady or even improves under pressure; he bats as well or better as strikes, outs, and base runners accrue, and his .309 batting average in postseason games is impressively close to his lifetime .317. Yet during the epic 2004 American League Championship Series, as his Yankees won the first three games and then *dropped four in a row* to allow the Red Sox to reach the World Series, Jeter hit barely .200.

Or consider Ben Hogan, one of golf's steadiest great players. On the final hole of the 1946 Masters, Hogan needed only to sink a two-foot putt to win. He completely missed the cup. In another notorious golf gaffe, Arnold Palmer, known for playing well in tight spots and being untouchable once ahead, choked the 1966 U.S. Open twice: he blew a five-stroke lead in the last four holes of regulation, and in the playoff the next day, he blew six strokes in the final eight holes, losing the tournament.

Collapses like these — classic chokes — appear to arise from the process known colloquially as "thinking too much" or "paralysis through analysis," and among cognitive scientists as "explicit monitoring." Explicit monitoring, says Beilock, is "conscious attention to normally automatized physical operations that destroys the athlete's normal fluidity."

This is the micromanaged putt, the aimed pitch, the overdirected free throw. This is the screwup your brother is trying to induce when he asks you, as you tee up, "Do you inhale or exhale on your backswing?" By consciously trying to direct a physical action that you've practiced until it's automatic, you botch it.

Bounteous research has confirmed that for polished athletes, the explicit monitoring of performance destroys performance. Beilock, for instance, demonstrated this by asking expert college soccer players to keep track of which side of which foot was contacting the ball as they dribbled through a series of pylons. When they did, they moved through the pylons more slowly and made more mistakes than they did normally. She regularly gets similar results when she asks good golfers to monitor, say, how far back they take their backswings.

"You need to monitor these mechanics while you're learning an action," Beilock notes. "But once you've learned it, you've got to leave it alone."

The classic advice for avoiding thinking too much is to "not think about it." But this is not easily done. You're better off, says Beilock, if you find something else to think about—a useful distraction, some simple mental task that occupies the mind enough to keep it from meddling.

Rob Gray, a professor of psychology at Arizona State University, demonstrated this a few years ago with an elegant two-stage experiment he conducted with high-level college baseball players in a batting cage. In the first part of the experiment, he asked the batters (whom he had already watched hit in order to establish a baseline performance) to listen for a tone while hitting so they could report where their bat was in the swing when the tone sounded. Unsurprisingly, this explicit monitoring made them hit worse. They missed more often, and their swings got measurably slower and more choppy.

Yet it was not the listening that messed them up; it was their attention to the swing. For when Gray asked the hitters to listen for a tone while batting and report merely whether the tone was high or low in frequency, the hitters swung as fluidly and hit as well as usual. Their bodies knew the hitting process well enough to do it with a distracted brain. But explicitly monitoring the process gummed it up.

Since then, Gray, Beilock, and others working such "dual-task" or "healthy distraction" experiments have shown that attending to a modestly demanding outside mental operation can reduce explicit monitoring and alleviate choking. Beilock has found, for example, that golfers under competitive pressure can prevent decrement by counting backwards to themselves while they putt.

"It's what I was doing when I sang during face-offs," says Beilock. "The simple mental task lets your body do what it already knows how to do."

Judicious Attention

Such findings have made explicit monitoring the blanket explanation of choking in sports. It's as if everyone agreed that while a bit of smarts can serve well at times—mostly for catchers, point guards, and quarterbacks—jocks had generally best leave their thinking brains in the locker.

Perhaps because she is both brain and jock, Beilock received this wisdom skeptically. As a grad student looking at choking research, it struck her that the prevailing model of performance under pressure rose from experiments that look almost exclusively at physical actions.

"Yet choking," as she points out, "is so clearly mental. If you study golf and study only the strokes, you'll have only one idea about how skills fail. But there are crucial skills in sports that rest on processes less physical. Part of sports is thinking." And there are chokes, she asserts, that arise not from overthinking but from poor thinking.

She offers evidence both anecdotal and experimental. For anecdote, consider golfer Colin Montgomerie in the 2006 U.S. Open. Montgomerie, 42 at the time and burdened with the unofficial title Best Golfer Never to Win a Major, began the tournament's last hole having just taken the lead with a gorgeous 50-foot putt.

To take the trophy he simply had to par the 18th. He put his drive in the middle of the fairway, leaving himself a straightforward 170-yard approach shot to the green. But after pulling a 6-iron from his bag—his usual club for a 170-yard shot—he suddenly worried about hitting too long.

He put back the 6 and pulled out the shorter 7-iron—and hit short. The ball landed in deep rough. His chip landed 30 feet from the hole, and he three-putted to lose by a stroke.

An even clearer example comes from the 1993 NCAA championship basketball game. University of Michigan star Chris Webber gained possession of the ball with 11 seconds left and called a time-out—only to discover that his team had no more time-outs. The resulting technical foul helped seal Michigan's elimination.

Beilock contends that such failures come not from unwelcome attention, as explicit monitoring does, but from a deficit of needed attention. "Sports aren't cognitively static," says Beilock. "Situations change, and you need to track things and make decisions. You can't just *not* think. There's a whole skill involved in knowing not just what not to think about, but when to attend to things that need tending. You've got to be able to control what you're attending to."

At the Sox-Indians game I saw with her, this made perfect sense. A typical at-bat requires coming to the plate with a plan of attack based on the hitter's skills and the pitcher's strengths and proclivities. Most batters focus on a hittable area of the strike zone they suspect the pitcher will find at least once with a particular pitch: fastball outside, perhaps, or slider in tight. As the at-bat progresses and the hitter gains or loses advantage by getting ahead or behind in the count, he must shrink or expand his swing zone.

When hitters step out of the box between pitches, it's usually to perform this recalibration: they zoom out from their deep focus to check the count, regauge their swing zone, then step in and zoom in again. If they don't do this or they think poorly or second-guess, they're more likely to get surprised—and to swing at pitches they should take or take pitches they should swing at.

Beilock holds that such faulty thinking amounts to a different sort of choke: a disruption of quick but vital data-checks, calculations, and recalibrations that the athlete must perform to play at optimum level. It's a failure of cognition. Call it a cognichoke.

Is that what was going on with Konerko? And how did it work?

Why White Men Can't Putt

Sports psychology goes back to 1898, when psychologist Norman Triplett found that cyclists ride faster in groups than they do alone. Since then, sports psychologists have had the arena of performance and its decrements largely to themselves. No one outside jock psych seemed terribly interested in what made people screw up.

This began to change, however, in 1995, when a Stanford psychology professor named Claude Steele, working with graduate student Joshua Aronson, published a study titled "Stereotype Threat and the Intellectual Test Performance of African Americans." The paper described how Steele and Aronson knocked down by a whopping 50 percent the scores of black Stanford undergrads taking sections of the Graduate Record Examination (GRE) simply by telling them the test measured intelligence.

The paper created a sensation, inspiring a rain of similar studies. Steele and Aronson subsequently showed you could drive down test scores merely by having black students declare their race on a pretest form. They and other researchers soon found that stereotype threat works on other groups too. Mention anything about gender or "innate ability" to women taking a math test, for instance, and they'll make more mistakes.

Though these stereotype-threat effects fairly reek of choking, several years passed before anyone examined them in the light of sports performance. Then, in 1999, Jeff Stone, a social psychologist at the University of Arizona, asked both white and black golfers to play a putting game framed as a test of either "sports intelligence" or "natural athletic ability." The results still astonish: among the golfers considering the putting game a test of "natural athletic ability," blacks did better than usual and whites did worse. Among those framing it as a sort of sports intelligence test, whites did better and blacks worse.

This result, replicated many times since, eerily echoes the GRE test-score plunge that Steele and Aronson induced in 1995. Yet that white golfers suffered a hit while being tested for "natural athletic ability" raises an intriguing question: if white male golfers in Arizona can be so easily derailed by an unflattering stereotype, who on earth is exempt from stereotype threat?

No one. Since those first studies, Stone, Beilock, and others have produced, with almost laughable ease, absurdly task- and stereotype-specific effects in groups of every sort. For instance, if you ask white men to jump both before and after calling the jumping test a measure of "natural athletic ability," they will jump significantly less high after the threat. White male engineers, meanwhile, will ace a math test if it's presented as a test of gender-based or innate math abili-ties—but tell them they're being compared with Asian male engi-neers, and they'll choke badly.

"We haven't found anyone," says Beilock, "that we can't screw up by suggesting that some group they're a member of is bad at some-thing."

Stereotype threat, it turns out, is a surprisingly democratic dy-namic. Obviously stereotypes such as bigotry and sexism are not applied equitably. But no one is immune to the mechanism that stereotype threat applies. For this reason, some psychologists are starting to call it "identity threat." As Jeff Stone put it, "We all have multiple identities, and they can all be discriminated against. It's the identities we carry that make us vulnerable here."

Emphasize the identity aspect, and the sports implications rap-idly expand. The many late-season and postseason failures by the Chicago Cubs, for instance, start to make more sense: in a pressure situation, any simple reminder that you're a Cub (like, say, your uniform) may cause enough decrement to make you drop fly balls, boot grounders, or monitor your way out of an at-bat.

Meanwhile, stereotype "lift"—a performance boost that some studies have found in people doing tasks their stereotyped groups supposedly do well—may lend extra advantage to the Yankees or (now that their two World Series wins in 2004 and 2007 seem to have lifted the Curse) the Boston Red Sox.

But how does stereotype threat work? The initial hypothesis about the Steele and Aronson African American test-taking results was that stereotype threat creates a self-fulfilling image of failure, a sort of role-playing in which the test-taker surrenders to the stereo-typed identity by disengaging emotionally and intellectually. In the last five years or so, however, researchers such as Beilock and the University of Arizona's Toni Schmader have done experiments sug-gesting that stereotype threat fouls performance primarily by oc-cupying working memory.

Working memory is the crucial mental faculty that briefly retains multiple pieces of unrelated data so you can use or manipulate them. You depend on working memory every time you read a para-graph, learn a new definition, perform a multipart math problem in your head, or try to retain a phone number while you finish a conversation. Working-memory capacity is closely tied to general powers of intellect and decision-making. When it's not working well, you're not as sharp.

In late 2007, Beilock found that when women under stereotype threat choked on a math test she designed for them, they choked almost exclusively on problems that relied on working memory; they fell short not because they were thinking too much, but because they couldn't keep in mind the things necessary to the task.

This working memory failure is a much different mechanism than external monitoring (which stereotype threat can also cause); instead of overmonitoring a physical operation, the athlete or test-taker is poorly attending to a mental operation. Beilock believes such misattention is at work when athletes commit mental stumbles like Colin Montgomerie's club switch. Montgomerie wasn't stupid to double-check his choice of club; calibrating club selection is essential to high-level golf. His mistake was in not working through the problem fully and leaving out the essential information: that conditions dictated that he should indeed use his regular club length. But with his cognitive machinery slowed by preoccupied working memory, he failed to think straight and miffed it. He cognichoked.

How do you fend off such effects of stereotype threat? As Jeff Stone notes, identity is partly a matter of context and even choice. "Usually, something in the context has to activate a stereotype threat. It has to be turned on. But you can also turn it off. To some extent, you can reframe things yourself." Asian women, for instance, do better on math tests if they focus more on their Asianness than on their gender.

"You can't dictate your genes," says Stone. "But among the many identities you have, you can choose which to operate from." Tiger Woods, for instance, has clearly forged an identity that transcends the potential vulnerabilities of his multiracial makeup. You can wallow in your most negative identity—the slow one, the over-thinker, the one who doesn't care—or you can foreground another identity, the one who is ready, the one who knows what's coming, the one who calmly attacks the problem.

Not that this comes easy. As Beilock notes, this second, cognition-based failure under pressure means "there are at least two things going on, running parallel, almost all the time": a physical track and a mental track. "And what might disrupt you—what might crunch under pressure—depends on what you're doing at a particular moment."

You can jump off the physical track by overmonitoring and fall off the cognitive track through inattention. And distraction greases the physical track and kinks the cognitive. To travel both smoothly requires knowing what to attend to and what not to attend to—or to put it another way, understanding what to distract yourself from (your physical mechanics) and what not to get distracted from (the score, the count, how many time-outs you have left).

This is a vision of athletic performance both alluring and daunting. Sports start to look a lot more like real life—and much more demanding.

"It's a lot more complicated than just 'Don't think about it,'" says Beilock.

Showtime

How did hitters handle this dual track? I wanted to ask Paul Konerko. So late that season of 2008, on August 29, I went to another White Sox game, the opener of a vital three-game series against the Red Sox in Boston. For pressure, this one easily beat the May game I'd watched with Beilock. Both teams were in drum-tight pennant races; the Red Sox were four and a half games out of first in the American League East and the White Sox up a game and a half in the AL Central. Both teams needed wins. Both knew they might meet a month later, in the postseason.

Despite the stakes, however, the White Sox clubhouse seemed a remarkably calm place three hours before game time. Several players sat watching a Cubs-Phillies game that ran quietly on a television. Another cluster studied laptops showing films of Boston pitcher Daisuke "Dice-K" Matsuzaka, whom they would face that evening. I found Konerko in a chair in front of his locker doing a crossword puzzle.

Konerko in person projects a warmth and quickness of expression that doesn't come across in photos or even video. He is a smart but modest man, and articulate and open in a way that had long made him a favorite interview target among Chicago sportswriters. He sat alone today, however.

His season had not gone well since I'd seen him strike out in May. After hitting .222 in April and .191 in May, he'd gone .250 in June and .209 in July, and so entered August hitting .214 with just nine homers, half his normal pace. The White Sox, desperate to produce more runs, dropped him two spots in the order, from the hallowed cleanup spot, fourth, to sixth; the Chicago press, meanwhile, was calling for his head.

On July 31 the team acquired slugger Ken Griffey Jr., and Konerko started seeing his name replaced on the lineup every few days by Nick Swisher, a 27-year-old outfielder–first baseman who until then had played the center-field spot now occupied by Griffey.

Whether it was the Griffey trade, the days off, or improving health, however, Konerko had started to heat up the first week of August. He got a hit almost every game that week, including three in one game in Detroit. The following week he went 6-for-20. He entered this crucial Boston series hitting .339 for the month.

In four weeks he'd become a different hitter. Surely, I figured, he would be able to describe some difference in how he felt now versus a month before, some mental or mechanical adjustment that explained his cleaner engagement with the baseball.

"It's kind of strange, actually," he told me. "Fact is, I don't feel any different. I mean, I feel happier when it's going well and I'm helping the team. But I don't really understand what goes on when I'm doing well versus when I'm doing badly. I've had whole years where I had 'good years' — good numbers, helped the team — but felt like I was struggling the whole time. I've had other stretches where I feel completely locked in — and things don't work out."

I asked him how he tried to adjust when things weren't going well or when a situation carried more pressure.

"You try to stay steady. Not change too much. You prepare. You do your work every day, so you're swinging well and you know your pitcher and the situation. Then you go in and try to focus and execute. In the box, keep it simple. I try to concentrate on tracking a pitch into a zone I've chosen to focus on, swing hard at those. Sometimes you get fooled. But you stick to your routine, stay focused. Don't overthink."

This message — sticking to a routine, not overexamining — was echoed by every hitter I talked to that day, on both teams: Boston's

free-and-easy slugger David Ortiz ("Don't be changing things!");
his tautly focused teammate catcher Jason Varitek ("Stay with your
game"); and Konerko's clubhouse mates Jim Thome ("Be true to
your program") and Ken Griffey Jr., who simply said, smiling slyly
and repeating himself precisely in tone and emphasis, "Every at-
bat the same. Every at-bat the same."

These were variations on "Don't think too much." But almost
every conversation also addressed, in ways more veiled, the tension
between when to think and when not to. The most revealing was a
comment Konerko made as I closed my notebook, ready to let him
return to his crossword.

"I wish you luck with this," he said. "It's a hard kind of story to
get people to talk about this time of year—a team like this, anyway,
in the middle of a pennant race. This is really kind of a spring training story."

Only later did I realize what he meant. During the season, hitters
in particular must guard against constant tinkering, or they'll tin-
ker away a season. You save the heavy refashioning—reworking
your stance or your swing, changing your focal tactics—for spring
training. Once play begins, you stick to your program.

Approaching every at-bat the same does more than prevent external monitoring. It ritualizes the mental processes—the zoom
out to check the situation, the zoom back in to focus, the oscillations between thinking and not thinking—that are as vital as the
physical execution. It creates a management of attention as proceduralized, if not quite as automatic, as your swing mechanics.

I considered all this later, as I watched Konerko confront the
mystery that was Daisuke Matsuzaka. Dice-K, 16-2 entering the
game, had all seven of his pitches going that night in Boston. He
was always on or near the edges of the plate and never over the
center; he threw an untrackable variety of trajectories and speeds;
he dipped, zipped, darted, and curved; he made the ball do everything but climb. The White Sox managed just two hits, and they
never came close to scoring. It was hard not to feel sorry for them.

Yet Konerko, though he went 0-for-3, looked good. Before each
at-bat, when he was on deck, he smoothly executed the same
stretching and swinging rituals, a sort of meditative entry. At the
plate, he stepped out of the box after each pitch with the same de-
liberation and rhythm every time, took the same easy-ripping prac-

tice swing, raised his bat, stepped back in. His body language did not convey the dismay and confusion that it had 14 weeks before. He was more evenly engaged. And he had good at-bats.

He didn't get much to hit, but he took the pitches he should take and swung at the ones he had to, and in the second he drove the one touchable pitch he saw, a nasty low fastball, deep to right-center, where it was gathered in by a sprinting Jacoby Ellsbury. He didn't get a hit. But he had righted himself.

Was he in the "zone," that hallowed place of effortless full focus? Perhaps; he certainly seemed to be there in the week that followed, as he went 10-for-28 with three homers, and for the rest of the pennant race, as he hit .260 with nine homers in September, despite a knee injury mid-month. He was the team's hottest bat as they claimed the American League Central Division by winning a one-game playoff after finishing the regular season tied with Minnesota. (They then lost the American League Championship to the Tampa Bay Rays in four games.)

The zone is a happy place. Yet if the zone lies at one end of a spectrum and the choke at the other, athletes spend most of their time laboring in the spectrum's inner bands, in a gray area between groove and gag. Playing on the happier end of this band requires almost numbingly proceduralized mechanics both physical and mental—a physical groove of automated motion and a mental groove requiring a disciplined oscillation of attention and thought.

"It'd be nice," as Konerko told me, "if it were as simple as not thinking. But you're always thinking. It's a matter of what you're thinking about."

MARK KRAM JR.

Life Goes On

FROM THE PHILADELPHIA DAILY NEWS

First of two parts

Chicago—Quietly, Sonia Rodriguez got out of bed and padded
into the other room, where the evening before she had laid out
her clothes for work. It was Wednesday, 6:30 A.M., and her husband
Paco was still asleep, the gray light of a cold Chicago dawn beginning to seep through the windows of the small house that the couple and their baby daughter shared with his parents. Sonia slipped
into the outfit that she had picked out, brushed her hair, and
stopped back in the bedroom to look in on Ginette, who slept in
the crib that was wedged against the wall. Sweeping up her purse,
she glanced over at Paco and told herself she would phone him
when he arrived later that day in Philadelphia. But as she stepped
out the door he called to her.

"Oh?" he said, blinking the sleep from his eyes. "Are you leaving?"

She looked over her shoulder and said softly, "Yeah."

"Come here," Paco told her. Sonia walked over and sat on the
edge of the bed. He reached up, drew her into his arms, and said,
"I want to say goodbye."

Goodbyes were not easy for them. In the five years they had been
together, they seldom had been apart. Even when they were still
dating, he would stop by and see her at the end of the day, if only
for an hour or so just to talk. But Sonia had not chosen to accompany her 25-year-old husband to Philadelphia, where that Friday
evening Paco had a 12-round bout scheduled at the Blue Horizon
with Teon Kennedy for the vacant United States Boxing Associa-

tion super bantamweight crown. Boxing had become a sport that Sonia looked upon with equal portions of acceptance and disdain. She accepted it because of the passion Paco had for it, and even now says that boxing was who he was. And yet part of her held it in disdain and she had stopped attending his bouts because of it, unable to cope with the queasiness that would send her fleeing from her ringside seat whenever Paco would engage an opponent in a toe-to-toe exchange. So when he asked her if she would like to come along to Philadelphia, he was not surprised when she smiled and told him, "No, you go. But hurry back to me." And he told her he would, adding as always, "I promise you."

An odd feeling had come over her in the weeks leading up to his departure that Wednesday. But she did not share it with Paco. Knowing how he was, she feared that it would only worry him — and he had been worried enough. In fact, he had been so overcome with anxiety that he was sure at one point that he was in the throes of cardiac arrest. At the emergency room, doctors told him he had had a panic attack, which Sonia ascribed to the pressure Paco had been under due to the approaching Kennedy bout. "Babe," he would remind her, "it's just three weeks away . . . it's just two weeks away . . . it's just a week away." But as excited as he appeared, he did not seem to be himself, and there was part of her that did not want to let go of him. While she told herself as he held her in his arms that morning that he would be back on Saturday, she would remember a conversation they had had a few days before, how engulfed it had been by this eerie edginess.

"What am I going to do without you?" he told her. "I am going to miss you so much."

"Be calm," she said. "Go over there and do what you have to do. And enjoy it."

"You are going to be very proud of me," he said. "This is going to really help us in the future. You and the baby and I are always going to be okay."

Every Sunday, they go to the Woodlawn Park Cemetery. As one-year-old Ginette plays amid the flowers that have been placed by the headstone, Sonia sits on the grass and ponders the tragic event that swept through their lives: one year ago this week, her beloved husband was lowered into the earth, the victim of head blows he received during his bout with Kennedy. For Sonia, 25, no words can adequately express the ache that dwells in her heart, which only becomes heavier when she thinks of Ginette and the journey that stands before them. When her daughter asks her one day what her dad was like, Sonia will explain to her that he was a hero, not for what he had accomplished in the ring but because he was a courageous man who loved them both and who helped prolong the lives of his uncle — and four people who were strangers to him. Francisco "Paco" Rodriguez was an organ donor.

Great need exists for organs, and it increases year by year: there were 109,138 people on the waiting list at the end of October, and 6,504 in the local Gift of Life Donor Program area, which includes eastern Pennsylvania, southern New Jersey, and Delaware. At the very moment that Paco was pronounced dead at Hahnemann University Hospital — Sunday, November 22, at 7:42 P.M. — there were five people who were waging battles with grave health conditions as bravely as he himself had ever engaged an opponent in the ring. One of them was his uncle in Chicago, Ramon Tejeda, who received a kidney in what is referred to as a "directed donation." Four others were people who had never heard of Paco before his organs saved their lives: Alexis Sloan, of Norristown, received his heart; Ashley Owens, of Spring City in Chester County, received both his lungs; Meghan Kingsley, of Gaithersburg, Maryland, received his liver; and Vicky Davis, of Clifford Township in Susquehanna County, received his other kidney and his pancreas. While Sonia says that Paco had not legally designated himself as an organ donor, she signed the consent form because it had been a subject the two of them had discussed.

"Francisco was always very giving and I did not want his death to stop that," says Sonia, seated at the dining room table with her in-laws. "We had talked it over and he had told me that it was something that he wanted to do. When they asked me if it was something we would like to do, I remember thinking: 'What if it were Francisco that was hanging between life and death, if he had been the one who had needed someone to be so giving?' I would have asked someone, 'Please, just do it. You are giving someone a chance at life.'"

Inside the doorway of the house, a small shrine has been set up in memory of Paco: a photograph of him adorned with a halo and angel wings; shelves with vases of white flowers; and a statuette of the Blessed Mother draped with rosary beads. Someone lights the candles at the base of it each day, the glow from which throws shadows across the bowed head of the porcelain Mary. Even a year later, the house remains a place of mourning, steeped in an unwillingness to let go. In a back room, the wall is covered with an inventory of the career that came to a sudden end that evening at the Blue Horizon. Wherever the eye turns there are boxing posters, gloves, and trunks, and up on hangers—carefully preserved beneath plastic—are colorful robes with "El Niño Azteka" scripted on the back. That was how he billed himself: "Kid Aztec." Elsewhere, the bedroom he shared with Sonia and Ginette remains just the same as it was when she said goodbye to him. The bureau is cluttered with beauty products; the bed is strewn with a tangle of sheets; and the crib still sits against the wall near a crucifix.

Gone is the serene smile that beamed from Sonia in her wedding pictures. In place of it are downcast eyes. While she speaks with clarity and precision, her voice has a quality that seems on the verge of shattering, as if it were a piece of fine china toppled over by the tail of a prowling house cat. She does not cry and yet one can see that she has, that there have been days that have been long and unbearable. Moving out of the house and in with her sister has provided her with some support, but she says there is "no way to explain how injured I feel." But she keeps herself busy and that has helped. There is Ginette and a job she has as a legal assistant and the accounting degree she is pursuing at DePaul University. And yet she has still not overcome the feeling that there is this hole in her heart, and she wonders to herself if it is ever going to heal. Sonia says, "You have to understand: he was the boy I had always dreamed of."

Even as she continues to grieve, Sonia has found some solace in the fact that her husband still lives on—in Ginette but also in the rejuvenated lives of the organ recipients. In an unexpected way, she has come to feel a certain bond with them, as if they were part of her extended family. On days when the weight of her loss bears down upon her, it reassures her to know that there are people who had suffered for so long who now have the chance to live life to the fullest because of Paco. Gradually, it occurred to her that she would like to contact them, if only to let them know who her husband was. And that with them would always be a piece of the love she has for him.

*

There is an irony here. Because long before boxing killed Paco, it very well might have saved him. As a boy growing up in the Logan Square section of Chicago, an area settled by a dense Hispanic population, he was surrounded by the presence of gang activity. The community has calmed down since then, but when Paco was 12, shots came through the front window, shattered the television set, and embedded in the wall. Apparently, someone had fired from a speeding car at someone else who had been running away down the sidewalk. No one inside the Rodriguez home was injured. But it was the type of trouble that Evaristo Sr. had always feared, which is why he told his boys: "Listen, you get home from school, you do your homework, get your stuff together, and we'll go to the gym."

The old man had been a fighter himself, a journeyman welterweight who always seemed called upon by promoters on short notice to fill out a card. Poor, he began boxing in Guadalajara, Mexico, came to Chicago as an illegal in 1979, and won just one of his seven bouts in the United States. To support his wife, Maria, and their three children—which included Alejandro (Alex) and Evaristo Jr. (Tito)—he found work as a busboy and later in a tool factory. While his boxing career ended in 1983, he still did some sparring here and there and passed along his passion for the sport to his sons. It was a way for them to keep out of trouble, yes, but the ring always has been looked upon in Latino culture as a place of honor, where boys prove themselves as men and, if they are good enough, ascend out of poverty into something better. Tito won the National Golden Gloves championship at age 17 in 1997 and is still considered one of the finest amateur boxers ever to come out of Chicago. But he did not turn pro because of a conflict with Evaristo Sr., and in the years that followed, it would become Paco who would carry on the dreams that had been thwarted in the others.

Evaristo Sr. could see there was an urgency building in Paco. While Evaristo Sr. says he had been undisciplined as a boy, choosing to stay home and play instead of applying himself at the gym, Paco seemed animated by the success that Tito enjoyed. By the age of 17, Paco would win a National Golden Gloves championship, five local titles, and a berth in the 2004 United States Olympic Trials. Overall, he won 76 of his 82 amateur bouts. With that solid background, he turned pro in January 2005 and emerged as a crowd favorite at the Aragon Ballroom and Cicero Stadium, the two Chicago-area boxing venues where he became a regular. Kid Aztec would bob up and down to the beat of a Mexican band as his entourage ushered him to the ring. Matchmaker Jerry Alfano says, "I tried to bring him up gradually by placing him with tougher and tougher opponents, so that we were building not just a record but a fighter." While Paco had suffered losses in two of his 16 fights, Alfano says that "everything was going pretty well."

Sonia stopped attending his bouts when friends began teasing her about how she would get up and run to the bathroom whenever the action heated up. But it just tore her up inside to see Paco in the ring, so she stayed away and waited for him to call from his dressing room with good news. They would then either go out to eat or swing by the emergency room, where Paco would have his face stitched up. When they would get home, she would hold ice on his bruises to ease the swelling. Two weeks before they exchanged vows at Our Lady of Grace Church, he was cut over both eyelids. Concerned how he would look on their wedding day—and in the pictures!—Sonia would have preferred that he not take the bout. "See, I told you," Sonia said when she saw his face. But Francisco told her the cuts would heal. And they did. No bride could have asked for a more handsome groom that August day in 2008. While they had been married in a civil ceremony two years before, Paco had promised her that one day she would have the church wedding she had always dreamed of. Paco had set aside some of the earnings from his bouts. They even had enough to go to Disney World for 10 days.

Inactivity became a problem for Francisco. Managed by Alex and trained by Evaristo Sr. and Tito, he turned down bouts in the Chicago area due to what Alfano says was a degree of overprotectiveness by his family; Tito says that the issue had more to do with the inability of Alfano to produce attractive enough purses. Whatever the case, Paco had had just one bout in the 15 months prior to his Philadelphia trip and had been working as a courier for a chiropractor. Sonia encouraged him to go back to school, which he would at Wright College, but only briefly. He had spoken to her of perhaps becoming a chef. When Ginette was born in August 2009, Evaristo Sr. even seemed to be of the belief that he should move on to something else. Paco told him, "Dad, you opened all these doors

for me and now you want to close them?" Evaristo Sr. told him
he would never do that. But whatever obstacles stood before him
seemed to fall away when Alfano told him of an opportunity that
had come up in Philadelphia.

On paper, it seemed like a good fight: Paco and Kennedy both
had had strong amateur pedigrees. In fact, Paco had beaten Kennedy as an amateur. "It was a crossroads bout for both of them,"
says Alfano, who served as the booking agent for Blue Horizon
promoter J Russell Peltz. The winner would be assured a Top 10
world ranking by the International Boxing Federation. While the
$6,500 he would earn for the Kennedy bout was above par for a
nontelevised bout, Paco could expect that his earning power would
increase if he beat Kennedy, who had emerged as a promising pro
on the Philadelphia scene. But even as Paco appeared to be on the
upswing professionally, he seemed to be struggling with something
profound.

Sonia could sense that he was unraveling. Two weeks before the
Blue Horizon bout, she found him in their bedroom with his hands
braced on the crib, gulping for air and unable to catch his breath.
She drove him to the emergency room at Illinois Masonic Medical
Center. On the way there, he had told her he was scared that he
was going to die. The doctors diagnosed it as a panic attack, so she
let it go at that. But a week later, he was once again in the grip of
what Sonia says he called "this weird feeling." He and Sónia were
taking Ginette to a well-baby checkup when Paco stopped in his
tracks, turned to her, and said: "Babe, I just have this feeling that I
am going to die before you." Sonia looked at him and said, "Why
would you say that?" The odd moment passed, yet he asked her
something that Sunday at church that surprised her, something
that he had never asked her before.

He turned to her and said: "Do you think the priest will bless
me?"

Sonia tossed in her sleep. It had been an anxious night, full of confusion. The bout had not gone well: Paco had been stopped by
Kennedy in the 10th round. But when Sonia did not hear from
him and he had not picked up his cell phone when she called, she
began to grow worried. To keep her calm, her brother-in-law Alex,
who had remained in Chicago, told her that Paco was at a hospital

having some cuts treated. The explanation gnawed at her: he still would have called. Sonia settled down Ginette and went to bed, only to be stirred awake at 3:00 A.M. that Saturday morning by the sound of the door bell ringing. Excitedly, she thought: Francisco! He took an early plane back! But when she looked through her doorway into the living room she saw Alex standing with her sister Celia. Both of them wore grave expressions.

Sonia got up.

Joining her was her mother-in-law, Maria.

"You know Paco is in the hospital," Alex began. "He has been badly injured. He hurt his head. We are not sure what is going on, but he is not doing very well."

All Sonia would remember is that she and Maria fell to the floor sobbing. In the fog that enveloped her, she thought back to the conversation she had with Paco the previous evening, before the bout. It was the last time they would speak. She was driving home from the job she then had at a bank. It was just small talk—how the baby was doing and so on—but they never got around to their prayer. They always said one before he stepped into the ring. But Paco knew she was behind the wheel and told her he would call her back if time permitted. When she did not hear from him, she looked at the clock—9:30 in Philadelphia, an hour earlier in Chicago—and began counting down the minutes. Quietly, she told herself as the evening progressed: Round 1 has to be over . . . Round 2 has to be over . . . To occupy herself, she played with Ginette and with her nephew. And she looked again at the clock.

For the 799 fans who showed up at the Blue Horizon that evening, it was a bout that proved to be just what Peltz had envisioned: "a terrific fight" not just on paper but in the ring. Paco was twice wobbled by Kennedy in the first round, but came back in the second throwing some big bombs of his own. The exchanges were fierce. Correctly, Peltz would say that by the end of Round 8, "the fight was up for grabs." But Kennedy won the ninth round decisively and the hard head and body shots he had connected with seemed to wear down Paco. Between the 9th and 10th rounds, the ring physician spoke with him and cleared him to continue. Twice in the 10th round Paco slipped to the canvas from exhaustion. When Francisco reeled into the ropes from a combination, referee Benjy Estevez waded in and stopped the bout at 1:52 of the round. And Paco labored back to his corner.

Scrambling up through the ropes to join him were Evaristo Sr., Tito, and cut man George Hernandez. Someone placed a stool under him and Paco sat down. As the ring physician, Jonathan Levyn, asked him some questions and peered into his eyes, Tito began cutting off the gloves. Evaristo Sr. looked on with apprehension. Paco had told him that his head hurt and that he was feeling sleepy. Evaristo said they would get him some aspirin later. When the ring physician stepped away, Tito asked someone to hand him an ice bag. Paco inhaled deep breaths as Tito sponged cold water on his back. Tito says that Paco became incoherent and he called for Levyn to come back. But Paco slipped into unconsciousness. EMS personnel strapped him to a stretcher and lowered him from the ring. As they passed through the crowd, Jason Barrett, a heavyweight who had appeared on the card, looked over at Paco and told local matchmaker Zac Pomilio: "Man, that guy looks dead."

Crazy with worry, Sonia boarded a 6:00 A.M. flight to Philadelphia. With her were Maria, Alex, her sister Lorena Ramirez, and her brother-in-law Noe Ramirez. Tito picked them up at the airport and drove them to Hahnemann, where Sonia would be stunned by what she saw. Paco had a breathing tube attached to him, and bandages encased his head. A craniotomy had been performed on him to alleviate the swelling inside his skull, but he was in "extremely critical" condition. Sonia would say later that she still held out hope, even as the doctors who spoke to her on Saturday evening attempted to prepare her for the inevitable. On Sunday morning, he began to show signs that he was beginning to become herniated. As the brain continued to swell, it pressed up against the hard shell of the skull. With nowhere to go, it collapsed and shut off blood to itself, which produced brain death. Examinations by two physicians six hours apart would officially confirm that: the first occurred at 1:45 P.M., the second at 7:42 P.M. It was at the latter that Paco was pronounced dead.

Sonia held the hand of the boy she always dreamed of that Sunday and wondered how she could ever let go of it. Vaguely, she became aware of visitors who stopped by the hospital, which included Kennedy and his father, Ernest. Tentatively, Kennedy stepped forward and offered his condolences. At the Third Annual Briscoe Awards in October, where his bout with Paco was honored as the "2009 Philly Fight of the Year," he would say impassively: "It could have been me." Ernest, a former boxer himself, knew only too well that it could have been. As he stood in the hospital and looked over at Sonia, he found himself reversing the characters in the tragedy before him. It was his son who was lying there. It was his family who stood at the bedside. He wondered: What would I do? What could I say? Gently, he told Sonia how sorry he was, but she was somewhere far away, thinking: Boxing is not even a sport. I hate it.

But there was still something to do that day, even if in her grief it seemed to Sonia to be so unreal. Given that Paco had been on a ventilator and had suffered a devastating neurological event, he was a candidate to become an organ donor. By 1998 law, hospitals in the United States are required to inform their area organ procurement organization of any person who is at or near death. According to president and CEO Howard Nathan, the Gift of Life Donor Program (GOL) receives 48,000 such calls each year. Of the 3,000 patients who are on a ventilator—which allows the organs to continue working until they can be recovered for transplant—only 439 last year ended up being donors. In the case of Paco, Hahnemann placed a referral call to GOL at 1:42 A.M. Saturday and updated them at 9:00 A.M. Sunday when his neurological status deteriorated. GOL transplant coordinator Janet Andrews came to the hospital and followed events as they unfolded. When Paco was pronounced dead, she introduced herself to the Rodriguez family, arranged at their request for a priest to come by, and at 10:30 P.M. invited Sonia and Alex to sit down with her in a conference room.

Someone had handed Sonia a program from the Blue Horizon card with Paco pictured on the cover. When she sat down, Sonia had flipped it across the table in disgust. Having collected preliminary information that Paco was a viable potential donor, Andrews asked Sonia and Alex if they had considered the possibility of organ or tissue donation. Sonia told her yes, but asked to have Evaristo Sr., Maria, and Tito step into the room. When Tito appeared uncertain, Sonia told him that it was something that she and Paco had talked over at one point and he had told her it was something he wanted to do. Maria said she had a cousin who was on the waiting list for a kidney and asked if he could be accommodated. Told by Andrews that he could, the family agreed.

Sonia signed the consent form at 11:30 P.M. And with the stroke of a pen, five lives were forever changed.

*

It was hard to know where to begin. Sonia remembered when they had first met. Tito was dating her sister and Paco had told him, "There has to be a Rosales girl for me." But when they dropped by to pick up Sonia from the job she then held at Target, Paco sat in the backseat of the car and would not say a word; they had just gotten back from an evening out bowling. Sonia would remember how shy Paco was, and how embarrassed he was when Tito looked over his shoulder and teased him. But when her sister later asked her if she would like to go dancing with him, she said yes and they would never again be apart.

Somehow it had become vital to Sonia in the year that has passed that the organ recipients know who Paco was, and how precious he had been to her. Increasingly, she began to wonder how they were faring, if the organs they had received had helped them regain their health. In her inconsolable grief, Sonia found it was healing to her to imagine that they had, that the piece of Paco that lived on in them would allow them to find some happiness. Given that anonymity is guarded and some recipients can be uneasy with contact with the donor family, Sonia was instructed to send a letter through GOL and told that it would be forwarded to any of the recipients who would welcome hearing from her. Sonia hoped that one day they would even be able to meet.

So one day she sat down and began writing, in part: "Dear Recipient: My name is Sonia Rodriguez, the proud wife of Francisco Rodriguez . . . Francisco was a very loving husband, father and friend and most importantly, of a truly humble and kind heart, which to me, made him extremely special . . . We shared five years together, the best five years of my life, as he made me the happiest woman in the world . . . We want you to know that you are always in our thoughts and prayers and sincerely hope that you are doing well. Hope to hear from you soon."

She then slipped a picture inside the envelope of Paco. And added: "By the way, he was very handsome."

Second of two parts: Blessed by Paco

Death was near. They told her that. Chances were it could be weeks —perhaps longer but not significantly unless she had a lung transplant. For years, Ashley Owens had known that she would not live to be 30 or even 25, that cystic fibrosis would sweep her away one day before she would have a chance to have a career or a wedding or children. It was a given she had come to accept. But now that she was coughing up blood and was in what her doctors called "the end stages," the sudden finality of her circumstances terrified her. All of it seemed to be happening too soon.

They told her that they would be moving her to the Hospital of the University of Pennsylvania. It was not something she wanted to do, if only because she had become accustomed to St. Christopher's Hospital for Children. She had been going there three or four times a year since she had been an eight-year-old and had befriended the nursing staff. But her doctors told her that there was a surgery that she would have to have, and that it was perhaps a good idea to become acquainted with the transplant team at Penn. Oddly, a feeling of calm settled over her at that point—what she would later describe as "a trance-like state." So she found a pen and some paper and began writing goodbye letters: to her parents, Bob and Charlotte; her young brother, Robert; and her boyfriend, Jesse, the young man who stood by her through her worst days.

With a shaggy beard and gentle bearing, Jesse Quinter swept her off her feet, both figuratively and literally. When she had been too weak to walk somewhere, Jesse lifted her then five-foot, 69-pound body up and carried her on his back. They had met each other in study hall at Owen J. Roberts High School in Pottstown. Ashley told him before their first date how sick she was, but he just shrugged and told her: "I like you for you." However worrisome her ordeal would become, Ashley would come to depend on Jesse to cheer her up. When she tearfully told him on the phone that day that she would be leaving for Penn, he left early from his job at the Warwick Child Care Center in Lionville and hurried to her side.

They talked. But she was upset and no words could seem to soothe her. Even when Jesse reassured her that she would be fine, she was in a forlorn place that seemed beyond even his reach. It was then that an idea popped into his head. He excused himself and said he had to get something from his car. When he came back, he sat down in a chair by her bed and resumed their conversation, which he always tried to keep light. Instead of dwelling on the sobering prognosis that faced her, Jesse would ask what she wanted to do when she got out of the hospital, where she would go to dinner and what trips she would like to take. It went on like that until he paused.

"I have to talk to you about something," he said.

Casually, Ashley replied: "About what?"

Jesse got down on one knee and displayed a diamond ring.

And with eyes wide, Ashley cried, "Oh, my God!"

On the very evening this scene was unfolding last year—Friday, November 20—Francisco "Paco" Rodriguez was preparing to step into a boxing ring at the Blue Horizon, where he had a scheduled 12-round bout with Teon Kennedy for the vacant United States Boxing Association super bantamweight title. Paco was stopped by Kennedy in the 10th round, passed out in his corner, and died of a head injury two days later at Hahnemann University Hospital. But it was there that one story ended and another began, the tale of how with a stroke of a pen on a consent form, a grieving widow bestowed life upon five people by offering seven organs from the body of her beloved husband for transplant donation. What began in a place of unutterable grief ended up in a realm of hope reborn.

Eighteen people die each day in the United States waiting for a transplant. In the case of the five people who received organs from Paco, each of their histories is tied together by a common thread: they had endured untold suffering in the grip of their various illnesses. Only days away from death in some cases, they looked upon themselves as fighters in the same very real sense that Paco had been. With the exception of his uncle, Ramon Tejeda, who received a kidney in a "directed donation," none of them had ever heard of the young boxer from Chicago. Given what they have received from him—a heart, a liver, two lungs, two kidneys, and a pancreas—none of them will ever forget him. While the recipients have not yet met, they share a bond that now unites them with someone they have come to cherish: Paco.

The five are:

• *Ashley Owens, 23, of Spring City, Chester County: Both Lungs*

As a 10-month-old baby, she weighed less than seven pounds. Initially, doctors suspected she had a tumor. But tests revealed that she had cystic fibrosis, which compromised her breathing and to some extent her digestion. Simple childhood pleasures such as running and swimming were beyond her ability. In and out of the hospital during her school years, she became an excellent student with the help of a tutor. Physically, she began "going downhill" at age 20 or so, a period during which her lung capacity dropped to as low as 20 percent. Without the help of oxygen her lips would turn blue. Concerned by the statistics that foretold an uncertain outcome for lung-transplant recipients, she held off going onto the waiting list until just hours before she suffered a collapsed lung on November 13, 2009. Of the pain her daughter endured, Charlotte Owens says, "Some days she would push through it. Other days it would be more than she could bear."

Ashley says: "Until the last two or three years, I had an okay handle on it. But when I was 20, I had stopped responding to the medication I was taking. My body had become so full of it that I had become immune. They told me I had two years to live. When I was 21, they told me I had one year to live. I was scared."

• *Meghan Kingsley, 26, of Gaithersburg, Maryland: Liver*

At 16, she was diagnosed with neurofibromatosis type 2, characterized by the growth of noncancerous tumors along the nerve that transmits information from the inner ear to the brain. An exceptional competitive swimmer who had dreamed one day of going to the Olympic Games, she underwent surgery in June 2001 for the removal of a tumor and was left deaf in one ear. In October 2007, she had decompression surgery on another tumor that doctors chose not to remove. In an effort to preserve what remained of her hearing, they instead carved away some bone that would allow the tumor room to grow. However, she began experiencing significant hearing loss and in September 2009 enrolled in a study for the experimental drug PCT299. By November, she was in the throes of liver failure.

Meghan says: "I became very, very ill and ended up in Johns Hopkins. I remember I was constantly burping; I had so much fluid in my stomach. I became jaundiced. [The whites of] my eyes were green and yellow. Mom said I looked like 'The Grinch.' I no longer had any bodily function. They later told me I was within 48 hours of dying."

• *Alexis Sloan, 27, of Norristown: Heart*

At 22, she was diagnosed with congestive heart failure, prior to which she had experienced symptoms that included a dry cough, fatigue, and shortness of breath. "A lot of big words were thrown at me," she says. "Scary." Within a year of her diagnosis, she received a biventricular pacemaker and defibrillator implant. Efforts to manage her condition with medication failed and in March 2007 she says she "coded," which is hospital slang for going into cardiopulmonary arrest. Doctors then equipped her with a left ventricular assist device (LVAD), which she found to be an unwieldy contraption. Battery-operated, it had internal and external components that left her feeling on some days as if she was a robot. To get on the waiting list for a heart, she had to fulfill a standard set of requirements that proved that she would submit to postoperative care. In May 2008, she had done that and was given a pager, with which she would be contacted when a heart was available.

Alexis says: "When they gave me the initial diagnosis, it was devastating. It seemed like a death sentence. There was a lot of confusion. When I got the LVAD, I was not happy with it. No young person should have to live that way. With the protocols I had to go through, it seemed like it was taking forever to get on the list. I became depressed and at one point even suicidal. I just thought: 'I am going to die anyway . . .'"

• *Vicky Davis, 58, of Clifford Township, Susquehanna County: Pancreas, Kidney*

At 37, she was diagnosed with diabetes, which through the years became progressively worse. In December 2005, she was told that her kidneys were failing. She went on dialysis in April 2006 and within a year was placed on the waiting list for a new kidney and pancreas. Initially, she says, she was told the wait would be just a few months. But whenever she received a call that there was a potential donor for her—and she says she received nine of them—the kidney and pancreas would end up going to someone else or there would be some other issue that would come up. For three and a half years, she spent three days a week on dialysis, a process by which the blood is cleansed of toxins.

Vicky says: "Going to dialysis was like having a job. I would have to be there by 5:30 A.M. and I would not get back until 10:00 A.M. And it was so draining. People would ask me, 'Do you work?' And I would say, 'No, I am on dialysis.' It takes a lot out of you."

• *Ramon Tejeda, 58, of Chicago: Kidney*

At 40, Tejeda had his left kidney removed because of kidney

stones. In December 2003, his right kidney began to fail. It was full of cysts and functioning at only 10 percent. He began dialysis and was placed on the waiting list for a kidney. Increasingly, the three-day-a-week, four-hour-a-day dialysis treatments began to wear on him. Depression set in. Though he says they were keeping him alive, they were not eradicating the underlying problem he had. Unable to continue in his factory job, he went on disability. On dialysis for six years, he had inched to the top of the waiting list when he received word last November that Paco had died and that his kidney was being offered to him in a "directed donation." Paco was the son of his cousin, Maria.

Ramon says: "I was not doing too well. I had been on dialysis for so long. When I heard what happened to Paco, I was so very sad, very depressed. I remember him as a boy. Knowing that the kidney would come from him was hard, but it was something I knew that Paco would have wanted me to accept."

Ramon pauses and says, "He was giving me a gift."

Jesse had told Ashley that evening when he proposed: "We have been through a lot of stuff, and we will have more stuff to go through. This is not the end. But whatever happens between now and whenever, I just want you to know that I will be here for you. Whatever happens, you can count on me."

And with that he slipped the ring on her finger, which had become so bony from her weight loss that it had to be reinforced with tape to keep it from slipping off. Ashley gazed at it as her eyes pooled with tears.

Immediately, the hopelessness that had engulfed her seemed to lift. From the hallway, the nurses came into the room to admire it, one after another. Suddenly, she says she found "the courage" to go over to HUP, where she was transported later that evening. There, she and Jesse had an impromptu engagement party. He ordered in pizza and wings. What they were unaware of as they sat there eating was that Paco was slugging it out with Kennedy at the Blue Horizon, the outcome of which he had hoped would propel his boxing career into a place where he could command larger purses and better support his wife, Sonia, and their baby daughter, Ginette. Uncertain of when she would get the transplant she so desperately needed, Ashley said good night to Jesse and went to sleep.

Whatever else the process of organ recovery and the ensuing transplant surgeries is, it is a synchronization of many moving parts. In the case of Paco, it began when he was declared brain dead on Sunday, November 22, at 7:42 P.M., at which point Janet Andrews, the transplant coordinator for the Gift of Life Donor Program, introduced herself to the Rodriguez family, offered her condolences, and arranged for a priest to come by at their request. At 10:30, Andrews sat down with them and offered them the option of organ and/or tissue donation. Sonia signed the consent form an hour later. Only when that occurred could Andrews move forward. She alerted the Illinois Organ Procurement Organization of the availability of a kidney for Ramon and arranged for Paco to undergo a series of tests to evaluate his suitability to be a donor, including an echocardiogram to test his heart. Until his organs were recovered, he would remain on a ventilator with his heart beating.

On Monday at 9:00 A.M., GOL began the organ allocation procedure: multiple potential recipients are identified and the organs are offered to the transplant surgeons, who assess them and reply via mobile device if they are interested or not. If they are, GOL contacts them by telephone and advises them of where they are on the list. By 1:00 P.M., the allocation procedure had been completed, the operating room space had been reserved, and the recipients had been contacted. Upbeat, Ashley says she prepared as if she was going to get better by taking a shower and braiding her hair. Told by her surgeons that they had found "a great liver," Meghan sat up in her hospital bed and said, "Let's go for it." Alexis was contacted not by her pager but by cell phone and told, "Come and get it. It's yours." At her dialysis appointment, Vicky was informed in a call and replied: "Are you sure?" Ramon could not help but think of Paco and how hard it had to be for Maria to lose a son.

That Monday at 6:30 P.M., four recovery teams entered the operating room at Hahnemann, where Paco was prepped and draped. Each organ has to be implanted within a certain span of time once it has been recovered. Says Howard Nathan, the president and CEO of GOL: "You have 3 hours for the heart, 6 for the lungs, 6 to 12 for the liver, 12 for the pancreas, and up to 48 for the kidney." In the course of the three-and-a-half-hour surgery, the heart and other organs were cooled by separate cold profusion lines and were removed one by one. At 9:07, the heart was recovered, triple bagged, and transported to the adjoining operating room for Alexis. At 9:15, both lungs were recovered and rushed to HUP for Ashley. At 9:50 P.M., the liver was recovered and flown by helicopter to Johns Hopkins Hospital in Baltimore for Meghan. And at 10:00 P.M., both kidneys and the pancreas were recovered. A kidney and the pancreas were hurried to Geisinger Medical Center in Danville, Pennsylvania, for Vicky, and the other kidney was flown the following morning to the Rush University Medical Center in Chicago for Ramon.

Given that Paco had been a highly trained athlete, his organs were exceptional. In fact, Charlotte Owens said that the surgeon told her that he had never worked with better lungs, which Ashley discovered worked wonderfully. Suddenly, she discovered that she could breathe deeply, and that she had stopped coughing. Within weeks of their operation, the other recipients reported excellent progress. Alexis says she could hear "the profusion of blood" running through her, "that ocean sound," and that each of her senses became amplified. "I could think better," she says. "I was even answering questions off of *Jeopardy!*" While Meghan has been hospitalized seven times since her transplant for periods ranging from four to 23 days and still has "dozens of tumors" in her body from her neurofibromatosis, she says she is "no longer dying but living." And Vicky and Ramon both say they have regained strength.

But curiosity set in. With the exception of Ramon, none of the others knew who the donor was. Confidentiality guidelines are such that the identities of the donor and the recipients are guarded and cannot be set aside unless either party agrees to share information. Consequently, there was always only speculation on the part of the recipients on the identity of the donor. While she was in her initial recovery, Meghan says that some friends tried to piece it together: the liver had come from Philadelphia from a 25-year-old male. When the friend told Meghan that a boxer of that age had just died in Philadelphia, she remembers thinking: "How bizarre! In this moment, I could not be fighting more."

Meghan says, "I just knew it was him. I could feel his presence."

Outside, a November rain was slanting from the gray sky in heavy sheets. But inside the third-grade classroom at Limerick Elementary School, it was dry and warm and filled with the enthusiasm of children, who were seated on the floor at the front of the room with their student-teacher, Ms. Owens. In preparation for a book the class would be beginning soon, *The One in the Middle Is the Green Kangaroo* by Judy Blume, Ashley asked them to predict what certain items she placed before them would have to do with the story: a jar of peanut butter; a doll with a broken leg; a kangaroo; and a green marker. Working individually and then in groups, Ashley recorded some of the suggestions on an easel.

She stepped back to look at them and said, "These are all good predictions, but guess what? None of them are right."

The children moaned: "Awwwwww!"

"So," she continued, "we are going to have to find out what happened compared to the predictions. Okay? It should be a lot of fun."

Scarcely taller than some of her students, Ashley had always hoped to become a teacher, specifically third to sixth grade. She enjoys the enthusiasm that the children bring with them to class each day. When she graduates this month from West Chester University, she plans to start looking for a teaching job in Pennsylvania or New Jersey, somewhere she and Jesse can settle down. Doctors have advised her not to teach children any younger than third grade because it would place her at an elevated risk for infections. Such warnings are heeded by her but not just because of her own health. She says she has a responsibility not just to herself but to "the gift" that she has received. To show her appreciation to Sonia, she has crocheted a pink blanket for Ginette.

It is something the others also say, that they feel a connection to Paco and his family. With the aid of Lara Moretti, the family services supervisor for GOL, Sonia reached out to the recipients in a letter to let them know who her husband was, how deeply she loved him, and how she hoped that they were doing well. Says Moretti, who vets each correspondence: "Typically, families look upon the donation as a small bit of good that can come out of something terrible." One by one, the recipients replied—again, through Moretti. They told of their ordeals and of how grateful they were, how the organ they received allowed them to become fully alive and be with their loved ones. In a way that she had not anticipated, Sonia found the letters she received to be helpful to her as she had moved through the stages of grief. Sonia says she hopes that she can remain in contact with them.

"The 25 years that Francisco lived were awesome," says Sonia, as a photograph of her husband looks down at her from the dining room of his boyhood home in Chicago. "He was healthy and enjoyed life to the fullest—and now [the recipients], who have suffered for so long, have that opportunity. I want to be sure they are okay and taking care of themselves, not just because they are carrying a piece of Francisco with them but because life is supposed to be lived. I pray for them every day."

Along with what Sonia has told them, the recipients have found out more information about Paco online, where there are portions of a few of his bouts. Alexis says that she became "obsessed" with learning more about him. Given that she is a big boxing fan, she says she is surprised she had not been at the Blue Horizon for his bout with Kennedy. It was an event she would have attended, and can only think that she stayed at home that evening because of her health. But she has looked into who Paco was and says "he was no slouch," not just a fine amateur and pro boxer but a good family man, "known for joking around and laughing." Says Alexis: "I was happy to learn that he had that kind of spirit."

The bond to Paco that they feel is a deep one. In the hard days that followed her surgery, during which she experienced periods of dementia, and in her subsequent hospital stays over the course of the last year, Meghan would find herself saying, "Come on, Paco! We can do it. Work with me on this." Once, she looked down at her hands, which for a period were covered with gloves. She said to herself: "Look! I am a fighter, just like Paco!" When she had a setback in March, she rubbed the scar at the site of her incision and promised Paco: "You know, if you get me out of this, we'll go see your wife and your little girl." Meghan says she hopes to do that at some point, if only just to thank Sonia and the Rodriguez family in person.

"I feel I am not just doing it for myself now, but I am doing it for him and his family," says Meghan, who is a graduate of Elon University in North Carolina. "I want to know how Sonia is doing. I want to know how Ginette is doing. I want to go there and visit, and see the gym where Paco boxed. Me, being an athlete, I understand the dreams he had. I had wanted to be a champion. So I want to be a part of that. I would like to think of them as my extended family."

Vicky has a photo of Paco taped to her refrigerator. "When Sonia wrote me, I read her letter three times," she says. "He was so young.

And she is young. But you could see there was this strong bond between them. I hope that we can become close. I would like that. Like the daughter I never had."

Vicky pauses and adds, "Somehow just saying thank you is not enough."

There will be a wedding. Bob Owens did not think he would ever have the chance to do it, but he will walk Ashley down the aisle and give her to Jesse. While there are still plans to be arranged, Ashley says she would like to have her wedding outdoors at the Valley Forge National Park and then honeymoon in Greece. Jesse says he would prefer to go to the United Kingdom, but says that Greece is fine, that he keeps telling her: "You set it up. Go where you want to go and I will follow. I want you to enjoy yourself."

Given that it is very likely she would have died were it not for the transplant, Ashley looks upon each day as precious, even if there are some worries as she moves forward. While her doctors have told her there is no physical reason she cannot have children, she is aware that the life expectancy statistics for lung-transplant patients are somewhat less encouraging than they are for the other organ recipients. "They say only 50 percent survive five years and 20 percent survive 10 years," says Ashley, who adds that she has also been told the absences of setbacks in the initial year are a positive indicator. But what also has her concerned is how she is going to continue to pay for the care she has to have, which includes 25 prescription drugs each day. While she and the other recipients have been covered by health plans, it has offset only a portion of the costs that they have incurred.

But Ashley does not dwell on any of this. Instead, she thinks of Paco and Sonia and Ginette; she thinks of her parents, Bob and Charlotte, and her brother, Robert; and she thinks of Jesse, who held her hand before she was wheeled into surgery and held it again when she came out. She thinks of what she can now do that she could never do before: get on a bike and go wherever she pleases; dive in a pool and hold her breath underwater; and slip on a pair of running shoes and just take off. It was something she did last March when she and her family were at Longwood Gardens. Seeing a big field stretched out before her, she challenged her brother to a race and shouted, "Daddy, take a picture!" And off she ran, the sun on her back, the wind rushing over her face.

CHRIS BALLARD

The Courage of Jill Costello

FROM SPORTS ILLUSTRATED

NEXT SPRING the NCAA women's crew season will begin again. On lakes and rivers across the country, fleets of skinny boats will skitter over the water like giant insects, their wooden legs moving in unison. Happen upon a race, and your eyes will be drawn to the powerful women in the bow of each boat, the ones with backs like oak doors who tear great gashes in the water, pushing and pulling and exhaling clouds of carbon dioxide until their chests are aflame and their temples thump. For a moment, though, it's worth shifting your gaze to the stern, to the wispy figure of the coxswain. She'll be the only woman facing forward, the only one without an oar. Indeed, she'll barely even move, instead just sitting there . . . talking. If you are unfamiliar with the sport, you might wonder about this small woman's purpose, wonder if she can even be considered an athlete. After all, how can you be an athlete when all you do is talk? What difference can a woman like that make, anyway?

You'd be amazed.

It started as a dull ache in Jill Costello's abdomen, the kind you get after a night of suspect Chinese food. Only it didn't go away. It was June 2009, and the Cal crew had just returned from the NCAA championships in Cherry Hill, New Jersey. The Bears had finished second, behind Stanford, continuing a remarkable run of six top-four finishes in seven years.

Jill came back to Berkeley elated. She had coxed the third boat at nationals, which meant she had a good shot at being in the top varsity boat as a senior. As for the nagging pain in her bloated stomach, she assumed it was stress-related — the product of late nights cramming for finals and early mornings practicing on the water. So when her good friend and teammate Adrienne Keller headed to the trainer to receive treatment for a balky back a few days after nationals, Jill decided to tag along; maybe she could pick up some pills before heading out for the summer.

When the two women walked into the training room, the tall, broad-shouldered Keller dwarfed Jill, who was small and thin, with porcelain cheeks, a cascade of brown hair, and an ever-present grin. Looking at the pair, you'd never have guessed they were teammates.

Understand, Jill never set out to be a coxswain. Nobody does. Growing up in San Francisco, she'd competed in the same sports as her friends: soccer, field hockey, cross-country. She had enough talent as a dancer to perform with the San Francisco Ballet as a nine-year-old, but she quit when told she'd need to devote herself to it full-time. She loved being part of a team too much for that.

There was only one problem. While her two older brothers kept growing, each eventually surpassing six feet, Jill stayed small. And no matter how hard she tried, it was tough to be a soccer goalie when she was the shortest kid on the field. By the time she was a senior at St. Ignatius College Prep, Jill had topped out at five-four and 110 pounds and was focusing her college aspirations on crew, the only sport in which her size was an asset.

The fit was more than physical. The coxswain's role is twofold. She's expected to steer the boat, factoring in the wind, tides, and at times the uneven stroking of her crew. (All coxes fear the moment when a rower "catches a crab" — that is, snags an oar in the water on the return stroke, jolts the boat, and even, in extreme cases, ejects herself.) The coxswain also acts as a surrogate coach, relaying information, determining strategy, and providing motivation.

This Jill could do. She'd always liked being in charge. One of her first phrases as a toddler was, *Me do.* Not long after, she began bossing around her older brothers. The way Jill saw it, life was too short to wait for things to come to you. While most of her teammates at Cal had a tough enough time juggling crew and school, Jill worked with Habitat for Humanity, was in a sorority, and was vice president of the Panhellenic Council, which governs campuswide Greek life.

At times her mother, Mary, found Jill's intensity exhausting. Even when shopping for clothes, Jill wouldn't buy a pair of pants unless they were perfect.

Such traits might have been grating in someone else, but pretty much everyone liked Jill. How could you not? If you looked sad, she'd puff out her cheeks, pull out her tiny ears, and make monkey faces until you laughed. If you were the new kid, she was the first to come up and start a conversation. When her roommate and best friend at Cal, K. C. Oakley, left school for a semester to go to Colorado, Jill texted her every day to say good morning and good night. It was Jill who nicknamed Cal crew head coach Dave O'Neill "the Coif" for his gravity-defying puff of blond hair and did a perfect imitation of the "jiggle-jaw" face he made when exasperated. (From anyone else O'Neill might have chafed at the jokes, but his bond with Jill was so strong that he asked her to be the godmother of his son, Dash.)

A goofball? Sure, but a dedicated one. As a sophomore Jill went to the DMV and took the test for a Class B license so she could drive the team van, and then she rose at 5:30 A.M. six days a week to pick up rowers for practice. And while most coxes avoid workouts — after all, their only physical requirement is to make weight (110 pounds for women) — Jill joined the team for cardio sessions and training runs. "She's as good an athlete as I've ever had as a coxswain," says O'Neill.

That's why no one thought twice about her stomach pain, including Jill. It came as a shock, then, when Linda "Smitty" Smith, the team trainer, told her that Friday after nationals, "Got some bad news, Jill. Turns out your lab tests are out of whack. Your white blood cell count is pretty high. You need to get to an ER, and you need to do it tonight. It's probably nothing serious, but better safe than sorry."

Jill called her mother and her aunt Kathy Morello, both nurses, and they drove her to the emergency room at California Pacific Medical Center in San Francisco. There Jill received a blur of diagnoses, each more frightening than the next: first she was told she had a serious infection, then grapefruit-sized cysts on her ovaries, and, a few hours later and most ominously, masses in her lung, liver, clavicle, and one breast. Radiologists came from across the hospital to peer at the results, disbelieving: a perfectly healthy 21-year-old nonsmoker with no family history of the disease had lung cancer, which three days later would be diagnosed as stage IV, the most advanced form. In just a few days Jill had gone from being a carefree college student to being told she probably had nine months to live.

There is no such thing as a good cancer, but lung cancer is just about the worst. The survival rate is 15.5 percent, and making matters worse, the disease comes with a stigma. Patients with lung cancer are assumed to have earned it, having inhaled toxins for years. Yet 20 percent of women diagnosed with lung cancer each year—about 21,000 in 2010, roughly the same number as new cases of ovarian cancer—never smoked. Because of lung cancer's reputation as a self-induced illness and its low survival rate, it rarely attracts big research money. In the last 40 years the survival rate hasn't budged.

Theoretically, at least, Jill stood as good a chance as anyone else of surviving. She was young and fit, so she could endure treatments that most other patients—whose average age is 71—couldn't. The chemo began within the week. Jill was told, as she wrote in her online journal, *to use only baby shampoo and soft toothbrushes, to get those protein shakes down and that weight up, to try on this wig and that hat, and to stock up on a list of drugs so long you'd think I was a dealer.* Her summer plans went from hiking in Tahoe to being spoon-fed blueberries in bed by Aunt Kathy.

When she asked her doctors about rejoining the team, they looked at her as if she were crazy. Crew? She'd need all her strength just to make it through each day. Jill didn't care. She told her mom she saw cancer as "just another thing on my plate." Besides, she'd had three goals for the better part of her adult life: to graduate from Cal, to cox the first boat, and to win nationals. She saw no reason to change them.

Rowing appeals to certain personality types. Converted swimmers do well at it, for example, because they are accustomed to monotonous practices. As O'Neill says, "It's a fitness sport, not a skill sport," which is another way of saying it's about desire. Consider: Cal has one of the best programs in the country, but its team includes both Olympians and women who are just discovering crew —as if the 12th man on the Duke basketball team were learning the game a month before the season.

The rewards are few. Crew has no professional league, no en-

dorsement contracts, little glory even at big events. Rare is the
sports fan who can name even one Olympic rower. What's more,
crew is rooted in suffering. As David Halberstam wrote in *The Amateurs,* his excellent book about 1984 Olympic hopefuls, "It was part
of the oarsman's unwritten code that one did not mention the
pain. That was considered unseemly and, worse, it might magnify
the pain and make it more threatening and more tangible. It was
as if by not talking about it, the pain might become less important."

Few sports, then, rely so much on inner fortitude. It is the coxswain's job to intrude upon each rower's silent battle, to find a way
to get the most out of eight disparate personalities. O'Neill, a former rower at Boston College, understands the difficulty of this task.
A thin, energetic 41-year-old whose staccato laugh masks the seri-
ousness with which he approaches his job, O'Neill likes to say that
"there is no defense in rowing." So while bitter rival Stanford has
sent assistant coaches to scout Cal—marking the team's splits and
the timing of its "moves" (power strokes)—O'Neill never changes
strategy from race to race. He likens his approach to that of a golfer
who plays the course, not the opposition. (O'Neill even refers to
rival crews not by their school names but by their colors: Stanford
is Red. Virginia is Orange.)

When it all comes together and eight oars are in sync, a crew can
reach a Zenlike moment referred to as *swing,* when the boat seems
to lift out of the water. This, more than anything, is the goal of rowing, when the whole is truly greater than the sum of its parts.
O'Neill's job is to put together boats that can achieve this chemistry, and it is a constant juggling act. At major competitions such as
nationals, points are awarded to each boat in three 2,000-meter
races: the varsity eight (the boat with the eight strongest oars and
the top coxswain), the second eight, and, finally, the four, a smaller
craft with only four rowers in which the cox must lie supine in the
bow. This means that from his pool of almost 50 rowers O'Neill can
choose only 20 to compete, and from his eight coxswains, only
three.

More so than most crew coaches, O'Neill recruits coxes. If a
prospect is shy, she doesn't stand a chance. He wants a firm handshake and a ready opinion. He wants leaders who are prepared to
sacrifice for the team, and he's a staunch believer that there is no

place in crew for prima donnas. When recruits ask him what it's like to be on the Cal team, O'Neill is fond of saying, "In one word: *hard*. In two words: *really hard.*"

This is his way of weeding out the women who aren't sure about the sport or who want to gain admission to Cal through crew and then, a year later, quit the team. When he gave Jill his one-word, two-words speech, she didn't blink.

"Cool," she said. "That's the kind of team I want to be on."

There are plenty of clichés about team sports, about the mystical nature of bonding and camaraderie. Sometimes they're even true. When Jill learned of her diagnosis, most of her teammates had already gone home for the summer. For many that meant Los Angeles; for others, such as Iva Obradovic, an Olympic-level rower, it meant Serbia. Still, within weeks, under the guidance of O'Neill, the team had filmed and sent her two videos. One was a collage of testimonials, the other an inspired mélange of karaoke and air guitar to the tune of Andrew W.K.'s feel-good song "Got to Do It." As W.K. sang, "When you're down on your luck, you gotta do it," rowers strummed their oars and assistant coaches played the drums on steering wheels. Watching from her hospital bed, IV lines protruding from her arms, Jill was overcome by emotion.

The support was only beginning. When Jill went home from the hospital, she felt as if the team had gone with her. During that summer and fall the Costellos' modest two-story house in southwest San Francisco often looked like a commune. Twenty, 30 kids—Cal rowers, Kappa Kappa Gamma sorority sisters, classmates from St. Ignatius, friends from the Bears' rugby team—camped out there. The Costellos would return from chemo appointments to find piles of food on their doorstep, full meals of salad and pasta and chicken. Letters and emails poured in from rowers at Princeton, Stanford, and Yale. Rivalries evaporated on the spot. The Stanford coach contacted Jill and said, "Whatever you need, just let me know." Her response: help her get in touch with this one oncologist at Stanford. Within a week the president of the university had assigned his assistant to Jill. Give her whatever access she needs, he said.

On June 14 Jill began a blog just so she could keep everyone up to date. In unflinching detail she described her treatment: the ra-

diation and the body molds and the chemo. *Well, it's Day 11,* one
entry read, *and despite the warnings to prepare for extreme nausea, vomit-
ing, low platelet count, depression, poor appetite, constipation, mouth sores,
and numbness/tingling, I've just been dealing with some aches and fatigue.
I guess this cancer wasn't aware that I'm used to doing six-minute elbow
bridges, have sat in the bow of a boat in eight inches of freezing water for an
entire two-hour practice, have climbed Half Dome three times in under 3½
hours, and can hold my own as 60 girls attack a feast of Kappa study
snacks during finals.*

While some patients might be embarrassed by the invasive treatments, Jill, ever the competitor, considered it a source of pride to
weather each new round. That's why she had her mom and aunt
keep track of every pinprick and every IV, the numbers scratched
into a notebook. Then, when those became too numerous, she settled for a record of every treatment. When the alumni magazine at
St. Ignatius wrote up her story and sent her an advance copy, she
read it with pride, then immediately emailed the writer. Thanks for
the story, she wrote, but you got the number of treatments wrong.
It's 14, not 9.

Just as she had directed her boat, Jill now drove her treatment.
She spent hours researching drugs. She emailed two top oncolo-
gists at UC San Francisco so often and struck up such a relationship with them that she began her messages, "Hi, boys!" With
Heather Wakelee, the Stanford oncologist, she exchanged texts
and took particular glee in pointing out whenever a Cardinal team
lost.

As all-encompassing as her treatments were, though, Jill couldn't
get rowing out of her mind. When school started again in the fall
her teammates began informal 6:00 A.M. workouts. While the rest
of Berkeley sipped Peet's coffee and blinked its way through the
fog, 50 young women in spandex met in the ergonomic room,
a cold, bare space under the track stadium. As techno music
thumped, the girls warmed up and, on O'Neill's cue, all began to
row as one, like one giant organism with ponytails. Jill used to love
those moments, walking from machine to machine, offering encouragement, checking erg scores, and then, when the workout
was done, drawing laughs by mimicking her friends, the tiny girl
on the big rowing machine. Now, staring out at the Pacific during

short walks on the beach with her mom, Jill thought about being on the water again. O'Neill had told her he'd save a spot on the team for her. What he didn't expect was that she'd take him up on it.

The winter brought encouraging news: the mass in her liver had shrunk, as had the tumor in her left lung. Still, the unrelenting treatments were taking a toll. Jill was back living on campus and taking two classes, but she spent a lot of time napping and used a scooter to get from class to class. *The only way I can describe the fatigue,* she wrote, *is like waking up the morning after running a marathon, but not having trained for the marathon, so your whole body is sore, weak, and achy.* Most of all, she hated not being able to schedule her life.

She had delighted in organizing her world, color-coding and endlessly updating the calendar on her iPhone, but now she was at the mercy of her body. She'd been the kind of girl who told her boyfriend at Cal, Bryce Atkinson, a tall and handsome former rower, to start planning a Saturday-night date a week ahead of time. Funny story, how they met. She'd chased Atkinson down when she was a sophomore, back when he was intent on not having a girlfriend. "Here's my number," she said one night, smiling and holding out a piece of paper. "You better use it." He was smart enough to comply. The two bonded over rowing, spent weekends in Tahoe, nights eating sushi. By junior year he was at every one of her meets, roaring from the shore.

Now, knowing it sounded nuts, Jill was telling Atkinson and her former roommate, Oakley, that she wanted to rejoin the crew team. She needed the connection. She'd kept in touch with her teammates during what they called "family dinners," at which a core of seniors and juniors would meet at someone's house each week. At one she brought the body mold she'd used during radiation treatments to use as a piñata. The rowers all took turns swinging at it, as if trying to smash the cancer right out of Jill.

In February she talked to O'Neill about returning. There would be plenty of obstacles. She'd be weak and susceptible to the tiniest illnesses—a common cold, for instance, could lead to pneumonia. And first, of course, she needed to convince her doctors and family that she could handle the rigors of competition.

Jill's biggest concern, however, was whether it would be unfair for her to return if she couldn't attend all the practices. "Look," said O'Neill, "you're the only coxswain we've got who's competed at NCAAs. You're the most experienced. If Iva got hurt and she couldn't practice until a week before Pac-10s, would she compete?" Jill nodded. O'Neill paused, then said, "Well, you're the Iva of coxswains."

Her first practice back was a Saturday morning in early March at Briones Reservoir, 15 minutes from the Cal campus. The team began with a two-mile jog, from the boathouse to the reservoir entrance and back. Jill sat in the boathouse clutching a cup of tea and watched as, one mile out, her teammates began changing color. All 50 of them tore off their sweatshirts to reveal yellow T-shirts that read CAL CREW CANCER KILLERS. All doubts she had about her decision vanished in the cool morning air.

After Jill's first practice the girls in her boat went up to O'Neill. Jill, they told him, had been awesome. Not because she was courageous or because she had made it through practice. Rather, because she was now a better coxswain. And as the weeks went on, O'Neill realized the rowers were right. He likes to say that there are three types of coxswain: the motivator, always rah-rah; the drill sergeant, ever demanding peak performance; and the airline pilot, cool and collected. Her first three years, Jill was more of a motivator, but now she had become an airline pilot. Maybe it was the cancer, maybe it was maturity, maybe it was a combination of the two. No matter what happened — a missed stroke, a slow start — Jill did not change her tenor. It would all be okay, she seemed to say.

Then there'd been the matter of her timing. For someone whose job was to call out the stroke rate — some schools' coxes say, *Stroke! Stroke! Stroke!* but Cal used a call of *Cha! Sha!* — Jill had terrible rhythm. She was always losing the flow of it, like a wallflower at a party hopelessly trying to snap along to a song. So at O'Neill's urging, she just stopped doing it. Watching the team in erg sessions, he'd noticed that the girls could maintain a rhythm without prompting.

O'Neill's other concern had been that Jill's illness might prove a distraction. That was clearly not going to be an issue. Not only did she refuse to use cancer as a crutch, but she didn't even talk about it. Before the first weekend of racing, in early April, Jill endured a round of chemo at Stanford on Friday, then called O'Neill — not to opt out of practice that afternoon but to say she'd be 20 minutes late because her treatment went long. The same day another rower called O'Neill to say she needed to skip practice: she had a fever of 99.1 degrees.

Smitty, the trainer, kept a close watch on Jill, expecting to be called upon often. She never was. "Honestly, Jill did not require anything of us," Smitty says. "She took care of the rest of us. She let us know if treatment was going to interfere with something we were going to do. She didn't want to focus on the illness or on her. Her attitude was, I am a member of this team and nothing more. She wanted to be like every other kid." In a way, Jill was finally like her teammates. *By not talking about it, the pain might become less important.*

By March, Jill had survived 14 rounds of chemo. The side effects included fatigue, night sweats, skin sensitivity, puffy cheeks, liquid retention, and swollen ankles and feet. Still, her attitude remained upbeat. *I'm going to keep on believing, JILL IS HEALTHY! until the doctors tell me I'm absolutely right,* she wrote.

The news relayed by the doctors got progressively worse, though. Scans in March showed that the masses in her left lung and her liver had grown, and a new mass had appeared in her right lung. Hoping for a miracle, Jill had applied in December to be one of about 40 people chosen to go with the Knights of Malta, a charitable group affiliated with the Catholic Church, to Lourdes, France, where the water at the Grotto of Massabielle is said to have healing powers. She was accepted and, with her mother and aunt, prepared to travel there for a week at the end of April and beginning of May. There was only one downside: she'd miss the season-ending Stanford meet.

So while Cal prepared to race its hated rival, half a world away Jill followed the team on Twitter and Facebook. When she saw a photo of the Cal uniforms for the race, she gasped. O'Neill had ordered special unitards in turquoise—Jill's favorite color—and navy rather than the familiar yellow and blue. Where there is usually a Cal bear, an emblem the girls like to focus on while rowing, there was now a silhouette of Jill, modeled after a photo of her taken the previous spring at nationals, holding high the team trophy. And where it usually read CAL in cursive, it now read JILL. The women's oars were also turquoise and navy. Inspired, the team swept Stanford. Jill read the news and danced around her hotel room.

Then she learned something else: Cal's top coxswain had been demoted to the second boat. The spot in the varsity eight was in play heading into the Pac-10 championships.

The good news came on May 8, the Saturday before Pac-10s. O'Neill had conducted an email poll of the top eight rowers, asking them to rank their top three coxswains. Six had put Jill first, even though she'd never coxed the top boat in competition. This was all the reassurance O'Neill needed. He was, as he says, "far too competitive" to make such an important decision based on sentimentality, but he'd seen the way Jill had worked the boats and had been impressed. Before practice he pulled her behind the boathouse. "I'm leaning toward you coxing the varsity this weekend," O'Neill said. "Are you up for it?"

It was what Jill had been waiting to hear since junior high, when she'd first dreamed of coxing an elite program. She smiled and said, "Yup."

Jill knew the job would be brutally taxing, but she was used to that by now. A couple of weeks earlier, on the eve of the Washington race, she had insisted on going to practice straight from a chemo session that had left her hardly able to stand. When her father, Jim, pulled up to the boathouse, rain was pounding down. Assistant coach Sara Nevin approached Jill as she got out of the car. "Jill, we have another cox," Nevin said. "You don't have to do this. Make a smart decision."

"I am," Jill replied.

The way Jill saw it, there was nothing more important to her recovery. If she could get in that boat, then she could keep fighting cancer. And if she could beat Stanford at the Pac-10s, then she could beat cancer.

It was all about managing her body. By this point her face was puffy, her abdomen bloated, and her feet so swollen that she couldn't wear shoes. (Instead she hobbled around in sandals.) But she had learned to conserve her energy. She'd be ready.

The heat didn't help. On Sunday, May 16, the day of the Pac-10s, it was 90 degrees at Lake Natoma, outside Sacramento, with only a whiff of a breeze. Waiting in the team tent, Jill drank water, trying to keep her temperature down. She'd awakened that morning from a feverish dream. Then she'd injected an anticoagulant into her leg and, as always, a dark bruise had immediately bloomed. Finally she'd gulped down 14 pills, the cocktail of cancer-fighting agents, vitamins, and painkillers that she needed to function. Pain was a constant now, but Jill didn't pay it much attention. "Her whole year was leading up to that moment," Mary Costello says. "She was going to finish it."

Gingerly, Jill joined her teammates in the boat. The morning's early races had gone well for Cal. Now, with only the varsity eight race remaining, Berkeley was in position to win the Pac-10 title. All the Bears needed to do was beat Stanford. On the sideline O'Neill tried not to think about the fact that this was the first time Jill had coxed the varsity eight. Usually there are preliminary heats and semifinals, but this year the Pac-10s had been compressed into one race. Jill was ready, O'Neill told himself over and over again.

In the boat Jill knew the time had come. She pulled out a vial and passed it to sophomore Kristina Lofman, who was immediately in front of her, and told her to pass it around. Lofman stared at it and asked, "Do I drink it?"

A few seats behind her Elise Etem, the powerful sophomore whose brother had been drafted by the Anaheim Ducks, thought perhaps her cox had lost her mind and brought the tiniest bottle of refreshment in the history of sports. "Um, I think we're good on water, Jill," Etem said.

"No," replied Jill, calm as can be. "It's miracle water."

And with that, each rower took a splash of the water, which Jill had brought back from Lourdes in plastic bottles, and, as if applying perfume, dabbed it behind an ear.

On the PA system, the race announcer said, "Attention!"

Their backs to the finish line, the eight rowers faced the small, puffy-faced girl with a blue Cal hat and a hands-free microphone. A thousand thoughts raced through their heads. In the fourth seat Etem thought that if Jill could be sitting there that day, then Etem could certainly row all-out for 2,000 meters. In the fifth seat Mary Jeghers thought how special it was that after being Jill's teammate for four years, this was the first time she had Jill as her cox. And in the eighth seat, only a foot or so from Jill, Lofman thought about what was to come.

Before the race O'Neill had pulled Lofman aside. "At a thousand meters I want you to look in Jill's face," O'Neill had said, "and be as brave as she is." Lofman had nodded her head, but she was scared. She didn't know if she could do it—be as brave as Jill. Later she would say that she had never gone for it as much as she did in that race, that she felt nothing was going to stop her.

The flag dropped, and the Cal team shot out like a waterborne rocket. Oregon State, Washington, and Washington State dropped back immediately. Only one team—Stanford, of course—would stick with the Bears. At 500 meters it was Cal by a nose. At 1,000 it was Cal by half a boat length. It was there that Lofman noticed something unusual: a dab of scarlet just below Jill's nose. Then the smudge grew, blood snaking toward Jill's upper lip. Jill saw the fear in Lofman's eyes and knew what had happened. With a quick, disdainful motion she wiped away the blood with the back of her hand. Lofman felt a surge of energy course through her. "It was like she wasn't going to let her body stop her from doing what she wanted to do," says Lofman. Already close to maxing out, Lofman dug even deeper.

With 300 meters to go Cal remained well out in front. But then, half a minute later, with only 100 meters to go, it happened: on her return stroke Etem caught half a crab, and moments later so did Kara Kohler, another port oar, causing the boat to rock violently. With a quick motion Jill grabbed the rope and yanked, pulling the shell back to starboard. "Finish strong" was all she said.

With that the boat righted and regained speed. Good thing too, for Stanford was now just 10 feet behind. The crews hit the finish line in a blur. There was a beat, and then a roar went up from the shoreline: the Bears had won by less than a second. By the slimmest of margins—half a point—the Pac-10 championship was Cal's.

If anyone questioned whether the girls had given their all, he had only to look at the boat. In their greatest moment of triumph, two of the rowers sagged over their oars, while another two were bent over the side of the boat heaving. Eventually the shell coasted into the shore, and the team piled out. Lofman, ankle deep in the water, wrapped her arms around Jill, later swearing that she could feel the joy in her coxswain bubbling into the embrace.

If there was any doubt about Jill's ability as a coxswain, it was gone. She would be Cal's varsity eight cox at nationals two weeks later.

If you were told you had a month left to live, what would you do? By May the prognosis for Jill had grown alarmingly dark. She paid it no mind. She'd learned early in her treatment to look at the world through a different lens. Her advice, as she wrote: *Your life is happening right now and this is the only moment you can control. This is the only minute that really matters. If you are constantly dwelling on something that happened in the past or feeling anxious about the future, you are missing out on YOUR LIFE. Do what makes you happy in this moment and your life will be full.*

What's more, Jill was part of something larger than herself now. For six months she'd been working with the San Francisco–based Bonnie J. Addario Lung Cancer Foundation, and she had agreed to become its director of public awareness after graduation. She funneled her energy into organizing a charity run in Golden Gate Park called Jog for Jill, which when it was held on a foggy Sunday in September would attract close to 5,000 people and raise more than $320,000. She spoke at Genentech, a cancer research firm, exchanged emails with half a dozen other cancer patients nationwide, and was interviewed on NPR as a voice of nonsmoker lung-cancer sufferers. She continued her schoolwork at Cal, as fastidious as ever. When, after a therapy-related extension, she handed in her final paper in International Trade, her professor gave her an A-minus without even looking at Jill's work. Naturally Jill was upset, believing she'd turned in a really good paper, one she'd worked diligently to finish. So she contacted the professor, who took a look and awarded her a straight A. The result: Jill had a 4.0 average in her final semester at Cal.

Why stop living? She persuaded her parents to get her a dog as her graduation present. Atkinson figured he'd go along with it, that she needed this. Later he realized that she was getting the dog as much for him and her parents as for herself, so there would be something of her left if she didn't make it. Jill chose a Maltese puppy, which she of course named Jack. She received the Pac-10 women's rowing Athlete of the Year Award and the Joseph M. Kavanagh Award, presented to the most inspirational athlete at Cal.

On May 18 Jill graduated, walking across the stage at Zeller-

bach Auditorium to thunderous applause while wearing her Pac-10
medal and a blond wig. Five days later her parents held a graduation party at their house for 150 people. Because Mary had traveled with her daughter to Lourdes, it had fallen to Jim, a laconic
water department supervisor, to organize the fiesta. "In 31 years of
marriage that was the first time he'd had to host an event," says
Mary.

Jill barely made it through the party, retiring to her room to rest
four times. The next morning she was back at practice, and again
on Tuesday, when her parents joined her for the final session at
Briones. The next morning the team left for nationals in Sacramento while Jill stayed behind for a doctor's appointment.

That afternoon she got the worst news yet. The treatment hadn't
stopped the growth of the tumors in her lungs, bones, and liver. It
was time to move, the doctors told her, from How do we cure this?
to How do we make your last few weeks as comfortable as possible?
In Natoma, O'Neill received the news in a text from Jill. After
months of holding it in, of playing the role of the stoic coach, the
ultimate optimist, he finally cracked. Gathering the whole squad in
the boathouse, he began a speech about teamwork, then brought
up Jill. "Guys," he said, "we can't control how many days she has
left, but we can control the quality of the days she has left." Then
O'Neill, who prided himself on never showing emotion, had to
stop. He turned away so the girls wouldn't see him crying.

That night no one expected Jill at the late practice, especially
because it was an unimportant one, devoted to rigging the boats.
But there she was. She had gone straight from the doctor's office
to meet with an assistant coach and with Obradovic, the star rower,
who'd had to stick around for a class, then traveled up to Sacramento. She was as upbeat as ever. Jeghers remembers marveling
that you'd never have known about Jill's diagnosis, that Jill didn't
once mention being tired. Even though she was having trouble
walking and keeping food down, Jill tried to show up to Saturday
afternoon practice. Only after O'Neill insisted did she relent and
stay at the hotel.

Just by making it this far, she'd defied the odds. Of all others
given a diagnosis of lung cancer in June 2009, more than half had
died by January. And here Jill was, six months later, about to race at
nationals.

There was so much wrapped up in this final race. Lying in bed that week, O'Neill had confided to his wife, Nicole, that while the rowers never talked about it, they felt that if they could win the NCAAs, then Jill could beat cancer. "It would be like Lance Armstrong all over again," he said. Saturday night, on the eve of the final race, O'Neill got up at the team dinner and said he thought it wasn't fair that everyone got to race as Team Jill except Jill herself. Then he'd pulled out a turquoise uniform for Jill.

The next morning, rowers were on hand from schools across the country—Princeton, Virginia, Yale—and many of them knew nothing about Jill. The trainer for Washington State, Barb Russell, knew only because she was friends with Smitty. So when the Cougars were knocked out in the semis, Russell couldn't contain herself any longer. She gathered the team around her. "Do you know why Cal is wearing those colors?" she asked. "Okay, let me tell you a story." Five minutes later all the Washington State rowers were clustered at the shoreline, cheering for Cal. They didn't stop until well after the boat had crossed the finish line.

The Bears' four finished second that day, and the second eight finished third. The field for the varsity eights, meanwhile, was extremely fast. In the first two heats, four boats had broken the course record. It would be no small feat, but if Jill's boat beat Virginia, Cal would be national champion.

In the final the Yale crew took an early lead, with Virginia and Princeton close and Cal in fourth. At 1,000 meters the Bears were a half-boat length back and looked out of the race. Knowing they needed to make a move, Jill exhorted the team to take a "power 10." Beat by beat it worked, and Cal gained on the Cavaliers. The Bears had found their swing.

Here it was, the dramatic comeback everyone was waiting for: after the fastest third leg of any boat by far, Cal was only 10 feet behind Virginia. On the shore O'Neill watched on the JumboTron and then, overtaken by the moment, began sprinting alongside the boat, yelling, "Go, Cal! Go, Jill!" In the stands Atkinson and Mary and Jim Costello were on their feet, Atkinson pumping his arms as if he might row the boat himself. The Washington State girls roared. The whole cosmos roared for Jill Costello, or so it seemed in that moment.

And then suddenly it was over. Cal ran out of water, finishing fourth, while Virginia came in second. Reality set in: the Bears had finished second at nationals. Lofman doubled over, bawling. Kohler, the six-foot freshman who looked like a Viking goddess, couldn't tell what was sweat and what was tears. None of them understood. No one had wanted it more than they had. Most schools would be ecstatic to finish second in the country; hell, the same girls had been ecstatic to finish second only a year earlier. But this was different.

The least upset girl was the one who had the most reason to be. Jill didn't break down and cry. She didn't scream out. She didn't wallow in the defeat. Instead she went to her mom and picked up Jack, then brought him back to the bleachers for the medal ceremony. That's where someone took the photo that Nevin set as her Facebook profile picture, the one that O'Neill included in the team training schedule, the one that Obradovic uses as her laptop background. It's the same shot that was in the program at Jill's funeral when she passed away less than a month later, on June 24, 2010. In the photo Jill is holding Jack aloft with one hand in front of the second-place trophy, smiling like the luckiest girl in the world.

If you look at the faces around her, of the teammates who should have been dejected, who had been so disappointed only minutes earlier, you'll notice something: they're smiling too.

WRIGHT THOMPSON

Above and Beyond

FROM ESPN.COM

COPIAPO, CHILE — On the eve of the biggest soccer game in the history of this remote desert town, the team knelt in prayer. The Regional Atacama players were one win from a championship and a promotion to the first division of Chilean soccer. The blue-collar mining community felt reborn. So, together in their locker room, they asked the local patron saint for help: please let us do this, for the people, for each other. They promised to visit the saint's roadside shrine after the game to give thanks. A few miles outside of Copiapo, built into a steep wall of rock, the place was an outdoor chapel where candles burned in wrought iron grates.

When the game ended, when Atacama had won, the players didn't even take off their uniforms. They ran from the stadium, up to Route 5, headed to the shrine. The whole team, Franklin and Diego, Mario and Ramon, all of them. They were young and strong. Their lungs filled with summer air, and a hundred or so fans gathered behind them, caught up in the joy. Everyone ran, shouting out praise, for five miles. The throng followed Atacama's powerful midfielder, the fastest player, the man who had scored the first goal in the team's history.

Everyone ran behind Franklin Lobos.

When the Cheering Stops

Almost 29 years later, on August 5, Lobos cranked his pickup truck to drive down into the San Jose mine. When he looked in the mirror, he didn't see the powerful young man those people followed. He saw a thick waist and a shiny bald head. But he remembered those days.

Just the week before, he had played with some of his teammates in an old-timers game. So revered was that 1981 squad that it, and not the current professionals, was invited to play the first game when the city opened a new stadium. Lobos, 53, loved hitting the field with his friends, even though his family couldn't understand why he spent so much time with these middle-aged men, reliving the past.

"Soccer players have their time," his mother-in-law would say.

The San Jose copper and gold mine had a reputation, even in a town of leathery miners. The locals called it the Kamikaze Mine. A miner had died several years ago, and earlier this year one lost his leg. Lobos got 30 percent more money, about $1,500 a month, for working there instead of a different mine. He knew it was dangerous, but he had bills. Soccer players didn't get rich in his time. All his former teammates had real jobs too.

He drove deeper into the mine, a coworker riding shotgun, passing another truck of friends, who soon came to the surface. Outside, his friends felt the mountain rumble. Later, they'd tell everyone that the cave-in surely had killed Lobos.

Down below, a slab of rock collapsed just behind Lobos. The daily routine turned into an action movie. Debris fell all around, a boiling cloud of earth turning everything dark. Lobos drove deeper into the mine. The tunnel dominoed behind him, huge sheets of thick earth landing near the back of the truck. The rocks buried a backhoe and a water tower. The whole mountain was coming down around them, but Lobos managed to make his way to the rescue chamber, where he found 31 fellow miners. They were trapped.

Everything was black. Hours passed. In the dark, they could only hear each other, and the voices sounded scared. The oldest miner was 62; he would lead them in prayer. The youngest was only 19; his family told reporters he was afraid of the dark.

Finally, the debris cloud cleared and everyone squinted into the dust. This was what they saw: 33 men in a tiny emergency refuge, 500 square feet, with limited water and just two days' worth of emergency rations. They were deep below the surface—almost two Empire State Buildings deep—and the rescuers didn't know where to look.

What happened next galvanized a country.

The foreman, Luis Urzua, took charge. He'd been a soccer coach, and his workers respected him. First, he had to make the food last as long as possible. Every 48 hours, he figured, each miner could have two teaspoons of tuna, a sip of milk, and half a biscuit. The men drained water-cooled machinery to stay hydrated. Urzua spent his time mapping out the tunnels around them, creating a drawing of their strange underground world, so they could spread out. He used the headlights of trucks to simulate day and night to keep the men sane.

A day passed.

A week passed.

Lobos heard the drills, grinding into rock, shaking the fragile mountain, blindly searching for 33 men in the dark. When the noise sounded close, his spirits rose. He felt alive. But each time, the drill pulled away, the noise fading to silence. Those hours felt like death to the miners. The food ran low. The men all lost weight, about 20 pounds apiece. One man wrote a poem: "Many days have passed without knowing. Here at the bottom, my tears begin to flow."

Day 16 arrived, blurring toward 17. The drill hummed close . . . achingly close . . . only to pull back again. The sound disappeared. Sores and rashes marked their bodies. The food ran out. Hope ran out. Lobos finally understood he was never going to leave this hole. He'd wait for a while longer, then he'd write a letter saying goodbye.

He sat in the cramped room and waited to die.

Losing a Hero?

The day after the mine collapse, word spread through Copiapo: Lobos, "the Magic Mortar," was one of the 33. The sports television and radio shows remembered his career.

Talk soon turned to 1980.

Copiapo existed on the edge of civilization. It was in the Atacama Desert, the driest place on earth. But in the late '70s, a surge in the local mining and agricultural industries set off a boom. The local university, now one of the best in Chile, was created in '81. Cranes dominated the skyline. In fact, they created the skyline; before, there were no tall buildings. And in April 1980, Atacama played its first game. The stadium was packed. Lobos scored the first goal and was a local hero. Everyone on the street knew his name, and when he and his teammates made it to the first division the next season, in the team's second year of existence, their place was secure. Like members of the 2004 Boston Red Sox or the 2009 New Orleans Saints, these guys would never pay for drinks. They aren't famous, per se. It's better than fame. They are beloved.

The promise of those years didn't last. The mining business faded, and the team eventually went broke and folded, replaced by a new club. Some of the players moved away. Some stayed in town and worked normal jobs. Lobos drove a cab, then took the job down in the mine. Life underground left little time for anything else. "Something happened when he began to work as a miner," says Ana Diaz-Torrejon, his mother-in-law. "He stopped practicing sports."

Still, every so often, the team would get together and play. The games sold out and the crowds sang the old songs and everyone remembered a different time. Even young people who had never seen them play called out their names.

"All this is in the heart of the people," says Ruben Sanchez, a member of the team. "The people remember all this until today."

Now, the fans tried to process the news. Former players, even those who had lost touch, began calling each other. In Santiago, Atacama star Mario Caneo's phone rang. It was the team's old equipment manager, Leonel Olmos.

"Franklin had an accident in the mine," Olmos said.

Caneo began to cry.

In his apartment in New York City, the team's tough defender, Ramon Climent, was watching the Chilean cable channel when the list of victims scrolled across the screen. The name of his old friend sent chills up his arms.

They all waited on news: the teammates and the city that loved them. In New York, on the 16th day, while Lobos lost hope deep below the surface, Climent almost got into a fight at a party with someone who told him, "Franklin is dead."

The next day, Climent was sitting in front of his television when it happened. He heard the entire story: the drill had found the safety chamber, and the miners attached a note in shaky, red hand-writing: *We are fine, in the shelter, all 33.*

Franklin Lobos was alive.

Life 2,300 Feet Down

People flooded the plazas all around the nation. Family members and friends tried to process the news. Down in the mine, the men felt born again. Communication was established, and the president of Chile, Sebastian Pinera, came on the line. He asked Urzua what the 33 needed.

"Mr. President," he said. "Don't abandon us."

"You won't be left alone," Pinera told him. "Nor have you been alone a single moment."

The rescue began. Chilean submarine officers helped devise a plan. South Africa, the U.S., and Canada sent their best mining brains. NASA sent scientists to advise on keeping people alive in outer space because that's essentially what the mine was like. Everything was new. Nothing was simple. Imagine: you are trapped in a subway tunnel with all the exits blocked and rescuing you means drilling a man-sized hole through almost 10 Superdomes. The crew members made it up as they went along, in the best sort of way, like something from *Apollo 13.*

In the first days, two narrow boreholes, nicknamed umbilical cords, were drilled to provide supplies. Each was a bit wider than an iPhone is long. One was for water, oxygen, and communications. The other was for sending packages up and down. Salvation arrived via eight-foot cylinders nicknamed *palomas:* doves.

One of the first things to go down into the mine was a video camera. The miners made a short film and sent it back up: an introduction to their world. It was like *Lord of the Flies.* They had built a society, with officials and rules, with someone in charge of food and another man in charge of their spiritual life. In a lot of ways, they had created a team.

Everything was carefully organized. A table for cards. A shelf for first aid supplies. One man hung a topless pin-up girl on the wall.

The miners figured out how to use the labyrinth of tunnels to which they had access. One tunnel was the latrine. One was for exercise. One was for smokers; two men finally badgered officials into sending cigarettes instead of nicotine gum. The miners put the smoking area in the hottest part of the mine and a long distance away: a walk of about five football fields. The telephone sat in a corner, so the men wouldn't see each other's tears.

Letters moved in both directions every day. The messages were lifelines. Carolina Lobos, Franklin's 25-year-old daughter, felt as if she was finally getting to know her father. One miner and his wife decided they should have a wedding in a church; they'd been married at the courthouse 25 years before. "Buy the dress," he told her. Another woman wrote that she would accept a marriage proposal that she had declined not long before. One man learned his wife had given birth to a baby girl. They named her Hope.

The men asked for tapes of Maradona and Pele. They asked for music. They asked for steaks and beer, but instead, they got elastic workout straps and strict exercise instructions: if they were overweight, they wouldn't fit into the rescue hole. The doctor on site had worked for a big Chilean soccer team; he helped the miners build aerobic stamina. He also got one of them, a trained paramedic, to send urine and blood samples up the pipe; the doctor sent vaccines back down—the time underground was erasing the men's immunity to common germs.

Each dove took 30 minutes to make the round trip. The men got a small television projector and antidepressants, dice and love songs. They got three meals a day and two snacks. They got media training to be prepared for the circus that awaited them outside; Lobos tried to tell them that fame did not come for free. They got tiny Bibles. They got jerseys from famous soccer players. Carolina told her dad that she wanted to send him a soccer ball but it wouldn't fit through the hole. The game was never far from Lobos's mind. He wrote a letter to the new Copiapo team, the one that replaced Atacama, which was playing a game to avoid relegation. Be as persistent as the miners, he said.

Mostly, the 33 miners stuck to the routine. Three eight-hour shifts, each group clearing the rock falling from the hole being drilled to rescue them. If they couldn't move the debris, they would be stuck in the mine. Every hour counted; in a briefing with the nation's health minister, Urzua said: "Keep it short. We have lots of work to do."

A month went by like this, then two. October arrived. Nobody had ever been buried underground as long. They felt happy because the end seemed in sight. They felt nervous about the specially constructed rescue pod, built by the Chilean navy. "Every day, I am more impatient," Carolina Lobos says. "My father too. We are anxious."

The men counted the days. They wrote letters. They read letters. The nation followed every development; in the middle of the ordeal, when the Chilean national soccer team played a match, the miners got to see the game, and through the magic of cameras and cables, the people of Chile got to watch them watch. The network broadcast cut to a live shot from the mine. The shot panned over to Lobos, who smiled a bit. A rough beard covered his face. He looked tired but safe. He fanned himself.

"Franklin Lobos is one of us," the announcer said. "To Franklin Lobos, a special hello."

A Bond That Never Breaks

In New York, with the rescue effort under way, Ramon Climent knew what he needed to do.

So many things had happened to him since the Atacama days, and even though he was three decades and 5,000 miles removed, he'd never really left that remote desert town, or that group of men. Athletes might grow old and apart, but they never stop being teammates.

He bought a ticket and flew to Copiapo, ending up in the square that once filled with fans after their games. This was where they had gone to celebrate after leaving the shrine so many years ago. Everything seemed vaguely the same, but the feeling he remembered, the hope of a city riding a boom, was gone. He got out his cell phone and dialed an old friend: Mario Caneo.

"I'm in downtown Copiapo," he said.

Caneo got on a bus in Santiago. Twelve hours later, he joined Climent. They called Diego Solis, who flew in from Buenos Aires,

Argentina. The men, once stars on Atacama, hadn't been together in a quarter of a century. That didn't matter. "It could be 1,000 years," Caneo says, "and I would have recognized them."

The time fell away. Solis laughed and stuck his finger in Ramon's ear. Climent made fun of Solis's lily-white skin. "The next Michael Jackson," he cracked.

The three walked around town. At a local café on the plaza, a crowd gathered. People stared and pointed. Their heroes had returned. Cameras flashed. Hands reached out. First there was joy, but then a sad feeling slowly came over everyone. The people of Copiapo realized *why* these three men were back in town.

They had come because an old friend was in trouble.

"We are not friends just of games," Caneo says. "We are friends of the heart."

The three men, in their fifties now, drove out to the mine last week. They passed the familiar roadside shrine where they had run 29 years ago; a homemade flag flapped above it asking not for a soccer victory but for the safe return of the miners. The terrain close to San Jose is often described as a moonscape. It's become a bit of a cliché, but it's true. Put it this way. If you were a location scout for a George Lucas film about the end of the world, you'd be getting a nice Christmas bonus. The place is barren, and the harsh desert alongside the gravel road to the mine made the men nervous. It was Caneo's turn to get chills. They imagined Lobos's last trip to this remote, lonely mine. They looked at the tall drills and tried to picture him buried down below. Anger spread throughout the car: how could a man who had brought so much joy to a city end up working in such a hell?

When they arrived at the dusty camp, the men milled around, waiting. They'd been told there might be a chance to speak with Franklin by phone. Olmos, the old equipment manager, met them there, across from the CNN truck, and he played the Atacama fight song on his phone. All three players met Carolina; they stood in a tight circle and listened to her explain the situation. She sounded so grown up. The last time they'd seen her, she'd been a baby. Now she was a woman. They asked questions, and she did her best to answer. She saw the concern on their faces, and, for the first time, she understood why they mattered so much to her father.

She understood they were brothers.

Campamento Esperanza

Climent stood on the dusty path and looked at the chaos around him. Straight ahead, teams drilled all day and all night, with three options reaching for the miners. Dozens of tents were pitched around the area, with smoldering campfires. Painted messages of hope covered rocks. Banners hung everywhere. Hundreds of Chilean flags flapped in the breeze. A crowd of priests performed Mass. Clowns tied balloon animals for children. People gripped letters that had arrived from the doves.

"This is crazy," Climent said.

Welcome to Camp Hope.

When the mine collapsed, the strange little tent city grew up around the rescue operation. The families moved out here into the desert, dealing with blistering days and frigid nights. It was a circus. Some folks wept openly. Others fought. One miner suffered the great misfortune of his wife and mistress arriving simultaneously. Carolina Lobos lived in a tent, chain-smoking cigarettes, getting up to three packs a day before Lobos was found alive. "I have to stop smoking when my father gets out of the mine," she says. "I promised him and God."

The television trucks followed, and they have moved in too. The networks and big cable operations, from around the world, have built wooden platforms for live shots, setting up satellites and booking every hotel room and Winnebago for miles. There are almost more reporters than family members, an impressive teacher-to-student ratio.

As weeks passed, some people began commuting from Copiapo. Carolina did that too, though she feels closer to her father at the mine than at home. Every night, she slept with the Adidas T-shirt they took out of his locker at the top of the mine. She slept with regret too. Before, she took family for granted. She cared for her father but never really took the time to show him. The accident made her realize what she had missed. With her father in a strange purgatory, not really dead or alive, she imagined what life would be like after he came back to the surface. She made plans. "To give him all the love that I never gave him," she says. "Help him. Take care of him. Protect him."

This past week, moving between her tent at Camp Hope and her breezy front porch in Copiapo, Carolina counted the days until her father returned. The end seemed near. She thought about all the little miracles of the past two months, about the middle-aged men who showed her what being a teammate truly meant.

"They are the most beautiful memories he has," she says. "He told me they were very important to him. These guys who helped him to be the soccer player and the man he is."

Brothers Forever

The men who played for Atacama have waited in hospital rooms and stood at the front of churches, traveled for weddings and for christenings. Many of them are godparents. They've always been there for each other, and now, three of them stood at the top of a collapsed mine, staring at a white office phone.

Lobos picked up his receiver a half-mile away, below their feet. He expected his daughter on the other end.

"We have a surprise," Carolina says. "Say hello to old miners from Atacama."

The old players crowded around the phone, leaning down to the speaker. They all started talking. Franklin heard voices from his past. He couldn't see their faces, but he knew them all.

Mario!

Diego!

Ramon!

They tried to keep it light, telling stories about a girl they all used to know, making fun of the billboards around Chile decorated with the miners' photos. Everyone took a turn, giving him encouragement, hoping to transport him, even if just for a few minutes, outside of the mine. Soon, their time came to an end. The laughter stopped. The conversation turned serious. In a few minutes, all the former players would go back to their car and ride away in silence, thinking about their brother stuck down in the earth. But at the phone, they first had to say goodbye.

"I'll come back when you get out to get a beer," Climent says.

"Goodbye, friend," Olmos says.

"I'm gonna stay here forever with you," Caneo says. "We are all with you, my friend."

Lobos began to sob. He had so many things to say. He could have told them about the beauty of his memories. He could have told them that the bonds they formed when everything seemed possible had survived the withering of time. Athletes might grow old and apart, but they never stop being teammates.

"I am crying," he said. "I never expected you to come here."

BILL PLASCHKE

A Gift That Opens Him Up

FROM THE LOS ANGELES TIMES

"W-W-W-WHAT IS THIS?"

As he tore open the brightly colored paper, the boy's heart dropped. It was flat, so it wasn't a baseball or a glove.

He ran his fingers across the blue vinyl cover, touched the white sheets of paper, slowly bit his lip to keep from crying. This wasn't a Christmas present, it was a school supply. It was a binder filled with blank pages. The boy looked angrily over at the balding man wearing a weary smile and a stray piece of tinsel on his shoulder.

"I-I-I can't play with this," the boy said.

"Yes, you can," the father said.

The awkward, stammering eighth-grader slapped Jackson Five and *Gilligan's Island* stickers on the binder to at least make it look cool, then tucked it into the bottom drawer next to his plaid shorts and forgot all about it. The next time he saw it was March, three months later, as he headed out to watch a sandlot baseball game. He had earlier announced to his family that when he grew up, he was going be a sportswriter, using the universal language of bats and balls to connect to a world he couldn't easily touch. On this day, he had finally worked up the courage to practice covering a game.

"Wait," said his father, emerging from the boy's bedroom, holding that dusty blue binder covered in stickers. "If you're going to be a sportswriter, you have to have a notebook."

"Oh y-y-yeah," the boy said. "My n-n-notebook."

And so he toted that binder to the baseball game, to a high school track meet the next day, somewhere new every weekend, wiping the dust off his giant glasses and pulling chewed pencils out of his wrinkled shirt pocket and filling that binder, reveling in words that worked, shouting in a voice that didn't stammer, adding exclamation points for the drama, *Bobby Kleinart hit the heck out of that baseball for a home run off the concession stands for Westport Chevron, boxes of Good N' Plenty went flying, what a play!*

Soon the white pages became full, and so more pages were carefully added, more baseballs clearing the fence, more snacks falling out of the sky, words written by a nobody for nobody, words meaning everything, the binder and the boy growing together.

"W-w-what is this?"

The gift sat in the basement, unwrapped, shiny and cluttered and weird. It was an electric typewriter given to a ninth-grader who had no idea how to use it. This wasn't a Christmas present, it was a third-period class.

"I-I-I can't type," the boy said.

"But I can," his mother said. "Bring me your binder."

Its stickers had worn down into bits of shiny strips, and its vinyl was cracked and frayed, but the binder's pages still exhaled the cluttered breath of scribbled observations— *the Ballard High cross-country team is one tough cookie!* His mother opened to his most recent story, turned a switch, started a strange whir, and began pecking.

"W-w-what are you doing?" the boy said.

"Don't you want this in that newspaper?" the mother said.

Oh yeah. That newspaper. It was a neighborhood weekly that needed stories to fill the space between school announcements and mortuary ads. A month earlier, the boy visited their storefront offices, opening his binder, showing the balding old boss his stories, watching him slowly shake his head.

"Your handwriting is terrible," the boss said. "Did you know that newspapers use typewriters?"

He could not begin typing class until the summer, so his mother spent hours every weekend tapping his stories to life. He scribbled, and she typed, word for word, her third full-time job, sometimes falling asleep between paragraphs, but always finishing in time to say, "Great story" and "Let's go."

Then, together, in the middle of every Sunday night, the mother

and the boy would ride through the darkened city to that newspaper's storefront, where the boy would slide that week's stories
into a mail slot, then rush back to the car for the relieved drive
home, the sportswriter and his ghostwriter.

"W-w-what is this?"

The gift was covered in light blue tissue paper, held together
with a frayed red ribbon. The young man opened it carefully,
forced a smile, scratched his head.

It was a scrapbook. But it was an empty scrapbook. It was two
covers of ornate brown leather held together by dozens of empty
pieces of gray construction paper. It was silly.

"Th-th-this is great, but w-w-what's going in it?" the young man
asked.

"You," his grandmother said.

So for the next seven years, she put him there, filling the scrapbook with everything the young man wrote, for now he was an amateur sportswriter being published in any newspaper that would
have him. The grandmother carefully cut and pasted every volleyball feature, shuffleboard column, and flag football game story,
everything from the neighborhood weekly, the high school newspaper, and soon even from the tiny college newspaper. She under-
lined phrases in her careful handwriting. She drew her own exclamation points after words with more than one syllable. The book
grew fat and messy as she grew old and frail.

The young man thought she was saving stories about other people. The grandmother knew better. She knew these would wind up
being stories about a young man, chronicling his increased confidence, his diminished stammer, the slow realization of his dream.

"Dad, what was your best gift ever?"

The middle-aged man is sitting with his three children around a
Christmas tree. He has been a sportswriter for more than half of
his life now, still chasing that dream, still thankful it is a journey he
has not taken alone. He looks at his children sitting amid the shiny
torn wrapping paper, the kids covered in the solitary pleasures of
iPods and Uggs and software programs that do things mothers and
electric typewriters could never do. He wonders if he can ever give
them what was given to him. He wonders if they will ever understand. One of them asks him again.

"Dad, what was your best gift ever?"

He looks up at a photo on the mantle. It is a 30-year-old family photograph. It contains the images of the father who still calls every other day to ask what he has in his notebook, the mother who now types him encouragement in emails, and the grandmother who died during his first year at one of this country's biggest newspapers. Before passing, she insisted that he stay on the job and skip her funeral. She insisted he write one more story for that scrapbook.

"Daaad! What was your best gift! C'mon."

He points to the photo. "They were," he said.

New Mike, Old Christine

FROM GQ

CHRISTINE HAD THE EYES all the girls wanted, translucent turquoise marbles fringed by strawberry blond lashes. And the smile. Wide and natural, but somehow coy and elusive too. You could work for years and not get that right. Her peach-colored blouse draped just so on her six-foot-one frame, the silky skirt skimming her calves. She had let her sun-streaked blond hair grow to chin length, and she helped it along by pinning on a little hairpiece that grazed her broad shoulders.

Amy LaCoe was an earthier, more androgynous type. At 59, a decade older than Christine, she didn't even bother to dye her hair as she grew it out, just wore it straight and silver, and stuck to jeans and pastel cotton V-necks, with a modest pink cameo on a chain around her neck. Like the rest of the transition group at the Los Angeles Gender Center, she marveled at Christine's feline grace in the summer of 2006, how everyone seemed to turn toward her, unconsciously, like a source of heat on a cold day.

Not that that would make it any easier for Christine when she went full-time, as she was planning to do in the coming year. Probably the opposite. The others had more marginal careers or at least less glamorous ones. Some were self-employed. Others, like Amy, a career counselor at a community college, could hide in academia, which was full of sympathetic hippie types. Christine's transformation from Mike Penner, a name that had appeared in the sports pages of the *Los Angeles Times* for 25 years as an NFL writer, an Angels beat reporter, a tennis columnist, was likely to be cataclysmic. Others could change their identity and never again speak their male names aloud, but a byline haunted you forever.

Anyway, Christine, who had chosen her new name to honor Christine Jorgensen, the first well-known transsexual, and two iconic Chrissies, Evert and Hynde, had no intention of living in anonymity as a diner waitress in Fresno or a 7-Eleven clerk along the Las Vegas strip. Being a sportswriter at the *Times* was everything she had wanted since she was a boy back in Anaheim, interning at the local daily while still at Cal State Fullerton.

But a transgender sportswriter? As a reporter, she knew it would be a big story. She remembered Renée Richards's transition in 1975, how the caustic tennis player who went to court to compete as a woman had been a media obsession for decades.

And then there was Lisa to worry about. Most of the 10 or so in the group had wives, but none had a marriage as symbiotic as Mike Penner and Lisa Dillman's. They'd been together for two decades, ever since they fell in love covering the U.S. Open in Flushing Meadows, New York. They even worked side by side — he'd long ago helped her move to the *Times,* where she covered tennis and had become the lead Olympics reporter. And because they'd never had children, they seemed even closer. Lisa played midfielder for the Scribes, a rec-league soccer team that Mike had cofounded and coached. On weekends their apartment in Long Beach shook with the sounds of Mike's music — he followed punk and indie rock, everything from the Clash to Nirvana to the Rapture, as closely as he did his beloved Arsenal of the English Premier League, and regularly sent his pals mix CDs labeled with his own personal radio call letters, KPEN. When other couples had dinner with Mike and Lisa, listened to them retell the story of how they fell in love, the wives would fuss to their husbands: *Look at them. So nice, so loving. Why can't we be like that?*

Lisa had known for years that her husband sometimes dressed as a woman, and she'd accepted it reluctantly as long as it was out of sight. But going full-time was a completely different thing, and Christine refused to dwell on how Lisa would react. Living without her was unthinkable, Christine told Amy on that first afternoon they went for something to eat after group. Lisa had been the best part of him for 20 years. Since they were kids. Since that day when he first met her, an open-faced midwestern girl barely out of her teens with *Minneapolis Star Tribune* press credentials dangling around her neck.

Hadn't other wives made their peace and stayed on, Christine reasoned as the waitress brought them their blueberry pie. What about Jennifer Finney Boylan, the Colby College English professor and novelist who had written that memoir, *She's Not There*, detailing how her wife stuck by her? It would be hard, sure, but not impossible: Lisa would come around. Surely she would realize that it wasn't about her; it was something Christine had to do to survive. She was the same person inside. She still loved soccer and the Raconteurs. She still needed Lisa as much as Mike had, maybe more.

Amy was quiet as the waitress refilled their coffees. In her experience, that just wasn't how it worked. The year before, when Amy told her wife of 39 years that she was a woman and planned to live as one, she had screamed obscenities and thrown Amy's estrogen tablets out the garage door. Called her a queer, a freak. Not that Amy blamed her for being upset. The poor woman hadn't signed on for this. Sure, she had known that Amy dressed on the sly for decades, that she kept plastic tubs of girl's things in the back of the station wagon. But hormones—that was too much. She had every right to expect to get old with the man she married, rely on retirement benefits from his job, play together with the grand-kids, die with him. Amy couldn't imagine how Christine thought it would all work out. She would be transgendering in the same work-place as her wife, something no one in the group had ever heard of. Lisa might not be the type to heave things, but that didn't mean she was going to adjust to it and carry on with a woman for a husband.

Still, it was hard not to get swept away by Christine's enthusiasm, her optimism. She clasped her hands to her chest at the sight of slingbacks that fit. She cooed at the flared poodle skirt on a rack at Countessa's Closet, a store in Studio City that catered to cross-dressers and transsexuals and let them keep lockers there. She never got tired of watching *Legally Blonde*. "I just feel so good," she would say, squeezing the arm of Amy's cardigan.

"It was contagious," Amy recalled recently. "She could make you forget all the things you came in worried about."

Maybe Christine would be the one in a million who could pull it off, Amy recalled thinking back then, watching Christine take out a compact—who used those anymore?—to put on fresh lipstick. Maybe she could do this and not lose everything. Wouldn't that be amazing?

*

"Old Mike, New Christine." That's the headline the editors chose for her coming-out column, which ran on April 26, 2007. Christine spent much of the previous night on the phone with Susan Horn, a pal she had met through Countessa's Closet. Horn, 49, a former lawyer who had been living full-time as a woman since January 2006, stayed on the line with her as Christine paced the tiny studio on Sepulveda Boulevard in West L.A., where she'd moved a few months earlier, each of them checking the Internet compulsively to see if the news had leaked out. "She was terrified," recalled Horn. "She was sure the response would be devastating, brutal." The column began:

> I am a transsexual sportswriter. It has taken more than 40 years, a million tears and hundreds of hours of soul-wrenching therapy for me to work up the courage to type those words. I realize many readers and colleagues and friends will be shocked to read them.
>
> That's OK. I understand that I am not the only one in transition as I move from Mike to Christine. Everyone who knows me and my work will be transitioning as well. That will take time. And that's all right. To borrow a piece of well-worn sports parlance, we will take it one day at a time.

The emails started streaming in at 2:00 A.M. By 6:00 P.M., there were more than 500, all but a handful supportive. Christine spent most of the day in tears, elated, says Horn. "She couldn't believe it; she just kept reading through them, weeping."

At first she hadn't wanted to write about it at all. It had been hard enough to tell her boss, sports editor Randy Harvey, a guy she had known since the 1980s, when they had both come to the paper as young pups: Randy a hotshot from the *New York Daily News,* Mike from the *Anaheim Bulletin,* the shitty little hometown daily where he had been made sports editor at 23. But Harvey had taken the news with remarkable equanimity. Christine later marveled to friends that he leaned back in his chair and said simply, "Okay, wow, how are we going to deal with this?"

Announcing the change to the entire world, though—that seemed overwhelming. Mike had never liked a lot of attention. Within the paper, he was widely acknowledged as one of the section's most stylish writers, a favorite of Harvey's but notoriously circumspect. Whatever emotion he had he seemed to put in his columns.

"Everyone thought of him as incredibly talented and really kind but standoffish," said Larry Stewart, a *Times* sportswriter for more than 25 years until he was laid off in 2008. "Sometimes halfway through a sentence you'd lose him. His eyes would go to the ground, and you'd wonder what had happened."

Christine's original plan was to retire the Mike Penner byline quietly and start writing as Christine Daniels a few weeks later. She had mapped out the timing during months of phone calls with Christina Kahrl, her guru in such matters. Kahrl, now 42, co-founded *Baseball Prospectus,* the stats bible, in 1996 and transitioned seven years later. She had done it gradually, without fanfare, and hadn't done interviews. The plan had worked well; Kahrl's transition had been as seamless as these things could be. The baseball world was just as eager for her pronouncements as it always had been. Her divorce was amicable; both her best man and the maid of honor remained her close pals.

"I told Christine that there's attention from every corner of your real life when you do this, that that's hard enough to deal with," Kahrl, a tall redhead with a square jaw, subtle jewelry, and finely arched eyebrows, recalled over tropical cocktails and tapas in a restaurant near her home in Chicago in January. "I thought that writing a column, doing this all so publicly, was a terrible idea, and I blame the paper for that. Christine wasn't ready for what it would bring."

But Harvey, a bearish man with gentle brown eyes, made a good argument. It was important for her to own the story, to control it, he told Christine. Otherwise, speculation would spread across the Internet like a fungus. "I knew she didn't want that 'gotcha' thing to happen," he said during an interview in his glassed-in office in the ornate, slightly bedraggled *Times* building downtown.

Christine's wasn't the only awkward, painful transition at the paper in the spring of 2007. Just two weeks before, the ailing Tribune Company accepted a buyout offer from Sam Zell, the irascible real estate billionaire. The specter of an unpredictable new owner and more layoffs made an already grim newsroom funereal. In that context, Mike Penner's travails seemed downright uplifting. "It gave people something to feel good about, made everyone feel as though they were breaking ground," said Kahrl.

"People figured that we were sports guys, that we'd be Neanderthals, but that just wasn't the case," said Harvey. "Sure, it was un-usual and some people had questions, but this is a pretty sophisti-cated place."

The reaction of Christine's own family was more mixed. Joan Penner had sent her son Mike to Catholic school for nine years, and she was horrified. The Dillmans didn't want anything to do with Christine either. But Christine's 42-year-old brother, John, who had followed Mike to the *Anaheim Bulletin* and now worked on the *Times* copy desk, was still talking to her, which she considered a great victory.

The national press, of course, went nuts. Hundreds of news-papers and the networks picked up the story, flashing the stilted snapshot from Mike's ID badge next to a blurry photo of Christine. There were countless interview requests, from NPR to the *Toronto Sun.* Evan Wright, an award-winning *Vanity Fair* reporter, was dis-patched to do a profile. David Kuhn, a well-known New York liter-ary agent, pursued her to do a book.

Christine was exhilarated by the response. "She really blos-somed," said Harvey. Billy Witz, an *L.A. Daily News* sportswriter who played for the Scribes, asked her to help coach his nine-year-old daughter's soccer team, and to everyone's surprise, none of the parents objected. A couple of trans friends persuaded her to join them performing a number from *Dreamgirls* for an AIDS fund-raiser at a local church. The annual CD compilation, cheekily re-labeled KGAL, arrived on schedule as spring melted into sum-mer. Long plagued by writer's block, Christine told people she had never felt more at home in her prose.

She even took Harvey up on his offer to write a blog, A Woman in Progress, about her transition. She began spending more time in the office than she ever had as Mike, stopping by colleagues' desks to chat and flirt. She laughed easily, covering her mouth with a well-moisturized hand. When she interviewed Vin Scully, the leg-endary Dodgers announcer, for a front-page profile, she gushed to colleagues that it was the best day of her life. "She hugged me on the walkway when I ran into her," said Larry Stewart, the former *Times* sportswriter. "She seemed really ecstatic."

You probably don't wake up in the morning glad for your penis. Maybe you run a hand through your hair or notice that your breath still reeks of scotch and the cigarette you wish you hadn't smoked last night, but if you're not a sex addict or a narcissist, you probably don't start the day thanking God or nature for your gender.

But if you're sure you aren't meant to be a man, your gender is everything. You open your eyes and reach for the only thing that can save you: a shiny tablet of estrogen or the syringe you jab into your glute. You can opt for the patch if you don't like needles, or ask the doctor to implant a time-release pellet under a buttock. The important thing is to get that daily hit; it's the air you need to survive. Only slightly less important is the anti-androgen. You wash the tab down with your coffee to block the effects of testosterone. Later in the day, you pull out another syringe and pump yourself full of progesterone to coax your breasts to swell. You will do anything to escape the hairy, stinky prison of your body. Anything.

No one knows how many men suffer from gender identity disorder—the official term used in the *Diagnostic and Statistical Manual of Mental Disorders*—but the American Psychiatric Association puts it at one in 10,000. Nor is there agreement on why some of us wind up believing we're the victims of such a cruel cosmic joke. A rough scientific consensus has emerged over the past decade that the disorder is at least partially explained by some sort of aberrant neurochemical reaction born of hormone exposure—or a mysterious lack of it—in utero. A few studies suggest that transsexual brains are measurably different from the brains of people who are comfortable in their gender, but transgendered people have normal hormone levels—until the pharmaceuticals kick in—and thus far no one has isolated a genetic or organic cause.

Gender discordance exists on a continuum. (Transvestitism, aka cross-dressing, is classified as a different disorder, a fluke of straight men who get a sexual charge from wearing panties or a skirt.) Most people who are convinced their genitals don't match their true gender will never go as far as getting sexual-reassignment surgery. Fewer than 1,000 such procedures are performed each year in the United States, where it can cost up to $30,000. (It's much cheaper elsewhere.) About three-quarters of the operations are male-to-female, partly because female-to-male surgery hasn't been perfected—it's a lot harder to add than take away.

Male-to-female technique has been so refined that the result is virtually indistinguishable from the real thing. The testicles are removed, and the penis is essentially inverted and reconfigured into a vagina, which is elongated with a graft of skin from the scrotum. You don't have orgasms like you used to — many newly minted females say they don't come at all — but most post-op transsexuals say there's plenty of sensation.

Anyway, sex is not really the point. "People assume that if you want to be a woman, then underneath it you really want to have sex with men and just can't deal with being gay," said Susan Horn. "But a lot of us aren't even thinking of whom we will have sex with. We're thinking about ourselves, that we want to be perceived by the world the way we perceive ourselves. We just want things to match."

Roughly half the men who become women wind up with another woman. "If you're interested in women before, you generally still are, even after you transition," said Horn. "Which, if you think about it, is the ultimate proof that gender and sex aren't as closely linked as we thought."

In the trans community, Christine was an instant headliner. "She was the public face everyone was hungry for," said Autumn Sandeen, who transitioned in 2003 and blogs for the popular LGBT website Pam's House Blend. "Someone with a visible career in a traditionally male field. Someone people couldn't ignore or diminish." Since January 2007, Christine had been a member of the Metropolitan Community Church in West Hollywood, where fashionable gay Hollywood worshiped. The Sunday after her coming-out column ran, the charismatic minister, the Reverend Neil Thomas, rhapsodized about her in his sermon.

She was the main attraction at a couple of major transgender gatherings that summer and fall, but the height may have been a giddy weekend at the National Lesbian and Gay Journalists Association conference in September. There were four transwomen in attendance: Sandeen, Ina Fried of CNET, Diane Barnes of Global Security Newswire, and Christine. Sandeen loaded them into her secondhand Hyundai, and they visited what passed in San Diego for gay bars, the only places that might not balk at the sight of them coming through the door. "We were four fairly large women stuffed in a small car, windows down, cruising down the freeway, incredibly, insanely happy," recalled Sandeen. Later they discussed whether they would stay in the public eye or attempt to lead a quieter life. "Christine told me she felt it was her responsibility to be out there," said Sandeen. "She didn't want the younger girls to have to go through what we'd gone through."

When David Beckham debuted that July with the L.A. Galaxy, Christine blogged about making her appearance at the press conference, her first, at the stadium.

> He arrived wearing a silver-gray Burberry suit, surrounded by a phalanx of assistants and yes-people, on his way to a temporary stage assembled on the Home Depot Center soccer pitch, where he would say hello to adoring fans and talk to the media about his new $250-million gig with the Los Angeles Galaxy.
>
> I arrived wearing a golden-hued top from Ross and a multi-colored paisley skirt from Ames and a pair of open-toed tan heels from Aerosoles, surrounded by nobody, just me and my press credential on our way to the far southwest corner of some very uncomfortable and unshaded stadium seats to listen to him talk and write about what he said.
>
> The details are not important. What mattered to me on Friday was: David Beckham arrived. And so did I.

The attention seemed to embolden her in ways that would have been anathema to Mike. Rick Reilly, who began his career in the Orange County bureau of the *Los Angeles Times* before going on to become the world's highest-paid sportswriter at *Sports Illustrated* and ESPN, was signing books at Borders in Westwood in May 2007 when he looked up to see a large woman with honey-colored hair staring at him. "It's me," Christine said. It took a moment for him to realize that this was the guy he'd played hoops with every Friday back in the late '80s at Mile Square Park near Huntington Beach.

"I was thrown briefly, but then, hey, whatever," Reilly said recently. "She seemed happier and more comfortable than he'd ever seemed." After the signing, Reilly and his wife, Cynthia, took Christine out and killed a couple of bottles of Chardonnay. Christine told them about playing princess dress-up with her male cousins as a child, how her need to dress as a woman, to be a woman, had escalated till it became unbearable, how she'd kept a red toolbox of women's clothes behind the headboard through the years with Lisa. She said it was transgendering or death. Christine became a regular that summer at the Reillys' house in Hermosa Beach. "She and Cynthia would sit on the roof deck, and my wife would tutor her on all the details of being a woman," said Reilly. "Where to get the best shoes, how to wear a push-up bra."

She talked a lot about getting the surgery. First she had to live full-time as a woman for a year—the Benjamin Standards, a medical protocol developed in the 1970s by German-born endocrinologist Harry Benjamin, required it. Next summer, she planned to go to Trinidad, Colorado, where Marci Bowers, a surgeon who transitioned more than a decade ago, practiced. The Reillys had a second home in Denver, where she would recuperate.

But there was one subject that always brought the mood down: Lisa. If only she would come around, Christine would say, as Reilly topped off her glass. If they could only still be close, everything would be so perfect. "Christine honestly couldn't fathom it," said Reilly, "I said, 'Dude, why would you think this would be okay with her?' But she couldn't let Lisa go."

In fact, the media attention was crushing Lisa, who had filed for divorce in January. "They had been really private about it, and that was bad enough, but now, all of a sudden, her tragedy, her pain— it was all out there," said Scott French, a cofounder of the Scribes, who met Mike at the Rose Bowl during the 1994 World Cup. Christine scrupulously avoided mentioning Lisa in interviews, but reporters kept pressing. "It's extremely painful," she told an NPR interviewer. "That's really a personal side of this conversation I'd rather not have."

Lisa was a stoic midwesterner, not some reality-show-ready California type who could easily spill her guts in public. She told her friends not to talk to the press and has never spoken publicly about her husband's saga. (She didn't respond to repeated requests to be interviewed for this story.) "What is there for her to say?" asked a fellow sportswriter who was close to both of them. "These were two people who were completely in love. Can you imagine what that's like?"

Everyone on the sports staff knew Lisa was suffering, and no one knew how to help. If Mike had been married to a suburban housewife, someone people hardly knew, it would have been different, abstract. Instead, Lisa was one of them. "People were nice to Christine, happy that she was happy, but they felt terrible for Lisa," said Larry Stewart. "Everyone in the newsroom sort of felt like they had to take sides. And they all chose Lisa. She's a lovely, fun person whom everyone loves. It wasn't an issue of Mike's becoming a woman; it was that Lisa was really broken up."

*

That giddy, golden summer of 2007 faded as the reality of being a midlife transwoman, single and lonely, set in: the stares as you passed on the street, the department-store salesgirls who whispered to one another as though you were deaf, the jarring sight of a stubbornly rugged jaw in the rearview mirror. "She would say that she had spent 45 minutes putting on her makeup and still she saw Mike staring back," Amy recalled.

In December, Randy Harvey called Christine at home to share a joke: the Olympic Committee had declared 2008 the Year of the Woman in sports. "I thought she'd get a real kick out it, but she got really offended," Harvey said. "I tried not to worry, but inside I knew there was something really wrong."

One night in February, Reilly was out late, getting hammered with Gene Wojciechowski, an ESPN colleague who'd worked with Reilly and Penner at the *Times*. On a whim, they dialed Christine to jaw about the old days. "She was totally touched that we included her," said Reilly. "She said she was going through a hard time with people she loved not accepting her. Then she cried, but I didn't think anything of it. Hell, she was always crying."

Around this time, Autumn Sandeen noticed that the activists had grown cold toward their poster girl. They sniped that she wasn't substantial enough, that A Woman in Progress spent too much time cataloging the new shoes in her closet and not enough mining the political turf. "They considered her frivolous," said Sandeen. "They didn't want to hear her talk about how great the *Times* had been about the transition or how Beckham gave her goose bumps. None of that highlighted the injustices and inequities that most transpeople go through. They wanted her to be a role model, a crusader. She was crushed. She just wanted to be Christine."

Then there was the matter of sex. Early on, Christine had dropped hints to Amy and Susan that she wanted to experiment with men, but as the weeks and months passed, she grew more withdrawn and uncertain. When they suggested she go out on a date to see how it felt, she demurred. "She said she had already had her great love," said Amy. "She said she couldn't fill that void."

It was late, almost midnight, when the phone rang at Amy's apartment in Redondo Beach. She knew right away who it was.

The death of Christine's mother the month before had been drawn-out and traumatic. Joan Penner had never accepted Christine and in her final dementia had vacillated between treating her as the daughter she never had and an abomination. The *Vanity Fair* piece that Christine hoped would show her as a complete, happy woman had fallen apart over differences about the photography and the direction of the reporting. "She realized that what she had envisioned, something glamorous and romantic, was never going to happen," said Sandeen. Then there was the divorce. Christine hadn't really believed Lisa would go through with it, but she could no longer ignore the documents that kept coming. They lay on the raw wooden table in her apartment amid tangled necklaces and a pile of old newspapers.

Amy had never had big expectations for her late-life transition — all she wanted was to die an old woman instead of an old man — but Christine had been convinced that becoming a woman would solve everything. Amy had tried to make her understand, from the beginning, that the act of becoming a woman itself wouldn't make you happy, any more than glasses would make you observant. But Christine just smiled that perfect smile. Until she didn't anymore.

She took a leave from the paper. Randy Harvey hadn't asked what was wrong, just told her to take care. She quit returning calls, even from Reilly. Mostly she sat in her apartment, the Audrey Hepburn posters on the wall failing to cheer her up, staring for hours through the sliding door to the dreary balcony and the busy street beyond.

So when Amy picked up the ringing phone, she braced herself. "I think I'm in kidney failure," Christine said.

Amy drove her to the hospital at Century Plaza. It was the third time in the past few months Christine had gone to the emergency room and the doctors had found nothing. But Amy couldn't let Christine go alone; hospitals were hard on the transgendered. The scanty gowns, the overworked staff poking and prodding you, some with barely concealed disgust. The fluorescent lights didn't do anyone any favors, even Christine, who had been so religious about electrolysis.

She was in bed in the ER, getting woozy from the sedative, when Amy took her hand. "I hope you won't be upset," Christine said,

her voice faint, "but I'm thinking of pulling the plug on my transition." She couldn't live without the warmth, she stumbled to explain as the drugs kicked in. Without Lisa.

It was like watching a tennis ball attached to a rubber band
stretched too tight and then released, Amy thought. It would snap
back, but not all the way. You couldn't go back. Not really. That
much Amy was sure of.

Christine came to stay at Amy's apartment after she got out of
the hospital, spending most days under a coverlet in the spare
room. She stopped taking her hormones, wasn't shaving her legs
or bothering with makeup.

When Amy's sisters invited her to visit them in Oregon in August, she couldn't say no. The girls, who shared a house on 10 wild
acres, had been surprisingly supportive when she told them their
only brother was going to become a woman. Going up there meant
flying as a woman for the first time — she worried about what would
happen if she couldn't pass and people stared on the plane — but
the fear was worth being able to drink iced tea on the deck and fish
on the river.

Christine got out of bed to drive Amy to the airport. They didn't
talk much on the way. Amy knew it was the last time she would see
Christine.

"You don't actually think Lisa will come back to you, do you?"
Amy asked quietly.

"No, not really," Christine said, her eyes on the steamy freeway
ahead. Amy didn't believe her, but what was there to say?

When Amy flew back into LAX two weeks later, Mike was waiting
for her in his old Toyota Camry. He was wearing jeans and sneakers
and a loose short-sleeve button-down shirt from Costco; his lank
blond hair was chopped to the shoulder. Amy kept things light in
the car, but it was hard. She had promised to be there for Christine
no matter what, but this felt like a death.

"It's okay if you want to call me Christine," Mike told her, his
voice a gruff whisper.

But Amy couldn't bring herself to do it; that would violate everything it meant to be trans. You got to be called what you wanted to
be, what you decided you were. That was the whole point.

"If you're Mike, you're Mike," she said.

He moved back to the apartment on Sepulveda. He was broke

and needed to go back to work. Randy Harvey tried not to ask too many questions, just limited it to "Will you be coming back as Mike?" Harvey suggested taking over "Totally Random," a short column of feature items. It was a simple assignment, a way to ease in. Before he returned, Mike asked the online editors to take down A Woman in Progress. They obliged by obliterating every trace of it in the system—not an easy task, and a first in the history of the paper. Harvey wasn't entirely comfortable with the idea of altering the record, but the guy's mental health was at stake, he told himself.

At first Mike came into the office every few days, like Christine had, but it was awkward. He was a shell, hollowed out to the rind. "He wasn't there anymore," said Harvey. Someone heard him make a reference to wanting to kill himself, and he wound up back in the hospital for a few weeks around Christmas.

After he got out, he stuffed Christine's clothes in plastic bags and brought them to Goodwill. Slowly he got rid of the jewelry stands shaped like little Victorian dolls that had brightened up the apartment; he gave Amy the necklace with the blue glass beads that she had always admired and a pair of peridot earrings.

Much of the trans community was angry with him, and he didn't blame them. Transsexual regret was a radioactive subject, especially with someone so well known. Fewer than 5 percent of transsexuals come to lament their decision, but there it was, a *USA Today* story about his reversal: "For Some, Shadow of Regret Cast over Gender Switch." Susan had dropped him, betrayed. The vibe at church the one Sunday he ventured back had been so hostile that Reverend Thomas later took a few bitter congregants aside.

When Thomas called to make sure he was okay, Mike told him he had never stopped being Christine but that he just couldn't take the expectations, the loneliness, the loss. "He knew it was irrational," Thomas said, "but there was part of him that believed he could get his old life back."

As 2009 wore on, Amy was the only one he seemed comfortable with. She had liked Christine better than she liked Mike, but she kept reminding herself not to be judgmental, that they were the same person in all the ways that counted. Fridays, after deadline, he would come to her apartment for dinner and a DVD. The night they screened a favorite, *Wonder Woman,* he gave her his Wonder

Woman costume, size 10. Christine used to wear it whenever they watched. Amy told him she would hold on to it, in case Christine ever came back. "She's not coming back," he said. "Christine is gone."

At least Lisa was willing to see him again, to have lunch or a cup of coffee; an hour with her made him happy. Amy could tell when he had seen her. His voice brightened on the phone, and when he came over, his eyes glowed turquoise again. "Lisa told him she was glad all that silly stuff was over, that she was happy he was back," said Amy. "He nursed some kind of hope it would develop beyond that."

But as the months slid into fall, the light dimmed. There were crushing bills, and no more mentions of Lisa's laugh over an afternoon latte. When Amy asked him if he'd seen her lately, he just said, "She's moved on."

November 2009 was unusually chilly for L.A., a damp cold that rarely settled over the city. The night before Thanksgiving, Mike called Amy and asked if she had a gun. "You know I can't help you with that," she said. She drove to his apartment, but when she got there he wouldn't talk about it. She dragged him to Marie Callender's for some chili, but he just stared past the chintz curtains at the cars whipping by in the darkness.

Amy was going to the home of a colleague for Thanksgiving dinner, a woman who had urged her to bring Mike along. "If you don't want to come, at least sit in my apartment and wait for me there," Amy pleaded.

"I'm driving through the Jack in the Box, and I have some errands," he told her. "Don't worry about it."

The call came in at 8:15 P.M. on Black Friday, the day after Thanksgiving. One of the neighbors and her boyfriend had spotted the Toyota as soon as they pulled into the parking structure below the stained stucco apartment building on Sepulveda. The motor was running, and a vacuum-cleaner hose snaked through the passenger-side window. A man was slumped against the seat. The boyfriend pulled him from the car, tried some CPR, and the girl dialed 911 on her cell phone.

By the time the EMS had taken Mike to the hospital in Culver City, the building manager had let two police officers into his apartment. At first, the 500-square-foot studio seemed like the typical lair of a transient single man: nothing on the walls, jeans draped over the generic pine furniture, the small fridge virtually empty. "Then I looked at the unopened mail," recalled Antonio Vasquez, one of the officers. "There was a lot of it, and most of it was addressed to a woman."

On the bed, in an envelope, was a handwritten note. For two decades, Mike Penner had crafted subtle sentences that teased the ironies out of the self-important world of sports; Christine Daniels, the woman he became for 18 months, added self-revelation and raw emotion to the mix. But in the end, there were only terse instructions. *Call my brother, John.* And Chris Foster, a close friend and colleague from the *Los Angeles Times.* And Lisa. Of course, Lisa. To her, "All my love."

Princess Di. Farrah. Cher. They are all here, or at least their wigs seem to be, at Christine's memorial service, on a Saturday afternoon in January at the Metropolitan Community Church. Some of the women sit together in the pews, reaching behind one another's broad backs to gently pat a shoulder; others come in alone, drawing fringed wraps or generously cut jackets around themselves to ward off the chill. By 5:00 P.M. the room is filled, both with full-timers and those who are living as men but have slipped away to pull on a dress and pumps to remember Christine.

There was a funeral in Long Beach a couple of days after Mike's death, a farewell to "Lisa and John's idea of who Mike was," said Scott French, who was asked to speak. "The story line was that he was depressed and had tried a lot of things and they didn't work." In the entryway there was a single image: a head shot of Mike, his mouth a closed-lipped smile. French and a few *Los Angeles Times* colleagues spoke about Mike's gentle impenetrability, his boundless love of soccer, the teammates who called him the Gaffer, British slang for "the boss." They praised his talent and mourned the sadness that dogged him. The only acknowledgment that their friend spent a year and a half as a woman was when Billy Witz got up to describe Christine's joy over the first goal by the shyest of the girls they had coached. The room was silent.

Amy was the only trans at the funeral, and she sat quietly in the back. John Penner had called to invite her; they had run into each other time after time at the hospital. Another transwoman, Michelle Evans, who had struck up a friendship with Christine through the blog, had shown up with her wife of 27 years, but Lisa had insisted that John turn them away at the door.

Six weeks later, at the Metropolitan Community Church memorial, an ebony-skinned transwoman in a black-and-yellow dress belts out "Walking Around Heaven All Day" like Cissy Houston. Amy La-Coe, nervous speaking in front of so many people, looks down at her notes and recalls that Christine was "as elegant in a pullover and jeans as she was in an evening gown." Susan Horn, a size 22 in a maroon silk sleeveless top, straps on a vintage Gibson ax and launches into "Travelin' Thru," from the soundtrack of *Transamerica,* which she and Christine often watched over trays of cocktail franks and glasses of Sauvignon Blanc. By the end of the song, the crowd is weeping. A photomontage flashes across the 50-inch screens that flank the stage. The music is Talking Heads, "Once in a Lifetime." Christine at an awards luncheon with a toothy smile. Christine at the microphone at a conference, her hand chopping the air. Christine in a soft blue sweater, her head thrown back with laughter.

> *And you may ask yourself*
> *What is that beautiful house?*
> *And you may ask yourself*
> *Where does that highway go to?*
> *And you may ask yourself*
> *Am I right? Am I wrong?*
> *And you may say to yourself*
> *My God! What have I done?*

Contributors' Notes

Notable Sports Writing of 2010

Contributors' Notes

CHRIS BALLARD is a senior writer at *Sports Illustrated*. He is the author of three books, including *The Art of a Beautiful Game,* and is currently working on a book about the 1971 Macon Ironmen baseball team. A graduate of Pomona College and the Columbia University Graduate School of Journalism, he has been at *SI* since 2000 and now lives in Berkeley, California, with his wife and two daughters. This is his second appearance in *The Best American Sports Writing.*

JAKE BOGOCH, a freelance writer and former editor in chief of *Skiing* magazine, has lived and worked in five NHL cities. The latest is home to the Blackhawks.

YONI BRENNER writes for film and television. He is a frequent contributor to *The New Yorker* and has also published short humor in the *New York Times, The New Republic,* and *Smithsonian* and on the sports website Deadspin.com. He lives in Brooklyn and roots for the Buffalo Bills.

HOWARD BRYANT is the author of *Shut Out: A Story of Race and Baseball in Boston,* which was a finalist for the Society for American Baseball Research's 2003 Seymour Medal; *Juicing the Game: Drugs, Power, and the Fight for the Soul of Major League Baseball;* and *The Last Hero: A Life of Henry Aaron.* He is a senior writer for ESPN.com and appears regularly on *ESPN: The Sports Reporters, ESPN: First Take,* and *Outside the Lines.* In 2010 he received the Online Journalism Award for Online Commentary.

STERRY BUTCHER is a reporter with the *Big Bend Sentinel* and Presidio International newspapers. She lives in Marfa, Texas, with her husband and son. "Gentling Cheatgrass" was her first story for *Texas Monthly.*

MEGAN CHUCHMACH is a television producer in the ABC News Brian Ross Investigative Unit. "The Coach's Secret" segment and a follow-up series of 17 broadcast stories about sexual abuse by coaches affiliated with USA Swimming, the sport's national governing body, won an Alfred I. duPont–Columbia University Award in broadcast journalism.

DAVID DOBBS has written features and essays for the *Atlantic,* the *New York Times Magazine, National Geographic, Wired, Nature,* and *Scientific American.* He is currently writing a book that explores the notion that the genes and traits underlying some of our most grievous mood and behavior problems may also generate some of our greatest strengths, feats, and happiness. He is the author of three books about science, culture, and the environment, including the acclaimed *Reef Madness: Charles Darwin, Alexander Agassiz, and the Meaning of Coral.* He blogs on these and other subjects at Neuron Culture, hosted at Wired Science. You can see more of his work at http://daviddobbs.net.

JASON FAGONE is the author of *Horsemen of the Esophagus,* an account of his year as a beat reporter on the competitive eating circuit. His journalism has appeared in *GQ, Esquire, Wired,* the *Atlantic, Slate, Philadelphia, The Penn Stater,* and Deadspin.com. He lives in southeast Pennsylvania with his wife and daughter and is working on a book about American inventors and super-efficient cars.

MICHAEL FARBER has been a senior writer at *Sports Illustrated* since 1994. He won two Canadian National Newspaper Awards for sports writing while at the *Montreal Gazette* and in 2003 received the Elmer Ferguson Award for distinguished hockey writing from the Hockey Hall of Fame. A native of New Jersey, Farber has lived in Montreal since 1979. He and his wife, Danielle Tétrault, have two children.

TOM FRIEND is a senior writer at ESPN.com and an on-air feature reporter for ESPN television. He has worked for the *New York Times,* the *Washington Post,* the *Los Angeles Times,* the *San Jose Mercury News,* and the *Kansas City Star* and was a columnist in the early 1990s for the now-defunct *National Sports Daily.* He has co-authored two books: *Educating Dexter,* the autobiography of an illiterate football player, Dexter Manley; and *Jack of All Trades,* the autobiography of baseball crony Jack McKeon. He is a graduate of the University of Missouri. His recent print work has been cited by Harvard University's Nieman Foundation for Journalism, and his television work earned a 2010 New York Festivals Award. He lives in southern California with his wife and two children.

NANCY HASS, a contributing editor at the *Wall Street Journal Magazine,* has written about culture and commerce for two decades. Her work is frequently seen in *GQ;* she has been on the staff of *Condé Nast Portfolio, Talk,* and *Newsweek;* and she spent a decade under contract as a featured writer at the *New York Times.* From 1998 to 2004 she was a member of the journalism faculty at the Arthur Carter Journalism Institute at New York University. She lives in New York City with her daughter, Dahlia, and her husband, Bob Roe, a longtime editor at *Sports Illustrated.*

PATRICK HRUBY is a freelance writer and frequent contributor to ESPN. com. He previously wrote for the *Washington Times,* holds degrees from Georgetown and Northwestern, and lives in Washington, D.C., with his wife, Saphira. This is his third appearance in *The Best American Sports Writing.*

SALLY JENKINS is a sports columnist and feature writer at the *Washington Post.* She is the author of several books, most notably the bestseller *It's Not About the Bike: My Journey Back to Life,* with cyclist Lance Armstrong, and *The Real All-Americans.* This is her third appearance in *The Best American Sports Writing.*

BRET ANTHONY JOHNSTON is the author of *Corpus Christi: Stories* and the editor of *Naming the World and Other Exercises for the Creative Writer.* His work has appeared in *Esquire,* the *New York Times Magazine,* the *Paris Review,* and the *Oxford American* and in anthologies such as *The Best American Short Stories.* He is on the core faculty at the Bennington Writing Seminars and is the director of creative writing at Harvard University. His website is www.bretanthonyjohnston.com.

CHRIS JONES is a writer at large for *Esquire* magazine and a contributor to Grantland.com. This is his third appearance in *The Best American Sports Writing;* he has also won two National Magazine Awards. More of Jones's work appears on his blog about writing and words, sonofboldventure.blogspot.com. He lives with his wife and two sons in a house that looks like the house from Scooby Doo in Port Hope, Ontario, Canada.

This is MARK KRAM JR.'s sixth appearance in *The Best American Sports Writing.* He has been a feature writer on the sports staff of the *Philadelphia Daily News* since 1987 and contributes an essay on American sports for the South African periodical *Business Day Sports Monthly.* He is currently at work on a book for St. Martin's Press on two brothers—after one brother was paralyzed by a football injury, the other became his caregiver, confidant, and conduit for his plea to end his life via an injection administered by Dr. Jack Kevorkian. Kram lives in Haddonfield, New Jersey, with his wife and is the father of two daughters.

JOHN MCPHEE began contributing to *The New Yorker* in 1963. He has
taught writing at Princeton University since 1975 and was awarded
Princeton's Woodrow Wilson Award for service to the nation in 1982.
McPhee has published 28 books, among them *Annals of the Former World,*
which won the Pulitzer Prize, and *Uncommon Carriers.* He lives in Princeton, New Jersey.

P. J. O'ROURKE is a political reporter who lives in New Hampshire. Once
every four years there's something political to report. This leaves him
ample time for bird hunting. He is an avid, if involuntary, practitioner
of catch-and-release grouse and woodcock shooting. He owns a splendid Brittany spaniel, Millie, which he attempted to train himself. She ate
the TV room sofa. His most recent book is *Holidays in Heck.*

AVNI PATEL is a television producer in the ABC News Brian Ross Investigative Unit. "The Coach's Secret" segment and a follow-up series of
17 broadcast stories about sexual abuse by coaches affiliated with USA
Swimming, the sport's national governing body, won an Alfred I.
duPont–Columbia University Award in broadcast journalism.

MARK PEARSON attended the University of Michigan on a wrestling schol-
arship and then returned to his home state of Pennsylvania, where he
worked as a journalist and pursued his interest in fiction. He earned a
PhD in English from the University of Georgia; he also has an MA in
English and creative writing from the University of California, Davis. His
fiction has appeared in *Aethlon, Blueline, Broken Bridge Review, Carve,
Gray's Sporting Journal, Short Story,* and *Stories.* He lives in Pottstown,
Pennsylvania, with his wife and two daughters.

BILL PLASCHKE joined the *Los Angeles Times* in 1987 and has been a sports
columnist since 1996. Plaschke is also a regular panelist on the ESPN
daily talk show *Around the Horn,* and he made his film debut with three
lines in the Will Smith movie *Ali,* playing a sportswriter. Plaschke was
recently named Man of the Year by the Los Angeles chapter of Big
Brothers/Big Sisters for his longtime involvement as a Big Brother. He
has also received a Pursuit of Justice Award from the California Wom-
en's Law Center for his coverage of women's sports. This is his seventh
appearance in *The Best American Sports Writing.*

JOHN POWERS has worked for the *Boston Globe* since 1973, writing for the
sports, metro, Sunday, magazine, and living departments. He shared the
1983 Pulitzer Prize for national reporting for a special *Globe* magazine
report on the nuclear arms race. As part of his international sports beat,
he has covered the Olympic Games since 1976 as well as seven men's
and women's soccer World Cups and has written stories from five conti-

nents. Powers is the author of *The Short Season, One Goal* (with Art Kaminsky), *Yankees* (with George Sullivan), *Mary Lou* (with Olympic gymnast Mary Lou Retton), *Seasons to Remember* (with Curt Gowdy), *The Boston Dictionary,* and *The Boston Handbook.* Powers, a 1970 cum laude graduate of Harvard and a former Poynter Fellow at Yale, lives in Wellesley, Massachusetts.

S. L. PRICE has been a senior writer at *Sports Illustrated* since 1994. This is his sixth appearance in *The Best American Sports Writing.*

SELENA ROBERTS is a senior writer for *Sports Illustrated,* where she has written the "Point After" column, investigative pieces, and features. She joined the magazine in January 2008 after spending 12 years covering pro teams and the Olympics and writing the "Sports of the Times" column for the *New York Times.* A graduate of Auburn University, Roberts began her sports writing career at the *Huntsville Times* in 1988 and then moved on to the *Tampa Tribune,* the *Orlando Sentinel,* and the *Minneapolis Star-Tribune.* She has written two books, *Necessary Spectacle: Billie Jean King, Bobby Riggs, and the Tennis Match That Leveled the Game* and *A-Rod: The Many Lives of Alex Rodriguez.*

ROBERT SANCHEZ is the senior staff writer at *5280* magazine in Denver, writing mostly long-form features and narrative stories. This is his second appearance in *The Best American Sports Writing.* A former reporter for the *Denver Post,* the *Rocky Mountain News,* the *Philadelphia Inquirer,* and the Associated Press, Sanchez has won or been nominated for multiple state and national awards, including the City and Regional Magazine Association's Writer of the Year, and he has twice been a finalist for the Livingston Award for Young Journalists. He graduated from the University of Missouri School of Journalism and is married to his high school sweetheart, Kristen. The two have a daughter, Alexandra, and a son, Michael.

BILL SHAIKIN is the national baseball writer for the *Los Angeles Times.* He has worked at the *Times* since 1997 and previously covered baseball for the *Riverside Press-Enterprise* and the *Orange County Register.* He also teaches sports reporting at the University of Southern California Annenberg School for Communication and Journalism and is the author of *Sport and Politics: The Olympics and the Los Angeles Games.* Shaikin graduated from the University of California, Berkeley, and he hopes to see Cal play in the Rose Bowl just once during his lifetime.

PAUL SOLOTAROFF is the author of *The Body Shop, Group,* and *House of Purple Hearts.* A contributing editor at *Men's Journal* and *Rolling Stone,* he has written features for *Vanity Fair, GQ, Vogue,* and the *New York Times*

Magazine. This is his sixth appearance in *The Best American Sports Writing.* He lives in New York.

WRIGHT THOMPSON is a senior writer for ESPN.com. He and his wife, Sonia, live in Oxford, Mississippi. This is his sixth appearance in *The Best American Sports Writing.*

WELLS TOWER, a native of Vancouver, grew up in North Carolina. He received a BA in anthropology and sociology from Wesleyan University and an MFA in fiction writing from Columbia University. He is the recipient of two Pushcart Prizes, the 2002 Plimpton (Discovery) Prize from the *Paris Review,* and a Henfield Foundation Award. Tower's first short story collection, *Everything Ravaged, Everything Burned,* was published in 2009.

CRAIG VETTER is a freelance writer living in Chicago. He is currently finishing a second novel.

Notable Sports Writing of 2010

SELECTED BY GLENN STOUT